THE GOSPEL
ACCORDING TO THE JEWS

JOSÉ FAUR

Copyright © 2012 José Faur

All rights reserved. This book or any portion thereof
may not be reproduced or used in any manner whatsoever
without the express written permission of the publisher
except for the use of brief quotations in a book review
and certain other non-commercial uses permitted by copyright law.

Printed in the United States of America

First Printing, 2012

ISBN: 0615699030
ISBN-13: 978-0615699035

Moreshet Sepharad Publishing

www.moreshetsepharad.org

All rights reserved.

To my sister Angélica, with whom I heard the "Jesus' story," told by our grandfather, and with whom I went together with our grandmother to see "Passion Plays" in Easter week.

IN MEMORIAM

With the Publication of this Important Work
We Honor the Memories of
my Dear Mother
Aurora Sofia Joli de Faur
and my
Paternal Grandmother
Malake Embe de Faur
Who taught me about the
Jewish 'Experience' in Sepharad

ת.נ.צ.ב.ה.

PREFACE

Western civilization prohibits the victim to speak up. History is the exclusive prerogative of the victor. Our knowledge of the victim must come, invariably, from the conqueror. The only exception is the Jews. Jews are the only victims in Western tradition that made their history known from their own perspective: Jewish history is history written from the standpoint of the vanquished. This is why *conquering* civilizations *hate* Jews.

No one was more implacable in the effort to muzzle its victims than the Church. The 'Gospel' or 'Good Tidings' announcing the coming of the Christian Savior became a handbook for the dissemination of hatred and violence against Jews.[1] No book in history—including Hitler's *Mein Kampf*—generated more intense hatred and violence against Jews than the *Christian Scripture*. To justify their enmity, the Church depicted the Jews as vile and debauched. Judaism was a prevarication of the truth, and the Law not only was dead but deadly; hence, the efforts to discredit Jewish memory. For almost two

---

[1] The sense of the term "Gospel" (standing for the Greek *evaggelion*) has been debated. It is widely accepted that it translates the Semitic word *besora*, a term that in Hebrew could mean either 'good' or 'bad' tidings. Naturally, traditional commentators of the *Christian Scripture* associate it with 'good' tidings, and argue vehemently that its usage was not derived from the Greek version of the *Hebrew Scripture* (=*Septuagint*). Therefore, although it is not *impossible* that it was used by Jesus, most probably it is a later interpolation by editors of the *Christian Scripture*. See Millar Burrows, "The Origin of the Term 'Gospel,'" *Journal of Biblical Literature* 44 (1925), pp. 21-33.

millennia, Jews were muzzled and could not properly develop the history of Jesus on the basis of Talmudic and Rabbinic sources and so answer adversarial questions posed by Israel's enemies. Proper response to Christian vilification was impossible: expulsion, confiscation of property, torture, and death would surely follow. Thus, Christianity stole the voice of Judaism. By portraying the Jew as perfidious and insincere, the ecclesiastic authorities succeeded in undermining trust in him. Jews were the only group in Western society that could not have a reasoned debate about their *own history*. This not only prevented the Jew from defending himself from Christian accusations, but also from telling the world what Judaism is all about.

Current times offer the Jew an exceptional window of opportunity to present the *Jewish* view on the life and death of Jesus, as registered by Jews who knew him and by his followers in the land of Israel.

It is not an idle pursuit. Silence may be eloquent indeed. Failure to seize this opening and to respond to two millennia of opprobrium may be defined negatively: as acquiescence to the key presumptions made by the *Christian Scripture* and the Church. The principal objective of this work is to examine the Jewish and Christian documentation on this subject from a *Jewish perspective*.

At the end of the *Foreword* to his *Jesus as Others Saw Him* (New York: Bernard G. Richards Co., 1925), Joseph Jacobs (1854-1916) made the essential point that, "It is only by knowing exactly where we [Jews and Christians] differ that we can hope ultimately to agree." A similar idea was proposed by Professor Neusner:

> It seems to me only when Christianity can see itself in the way in which the Church fathers saw it—as new and uncontingent, a complete revision of the history of humanity from Adam onward, not as a subordinate and heir to Judaism—and when Judaism can see itself in the way in which the sages and the oral Torah saw it—as the statement of God's Torah for all humanity—that the two religions will recognize this simple fact: they are really totally alien to one another. Dialogue will begin with the recognition of difference, with a search for grounds for some sort of communication, rather than with

the assumption of sameness and the search for commonalities.²

This is precisely the purpose of this work. The view urged here is to consider the life and death of Jesus on the basis of Talmudic and Rabbinic sources, and read the *Christian Scripture critically*. Surprisingly, both the Jewish and Christian sources coincide, providing that one dares read the texts *analytically*—that is, like a Talmudist.

As we shall see in the course of this work, the most important piece of evidence that the Church tried to suppress is the story of Jesus as known to the Jews.

José Faur
Netanya Law School
Netanya, Israel
5 *Mor-Ḥeshvan,* 5773
25 October 2012

---

² Jacob Neusner, *Jews and Christians: The Myth of a Common Tradition* (Binghamton, N.Y.: Global Publications, 2001), p. 119. For a bold and lucid response to Christian vilification of Jews and Judaism, as well as the spiritual abyss separating Judaism from Christianity, see R. Henry Pereira Mendes (1852-1937), *The Jewish Religion Ethically Presented* (New York: Published by the Author, 1904), especially chapter 51, "The Attitude of Judaism to Christianity."

PROLOGUE

I was born into a Sephardic family where the Iberian experience marked a pivotal point in time. Central to the Sephardic mindset is the emphatic 'No' given to Christianity, both in and outside the Iberian Peninsula. It was an intelligent, rational 'No.' In my case, it began being instilled early in my childhood, during Easter week, when my grandfather would gather the family and recount the *Jewish* version of "Jesus' story." During the same week, my grandmother would take my oldest sister and me to see one of the many "Passion Plays" being shown in the neighborhood. The result was a view of the subject that was both fair and balanced. This helped me, not only to come to grips with my own Jewish tradition, but also to gain a better insight into the problems facing the faithful Christian wishing to understand Jews and Judaism.

Books, like poems, are born in the strangest of places and circumstances. This book came about in my younger days, when I was a graduate student at the University of Barcelona. My teacher, who directed my Ph.D. thesis, was a Catholic priest, Alejandro Díez Macho, M.S.C. (1916-1984), who occupied the prestigious Chair of Rabbinic Literature at the University of Barcelona. He had dedicated his life to the study and teaching of Hebrew texts. At all times, he would go out of his way to make sure that I was able to comply with even the minutest details of Jewish law. During the winter, when the afternoons were short and his seminars run way after sunset, we had a special arrangement. When the sun was about to set, I would point to my watch. This served as a signal that it was getting late for the Afternoon Prayer (*Minḥa*). He would then stop lecturing and give the class a break. To make sure that nobody would disturb me, he would let me use his office. In this manner, I was able recite the Afternoon Prayer (*Minḥa*) at ease.

Once, he invited me to read the *Gospels* together with him. He reasoned that since initially, the *Gospels* were written for Jews, Jewish scholars were particularly qualified to interpret them. "From reading your Scripture," I replied, "it is obvious that for the authors of the *Gospels*, Jesus' death was much more important than his life. Don't you think that before you learn about how he died you should learn about how he lived?" He agreed. "But how are we going to find out about the historical Jesus," he asked. "A first step would be learning *The Gospel according to the Jews*," I replied. Circumstances beyond our control prevented us from realizing this project. But it was at that moment that the idea of this book was born.

I wish to express my gratitude to my son, R. Abraham Faur, for having read the text and made substantial suggestions, both at to style and content.

I owe a special note of gratitude to Eli Bildirici, Alex Schindler, Jaim Harlow, Eli Shaubi, Shemuel Aiello, Shelomo Nahari, Raymond Habbaz and Daniel Sayani for going over the text and the indices, thoroughly and conscientiously.

Above all, I want to acknowledge my wife Esther for the bliss of her fellowship, without which, studying Tora would not have been—and continue to be—as rewarding.

CONTENTS

PREFACE i
PROLOGUE v
HEBREW TRANSLITERATION TABLE.. xi
ABBREVIATIONS xii
INTRODUCTION.. 1
SECTION I: *A Clash Of Civilizations*, Myth *Vs.* Book 39
   1. Myth and Book... 40
   2. The Medium of Myth 49
   3. Invariant Structures of Mythological Thought 56
   4. Myth and Media.. 62
   5. Israel's Medium: Speaker-'*I*,' Addressee-'*you*' 72
   6. The Publication of a Vowel-less Text and the Formation of the Hebrew-Self.. 78
   7. Masks and the Absentee Society 85
   8. Escape from Myth.. 93
   9. Christianity, Religion of Myth 100
SECTION II: *Jesus, His Life And Ministry*, A Jewish Reading of The Christian Version 107
   10. Christianity and the *National Memory* of Israel........... 108
   11. Jesus' Life-Style.. 112

12. Jesus, Amicus Publicanis 123
13. Jesus, *Adversus* Pharisees 129
14. Who was the 'Good Samaritan'? 133
15. The Sin of *Minut* 137
16. Taking Pleasure in the Mystery of the Kingdom 143
17. Why were the Judeo-Christians expelled from Christendom? 148
18. Paul, Saint *and* Mimic Actor 157
19. Jesus as Jews and Pagans saw him 161
20. The Perception Issue 169

SECTION III: *Jesus' Trial*, A Passion Play 177
21. Jesus' Earthly Life and Death 178
22. *Kyrios* Jesus, Tax Collector 184
23. The Christian Account of Jesus' Trial 190
24. Consuming Jesus Flesh and Drinking his Blood 193
25. The Remaining Twelve 203
26. 'Gospel-Truth'—Truly? 212
27. Alexandria, Cradle of the First Pogrom 225
28. The Alexandrian Precursor of Jesus 231
29. Theater and the New Faith 239
30. Jesus of Alexandria 244

SECTION IV: *The Alliance Cross-Sword*, Megalomania and The Culture of Obedience-Submission 251
31. Defrocking Israel and Dethroning the God of Sinai 252
32. Israel's Primordial Struggle 257
33. The Theology of Power 261
34. A Heavenly *Cosmocrator* 267

35. The Divine Right of Tyrants 271
36. The Alliance Church-Monarch 277
37. The Banality of Evil 281
38. *Nova creatura* and *Humanitas* 290
39. The *Tora*—an Evolutionary Gift to Humankind 296
40. Thinking *Shalom* 301

EPILOGUE 311

APPENDICES 313
    Appendix 1 313
    Appendix 2 315
    Appendix 3 319
    Appendix 4 321

INDICES 323
    Index of References 323
    Names, Places and Subjects 335

BIBLIOGRAPHY 347

HEBREW TRANSLITERATION TABLE

א	ʾ
ב	b
ג	g
ד	d
ה	h
ו	v, w
ז	z
ח	ḥ
ט	ṭ
י	y
כ, ך	k, kh
ל	l
מ, ם	m
נ, ן	n
ס	s
ע	ʿ
פ, ף	f, p, ph
צ, ץ	ṣ
ק	q
ר	r
ש	sh, s
ת	t

ABBREVIATIONS

Ch	Chronicles
Col	Colossians
Cor	Corinthians
Dan	Daniel
Dt	Deuteronomy
Ec	Ecclesiastes
Eph	Ephesians
Est	Esther
Ex	Exodus
Ez	Ezekiel
Gal	Galatians
Gn	Genesis
Gr.	Greek
Heb	Hebrews
Hos	Hosea
Is	Isaiah
Jer	Jeremiah
Jn	John
K	Kings
Lk	Luke
Mal	Malachi
Matt	Matthew
MT	Mishne Tora
Mk	Mark

n.d.	no date
n.p.	no place; no pagination
Neh	Nehemiah
Nu	Numbers
Pet	Peter
Rom	Romans
Sam	Samuel
Song	Songs Song of Songs
Thess	Thessalonians
Tim	Timothy
Zeph	Zephaniah

INTRODUCTION

From time immemorial, Jews crossed paths with countless cultures and creeds without encountering a single *religious* enemy. Of course, like every other people, Israel had her assortment of *political* foes, but never a *religious* enemy. There was a good reason for that. Central to the Hebrew ethos is the concept of religious humanism; a concept grounded on the belief that all humans are created in God's image (*Gn* 1:27). Before proceeding with an analysis of this concept, it would be advisable to comment briefly on the Hebrew idea of *'aboda zara*—mistranslated 'idolatry,' but actually meaning 'alien cult.' Patriarch Jacob first designated pagan idols "foreign deities" (*Gn* 35:2, 4). The sense of this expression will be clear upon considering that a married woman is also designated 'alien'; i.e., she is forbidden to *you*, not because she is evil, but because she is *not* your wife. Likewise, *'aboda zara* is forbidden to Jews because it is a cult *alien* to Judaism. Jewish regulations of *'aboda zara* apply to gentiles residing in the land of Israel, for the simple reason that it is expected from every alien to respect the laws and regulations of the host country.[1] The destruction of idols in Biblical and post-Biblical times, apply to idols in the *land of Israel*.[2] These were state-sponsored symbols, representing

---

[1] For an in-depth analysis of this subject, see my *Horizontal Society* [henceforth: *HS*], 2 vols. (Boston: Academic Studies Press, 2008), vol. 2, Appendix #11, pp. 32-34.

[2] The law also applies to idols in the possession of an Israelite. Explicitly, the rabbis exempt someone worshiping an idol "out of love or fear" from the sin of *'aboda zara*; see *Shabbat* 72a, *Sanhedrin* 61b; *Mishne Tora* (standard edition, henceforth: *MT*)

alien domination in the Promised Land. In this connection we should bear in mind that in Antiquity, the worship of alien deities was regarded as a 'political' crime against the state, rather than a 'religious' offense. Let me quote a pertinent passage on this subject from Reverend Jonathan Mayhew (1720-1766):

> It is to be remembered that Judaism was at least as much a *political* as a *religious* institution. The *Jews* had God for their immediate *king* and *lawgiver,* both in *church* and *state.* Their *civil* and *ecclesiastical* polity were blended together; and being derived from the same source, every violation of the law of *Moses* might be considered and punished as an offence against the state, in a greater or lesser degree: And *idolatry* being in these circumstances equivalent to *high treason,* it is not strange that a capital punishment should be annexed to it.[3] [Italics in original]

There is, however, a major difference between alien *idols* in the land of Israel, standing for pagan *dominion* over the Holy Land, and *deities* worshiped by the faithful pagan. When speaking to gentiles, Jews refrained from referring to their deities in a derogatory manner, as a matter of human fellowship and sensitivity, not theology.[4] In this spirit, the official translation of the *Tora* in Aramaic rendered the Biblical expression 'other deities' *ṭa'uta,* 'error'—a term bearing no opprobrium.[5] (From the Judeo-Aramaic, this term entered the Arabic in the form *ṭa'a*; in the sense of 'submissive,' 'obedient,' someone who is fulfilling a 'religious duty'). In the same spirit of fellowship, the *Tora* prohibits blaspheming alien deities. The plain sense of "his god," in the verse, "Whosoever cursed his god (*elohav*) shall bear his

---

MT *'Aboda Zara* 3:6; cf. ibid, 1:2; 1:3. For a full examination of this subject in *rabbinic* law, see my *Studies in the Mishne Tora* (Heb.) (Jerusalem: Mossad Harav Kook, 1978), pp. 219-227.

[3] Reverend Jonathan Mayhew, in *Seven Sermons,* reprinted in *Religion in America* (New York: Arno Press, 1969), pp. 68-69. Cf. Albert Barnes, *The Book of Job,* vol. 1 (New York: Leavitt, Trow, & Company, 1845), pp. xxviii-xxix.

[4] Obviously, Jews believed these deities were pure nonsense, often accompanied by awful rituals; see *Megilla* 25b and *Sanhedrin* 63b. However, Jews saw no point in offending the faithful pagan; see the quotation from Philo, below n. 8.

[5] See *Targum* to *Dt* 4:28; 28:36, 64; 32:5, etc.

sin" (*Lev* 24:15)—is *any* god—as per the *Septuagint* (Greek translation of the *Tora*).⁶ Let us note that in this case, the culprit does not face capital punishment. Hence the difference between this offense, and the offense stated in the next verse: "And he that blasphemed the name of the Lord (YHWH) shall be put to death" (*Lev* 24:16). In a similar vein, the manifest sense of *Ex* 22:27(28) is, as per the *Septuagint*: "Thou shall not revile the gods (*elohim*)," that is, of pagan deities.⁷ It is on the basis of these verses that Philo (20 BCE-50 CE) warned against those who,

> ...revile with an unbridled tongue the gods whom others acknowledge, lest they on their part be moved to utter profane words against Him Who truly is. For they [the pagans] know not the difference, and since the falsehood has been taught to them as truth from childhood and has grown up with them, they will go astray.⁸

Similarly, Josephus (37-100) wrote: "Let none blaspheme the

---

⁶ This point was first made by R. Elie Benamozegh, *Em la-Miqra*, 5 vols. (Leghorne, 1862-1863), vol. 3, 59b-60b, 72b. He also called attention to Philo's and Josephus' view on this matter, and noted the remarkable fact that a similar interpretation appears in the *Zohar*, vol. 3 (Leghorn: 5611/1851), 106a-b. To my mind, the Aramaic version in *Ms. Neophyti 1, III, Levítico*, ed. Alejandro Díez Macho (Madrid-Barcelona: Consejo Superior de Investigaciones Científicas, 1971), 24:15, p. 178: "*shema de-elah*," is to be translated "the name of *a* god," that is, of *any* god, including a pagan deity.

⁷ We should not be surprised to discover that after the defeat of Bar Kokhba (132-136), when the Romans committed one of the greatest genocides in human history, greater than Nazi Germany——between 80% to 90% of the Jewish population in Judea were exterminated—'gods' was replaced by 'judge.' For some vestiges of the original 'gods,' see R. 'Aqiba, *Mekhilta de-R. Yishma'el*, eds. H. S. Horovitz and I. A. Rabin (Jerusalem: Wahrmann Books, 1970), *Mishpaṭim*, XIX, p. 317; *Mekhilta de-R. Shim'on bar Yoḥai*, on *Mishpaṭim*, 22:27, p. 213; and *Sanhedrin* 66a where this verse is interpreted as blaspheming a deity, not as cursing a judge. Concerning the Roman genocide of Jews, Yehoshafat Harkabi, *The Bar Kokhba Syndrome* (Chappaqua, N.Y.: Russel Books, 1983), p. 48 wrote: "No pogrom is commensurate with that which the Romans perpetrated against the inhabitants of Judea."

⁸ Philo, *The Special Laws*, I, 53, in *Philo Complete Works*, 10 vols., and 2 vols. Supplements (Loeb Classical Library), vol. 7, p. 129, see tr. n. *c*. Cf. idem, *Moses*, II, 198-206, vol. 6, pp. 549-551.

gods that other cities revere."⁹ The same applies to pagan rituals and ceremonies, "For it is our traditional custom to observe our own laws and to refrain from criticism of those of aliens."¹⁰

The purpose was not merely good-neighborly relations, as anti-Judaic cynics would argue. Rather, it springs from a deeply ingrained feeling of what may be properly described as Hebrew humanism—a humanism rooted in the belief that we are all created with the image of God within. Given that there *is* a *single* God, this not only means that all humans are *created* equal, but that everyone, although individually unique, is equivalent to everyone else. Put in simple terms, Hebrew humanism proposes what at first sight may appear as a paradox: although each individual is fundamentally different from anybody else, past and present, we are all fundamentally equivalent. The principle applies, first and foremost, at the religious level: before you censor someone, have you fulfilled *your* religious responsibilities, in accordance with *your* possibilities? In the Hebrew economy of ideas, the person having *more* religious responsibilities is the High priest, whereas the person having *less* religious responsibilities, within the Jewish faith, is a woman. Outside the Jewish faith, "the seven Noahide precepts," are incumbent upon a pious gentile. One could therefore assume that a Jewish High Priest is *ipso facto* 'holier' than a 'pagan.' R. Me'ir (2ⁿᵈ century), however, taught differently: "An alien engaged (*'oseq*) in the *Tora* is like a High Priest."¹¹ On the basis of this

---

⁹ *Jewish Antiquities*, IV, 207, in *Josephus* (Loeb Classical Editions), vol. 4, p. 575. Reflecting the narrow-mindedness peculiar to scholars dealing with 'Jewish' subjects, the tr. ibid, note d, saw a contradiction between the ruling to destroy pagan idols, and what Josephus wrote here. Most people, however, will have no problem in understanding that although one might strenuously object to symbols of foreign domination oven his own country, still he could behave respectfully with citizens of that nation, and refrain from saying something that could hurt their feelings.

¹⁰ *Against Apion*, II, 237, *Josephus,* vol. 1, p. 389. According to the *Tora* one should only ensure the faults of you and your "people" (*'amitekha*; root 'AM, 'nation,' *Lev* 19:17)—not of 'others'—while postulating, by default, that you and your people are immaculately pure. According to the rabbis, the only worthy criticism is one that you make about yourself, for your personal failures; see *Massekhet Kalla Rabbati*, ed. Michael Higger (Brooklyn, NY: Moinester Publishing Co., 1936), III, 20, p. 243.

¹¹ *Baba Qamma* 38a; cf. *Sanhedrin* 59a. R. Me'ir's source is the story mentioned be-

doctrine, R. David ha-Kohen (15th and 16th centuries), concluded: "A gentile fulfilling the seven Noahide precepts, and a woman fulfilling the precepts incumbent upon her, equal [the sanctity of] a High Priest."[12] Conversely, we may infer that a High Priest *not* fulfilling all his religious duties is less than a woman or pagan fulfilling all of their respective duties.[13] This leads to another revolutionary concept, implicit in the rabbinic doctrine that, "God does not act with His creatures as if He were a Tyrant."[14] That is, the God of Israel will never reproach an individual for failing to accomplish something for which He never gave him the actual means to fulfill.[15] Therefore, even wisdom and personal achievement, ranking high in the Jewish mindset, are relative to the specific circumstances and possibilities available to each person.

Let me illustrate. Suppose that in a level from 1 to 10, A, because of his natural, social, and educational possibilities, could reach level 9, and B could only reach level 7. Level 7 of B equals level 9 of A. Now, suppose that out of complacency, etc., A reached only level 7. Level 7 of B is higher than level 7 of A.[16] Therefore, "every one

---

low, n. 13. The sense of *'oseq* is not 'study' and 'contemplate' in the abstract, but of examining how to implement a particular duty in deed and in action. Evidence to this is that the rabbis (*Baba Qamma* 38a) associated the term "*'oseq*" with the verse (*Lev* 18:5), "which a man shall <u>do</u> and live by them." This answers the objection raised by R. Ḥezqiya de Silva, *Peri Ḥadash* (Amsterdam, 5490/1730), against *Bayit Ḥadash*, *Ṭur Oraḥ Ḥayyim* 47:5, 2a *s.v. ve-noshat*.

[12] R. David ha-Kohen, *Teshubot ha-Radak* (Constantinople, 5297/1537), #XVII, 9, 11b.

[13] See the awe-inspiring story, in *Yoma* 71a-b, taking place in the 1st century BCE. For an analysis, see my *In the Shadow of History* (Albany, NY: SUNY, 1991), p. 201.

[14] *'Aboda Zara* 3a.

[15] Since our mental capacities are conditioned by biological factors, etc., see *Nidda* 16a, each individual is judged according to her or his competence and possibilities. This answers the objection raised in *Haggahot Maimoniyot*, MT *Teshuba* 5:2 [a]. See below, n. 17.

[16] For the rabbinic sources and development of this concept, see R. Moses de Ṭrani, *Bet E-lohim* (Venice, 5336/1576), "Introduction," 2a-c. A similar idea was independently developed on the basis of other rabbinic sources, by R. Joseph Ṣarfati, *Yad Yosef* (Amsterdam, 5460/1700), 175b-c. Within this concept the parity

can be like Moses"; i.e., he can reach his full potential.[17]

Given that all humans are endowed with the image of the same God, the 'alien' is not a sub-human, incapable of 'good,' but as the rabbis taught, every human is "a full integral world."[18] In his address to the Nation of Israel, at the inauguration of the Temple in Jerusalem—that glorious moment in *human* history—King Solomon extended an invitation to "the stranger that is not of Thy people Israel" (1*K* 8:41). Turning to God, he asked Him: "to hear their prayer and their supplication, and maintain their cause" (1*K* 8:45). According to Jewish law, a pagan may offer sacrifices at the Temple. The rabbis explained: "A pagan has his heart focused towards Heavens."[19] Speaking in the name of God, Prophet Isaiah declared: "For My house," that is, the Temple in Jerusalem, "shall be called a house of prayer for all peoples" (56:7). Prophet Malachi went a step further: "For from the rising of the sun even unto the going down of the same, My name is great among the nations; and in every place offerings are presented unto My name, even pure oblations; for My name is great among the nations, said the Lord of hosts" (1:11).[20]

Therefore, it is wrong to say that Judaism regards all forms of pagan humanity as wicked and worthless. The rabbis warned against assimilating the bad habits rampant throughout the pagan world. The problem with assimilated Jews is that invariably, they pick up the worst traits of pagan society, as illustrated by the self-hating Jew (des-

---

of men and women in rabbinic tradition is clearly understood; see R. Isaac Adrebe, *Dibre Shalom* (Venice, 5346/1586), 89c-d.

[17] See *MT Teshuba* 5:2.

[18] Mishna *Sanhedrin* 4:5; see *HS,* vol. 1, p. 107 n. 54.

[19] *Menaḥot* 73b.

[20] For reasons explained above n. 7, the rabbis departed from the plain meaning of this verse; see *Vayyiqra Rabba, Ṣav,* VII, 3, in *Vayyiqra Rabba,* ed. Mordecai Margulies, 5 vols. (Jerusalem: American Academy for Jewish Research, 1956), vol. 1, pp. 155-156, and *Menaḥot* 110a. The *Targum* to *Mal* 1:11, too, reflects the same attitude; see *The Bible in Aramaic,* vol. 3, ed. Alexander Sperber (Leiden: E. J. Brill, 1962), p. 501.

ignated *min* in rabbinic literature).²¹ Addressing this sort of Jew, the sages of the Talmud explained:

> One verse says: "You have done after the laws of the nations around you" (*Ez* 11:12). While another verse says: "neither have you done after the ordinances of the nations around you" (*Ez* 5:8). How are we to explain this? Like those who are upright among them (the nations)—you haven't done; but like those among them that are corrupt, you have done!²²

Judaism never regarded 'gentiles' as a single homogeneous mass. The rabbis were the first religious leaders to teach that people *outside their own faith*, may be saved: "the pious among the nations of the world," i.e., non-Jews, "have a portion in the world to Come."²³ They also promoted reverence for gentile men of wisdom. In accordance with the principle that there is "wisdom among the nations," the rabbis treated "the sages from the nations" with deference. "Whoever pronounces a word of wisdom, although from the nations (i.e., a gentile), he should be entitled 'sage' (*ḥakham*)."²⁴ Remarkably, they believed that pagan sages were their natural allies, and would defend them against their own Tyrants.²⁵ In token of respect, when meeting

---

²¹ See below n. 67.

²² *Sanhedrin* 39b. See *Genizah Studies*, ed. Louis Ginzberg, vol. 1 (New York: Jewish Theological Seminary, 1928, pp. 225-226; *HS*, vol. 1, pp. 354-355. Therefore, rabbis often censured their congregants for failing to emulate the *good conduct* of their gentile neighbors; see, for example, R. Saul Levi Mortera, *Gibʻat Shaʼul*, (Brooklyn, NY, 5751-1991), p. 257; R. Moshe Israel Ḥazzan, *Words of Peace and Truth* (London, Samuel Meldola: 5605/1845), pp. 13-14; etc.

²³ *Tosefta Sanhedrin* 13:2, ed. M. S. Zuckermandel (Jerusalem: Wahrman Books, 5035/1975), p. 434. See *Sanhedrin* 105a, and *HS*, vol. 2, p. 33. Fortunately, the rabbis were not the *last*, I am thinking of Roger Williams in America; see Oscar S. Straus, *Roger Williams: The Pioneer of Religious Liberty* (New York: D. Appleton-Century Company, 1936). It is high time for American Jewry to recognize these great Christian champions of freedom of conscience. May I suggest to begin with naming Jewish Schools in honor of men like Roger Williams and Jonathan Mayhew.

²⁴ *Megilla* 16a.

²⁵ The rabbis in *Midrash Rabba, Ester* VII, 13, 12c, and *Aggadat Ester* (S. Buber), 16b-17a taught that when King Ahasuerus, "consulted with the sages from among the

a pagan sage, one should say: "Blessed art thou God, our Lord, King of the Universe, for having bestowed of His Wisdom to a human being."[26] Even more important is the fact that the rabbis did not refrain from consulting with "the sages from among the nations" as expert witnesses in matters concerning Jewish law. On one such occasion, when a dispute arose between "the sages of Israel and the sages from among the nations," the Jewish Court relied on the expert testimony of the sages among the nations.[27] We should also mention that according to the rabbis, the special courtesy urged by the *Tora* towards the elderly (*Lev* 19:32), must be extended to non-Jews.[28] The same holds true for the distribution of alms, visiting the sick, burying the dead, and comforting those who had lost loved ones.[29] Likewise, when dealing with pagans, any form of fraudulent representation, even when not resulting in monetary loss, is strictly prohibited.[30] Accordingly, we should not be surprised to discover that throughout her long history, Israel only came in conflict with pagan monarchs—

---

nations," whether or not to proceed with Haman's plan to exterminate the Jews, they replied:

> Who has counseled you with the folly of destroying Israel? Were you to destroy them, the world will no longer subsist, since it subsists but for Israel and the *Tora* which was given to Israel.

[26] *Berakhot* 58a; see *MT Berakhot* 10:11; *Shulḥan 'Arukh, Oraḥ Ḥayyim*, CCXXIV, 7.

[27] *Pesaḥim* 94b. For an extensive treatment of this subject, see José Faur, "*Ve-Nishu Ḥakhme Ummot ha-'Olam et Ḥakhme Yisrael*," eds. Chief Justice of Israel Aharon Barak and Professor Menashe Shawa, *Minḥa Le-Yisḥaq* (Jerusalem: Lishkat 'Orkhe-Din, 1999), pp. 113-133.

[28] See *Qiddushin* 33a; *MT Talmud Tora* 6:9; *Shulḥan 'Arukh, Oraḥ Ḥayyim* CCXLIV, 7. I remember with fondness and pride, as both my grandfather and my father would instruct me to kiss the hands of elders from the Christian and Moslem communities that came to visit us.

[29] Concerning the distribution of alms, visiting the sick, and burying the dead, see *Gittin* 61b; and cf. *MT 'Aboda Zara* 10:5; *Mattanot 'Aniyyim* 1:9; *Abel* 14:12; *Melakhim* 10:12. For further sources, see Mishna *Shebi'it* 4:5; 5:9; *Gittin* 5:8; *Tosefta Gittin* 3:14, and the comments of Professor Saul Lieberman, ad loc., *Tosefta Kifshuṭah*, vol. 8, pp. 849-850.

[30] See *Ḥolin* 94a, *MT De'ot* 2:6, *Mekhira* 18:1; *Shulḥan 'Arukh, Ḥoshen Mishpaṭ* CCXXVIII, 6.

never with pagan priests.[31]

Given that in the Jewish mind, 'gentiles' are God's creatures, and every person is "a full integral world," the rabbis never generalized.[32] Concerning Christians, Samuel (2nd and 3rd centuries), one of the pillars of the Babylonian Talmud, would visit Be-Abidan, a kind of 'Academy,' where scholars would meet and discuss matters of common interest. These gatherings included Christian sages.[33] Arius (256-336), the great Christian sage famous for his opposition to the Trinitarian doctrine, had contacts with rabbinic sages.[34] For reasons of prudence (rather than 'religion'), the rabbis' policy was not to discuss theological matters with Christian and Muslim sages. However, when circumstances permitted, Jewish sages did not hesitate to engage their counterparts in the Christian and Muslim communities, about 'neutral' subjects; i.e., matters of grammar, philology, and lexicography. The purpose of these contacts was human fellowship, rather than the acquisition of knowledge.[35] In this spirit, although it is

---

[31] See *HS*, vol. 1, Chapter 25. Although targeting Jewish religious institutions, Antiochus Epiphanes was motivated by political, not religious concerns; see Elias Bickerman, "The Maccabean Uprising: An Interpretation," *The Jewish Expression*, ed. Judah Goldin (New Haven: Yale University Press, 1976), pp. 66-86. See below, Section III, n. 146.

[32] Mishna *Sanhedrin* 4:5. See above, n. 18.

[33] See *Shabbat* 116a. Be-Abidan was an Academy at a pagan Temple, containing a library, attended by gentile sages who met to discuss matters of common interest. Among the participants, there were Christian sages of Jewish background; see *Perushe R. Ḥanan'el*, ed. Chief Rabbi David Masger (Jerusalem: Leb Sameah, 5750/1990), ad loc., 252b. Cf. *Perush R. Ḥanan'el*, *'Aboda Zara* 17b. For further insights, see R. David Cohen de Lara, *Keter Kehunna* (*Lexicon Thalmudico*) (N.p. 1667), 1c, line 43-47. Let us mention, in passing, that Samuel was friendly with Plotinus (204/5-270); see *Em la-Miqra*, vol. 5, 153a, 175b. On one occasion, when Plotinus inadvertently touched a flask of wine, he alerted Samuel not to drink from it, as that would contravene Jewish law; see *'Aboda Zara* 30a.

[34] There is a long, analytical note in *Em la-Miqra*, vol. 5, 4a-6a, 8b-10b about Arius in rabbinic literature.

[35] See R. Moses ibn 'Ezra, *Kitab al-Muḥadara wal-Mudhakara*, ed. and tr. A. S. Halkin (Jerusalem: Mekize Nirdamim, 1975), p. 227; R. Joseph ibn 'Aqnin, *Hitgallut ha-Sodot*, ed. and tr. A.S. Halkin (Jerusalem: Mekize Nirdamim, 1964), p. 494. The precedent for this type of consultation is to be found in *Yerushalmi, Baba Batra* VIII,

prohibited to teach *Tora* to non-Jews,³⁶ Maimonides (1135-1204) permitted to teach the *Scripture* to Christians, since they (unlike Muslims) admit its sanctity.³⁷

On the basis of Hebrew humanism, Jewish sages believed that despite their irreconcilable differences with Judaism, in the course of time, Christianity and Islam would come closer and closer to the basic principles of the *Tora*. Even before that glorious moment, Maimonides acknowledged the contributions to pagan humanity made by these religions. "And were it not because of the extent to which the existence of God is now propagated [by Christians and Muslims] among the nations, our days now would have been darker than then, but in a different form."³⁸ R. Judah ha-Levi (ca. 1075-1141) offered a beautiful metaphor to illustrate how, in spite of their continuing pounding against the Law of Moses, and changing and reshuffling of its core teachings, in the end, Christianity and Islam will result in a system pretty much like the *Tora*. The Law of Moses is a seed, he explained, which once deposited in a fertile ground, appears to have been destroyed by the forces of nature pounding against it. And yet, at the right moment, the seed will sprout out from the entrails of the ground, transformed into the very tree that bore the fruit carrying it within.

> Every religion coming after it (the Law of Moses), is in reality evolving towards it, seeking to become like it. Their distance from it (the

---

8, 16c. Cf. Saul Lieberman, *Greek in Jewish Palestine* (New York: Philipp Feldheim, 1965), p. 26 n. 76. On the limits of this cooperation, see my *Golden Doves with Silver Dots: Semiotics and Textuality in Rabbinic Tradition* [henceforth: *Golden Doves*] (Bloomington, Indiana: Indiana University Press, 1986, pp. 123-124.

³⁶ *Sanhedrin* 59a, *MT Melakhim* 10:9.

³⁷ *Teshubot ha-Rambam*, ed. and tr. J. Blau, 4 vols. (Jerusalem: Mekize Nirdamim, 1975-1986), #149, vol. 1, pp. 284-285.

³⁸ Maimonides, *Guide*, III, 32, p. 379 (l. 12). See my *Homo Mysticus* (Syracuse, NY: Syracuse University Press, 1999), p. 151. All references to Maimonides' *Guide* are to the Arabic original, *Dalalat al-Ḥa'irin*, eds. Issachar Joel and Solomon Munk (Jerusalem, 1931). A similar view was expressed by Aimé Pallière, *The Unknown Sanctuary*, with a Preface by Abraham I. Carmel (New York: Bloch Publishing Company, 1971), pp. 234-235.

Law of Moses) is superficial. Actually, these religions are the preparatory groundwork and a preamble to the Messiah that we (Jews, together with these religions) wait for. He (the Messiah) is the fruit! At the end of days, when they would acknowledge him [these religions] will become his fruit—and the tree will be one [cf. *Ez* 37:19]. It is only then, that they will honor the root [Israel], which they had previously despised.[39]

Carrying this vision further, Maimonides proclaimed that eventually, members of these three faiths would be "standing shoulder to shoulder" to welcome the Messiah.[40]

Israel never perceived Christianity and Islam as *religious* enemies, simply because Israel never had and never will have a *religious* enemy. Such a notion would stand in stark contrast with the Jewish belief that every human being is endowed with the "image of God" and is, as the rabbis taught, "a full integral world" unto himself.[41] Prior to

---

[39] R. Judah ha-Levi, *Kuzari* IV, 23. Our translation comes from the original Arabic, *Kitab al-Radd wa-al Dalil fi-al Din Dhalil*, ed. H. Baneth (Jerusalem: Magness Press, 1977), p. 172. For the Hebrew version, see *Kuzari*, ed. and tr. Yehuda Even Shmuel, (Tel-Aviv: Dvir Publishing, 1994), p. 178. Further developing this metaphor, some later rabbis depicted Judaism and Christianity as "two branches of one tree"; see my "Sephardim in the Nineteenth Century: New Directions and Old Values," *Proceedings of the American Academy for Jewish Studies*, 44 (1977), p. 46. On the principle that there is an evolutionary movement in Christianity towards Judaism, let me copy the following lines from Aimé Pallière, *The Unknown Sanctuary*, p. 182:

> Christians of all communions, orthodox, liberals, and those among them who have ceased to believe, all of these are made aware of this evident fact, that all the reforms at present within Christendom are really tending toward Judaism. The dogmas which are decidedly crumbling after having been considered during centuries as impregnable fortresses, without which no Christian faith was possibly, are precisely those which Israel stubbornly denied for nineteen hundred years. The ideal which little by little emerges from the haze of dogmatics, and in which certain spirits, keener than they knew, saw evidence of the Judaization of the Christian people, is the ideal of the prophets, and Christianity tends more and more to transform itself into *Messianism* in conformity with the Jewish conception.

[40] See quotation below Section IV, n. 126.

[41] Mishna *Sanhedrin* 4:5; see above n. 18. On Jewish attitude towards Christianity, see Maimonides, *Teshubot* #149, vol.1, pp. 284-285; *Guide* III, 29, p. 379 (ll. 13-15), and *Homo Mysticus*, pp. 135, 151. On the Jewish attitude towards Islam, see *MT*

Christianity, no people ever claimed that Jews were their *religious* enemy, or that they had been the victims of Jewish *religious* hatred.[42] In Antiquity, wars were motivated by political and economic considerations—not by 'religion.' The idea of a 'religious enemy' was alien to the Ancient world. It was first invented by Christianity to target Jews. Without the creation of a 'religious enemy,' Christianity would have been indistinguishable from any of the multitude of religions flourishing in the pagan world. As we will see in the course of this work, if one were to discount the elements 'borrowed' from the *Hebrew Scripture* (to use rhetorically *against* Israel), then we will soon discover that *every single detail* 'peculiar' to the Christian religion—including the Immaculate conception, Incarnation, Atonement, Resurrection, as well as the cult of the Eucharist, etc—come from the pagan world (see below Chapter 24). The single contribution made by Christianity to religion—previously unknown to both Jews and pagans—is the invention of a '*Jewish* religious enemy.' Thus, anti-Jewish writers of the sort of Sir Edward Gibbon (1737-1794) excused Christian misanthropy by blaming, who else, the Jews! Assuming that Christianity had adapted *every single detail* from the Jewish *Scripture*—from the prohibition of cooking meat with milk to circumcision—Gibbon made this vile allegation: "The inflexible and, if we may use the expression, the intolerant zeal of the Christians, derived, it is true, from Jewish religion."[43] This is a shameful lie! As made abundantly clear by R. Elie Benamozegh (1822-1900):

> Yes, the religious enemy is a creation altogether Christian, unknown

---

Ma'akhalot Asurot 11:7; *Teshubot* #448, vol. 2, pp. 725-727; cf. *Guide* III, 29, p. 379 (ll. 13-15).

[42] See *In the Shadow of History*, p. 198. The fact that Christian anti-Semites had to fabricate 'blood-libels' and all kind of diabolic rituals to justify their neurotic fear of Jews, proves that there was nothing outside their demented mind that could corroborate these accusations.

[43] Edward Gibbon, *The Decline and Fall of the Roman Empire*, XV, vol. 1 (New York: The Modern Library, n.d.), p. 383. About Gibbon's 'malicious erudition' against Jews, see *HS*, vol. 2, Appendix #20. Concerning Christian misanthropy, see *HS*, vol. 2, Appendices ## 21, 24.

to Judaism, *impossible* even at the moment that it admits that eternal salvation is not the exclusive heritage of the Mosaic Law.[44] [Italics in original]

As mentioned earlier, *all* of Christian religious doctrines, including the cult of the Eucharist, come from the pagan world. It is only when addressing a public barred from exploring Jewish life and values that Christianity can boast of her superlative 'Biblical virtues.' However, were one to compare the *practice* of Biblical virtues in Christendom with the *practice of the same virtues* within the Jewish communities *throughout the world*, then the Christian self-congratulatory arguments would ring hollow and vastly overrated: a gross caricature of the misery facing the poor, the sick, and the disadvantaged in the midst of Christian opulence. Thus the greatest fear of the ecclesiastic authorities was having the faithful look at Jews and Judaism with their own eyes.[45] It is only by demonizing the Jews and Judaism that

---

[44] Elie Benamozegh, *Jewish and Christian Ethics* (San Francisco: Emanuel Blochman, 5633-1873), pp. 83-84. In my view, only in the Holy Land are 'pious gentiles' required to observe the Seven Noahide Precepts; see *HS*, vol. 2, Appendix #11.

[45] This theme underlies Yshac Cardoso, *Las Excelencias de los Hebreos* (Amsterdam: David de Castro Tartas, 1679). On this book and its author, see the masterful work of Yosef Yerushalmi, *From Spanish Court to Italian Ghetto* (New York: Columbia University, 1971). This is how Pallière described the impact of seeing Jews praying at the conclusion of the *Yom Kippur* services, *The Unknown Sanctuary*, p. 24:

> This is what I realized on that day. In saying that it was not the Jewish religion, but the Jewish people which revealed itself to me at that moment, I set down a fact that was only clear to me personally.

I would like to call attention to a remarkable passage by James Michener (1907-1997), *The Source* (New York: Random House, 1965), p. 468, describing a Friday evening service, by one of his characters, Cullinane, an archaeologist digging in Israel.

> So as the summer passed, John Cullinane became less a Catholic and more a Jew, immersing himself in the weekly ritual that had kept the Jews together through dispersions that would have destroyed a lesser people. In fact, he grew to love the Friday sunset, when Jewish men, freshly washed and dressed, walked like kings to the synagogues to go through the rites of welcoming Queen Shabbat. More sacred than any day of the Hebrew calendar was this Shabbat, when the creation of the world and God's compact with the Jews were remembered, and it occurred once each week, more sacred perhaps than Easter to a Christian or Ramadan to a Muslim.

Christianity could offer her conceited and depraved view of the Law and the people of Israel. Hence the Christian imperative to invent the equation 'Jew= religious enemy.'

In this fashion, Christian authorities ended up transforming Christianity into a *persecuting* religion, the first of its kind! To this end, it raided the *Tora*, given as a holy patrimony to Israel, and used it as an instrument to launch 'religious wars' against humanity. The two most important ideas that the Christian authorities 'borrowed' from the Jews—'monotheism' and 'love'—became excuses for *aggression* and *domination*. For the ecclesiastic authorities, the purpose of 'monotheism' is not to teach that there is only One God—the Mystery of the Holy Trinity makes this point abundantly clear—but that there is only *One Religion*, which you must accept, or else…[46] The same is true of Christian 'love.' It is a psychological mask designed to justify disorderly behavior (see below, Chapter 7). It demands total surrender. If you refuse to accept her advances, you are the 'enemy.' In law, this is call 'rape.' By contrast, the love taught by Israel is grounded on respect for the uniqueness and autonomy of the 'other'—best symbolized by the Hebrew idea that every individual is created "in the image of God," and the subsequent rabbinic doctrine that "the pious among the nations of the world," i.e., non-Jews, "have a portion in the world to Come." So, if there is one thing about which Christianity *cannot* teach Jews that is 'love.'

I believe there are plenty of Christians that would agree with that. Let me narrate an episode, taking place over one hundred and fifty years ago. It concerned Andrew Bonar (1810-1892), a well-known Christian missionary, and R. Judah Bibas (1780-1852), whom he described as "a genuine Pharisee of the old school, rigidly observing the Jewish law." Like many devout Christians, Bonar believed that 'Christian love' mandates the conversion of the Jews. At the end of their meeting, Bonar mentioned to R. Bibas that his missionary work was moved by love of Israel.

---

[46] See, however, Paul Tillich, *Dynamics of Faith* (New York: Harper & Row, 1957), pp. 122-125.

On our rising to take leave, and mentioning that love to Israel had brought us to visit him, he [Rabbi Bibas] declared that he loved Christians exceedingly, and that no Christian loved the Jews more than he did Christians.

I am convinced that Bonar believed him. In fact, later on, he referred to him as "our friend Rabbi Bibas."[47]

One may argue that the Trial of Jesus and the Jewish refusal to accept him *compelled* the Christian authorities to demonize Jews. In the course of this work we will see that Jesus' Trial and Passion, as presented in the *Christian Scripture*, were never intended to be taken as court proceedings. Rather, they were modeled in the fashion of the many popular 'mock-trials,' performed throughout the Roman world to incite violence against Jews. But let us concede, for argument's sake, that the *Christian Scripture* is actually reporting indisputable 'facts'—something that nobody knowing Roman or Jewish law would concede—still, what was the point in demonizing the Jews? Why could one not argue, as Benjamin Disraeli (1804-1881) did in his *Tancred*, that if true, then Christians should kneel down to Jews for having supplied not only the sacrifice but also the immolators.

> The holy race [the Jewish people] supplied the victim [Jesus] and the immolators [the Jewish authorities]… Persecute us! Why if you believed what you profess, you should kneel to us! You raise statues to the hero who saves a country. We have saved the human race, and you persecute us for doing it.[48]

---

[47] The quotations proceed from Andrew A. Bonar, *Mission of Inquiry to the Jews* (Philadelphia: Presbyterian Board of Publication, 1839), p. 526, p. 393 and p. 395. For some biographical notes on R. Bibas, see my "Early Zionist Ideals Among Sephardim in the Nineteenth Century," *Judaism* 25 (1976), pp. 60-62; and "Sephardim in the Nineteenth Century: New Directions and Old Values," p. 47. A most glaring example of this type of friendship is Ezra Stiles and R. H.I. Carigal; see George A. Kohut, *Ezra Stiles and the Jews* (New York: Philip Cowen, 1902), pp. 114-133, and cf. pp. 79-98. For a sample of Jewish respect and admiration for Christian Hebraists, see the long list mentioned in the dedication of R. David Cohen de Lara, *Keter Kehunna*.

[48] *Tancred* Bk III, Ch. 4.

It would have taken less theological ingenuity to teach the above, than to teach about the Mystery of the Holy Trinity: how 'one' is really 'three' and 'three' really 'one.'

Together with the notion of a 'religious enemy,' Christianity has the distinction of introducing the idea of 'Holy War,' the first of which were the Crusades against 'Islam,' during the 11th-13th centuries. Later on, when war against 'Islam' was no longer practical, 'religious wars' between different Christian denominations followed—principally from ca. 1524-1651, but continuing, in one way or another, until our days (for example, the conflict between Northern and Southern Ireland). When a religious war against another nation was not expedient, atrocities against Jews, in the form of Expulsions, Inquisitions, pogroms, and wholesale extermination, could help pump up the spirit of the faithful.

The Christian notion of 'monotheism,' as a supreme mandate to impose the 'true' religion on humankind, if necessary by the point of the sword, yielded unexpected fruits. Christianity has the unique distinction of having generated *another* 'monotheistic' religion in *her* image. All the beautiful and exalting ideas that Islam offered the world are subservient to the Christian equation, 'monotheism'='Holy War.' The semantic equivalent of 'religious enemy' in Arabic is *kafir*, and of 'Holy War', is *ijtihad*. Those carrying this 'Holy Mission' are call *mujtahidin*—the semantic equivalent of *Milites Christi* in Latin. (Some historians consider the impending war between the Christian and Muslim nations as a 'Clash of Civilizations.' I believe that a more accurate description would be a 'Clash between *Milites Christi* and *mujtahidin*).

Surveying our arguments thus far, Jews and Judaism never regarded Christianity or any other religion as a 'religious enemy.' Christianity created the first religious enemy in history in order to justify the persecution of Jews, and the despoiling of their properties and religious monuments. Before the spread of Christianity, Israel had no *religious* enemies. This explains the curious fact that until the arrival of missionaries in modern times, anti-Semitism was unknown in the Far

East and Central Africa. Citing these points we ask: why did Christianity choose to demonize Judaism and persecute Jews? It has to do with the fact that 'religion,' whether 'polytheistic' or 'monotheistic,' will become evil when sponsored by a Rex. Inevitably, the result of such an alliance would be rendering God's word a *tool* to advance the monarch's political schemes. An entire 'Weekly Section' (*parasha*) of the *Tora* is dedicated to teaching the disastrous consequences of the alliance Rex-Prophet (*Nu* 22:2-25:9). Balaam, the main character of the story, was a pagan prophet who occasionally communicated with God. Responding to an appeal by King Balak, he decided to use his special relationship with God to curse Israel. God tells him *not* to curse Israel (*Nu* 22:12). Now, Balaam had the power to curse and to bless (*Nu* 22:6). Therefore, he could have soothed the king's fear of Israel, by *blessing* him and his people. Instead, Balaam decided to *manipulate* God by every which way, and have Him *curse* Israel. To properly understand this story, two notes are of the essence. First, for Balaam, the God of Israel was one among many deities. Yet, God communicated with him. This means that God communicates with polytheistic people (cf. *Gn* 20:3-7; 31:24). Second, there was nothing immoral or offensive in his prophecy. Balaam's fault was in *manipulating* God's word and attempting to use it as a tool to serve the king's designs. When he failed, he decided to *manipulate* the king to erect altars at diverse places. When these maneuvers were unsuccessful, and he realized that he could not manipulate *God*, instead of desisting, he counseled the king to *manipulate* the *women*, so that they would *manipulate* the *Jewish men* to participate in their cult (see *Nu* 24:14; 25:1-3). Balaam's advice, rather than his curse, yielded results. As a consequence, one of the leaders of Israel succumbed, sinning with a Midianitish woman, in what involved a sexual pagan cult. The man challenged Moses and Aaron. Mayhem broke out in the camp, and Moses and Aaron found themselves helpless (see *Nu* 25:6). It is at this critical moment that Phineḥas arose and slew the political leader and the woman. Thus, he established the precedent that political leaders, too, are bound to the Law, just like everybody else.

A few brief observations should be made in closing. The rabbis associate Phineḥas with Prophet Elijah, given that both confronted the political ruler in the name of the Law. They also associated Balaam with Christianity. As with the proverbial Balaam, invariably, the Church was sponsored by a *political* system that victimized Jews as a matter of *national policy*, thus enabling the ecclesiastic authorities to promote a system *requiring* the eventual *abolition* of Judaism and the *elimination* of Jews. In both cases, the word of God is manipulated to serve as a tool in the service of the monarch's anti-Jewish policies. Both these aspects are functionally linked. Alone in history, Israel stands for the supreme rule of the Law, rather than the monarch; cursing Israel serves to silence the people that witnessed God's Theophany at Sinai. There is another aspect worth considering. As with the proverbial Balaam, the 'monotheistic religions' use God's word, not to bestow blessing on their own people, but in their vain task to curse Israel.[49]

Let me add, that Judaism and Christianity are guided by two

---

[49] Balaam is a historical figure; see *'Olam ha-Tanakh, Bemidbar* (Jerusalem: Rebibim, 1985), pp. 137c-138c. He is mentioned in the *Mishna Sanhedrin* 10:2, and *Abot* 5:19. Alluding to the fact that Christianity is not a nation, the rabbis expanded on the name 'Balaam' (*bal* 'no'+ *'am* 'nation'= 'no nation') and used it as a code name for 'Christianity' ('Jesus' or 'Paul'); see *Sanhedrin* 105a. On the association 'Jesus/Balaam' in *Abot* 5:19, see H. R. Charles *The Apocrypha and Pseudepigrapha of the Old Testament*, vol. 2 (Oxford: Clarendon Press, 1979), p. 709 n. 22. On the association 'Jesus/Balaam' in rabbinic literature in general; see R. Travers Herford, *Christianity in Talmud & Midrash* (London: Williams & Norgate, 1903), pp. 63-78; cf. below, Section II, n. 156. R. Travers Herford, *The Ethic of the Talmud: Saying of the Fathers* (New York: Schocken Books, 1962), pp. 142-143, properly noted that not in all cases 'Balaam' stands for 'Jesus.' On Balaam refusal to use his power to bless his own people, but only to curse Israel, cf. R. Isaac Caro, *Toledot Yiṣḥaq* (Riva di Trento, 5318/1558), 93b *in fine*-94a. This is why, one of the characteristics of Balaam's disciples is "meanness" (= *'ayyin ra'a*, see *Abot* 5:19). It is a peculiar strategy used by anti-Semites. On the one hand, they envy the accomplishment of the 'Jew,' while at the same time, instead of striving for excellence, they bad-mouth him to hide their feelings of inadequacy; see the quotation from Fromm, Section IV, n. 8. On the association 'Phineḥas/Prophet Elijah,' see *Yalquṭ ha-Tora* (Venice, 5326/1566), #771, 244b-c; and cf. Rashi on *Baba Meṣi'a* 114b *s.v.* 'ervat. For an intelligent study of the misuse and manipulation of religion, see Charles Kimball, *When Religion Becomes Evil* (San Francisco: Harper San Francisco, 2002).

radically different principles. For the Jew the "image of God" within involves the idea of a God whose *conduct* is marked by 'goodness' (*tob*) and 'kindness' (*raḥamim*) to all (see *Ps* 145:9). From this point of view, your most sublime responsibility to the 'other' is not to convince him that he is 'wrong' and you are 'right,' but to give him/her a helping hand. Therefore, the earmark of the Jew is not his 'faith,' but his kindness to others (*raḥamim*). It is a matter of human fellowship, pure and simple. The gold-standard in treating 'others,' including heathens and servants, explained R. Yoḥanan (ca. 180-ca. 279), is Job's standard: "Did not He that made me in the womb make him? And did not One fashion us in the womb?"—not as a matter of law, but as a matter of human fellowship.[50] The point of Judaism is that *your* theological views are between *you* and *your* Maker, and please don't tell me about them. Instead, let us see how *we* can gird our loins and together stretch out a helping hand to the poor, the orphan, and the wronged. The guiding principle in Christianity is 'theology'—Salvation, Original Sin, the Calvary, Hell, Damnation, Atonement, etc. Theology breeds conflict. Kindness (*raḥamim*) builds bridges.[51]

* * *

Properly understood, Christianity and the *Christian Scripture* represent an older form of spirituality and devotion than Judaism. Biblical Nimrod, the first tyrant in history, and Patriarch Abraham, the father of Judaism, were contemporaneous and 'made' each other. Early in his childhood, so Jewish tradition recounts, Abraham broke the local idols. Significantly, he was summoned, not by the priests,

---

[50] *Yerushalmi Ketubbot* V, 5, 30a; cf. *Baba Qamma* VIII, 5, 6c. See *MT 'Abadim* 9:8; *Melakhim* 10:12. For the rabbinic sources, see Maran Joseph Caro, *Kesef Mishne*, ad loc. Kindness (*raḥamim*) is one of the three fundamental traits peculiar to the Jewish ethos; see *Yebamot* 79a and *Debarim Rabba*, ed. Saul Lieberman (Jerusalem: Wahrman Books, 1974), *'Eqeb* IV, pp. 85-86. In this spirit, my mother and sisters would personally serve the maids before they waited on us.

[51] See below, Section I, n. 158; Section II, n. 68. In Judaism matters of faith are not justifiable in a court of justice; see *HS*, vol. 1, pp. 79-81.

but by tyrant Nimrod. In a totalitarian state, 'religion' is just another arm of the political establishment designed to enslave its subjects from within. In regards to Abraham, the true god was not the idols that the people worshiped, but the *Übermensch*-Nimrod who had the power to tell the people which idols to worship and which not to worship. Thus, when you challenge 'religion,' you are challenging the absolute authority of the tyrant. Tyrannical authority was exercised for the first time in history, when Nimrod threw Abraham into a furnace of fire. Out of this clash were born, simultaneously, the first tyrant and the first Jew. Josephus wrote that after the Deluge, Nimrod incited the people against their Maker.

> They (the people) were incited to this insolent contempt of God by Nebrodes (=Nimrod), grandson of Ham the son of Noah, an audacious man of doughty vigor. He persuaded them to attribute their prosperity not to God but to their own valor, and little by little transformed the state of affairs into a tyranny, holding that the only way to detach men from the fear of God was by making them continuously dependent upon his own power. He threatened to have his revenge on God if He wished to inundate the earth again: for he would build a tower higher than the water could reach and avenge the destruction of their forefathers.
>
> The people were eager to follow this advice of Nebrodes (=Nimrod), deeming it slavery to submit to God; so they set out to build the tower with indefatigable ardor and no slackening in the task.[52]

Abraham was the first man to refuse a direct command from the sovereign; Nimrod was the first ruler to throw someone to the fire for failing to comply with his command. Without Abraham refusing to bow down to Nimrod's gods, Nimrod could not have exercised tyrannical authority; conversely, without an absolute tyrant demanding unconditional submission, there would not have arisen an

---

[52] *Jewish Antiquities*, I, 113, *Josephus*, vol. 4, p. 55. Cf. "On the Giants," 66, *Philo*, vol. 2, p. 479. See *'Erubin* 53a; *Pesaḥim* 118a. For an intelligent analysis of this issue, see Silvano Arieti, *Abraham and the Contemporary Mind* (New York: Basic Books, 1981), pp. 53-55.

individual with the guts to say 'No!' to the *Übermensch du jour*. The history of Israel is the continuing unfolding of this primordial struggle.

God revealed Himself to Abraham *after* he was thrown into the flames. There was a good reason for that. People inhabiting the realm of the *Übermensch* are impervious to God's word. To hear His word, Abraham had to first shatter Nimrod's idols. The process took a long time. Early in his childhood, he "pondered and attempted to understand" on his own, about God and the world. After years of endeavor, he finally discovered the truth, "out of his own precise intelligence."[53] What made Abraham's truth exceptional was the fact that he deemed it trustworthy and was ready to die for it, not because some *Übermensch* told him that it was so, but because "his own precise intelligence" showed him that it was so! People controlled by *Übermensch*-idols can obey orders, but cannot enter into a dialogue with anyone, for the simple reason that they cannot exercise personal judgment without prior approval from the *Übermensch*. At this level of human development, 'knowledge' is a function of obedience. People know what they know because somebody above told them that it is so! This explains the strange fact that the *Hebrew Scripture* did not record Abraham's smashing of the idols or Nimrod's attempt to burn him alive. The *Hebrew Scripture* is not for everyone. An absolute prerequisite for processing the *Hebrew Scripture* is having previously crushed the idols erected by the *Übermensch*, on your own.[54] Otherwise, the voice of the God of Israel will be quelled by the racket and clamor of all kind of minor and major Nimrods.

Israel in Egypt, too, had the fortitude to smash the idols erected by tyrant Pharaoh. They, alone among multitudes of slaves, had the

---

[53] See Maimonides' *MT, 'Aboda Zara* 1:3. The source is Philo, see the quotation below, Section I, n. 168.

[54] In this connection it should be noted that before a child is taught the first letters of the *Hebrew Scripture*, his father must teach him two verses from Scripture *Dt* 33: 4 and *Dt* 6:4; see *Sukka* 42a, *MT Talmud Tora* 1:6, *Shulḥan 'Arukh, Yore De'a* CCXLV, 5.

mettle to recognize that they were nothing but slaves in a nation of slaves. It was at that pivotal moment in history that the people of Israel raised their voices in anguish to God, "out of their bondage," and began their journey towards freedom (see *Ex* 2:23-25). Like Patriarch Abraham, Moses had the grit to say 'No' to Tyrant Pharaoh (see *Ex* 2:11-14). There is a remarkable similarity between the tactics chosen by Moses and Abraham. Both concluded that people bowing down to the idols of a *Übermensch* are impervious to God's words, and that to hear God's words you must first leave the tyrant's territory. God spoke to Abraham *on his way* towards the land of Israel (see *Gn* 12:1), and to Moses when he was in the Sinai Desert (see *Ex* 3:1-3). What about the Jewish people? Did they possess the mental and linguistic apparatus to process God's message at Sinai? The answer is an unqualified 'Yes!' To ascertain this pivotal point, Israel was subjected to the most exhaustive psychological test ever—a test designed by God Himself.

Israel's phenomenal discovery—first (and last?) in the annals of history—that they were slaves, led to another, equally phenomenal discovery. Freedom is incompatible with belief in any sort of a *Übermensch*—regardless of whether you call him 'Nimrod,' 'Pharaoh,' or something else. People requiring the approval of a *Übermensch* to validate their own experiences, would not—could not—hear God's voice. Now, if there ever were a man worthy of bearing the title *Übermensch*—that man was Moses (see below Chapter 33). The Ten Plagues he brought into Egypt, his triumph over Pharaoh, and then the splitting of the sea, so that a group of slaves could cross over into freedom, would certainly qualify Moses for that title. What proved beyond a shadow of a doubt that Israel had broken the chains of bondage was the fact that they refused to believe that Moses was a *Übermensch*—a kind of a benevolent Nimrod or Pharaoh, if you will. To underline this point, we are told that after crossing the Red Sea, "Israel saw the great work which the Lord did upon Egypt, and the people felt awe for the Lord"—not for Moses—"and they believed [first] in the Lord, and [then] in his servant Moses" (*Ex* 14:31). That is exactly the opposite of what takes place in the minds of slaves. People inhabiting the realm of a *Übermensch* would have first believed in Moses, and *then* in whatever god he would propose. In the minds of slaves, the fact that Moses pointed at the sea and thereupon it split, would constitute irrefutable proof of Moses' power. As a matter of fact, the Egyptians believed that on account of the miracles he performed, "Moses was very great" (see *Ex* 11:3). Israel did not think so. They first "believed in the Lord," and *then* "in his <u>servant</u> Moses" (*Ex* 14:31)—not the other way around. You need to free yourself first from the earthly master, so that you can recognize the God of the *Hebrew Scripture*. Otherwise, you will end up identifying 'God' with your earthly master. The problem with the 'monotheism' of pagan humanity (Christianity and Islam) is that they did not break the bondage of their *political* master, Nimrod/Pharaoh, *before* hearing the word of God, Creator of Heavens and Earth. Hence the abysmal distance between the God of Israel and the God of Christianity and Islam. Invariably, people in mental bondage, first believe in their *Übermensch* and then in a deity tailored to fit him; god, religion, etc., are ancillary concepts designed to support, and further enhance, the *Übermensch*'s power. Did Moses ever feel insulted because Israel refused to attribute the miracles to *his* power? Was there consequently a strain between the people and him? Quite the contrary, "Then sang Moses <u>and</u> the children of Israel this song unto the Lord, and <u>they</u> (*vayyomeru*, pl.: Moses <u>and</u> the people of Israel) spoke, saying: I will sing unto the Lord, for He is highly exalted; the horse and his rider, <u>He</u> threw into the sea" (*Ex* 15:1), etc., etc. Unlike hierarchic societies, where the tension between the ruler and the ruled is constant, in a horizontal society the people and the leadership march ahead toward the same goal, singing together in harmony.

* * *

The central thesis of the First Section is that the *foundational* difference between Judaism and Christianity pertains neither to 'religion' nor 'spirituality,' but to the *medium* of communication. In pagan humanity, the constitutive values of society are transmitted from top to bottom. 'Authority' warrants a *Übermensch*, issuing commands from a 'first-party platform'—speaking as 'I/we'—to a 'third-party platform.' As such, the 'third-party platform' is banned from entering into a direct dialogue ('I-you') with *Übermensch*. (Hence, the need for a 'Holy Ghost,' or intermediary between God and man, in Christian theology). The sole function of people inhabiting the 'third-party platform' is obedience. To accomplish this, the individual must suppress 'his own precise intelligence' on behalf of the pronouncements of the *Übermensch*. It is by this act of self-suppression that members of the third-party platform actually know that the *Übermensch*'s pronouncements are the absolute 'truth.' According to this system, the concepts 'truth,' *Übermensch*, 'first-' and 'third-party platforms' are interdependent. Invariably, the '*Übermensch*' announces the 'truth' from the 'first-party platform.' The 'truth' proclaimed from 'first-party platform' is absolute, because it was said to be so by the '*Übermensch*.' At the same time, members of the 'third-party platform' can positively know that they are privy to 'the truth,' since the 'first-party platform' said that it is so. The overall effect of this system is that the 'third-party platform' must accept as apodictic 'truth' the pronouncement made from the 'first-party platform,' given that it was made by the '*Übermensch*.' In the same Section we propose that 'myth' does not depend on the content, but on the medium of transmission: '*Übermensch*'/'first-party platform' → 'third-party platform.' Accordingly, it would be irrelevant whether the message is '1+3=4,' or '1+3=1.' In either case the message equals 'myth,' given that members of the 'third-party platform' are barred from analyzing the 'truth' according to their 'own precise intelligence.' A significant aspect of the '*Übermensch*'/'first-person platform' system is that, necessarily, it warrants the division 'superior/inferior.' Thus, all mythical civilizations are hierarchically structured (and vice versa). 'Order,' 'organization,' etc., require *submission* of the 'lower' to the 'higher' echelons, not on the basis of pragmatic considerations, but, solely, on the fact that in the quality of a 'third-party,' the 'faithful' must express 'faith' in the infallibility of those standing 'above.' This will explain why a myth *ought* to be unprovable: its authority must depend, exclusively, on the fact that it was so proclaimed by the first-party platform. Questioning the validity of a myth on the basis of one's 'precise intelligence,' as Patriarch Abraham, is an affront to hierarchic authority.[55]

There are *political* implications to the Hebrew concept that every human being is created in the *image* of God (*Gn* 1:27). One of which is that an individual need not surrender 'his own precise intelligence' on behalf of the *Übermensch*. Israel rejects the very idea of a hierarchic humanity, divided into 'superior/ inferior.' The constitutive values of Israel, in both the 'written' (=*Hebrew Scripture*) and 'oral' (=rabbinic tradition) forms, were *not* proclaimed from a first-party platform to an audience acting in terms of a third-party, whose function is to obey. Jewish Law is the result of a *horizontal* accord. In Sinai, God spoke in the first-person singular, 'I' (*anokhi*), to each member of Israel, in the second-person singular (*/kha*), thereby setting up a dialogue, where second-person 'Israel' can turn and speak, in quality of first-person 'I,' to the second-person 'God.' At both Sinai and Moab, the covenant required and obtained the ratification of the people, thus instituting the principle that government requires the consent of the governed: even when the governor is God, Creator of Heavens and Earth. It follows, that the 'Hebrew Law' is the Supreme authority of Israel, not because some sort of a *Übermensch* imposed it, but because both parties to the covenant, God and Israel, wished to establish it.

In the Hebrew mind, the most exclusive characteristic of the God of Israel is not His 'power'—after all, He is the Creator of everything—but that He operates within the confines of the very 'Law'

---

[55] In my view, the fact that Indo-European languages admit the 'third-person' as a grammatical person, equal to the first and second persons, proves conclusively that their 'persons' are not *linguistic* persons; see below Chapter 1, and the quotations at notes 14, 135. This linguistic phenomenon may be connected to the fact that Indo-European societies are hierarchically organized and therefore find it difficult to apprehend the linguistic equality intrinsic to the act of speech 'I/you.'

that He contracted with Israel. The God of Israel does *not* act as a *Übermensch*. At both Sinai and Moab, God's proposal to establish a covenant required *ratification by the people*. A unanimous "Amen," too, ratified the *sanctions* of the covenant.[56] At the Synagogue, too, the congregants express approval to the prayers by responding 'Amen!' In Judaism, the precentor leading the prayers *does not* represent a 'higher authority' to which the congregation must submit. Rather, as per the Hebrew denomination, he is the *Sheliaḥ Ṣibbur* or the 'Congregation's Envoy.' Therefore, to conduct the services, he requires the *unanimous* consent of the congregants. This means that

> even a single member of the congregation may prevent his nomination, and state: 'I do not wish that he should be the precentor.'[57]

Were he to attempt to lead the services without obtaining their consent, the public should refrain from answering 'Amen.'[58]

Intimately connected with this principle is the Hebrew concept of 'Book.' A Hebrew 'Book' has two exceptional characteristics. First, it is a national publication, transmitted in perpetuity *by* the nation of Israel *to* the nation of Israel. Second, it is inscribed only in consonants. Vowels are formally excluded from the text. A vocalized Scroll of the *Tora* is ritually void and may not be used for public reading. Thus, Hebrew 'reading' involves the active participation of the 'reader' (=second-person), who provides the vowels to the 'consonantal text' (=sacred text, first-person).[59] A 'Book' is the effect of the inter-

---

[56] See *Dt* 27:15-25. On other occasions, when addressed by the political leader, the people of Israel gave their unanimous consent in a similar manner; see *Neh* 5:13 [cf. *Ps* 106:48; 1*Ch*16: 36], 8:6. At the end of his career, when proposing to the people to accept God's Law as *the* Law of the land, Joshua sought and received, the explicit consent of all the people; see *Jos* 24:1-28, specially, vv. 21-28. Even a woman suspected of adultery, needs to give her consent to the invocation of the priest, and respond "Amen!" See *Nu* 5:26. More significant is the rule requiring that the congregants respond with an approving 'Amen' to the priestly blessings at the Synagogue; see *MT Tefilla* 9:3.

[57] Maran Joseph Caro, *Shulḥan 'Arukh, Oraḥ Ḥayyim* LIII, 19.

[58] Rama, *Shulḥan 'Arukh, Oraḥ Ḥayyim* DLXXXI, 1.

[59] In this fashion, the Hebrew 'reader' is in effect the 'writer' of the *Scripture*; see

action 'sacred text'-'reader' that brings it to life. A consequence of this principle is that the *Tora* "is no longer in the Heavens"; that is, the Heavens cannot impose the meaning of the 'Book' on the 'people of the Book.'[60] This follows a general linguistic principle, whereby in the act of speech 'I/you,' the semantics of the sentence is determined by the second, not the first, person. Accordingly, the meaning of the 'Law' must be established by second-person Israel, and her duly-recognized judicial and legislative representatives.[61]

In short, in the First Section we propose that the conflict between Christianity and Judaism stems from two mutually exclusive systems of transmission. One hierarchic, where the 'public' knows the 'truth' because it was so announced by the *Übermensch* and approved by the first-party platform; and another, horizontal, where the 'Law,' 'truth,' and 'authority' are the effect of a *berit* (a covenant), freely negotiated by the linguistic persons 'I' and 'you.' Myths do not allow for dissention or diverse interpretation. The rabbinic principle, "the *Tora* expresses itself in the language of man," serves to define the linguistic reciprocity 'speaker-God/addressee-people.'[62] An important outcome of this principle is that the 'meaning' of the sacred text is established through dialogue and persuasion, as beautifully illustrated by the sages of the Talmud. It also serves to explain why Jews pay little attention to theological bullies: mostly, victims of severe delusions of grandeur.

* * *

The different media of transmission dividing Christianity and Judaism lead to two conflicting biographies of the 'real' Jesus. Christian knowledge of Jesus is contingent on having previously accepted

---

HS, vol.1, pp. 3-4.

[60] See *Baba Meṣi'a* 59b; cf. *Golden Doves,* pp. 13-14, 119; *HS,* vol. 1, pp. 5, 58, notes 29-30.

[61] For a detailed analysis of these basic concepts, see *HS,* vol. 1, Chapters 5, 6, 44.

[62] See *Berakhot* 31b; *Golden Doves,* p. xxi and corresponding note, pp. 151-152.

the infallibility of the editors of the *Christian Scripture* and ecclesiastical authorities. According to the medium of myth, it is axiomatic that neither the *Übermensch* nor members of the first-party need to provide evidence: it is so because *it was said* that *it is so*. Only on the basis of this postulate can the faithful accept as apodictic truth the Christian version of Jesus' Birth, Ministry, Trial, Crucifixion and Resurrection. Conceptually, it demands that the faithful should process Jesus' biography backwards: from *end* to *beginning*. Once Resurrection is accepted as an incontrovertible fact, then and then only is it possible to proceed to interpret backwards the significance of the Crucifixion, his Trial, Ministry, Birth and Miraculous Conception. All of these 'facts' are known with absolute certainty, because they were said to be so by the proper authority. A condition for this sort of knowledge is that, in contradistinction to the Patriarch Abraham, the faithful forfeits his own precise intelligence on behalf of the truth revealed by the *Übermensch*. The story of Jesus' birth, as well as his life and death, would amount to nothing unless we accept, as an apodictic truth, that "God sent forth his Son, made of a woman" (*Gal* 4:4). It is on this basis that the faithful must conclude that Jesus is "The Son of God with power, according to the spirit of holiness, by the resurrection of the death" (*Rom* 1:4).

* * *

Jews knew Jesus when he was living and preaching in the land of Israel. They spoke with him face to face, argued with him, and exchanged views with his followers. There were fundamental disagreements between his teachings and the faith of Israel, but Judaism has always been a pluralistic society. In the Second Section we examine Jesus' life and ministry, as they appear in Jewish sources. The point of departure is that, far from being a "helpless-baby in the manger," Jesus "was close to the ruling circles"—the infamous publicans, who paid huge sums of money to the Roman authorities for the right to extort taxes from the working class: the small farmer, the shopkeeper, the artisan, and the laborer (see Chapter 12). The sumptuous tomb of Jesus' family found in modern Talpiot (on the outskirts of modern Jerusalem) provides archeological evidence that this was the resting place of men and women of immense power and wealth.[63] A close reading of the description of Jesus' life found in the *Christian Scripture,* corroborates this pivotal point: his intimate association with, and steadfast defense of, publicans and their lady-companions, his eating and drinking habits, his obsession with foot-massage and similar luxuries—all these indicate that we are not dealing with someone unaccustomed to the pleasantries of high-living (see below, Chapters 11-12).[64]

In the same Section we propose that the conflict between Jesus and the Pharisees was a clash between two political camps. One made up of publicans and their associates, and the other made up of the Jewish masses, standing up against enemy-collaborators and informers. Jesus spoke to the Pharisees with contempt, for the same reason that men of 'rank' speak with scorn and derision to people 'below.' This explains the notable fact—somehow unnoticed by exegetes and historians—that, *as reported in the Christian Scripture*, there never was a publican or a prostitute whom Jesus did not treat with deference, nor a Pharisee and rabbi whom he did not insult.[65] In this connection we should note that although Jesus was very polite and loving with prostitutes, he was disrespectful to his mother (see *Mk* 3:33-34). We should also note that while some prostitutes came to visit his tomb, according to *Matt* 28:2, his mother did not (see Chapter 13).

This brings up another key point. In rabbinic literature, Jesus and his followers are referred to as *minim* ('sectarians,' 'dissidents'),

---

[63] See Simcha Jacobovici and Charles Pellegrino, *The Jesus Family Tomb* (San Francisco: Harper, 2007), and below Chapter 12.

[64] In Chapter 22 we propose that Jesus' involvement with tax-collection may have been the reason for his clash with the Roman authorities.

[65] Concerning Jesus' association with disreputable women, see Hyman E. Goldin, *The Case of the Nazarene Reopened* (Clark, NJ: The Lawbook Exchange, 2003), pp. 696-697, n. 228.

and their religious ideology as *minut* (Chapter 15). These terms refer to a variety of groups, holding all sorts of views about cult and basic doctrinal matters. They all, however, shared one common denominator: they were connected, directly or indirectly, to the rapacious *qarob la-malkhut*-circles: self-hating Jews, perennially pandering to the Roman authorities, while censuring fellow Jews. The rabbis referred to them as 'flatterers' (*mahanifim*), and 'hypocrites' (*hanifim*, Chapter 11). Duplicity was the name of their game: perennially hiding the ugly face of cynicism and debauchery under a mask of sanctity (Chapters 15-16). One aspect in particular, having nothing to do with 'religion,' made the *minim* odious in the eyes of Israel. They acted as the proverbial self-hating Jew: forever bowing down to the Romans, while pointing an accusing finger at their own brothers.[66] As among all self-hating Jews, the *minim* spared no effort to delegitimize the God of Israel and to make Him appear "insufferable" in the eyes of the world.[67] Because they could always count on with the 'support' of the Romans, they thought themselves superior to the rest.[68] They were bossy and vociferous and would not hesitate to disturb the services, first at the Temple and then in the Synagogue.[69] Symptomatic of their

---

[66] On this type of 'Jew,' see Sander L. Gilman, *Jewish Self-Hatred* (Baltimore: Johns Hopkins University Press, 1986). For an analysis of their personality and main characteristic, see ibid, Chapter 1. The worst case is the abominable 'self-hating Jew,' thriving in and outside the land of Israel, past and present; see *Is* 49:17, and Rashi and Radaq ad loc.

[67] See *Sifre Debarim*, ed. Louis Finkelstein (New York: The Jewish Theological Seminary of America, 1969), CCCXXXI, s.v. *ma*, p. 381; and *Shabbat* 116a.

[68] The expression "*la-minim li-rdot aharekhem*," in *Tosefta Yom ha-Kippurim* 2:10; implies 'persecution, coercion and bullying.' The term "*lirdot*" also implies hierarchic superiority, as from a human to an animal; cf. Mishna *Para* 3:2, and Maimonides, *Perush ha-Mishnayot*, ed. and tr. R. Joseph Qafih. 7 vols. (Jerusalem: Mossad Harav Kook, 1967), vol. 7, p. 421. Cf. *Sifra, Dibbura Di-Ndaba*, II, 5 (Warsaw, 1866), 4a; *Sifre Bemidbar*, ed. H. Horovitz (Jerusalem: Wahrman Books, 1966), CXLIII, p. 191; *Tosefta Ki-Fshutah*, vol. 4 (New York: The Jewish Theological Seminary of America, 1962), p. 776.

[69] On the theological doctrines of the *minim*, see *HS*, vol. 1, Chapters 25, 26, and vol. 2, Appendix #24. On the *minim* in Mishna *Berakhot* 9:7 and Talmud *Berakhot* 63a, see *HS*, vol. 2, pp. 95-97. On the *minim* in general, see *HS*, vol. 2, Appendix

haughty temper was their "malicious complaint" (*tar'omet*) against fellow Jews.[70] When they could not get their way, they would involve the Roman forces, causing havoc in the Synagogue.[71] In addition, they used the Synagogue to spy on fellow worshipers on behalf of the Roman authorities.[72] In this manner, they were constantly sowing "distrust, hatred, and rivalry" within the Jewish communities.[73] Taking advantage of the utter misery befalling the Jews after the Destruction of the Temple (68 CE) and the defeat of Bar-Koziba (d. 135), some of the *minim* decided to set themselves apart, by invoking the Holy Trinity in their daily greeting: "May you be blessed by the Father, the Son, and the Holy Ghost" (*Barukh Mar! le-Abba, wu-Bra, ve-Ruḥa de-Qudsha*"!).[74] Finally, although these *minim* practiced some aspects of Judaism, the rabbis decided to expel them from the Synagogue. With this purpose in mind, they instituted a special petition in the Daily Prayer (ca. 140 C.E.).[75] In the standard Sephardic Prayer-

---

#55. For some general remarks on the *minim* in the *Berakhot* 28a, see Isaak Halevy, *Doroth Harischonim*, vol. 5 (Frankfurt: Louis Golde, 1918), pp. 171-174. For an analysis of *Tosefta Berakhot* 3:25, see Saul Lieberman, *Tosefta Ki-Fshuṭah*, vol. 1, pp. 53-54.

[70] See *Berakhot* 12a and *Pesaḥim* 56a; *Mekhilta de-R. Yishma'el, Beshallaḥ, Masekhta de-Vayyisa'*, I, s.v. *vayyabo'u*, p. 155. A slightly different version is found in *Yerushalmi Berakhot* I, 4, 3c; see Louis Ginzberg, *A Commentary on the Palestinian Talmud* (Heb.), vol. 1 (New York: Jewish Theological Seminary, 1941), pp. 166-167. As indicated by R. Benjamin Musafia, *Tosefet he-'Arukh, s.v. tar'omet*, this is an Aramaic term, used in the *Targum* to translate the Hebrew root LWN, indicating 'murmur,' 'baseless complaint.' It appear, exclusively, in connection with the Jews leaving Egypt and their children; see *Ex* 15:24; 16: 2, 8, 9; *Nu* 14: 2, 27, 29, 34, 36; 17: 6, 20, 25; *Jos* 9:18. It may also imply affront to God's authority; see *Targum Nu* 21:5, 7. In rabbinic literature it generally refers to a frivolous suit; see *Mishna Baba Meṣi'a* 5:6; 6:1; *Tosefta Baba Meṣi'a* 4:22; 7:1, etc. For an exception, see *Baba Batra* 145b.

[71] See "The Jewish Christians," (Heb.), *Proceedings of the Israel Academy of Science and Humanities*, II (1966), p. 185.

[72] See "The Jewish Christians…," pp. 185-186.

[73] See *Shabbat* 116a; *Tosefta Shabbat* 13, 5, pp. 58-59; *Sifre Debarim*, ed. Louis Finkelstein (New York: The Jewish Theological Seminary of America, 1969), CCCXXXI, s.v. *Im*, p. 381; *Tosefta Ki-Fshuṭah*, vol. 3, pp. 206-207.

[74] For full citation and reference, see *HS*, vol. 2, p. 96.

[75] See *Berakhot* 28b-29a; *Megilla* 17b; *Yerushalmi Berakhot* IV,3,8a and *Ta'aniyot* II,7,65c; *Tosefta Berakhot* 3:25, pp. 17-18. Cf. *Midrash Tanḥuma, Vayyera*, I, ed. S.

Book, the petition reads as follows:

> May the sectarians (*minim*) and collaborators find no hope, and the merciless all swiftly disappear. May all your enemies and those who hate Thee be speedily cut down. May the Empire of Evil [=Rome] quickly be uprooted, and broken, and humbled, rapidly, in our days! Blessed are Thou, Lord that breaks the enemies [of Israel] and humbles the merciless.[76]

It is important to take note that the "sectarians" (*minim*) and "collaborators" are cited together with the "Empire of Evil" (=Rome), and the "enemies" and the "merciless"—these are references to political, not to religious foes! Israel has always been kind and liberal with dissidents, up to the point that they collaborate with the enemy, and behave pitilessly with their own people.[77] The dependence of the *minim* on the imperial sword explains why, once Roman occupation ended with the Arab Conquest of Jerusalem (638), the Judeo-Christian groups left the land of Israel altogether.[78]

Christian opposition to the 'Jesus' of history is stronger than Israel's opposition to the 'Jesus' of myth. "The known facts of his [Jesus'] life," registered in the *Christian Scripture*, "are meager in the ex-

---

Buber, vol. 1, p. 83; Professor Luis Ginzberg, *A Commentary on the Palestinian Talmud* (Heb.), vol. 3 (New York: The Jewish Theological Seminary, 1941), pp. 271-272, cf. ibid, p. 245. For further analysis and discussion, see *Tosefta Ki-Fshuṭah*, vol. 1, pp. 53-54. According to Joseph Derenbourg, a similar formula had been in use before the destruction of the Temple; see his "Mélanges Rabbiniques," *Revue des Études Juive*, 14 (1887), p. 31 n. 1.

[76] For an overview of the variants in the Sephardic Prayer Book, see R. Shem Ṭob Gaguine, *Keter Shem Ṭob* [vol. 1] (England, 5694/1934), n. 90, pp. 57-58.

[77] In this connection we should mention the variety of groups and ideologies flourishing within the Jewish public throughout history. On rare occasions, there may be found a group holding doctrines substantially similar to Christianity. For a modern example, see R. David Berger, *The Rebbe, the Messiah, and the Scandal of Orthodox Indifference* (The Littman Library of Jewish Civilization: 2006). Yet, since they never distanced themselves from the Jewish people, and on the contrary, they excel in deeds of loving-kindness, always expressing full solidarity with the land and the people of Israel, they are highly cherished and respected, despite fundamental differences in matters of doctrine.

[78] See "The Jewish Christian," pp. 170-216.

treme." Significantly, all that "has been said and done by Jesus in all four gospels, could not have occupied more than three weeks."[79] Furthermore,

> The records of his life are confused, and Bible critics are left with scores of unsolved problems, which have been the source of heresies that have racked Christendom from its beginnings. Scholars have been perplexed by the contradictions, inconsistencies and improbabilities in the canonical gospels alone, which they have never been able to reconcile.[80]

The reason for the 'confusions' may be deliberate. A historical 'Jesus' would clash with 'Jesus' the *Übermensch* (Chapters 14 and 31). That is why the editors of the *Christian Scripture* may have wanted to suppress some material pertaining to the Jesus of history. They succeeded. As noted by a serious reader of the *Christian Scripture*: "Thus the personality of the historical Jesus can no longer be reconstructed and is also not at all important."[81] The second part of the sentence may be true for the faithful Christian. To a Jew, however, victim of countless pogroms and attacks, the historicity of Jesus often was and is a matter of life and death.

In their efforts to suppress the historical Jesus (see Chapter 21), the ecclesiastical authorities ended up expelling the *Jewish* followers of Jesus; namely, *those who knew him personally and followed him during his life*, together with their children and disciples. The official explanation was their adherence to some aspects of the Law. The issue has been elegantly expressed in the *Catholic Encyclopedia*. When introducing the article on the "Ebionites," one of the earliest Jewish followers of Jesus, it was explained: "By this name was designated one or more early [= 'Jewish'] Christian sects infected with Judaistic errors."[82] The

---

[79] Benjamin Walker, *Gnosticism* (Wellingborough, Northamptonshire: The Aquarian Press, 1983), p. 70.

[80] *Gnosticism*, p. 70.

[81] Alfred Ribi, *Demons of the Inner World* (Boston: Shambhala, 1990), p. 110.

[82] J. P. Arendzen, "Ebionites," *Catholic Encyclopedia*, (New York, 1907), vol. 5, cols. 242b-244a. This, of course, runs contrary to Origen: *Contra Celsum*, tr. Henry

'infection' refers to the fact that these Jews actually knew the Jesus of *history*, and could not accept the Jesus of *myth*. Nothing is more dangerous to ecclesiastic authorities than knowledge of the historical Jesus. To make sure that the rupture with historical Jesus would be total, not *a single Jewish rite* was admitted: the 'Law' of Moses is not only dead, but also deadly. All Christian rites must come exclusively from the pagan world; e.g., the mysteries of Demeter and Orpheus, "most obviously in the myths and rites of the Virgin and the Mass."[83] Jesus' 'biography' too, including his birth, childhood, and life comes from pagan lore. To make sure that the brake with Judaism is total and irrevocable, *Christian Scripture* was careful to portray *a* 'Jesus' whose earthly *lifestyle* and foundational religious *practices* are unacceptable to Jews (see Chapters 16-17, 19-20). The editors of the *Christian Scripture* went on to 're-write' any story that may reflect a modicum of cordial relations between Jesus and Jews. A point in case is distorting the story of the 'Good Samaritan' (see Chapter 14). Within this context, anti-Semitism and the vilification of the wretched 'Pharisees' and diabolical 'rabbis' played a pivotal role. It not only protected the faithful from the "infections" caused by "Judaistic errors," it also excused Christian authorities from common civility when dealing with 'Jews' and 'Judaism.' Accordingly, rather than debate the differences, mud-slinging would suffice.

* * *

In Section III, we examine a key question affecting Jewish relations with Christians. Did the Jews kill Jesus? Were they in any way responsible for his death? Before I review the Jewish and Christian

---

Chadwick (Cambridge: Cambridge University Press, 1953), p. 66; cf. pp. 311-312, 314.

[83] Joseph Campbell, *The Masks of God: Occidental Mythology* (Penguin Compass, 1991), p. 28. This sort of belief was not uncommon among primitive man; see Lucien Lévy-Bruhl, *The Notebooks on Primitive Mentality*, tr. Peter Riviere (New York: Harper and Row, 1978), pp. 10-11.

accounts on this subject, I must relate an encounter I once had with an Iranian diplomat. It took place on a flight from Istanbul to Tel Aviv, in the month of July, during the mid-sixties.

At the time, Turkish Airlines did not have a Kosher meal program. Nonetheless, I approached someone at the counter and asked him whether he could arrange for a Kosher meal, since otherwise I would not be able to eat. The person in charge was Armenian. He was married to a Jewish girl and was sympathetic to my request. We spoke for a while, and then he made a note of my request. When I asked him how he was going to get me a Kosher meal, he responded, "Don't worry. I know what to do." To my surprise, when it was time to check in for the flight, I discovered that he had upgraded my ticket to First Class. I got the window seat. Next to me sat a gentleman. He was an Iranian diplomat stopping for a short time in Israel. We spoke for a while. When they began to serve the food, I received two beautiful trays. One contained a green salad, with olives, lemon, oil, salt and pepper on the side to garnish. The other tray contained an assortment of fruits. Turkish fruits and vegetables are delicious. I don't know whether it was because I was so hungry, or because of the excitement of the situation, but I still think that it was one of the best meals I had on *any* flight (sorry EL AL!). Apparently, the Iranian diplomat was touched when I told him that I kept a kosher diet. After the meal, he told me, "You appear to be learned. There is a question about Judaism for which I never could find an adequate answer. Perhaps you could enlighten me on this matter." He then proceeded, "How could you justify the Jewish killing of Jesus?"

A fundamental trait of Sephardic tradition is Jewish *national* pride. Sephardim never permitted gentiles to trample upon Jewish *national* reputation, or to treat the Jewish *nation* as some sort of international pariah needing to justify herself to a higher court of justice. R. Ḥayyim Palaggi (1788-1896), one of the foremost rabbinic authorities in modern times, pointed out that 'humility' (*'anava*), which is a much prized virtue in Jewish ethics, "must be reserved for internal relationships, between a Jew and a Jew." A Jew should treat gentiles neither as superiors nor as inferiors but as equals, even when dealing with the highest aristocracy. "However, when I find myself in the company of the gentile aristocracy," he wrote, "I feel a great aristocrat myself...because we are the children of Abraham, Isaac, and Jacob."[84]

"Are you aware that at the time of Jesus, Israel was an autonomous state?" I asked the Iranian diplomat. "Of course," he responded. "Did you know that Jesus was a Jew, and a citizen of that state?" Again, the answer was in the affirmative. "Now, how would you respond to a foreign government or a foreign citizen, demanding that you justify the right of an Iranian court of law to try an Iranian citizen? The same is true of Jesus. The Jewish people *were* and *are* an autonomous nation. Jesus was Jewish, and therefore whatever transpired between him and the Jewish people is a purely internal matter. A Jew may indeed have the right to ask me about it, because he is a member of the Jewish nation. But to respond to the demand of a non-Jewish entity on this matter would impugn our autonomy and sovereignty as the nation of Israel." "It is the best answer I ever heard!" he responded.

I believe he was sincere and not just diplomatic. As a matter of principle, this is the answer I give to non-Jews. It is none of their business! Jews need not justify themselves to a bunch of hypocrites, guilty of the worst abominations in history, including the Inquisition, the mass genocide of Amerindians—the largest in world-history—and the extermination of 6,000,000 million Jews, counting among them over 1,000,000 children (see below Chapter 37). To this sort of people, Matthew's words fits best: "Thou hypocrite, first cast out the beam out of thine own eye: and then shall thou see clearly to cast out the mote out of thy brother's eye" (*Matt* 7:5).[85]

In Section III we propose that there was malice on the part of the ecclesiastic authorities in attributing to the *Gospels* a historical

---

[84] R. Ḥayyim Palaggi, *Birkat Moʻadekha le-Ḥayyim*, vol. 2 (Izmir, 5611/1851), 143d.

[85] This proverb comes from the Talmud, *Baba Batra* 15b, *ʻArakhin* 16b; cf. *Sanhedrin* 19a.

dimension (see Chapter 28). The principal thesis of this Section is that the Trial, Crucifixion, and Resurrection of Jesus, as *portrayed* in the *Christian Scripture,* were not written as if they were 'history.' Specifically, the authors of the *Gospels* did not have the foggiest idea of what an actual trial is. Not only did they repudiate Jewish 'Law,' but they had neither interest nor knowledge of law in general, Jewish or Roman. One thing that their description of Jesus' Trial makes clear is that the writers of the *Gospels* never witnessed an actual trial in their lives (in either a Roman or a Jewish court of Justice); but, even if they did, they still would have lacked the intellectual skills to describe what they saw (see Chapters 28-29). We will see that the only 'trials' that the authors of the *Christian Scripture* witnessed were the mock-trials carried for and by the unruly mobs in the arenas and theaters of Alexandria (see Chapter 28). A close reading of Jesus' Trial will reveal that it was modeled on a famous mock-trial described in detail by Philo. We will also see that the architecture of the early Church resembled the style of the civil basilica, and the sanctuary functioned like an auditorium, where the greatest drama in history, Jesus' Trial and Resurrection, was performed (see Chapter 29). This is consistent with the Christian repudiation of the Jesus of history, in favor of the Jesus of myth.

* * *

Section IV examines the ideological consequences of the alliance Cross-Sword, established between Emperor Constantine and the ecclesiastic authorities in the 4th Century. It is the matrix of the culture obedience-submission, dominating Europe until present days. In the same Section we also propose that much of the socio-political movements flourishing in secular Europe from the late 18th century on, both to the right and to the left of the spectrum, are directly dependent on the ideology of obedience-submission promoted by the Church.

Earlier, we mentioned the disastrous consequences of the alliance between King Balak and Prophet Balaam. In my view, it is a paradigm applying to all religions: a religion *will become evil when used as a tool* to implement the policies of political tyrants. Within this context, let us consider four closely related points, resulting from the alliance Cross-Sword: [1] The creation of a religious enemy, thus leading to [2] Christian anti-Semitism, [3] the changing of the Hebrew idea of 'One God' into 'one exclusive religion,' thereby [4] transforming Jesus' teachings into a persecuting religion. As noted in beginning of this "Introduction," Christianity is the first religion in history to have introduced the idea of a religious enemy [1]. This was a direct consequence of becoming the official religion of the Empire (see below, Chapter 36). Politically, Israel and Rome have been mortal enemies. The net result of the alliance Church-Rome was the changing of the religion taught by Jesus and his disciples into an imperial tool, to be used against Rome's archenemy: Israel (see below, Chapters 15, 17). [2] In this respect, anti-Semitism is central to Christianity. To justify her enmity, Christianity *had* to demonize Judaism and *vilify* the Jews (see below, Chapter 38). [3] With this objective in mind, Christianity changed the Hebrew concept of 'One God,' into 'One, Exclusive Religion,' [4] to be imposed on everybody, if necessary by the Rex's sword and the flames of Inquisition. We can now best appreciate the enormous contribution to 'religion'—to my mind, the greatest contribution in modern times—made by the United States. The separation of 'Church' and 'State' is, first and foremost, a repudiation of the alliance bargained by the ecclesiastic authorities with Constantine. It is also a solemn promise by the political authorities *not* to use religious institutions as a political tool, and by the religious authorities *not* to use political institutions as a religious tool (see below, Chapter 40). This is one of the reasons why the American people are the freest in the world.

SECTION I

A CLASH OF CIVILIZATIONS

MYTH *vs.* BOOK

1. Myth and Book

There are two different processes by which social and cultural continuity is conveyed: Myth and Book. Myth, as it is known from Greek literary sources, is extremely difficult to define.[1] Our purpose here is to consider Myth and Book as means designed to express and pass on the constitutive values of a society. I shall therefore begin by setting out their relevant features.

[1] 'Myth,' from the Greek *mythos*, refers to *stories delivered by way of mouth*. The myths coming to us from antiquity were not invented in historical time. Before they were put into writing, they existed in the form of oral poetry, epic tales, etc. Even epic poems, like the *Iliad* and the *Odyssey* were originally conveyed orally.

[2] Myths are much more than entertaining stories: they served as mental models permitting psychological representations of 'reality.' In this manner, they brought about cultural and social cohesion.

[3] Myths need not be provable. They depend, exclusively, on invocation; that is, the authority of the first-party platform addressing the audience. "Once told, that is, revealed," explained Eliade (1907-1986), "the myth becomes apodictic truth; it establishes a truth that is absolute." By way of illustration, Eliade pointed to the Netsilik Eskimos that confirm their faith and sacred history by the fact that it has been said so: "It is so because it is said that it is so."[2]

---

[1] See Mircea Eliade, *Myth and Reality* (New York: Harper & Row, 1963), Chapter 1.

[2] Mircea Eliade, *The Sacred and the Profane* (San Diego: Harcourt Brace and Company, 1987), p. 95. Similarly, in *Myth and Reality*, p. 6: "Because the ancestors so commanded it." On the form of political and social organization of 'primitive' man, as well as on some of their basic beliefs, see Paul Radin, *Primitive Religion* (New York: Dover Publications, 1957), pp. 51-55.

[4] Myths function like graffiti, or a signpost, where the message is captured by everyone equally. Ambiguity is categorically excluded, leaving no room for interpretation; just like there cannot be any room for interpreting the sign 'Stop' or the traffic lights 'Red/Green.'[3] Myths expect total affirmation, and do not allow for dissention or diversity.

[5] Myths exclude dialogue, that is, 'the act of speech' between the first and second person. The conveyance is always hierarchically structured from the first-person platform, *pronouncing* the myth to *a public that is excluded, in quality of absentee, from questioning the speaking subject*.[4]

[6] Myths unfold in a realm immune from the categories of time and space, so that neither of these categories can affect mythical thinking.[5] This is why the mythological world appears chaotic and populated by psychotic fantasies.

[7] Mythical man can reason and conduct rational discourse. However, given that his rationality is conditioned to apodictic truths known to him by the fiat of authority, his 'truth' may be wanting. Hence it could be irreconcilable with another such 'truth,' expressed in different words or derived from a different set of apodictic truths.[6]

[8] Mythical thinking is akin to a thought process that Silvano Arieti (1914-1981) designates "paleologic thinking," where identity is estab-

---

[3] See *Golden Doves* [henceforth: *GD*], Chapter 1.

[4] See *The Sacred and the Profane*, p. 95; *Myth and Reality*, p. 69; José Faur, *Homo Mysticus*, p. 150.

[5] See Lucien Lévy-Bruhl, *The Notebooks on Primitive Mentality*, tr. Peter Riviere (New York: Harper and Row, 1978), pp. 184-185, 193-194.

[6] Myth-variations are tolerated only when proceeding from an acknowledged first-person platform; see below n. 37.

lished on the basis of similar predicates, rather than similar subjects. This mode of thinking serves as the basis for myth and magic:

> Paleologic thinking seems to be the foundation of many societal or collective manifestations—rituals, magic, customs, and beliefs—that are transmitted from generation to generation and accepted without questions being raised as to their validity.[7]

[9] In a myth-dominated culture, writing is a secondary tool. It may be used as a mnemonic device, to help memory, but it can never substitute the voice of the first-party platform, invoking the truth. Oral transmission is a more effective medium, because of the possibilities of staging, voice manipulation, and the numerous devices provided by theatrics and oratory.

The alternative to the culture of myth is the 'Book' as *defined in Jewish tradition* (see below).

[1] The values and institutions designed to bring political, social, and intellectual cohesion in Israel are the effect of a bilateral 'covenant' (*berit*), contracted at Sinai by "the children of Israel" and God (*Ex* 19:3). The specifics of the covenant, the historical and foundational beliefs of the people contracting the covenant—including its further developments, as well as the clarifications brought about during the forty years in the Desert—were inscribed by Moses in a Book known as *Tora* (the 'Law' or 'Pentateuch'). Before his death, Moses conveyed the *Book* containing the text of the *Tora* (*Sefer ha-Tora*) in a formal ceremony. The ceremony consisted of depositing the Book of the *Tora* next to the Ark, in the presence of the Elders of Israel. Thus was published the first *National Book* known to humanity.[8]

---

[7] Silvano Arieti, *Creativity* (New York: Basic Books, 1976), p. 72. On paleologic thinking, see ibid., Chapter 5; *Homo Mysticus*, pp. 66-67; cf. ibid. pp. 62, 64, 80, 211, and below n. 41.

[8] *HS*, vol. 1, Chapter 7.

[2] In the course of history, the Nation of Israel published other books. They are contained in two collections, the 'Prophets' and 'Hagiography.' Together with the *Tora* these Books constitute the *National Books* of Israel, commonly known as the '*Hebrew Scripture.*' These Books, too, were designed to convey the foundational beliefs and institutions, developed in the course of Jewish history. The status of these Books is predicated on the fact that they are *national publications*; that is, they were *published by the Nation of Israel* and conveyed by the *people of Israel to the people of Israel in perpetuity*. The act of publication consisted in depositing these Books in the Temple's archives by the Supreme Court of Israel (*Sanhedrin*), just like Moses had previously deposited "the Book of the *Tora*" (*Sefer ha-Tora*) next to the Ark at the Tabernacle.[9]

[3] The function of *publication* is to break the link author/book. By depositing the book in the Temple, the author transfers the book from his *private domain* to the *public domain* of Israel.[10] Accordingly, the National Books of Israel are designated *Kitbe ha-Qodesh*, mistranslated 'Holy Books.' In Hebrew, *qodesh* is a noun—not an adjective—and it stands for the 'Sanctuary' in Jerusalem.[11] The correct translation of *Kitbe ha-Qodesh* is "Books" of or at "the Sanctuary." That is, Books

---

[9] See *HS*, vol. 1, pp. 64-65.

[10] This is somehow analogous, but by no means similar, to the dissolution of authorship effected by the hypermedia; see Ronald J. Deibert, *Parchment, Printing and Hypermedia* (NY: Columbia University Press, 1997), p. 183: "all the expressions once contained in books or films strips or newsletters—will exist either as pure thought or something very much like thought"; quoting John Perry Barlow, "The Economy of Ideas: A Framework for Rethinking Patents and Copyrights in the Digital Age," *Wired* (March, 1994), p. 86. Cf. Jorge Luis Borges, in Amelia Barili, "Borges on Life and Death," *New York Times Book Review*, July 13, 1986), p. 28, cited in José Faur, *The Naked Crowd: The Jewish Alternative to Cunning Humanity* [henceforth: *NC*] (Fort Lee, N.J.: Derusha Publishing, 2009), p. 48.

[11] See *HS*, vol. 1, p. 65 n. 70; *Homo Mysticus*, p. 201. For reasons better left unexplained, the distinguished scholars pontificating 'scientific-wisdom' to the people of Israel standing below, find it intellectually difficult to distinguish between a Hebrew noun and an adjective.

which were *deposited in the Jewish Sanctuary* for publication, and thereby transferred to the *public domain of the people of Israel*. Books that were not deposited in the *Qodesh* are known as *sefarim ḥiṣoniyim* or 'Outside Books'; i.e., books that, for whatever reason, were not deposited in the *Qodesh* for publication.

[4] As a *consequence* of having been formally accepted into the Sanctuary, the Books comprising the *Hebrew Scripture* are said to have been written "*be-Ruwaḥ ha-Qodesh*"; a term mistranslated as 'Holy Ghost' or 'Holy Spirit,' but actually meaning the 'Spirit from the *Qodesh*,' i.e., the Temple in Jerusalem.[12] By virtue of having been deposited for publication at the Temple, these Books convey the 'Spirit' of the Temple (cf. *Is* 63:11; *Ps* 20:1-4; etc.). We can thus understand why, traditionally, reading the *Hebrew Scripture* was regarded as a virtual visit to the *Temple* at Jerusalem.[13]

[5] At Sinai, God addressed every member of Israel in the second person singular. To appreciate the significance of this usage, it would be valuable to recall that Hebrew grammatical theory recognizes only two personal pronouns: the first person (*medabber*) or 'speaker'—posing himself as the speaking subject '*I*,' and the second person (*nokheaḥ*) or 'addressee' '*you*,' to whom the speaking subject talks. In turn, the second person (*nokheaḥ*) is defined as the person that can *address* the speaking subject '*I*' as '*you*'; inverting, thus, the role 'speaker/addressee.' This fundamental condition of 'linguistic person' has been explained by Émile Benveniste (1902-1976):

> Consciousness of self is only possible if it is experienced by contrast. I use *I* only when I am speaking to someone who will be a *you* in my address. It is this condition of dialogue that is constitutive of *person*, for it implies that reciprocally *I* becomes *you* in the address of the one who in his turn designates himself as *I*.

---

[12] See *HS*, vol. 1, pp. 63-64.

[13] See *HS*, vol. 2, Appendix 58.

Invariably, the speaking subject *I*, "posits another person, the one who, being, as he is, completely exterior to 'me,' becomes my echo to whom I say *you* and who says *you* to me."[14] [Italics in original]

'Speech,' in contradistinction to 'communication', is the act of first person *I* addressing second person *you*. 'Linguistic person' involves reciprocity between 'speaker' and 'addressee'; together, they constitute 'a dialectical person.' It follows that there cannot be a linguistic *I* without a corresponding *you*, and vice versa. The third person, however, is excluded from the act of speech. In Hebrew grammatical theory, the third person is designated 'absentee' (*nistar*) or 'non-person': he can be spoken to, but it cannot speak back to the first person. Therefore, neither the party speaking from the first-party platform, nor the third-party absentee, stand for a 'linguistic person.'[15] At Sinai, God addressed every member of the people of Israel in the first person singular (*anokhi*), to a public made up of individual second person singular (*Ex* 20:1). Accordingly, every Jew is expected to assume the *speaking subject I* and address God in the second person singular *you* (*atta*).[16] The dialogue Jew-God is never ending. 'Jewish atheists' are not unbelievers, but people 'angry' at God's response: interrupting their silence, occasionally, to reproach their interlocutor.[17]

---

[14] Émile Benveniste, *Problems in General Linguistics* (Coral Gables, Florida: University of Miami, 1971), pp. 224-225. See *HS*, vol. 1, p. 22. On linguistic subjectivity, see *GD*, pp. 41-44, 47-48.

[15] See José Faur, "The Third Person in Semitic Grammatical Theory and General Linguistics," *Linguistica Biblica*, Bonn, 46 (1979), pp. 106-113; and *GD*, pp. 44, 47-48.

[16] Indeed, in the Hebrew Prayers, to be said morning, afternoon, and night, the faithful addresses God in the singular *atta* '*you*.'

[17] A case in point is the story mentioned by Elias Canetti, *The Torch in my Ear* (New York: Farrar, Strauss and Giroux, 1982), p. 341. The Hebrew lexicon does not have a term for 'atheist.' The term *apiqoros* in rabbinic literature is the Greek 'epicurean.' However, rather than someone actually denying the existence of God, he is a libertine, *acting* as if there would be no God. On Jewish 'heresy' in general, see *HS*, vol. 2, Appendix 55. The Hebrew *kofer*, root KFR stands for someone who 'covers' something deliberately, in order to avoid responsibility—not for an 'unbeliever.'

[6] The *Hebrew Scripture* are structured *horizontally*, from the author (first person) to the reader (second person). These Books are not only intended to be 'read,' but 'expounded' and generate meaning: a condition of the National Books of Israel is that they warrant exegesis (*nittena le-hidaresh*).[18] Consequently, diversity of interpretation, as exemplified in rabbinic literature, is a dimension of Jewish reading. As Kafka (1883-1924) commented to a friend, "One reads in order to ask questions."[19]

[7] The nations of the world have left inscriptions and written documents. 'Writing,' however, does not equal a *Sefer Tora*. A *Sefer Tora* is a *National Book*, published by the *national* authorities of Israel, and acknowledged as such by the *congregation* of Israel.[20] Even though all *Tora*-related writings require especial care and deference; e.g., they may not be thrown away and must be deposited in a special place (*geniza*), they are not the same as a 'Book.' A 'Book' is an autonomous entity (representing the Temple) and must be inscribed in a special material, prepared in a particular manner, written with a special type of ink, etc. Referring to "the Scroll" containing the Five Books of the *Tora*, which serves as a paradigm for the other books of the "*Hebrew Scripture*," Maimonides enumerates twenty conditions for a Scroll of the *Tora* to acquire the status of 'Book.' Should any one of the twenty conditions be amiss (e.g., if the parchment was not prepared according to the specific rules designated for inscribing the *Tora*), the Scroll is liturgically void (*pasul*), "and may not be used for public readings" (=formal conveyance).[21]

[8] The Hebrew alphabet consists of only consonants. On the basis

---

[18] See *GD*, pp. 104-107.

[19] Alberto Manguel, *A History of Reading* (Viking, Penguin, 1996), p. 89; quoting Gustav Janouch, *Conversations with Kafka* (New York, 1971). Cf. *GD*, p. xxvii.

[20] See *HS*, vol. 2, Appendix 6.

[21] *MT Sefer Tora*, 10:1.

of rabbinic sources, post-Talmudic authorities stipulated that a Scroll of the *Tora* that has been vocalized is liturgically void (*pasul*) and may not be used for public readings (=formal conveyance).[22] Thus, the following paradox: to be ritually suitable, the reading must be carried on from a text made up of only consonants and therefore unreadable! The theory of this rule has to do with the Hebrew concept of 'alphabet' and 'reading.' In Hebrew, a 'letter' must be inscribed in a blank, *writable* space, on all its sides.[23] In this manner, each letter is formally separated from the other. Reading a purely consonantal text, involves multiple choices. I do not by any means wish to suggest a simple parallel, much less to assert a symmetry, but there is some similarity between interpreting a purely consonantal text and interpreting a mathematical formula. In both cases, ciphers and letter must be separate from one another, and it is incumbent on the 'reader' to spawn meaning from the ciphers and consonants and give them sense. Put more simply, unlike a vocalized text that is immediately recognized by the reader, in a purely consonantal text the reader must process the letters and generate meaning thereof. In a vocalized text, such as that of the *Christian* and *Muslim Scriptures*, where the consonants have been provided with vowels, the reader is passive. His role is marginal and submissive. He just 'lifts up' the sound from the script and 'recites' it.[24] The rule requiring that the public reading of the *Tora* (=conveyance) should be carried on from an unvocalized text, proposes that the reader be the actual writer of the text.[25] Thus, the reader *knows* the text because *he has written it*.[26]

---

[22] See *HS*, vol. 2, Appendix 1.

[23] Vowels, however, link the letters and words *semantically* to one another, canceling, thereby, the blank space between the letters. See *GD*, p. 116; *Homo Mysticus*, p. 7.

[24] See *HS*, vol. 1, p. 4. Hebrew reading warrants *successive synthesis*; see *GD*, pp. 30-35. A vocalized text allows for *simultaneous synthesis*, where the reader plays a passive role; see *GD*, pp. 118-123.

[25] See *HS*, vol. 2, Appendix 1.

[26] See *HS*, vol. 1, pp. XV, 4-5, 10; and Ludwig Wittgenstein, *Notebooks*, 1914-1916 (New York: Harper & Row, 1961), 15.4.16, p. 71e.

[9] A consonantal text consists of a series of letters challenging the reader/addressee to generate meaning. Given that more than one arrangement is possible, competing interpretations are accepted. In the language of the rabbis, there are "seventy faces" to the *Tora*.[27] Another principle stipulates that the *Tora* expresses itself "in the parlance of man," that is, the addressee.[28] An extension of this principle is that authorial intent is irrelevant, even if the author is God! Accordingly, the rabbis concluded that if a conflict of interpretation arises between God and Israel, the meaning of the text is to be determined by Israel, not God![29] Thus, in Israel "the truth it is not so just because it is said so," but because the addressee concluded that it is so.[30]

In matters of governance, textual ambiguities in the *Tora* are to be resolved by the *national* authorities, that is, the *Sanhedrin* or Supreme Court of Israel. Their interpretation, however, is only binding in the *application* of the Law.[31] Matters of faith may be right or wrong, but are not justifiable in a court of justice. Therefore, competing interpretations, not challenging the right of the court to execute their decision, are allowed.[32] That is why the Geonim and the ancient Sephardic commentators to the Scriptures did not hesitate to present alternative interpretations, since they were dealing with textual analysis and *not* with the application of the Law. Lastly, even the court's *judicial interpretations* of Scriptures may be reversed by another court.[33]

---

[27] Some propose that there are "600,000 faces," according to the number of Israelites standing at Mount Sinai; see *GD*, p. 120.

[28] *Pesaḥim* 6b; *Sanhedrin* 49b; etc. Cf. below n. 118.

[29] See *HS*, vol. 1, pp. 57-58, 60.

[30] See below n. 119.

[31] See *HS*, vol. 1, Chapter 10.

[32] See *HS*, vol. 1, Chapter 11.

[33] See *HS*, vol. 1, pp. 74-78.

2. The Medium of Myth

Joseph Campbell (1904-1987), one of the great specialists in world mythology, opened his *Hero with a Thousand Faces* (1949) with these golden lines:

> Throughout the inhabited world, in all times and under every circumstance, the myths of man have flourished; and they have been the living inspiration of whatever else may have appeared out of the activities of the human body and mind. It would not be too much to say that myth is the secret opening through which the inexhaustible energies of the cosmos pour into human cultural manifestations. Religions, philosophies, arts, the social forms of primitive and historic man, prime discoveries in science and technology, the very dreams that blister sleep, boil up from the basic, magic ring of myth.[34]

But, what is myth? Anthropologists and psychologists define 'myth' in terms of content. However, if we accept McLuhan's (1911-1980) principle that "the medium is the message," then the content of the myth, including its conceptual aspects, are secondary to the medium by which it is conveyed.[35] Furthermore, borrowing from modern communication theory, since we all "live in a network of communication,"[36] the medium by which the social and cultural values of a people are conveyed is the primary factor in the formation of the people. As acutely observed by one of the foremost scholars on the subject:

> ...myth is the canvas upon which both oral narrative and written literature depict their message, each with such freedom that divergences between different traditions and innovations that certain authors introduce neither scandalize nor are even difficult to accommodate

---

[34] Joseph Campbell, *The Hero with a Thousand Faces* (London: Fontana Press, 1993), p. 3.

[35] See Marshall McLuhan, *Understanding Media* (Cambridge, Mass.: MIT Press, 1998), Chapter 1.

[36] W. Barnet Pearce, *Communication and the Human Condition* (Carbondale and Edwardsville: Southern Illinois University, 1989), p. 13.

from a religious point of view. If the myths can vary in this way from one version to another without damaging the balance of the general system it must be because what matters is not the way the story is told, which can vary from one account to the other, but rather the mental categories conveyed by the stories as a whole and by the intellectual organization that underlies all the various versions.[37]

Accordingly, a speaking snake in the medium of Book is a metaphor, whereas 2+2=4 in the medium of myth is magic.

Citing these points, we ask: what are the components making up the medium by which 'myth' is conveyed? For our purpose, the distinctive features of myth-conveyance are six:

[1] The conveyance of myth requires hierarchic societies, on top of which rules a man or group of men, *invoking* and further expounding the myth. In this manner, the message descends in a variety of forms from one stratum to the other, via a scale of superior/inferior; whereby the lower stratum must *acknowledge* by fiat of *rank*, the message conveyed by those above. Accordingly, myth demands total affirmation; rejection of myth equals insubordination.

Hierarchic rank prohibits the third-party addressee to address the first-party invoking the myth in the second person; thus, it excludes linguistic reciprocity between the subjective 'I' and the addressee '*you.*' Therefore, rather than an act of speech between *linguistic persons*, conveyance of myth involves *communication*, consisting in the dissemination of information from the first-party platform to the third-party audience. This sort of conveyance is essentially not different than when a bee announces the discovery of a source of food to the rest of the colony.[38]

[2] In myth, the function of 'words' is to elicit visual images, as with

---

[37] Jean-Pierre Vernant, *Myth and Society in Ancient Greece* (New York: Zone Books, 1990), p. 224; see ibid. p. 223. Myth-variations are only tolerated when invoked from an acknowledged first-person-platform; cf. above n. 6.

[38] See *GD*, pp. 42-43.

slogans (and graffiti), where 'meaning' and 'sound' are one and the same.[39] The verbal message is void of conceptual content; *words* are a vehicle for the conveyance of a special type of imagery. Concerning this type of imagery, Arieti wrote:

> The more primitive the way of thinking, the more limited is the use of the conceptual and the greater the use of the perceptual order. Thus visual images tend to replace the verbal.[40]

The imagery originates in the archetypal structures of the group. That is why it is unaffected by "tangible reality." The foundational principle of these structures has been discussed with great insight and authority by C. G. Jung (1885-1961).

> The archetype does not proceed from physical facts, but describes how the psyche experiences the physical fact, and in so doing the psyche often behaves so autocratically that it denies tangible reality or makes statements that fly in the face of it.[41]

Consequently, *similar* myths conveying *similar* archetypal images are *fundamentally* different and may not be tolerated by members of the group.

In this connection it would be helpful to recall that at an early stage of mental development, man could not distinguish between 'memories' generated by his mental associations, and experiential memory, gained through sensory perception. Concerning 'primitive' man, Jung observed, "it is often next to impossible to find out whether he merely dreamed something or whether he really experi-

---

[39] See *GD*, Chapter 1. As per *modern* opera and Arabic songs, in which people having no clue of the language are intellectually inspired and emotionally moved.

[40] Silvano Arieti, "Primitive Intellectual mechanism in Psycho-Pathological Conditions," *American Journal of Psychotherapy* 4 (1959), p. 11. See below n. 52.

[41] C. G. Jung, "The Psychology of the Child Archetype," in *Essays on a Science of Mythology* (Princeton, N.J.: Princeton University Press, 1993), p. 73. Cf. *Homo Mysticus*, p. 16. On the role of archetypes in religion in general, see Heinrich Zimmer, "The Significance of the Tantric Yoga," in ed. Joseph Campbell, *Spiritual Disciplines* (Princeton: Princeton University Press, 1985), pp. 23-24.

enced it."⁴² A fundamental aspect of this sort of discourse is that neither the party invoking the myth nor the audience can actually *understand* the myth.⁴³

[3] Mythical knowledge is absolute. The truth invoked from the first-party platform demands absolute submission. This is not to say that myth-centered societies cannot be 'rational.' Indeed, the great civilizations of the Ancient Near East were capable of great achievements, impossible without an advanced knowledge of mathematics and technology. However—and that is the crux of the matter—their rationality is conditioned by 'the apodictic truth' invoked from the first-party platform. This condition led to the development of what Arieti designated "paleologic" thinking. Given that reason is to be subjected to the 'apodictic truth,' no issue could be *fully* investigated. Consequently, identification between *A* and *B* can only be established on the basis of *similarities*. Drawing from the field of psycho-pathology, Arieti explained, "The patient focuses on the common element and ignores the rest, which does not count." Invariably, "the identifying link" is something trivial. For instance, in paleologic thinking, an apple might be identified with the mother's breast, since "the breast and the apple have a similar shape."⁴⁴ This type of reasoning is central to myth-centered societies. Quoting Arieti, again:

> Paleologic thinking seems to be the foundation of many societal or collective manifestations—rituals, magic, customs, and beliefs—that are transmitted from generation to generation and accepted without questions being raised as to the validity.⁴⁵

---

[42] C. G. Jung, "The Psychology of the Child Archetype," in *Essays on a Science of Mythology*, p. 73.

[43] See Octavio Paz, *Claude Lévi-Strauss: An Introduction* (New York: Dell Publishing, 1978), p. 39; cf. ibid. p. 44.

[44] *Creativity*, p. 69.

[45] *Creativity*, p. 72; cf. ibid, p. 71. For further details, see Silvano Arieti, "Some Basic Problems Common to Anthropology and Modern Psychiatry," *American Anthropologist* 58 (1956), pp. 26-30.

Mythical knowledge is static. An essential characteristic of mythically centered societies is resistance to progress and or the accumulation of knowledge.

[4] Conveyance of myth is possible only in an oral culture, where 'reality' depends, exclusively, on *who* said *what*, not *what* was *said* by *whom*. This is so, not only because oral transmission permits the establishment of a hierarchic relation between the first and third person, but also, because oral communication, through staging and voice manipulation, can elicit a wide range of emotions that will *enchant* the audience, as if per magic.[46]

[5] The message invoked by the first-party platform has an autonomous existence, immune from the constraints of time and space.[47] Within this context, 'time' is circular and related to the myth of the "eternal return," common to archaic religions, where the same reality is made and unmade in periodic cycles of creation and destruction.[48] In less elegant terms, as it is commonly taught, 'history repeats itself,' etc. This is possible because in mythical thought, time and space are disconnected from each other. Space is static, as in Euclidian geometry, with rigid and invariable distances between points. It has nothing to do with time that is *cyclical and reversible*. Therefore, there isn't—there could not be—any relationship between (cyclical) 'time' *and* (linear) 'space,' let alone a space-time continuum. Accordingly, there is no cogent reason why *the same object* cannot be in *two* different *places* at the *same time*.[49]

In fact, Lucien Lévy-Bruhl (1857-1939) showed that since "for the primitive mind," there is "an objectivity which is independent of the conditions of possibility" (=time and space), it is also possible to

---

[46] See *HS*, vol. 1, pp. 29-31.

[47] Cf. Mircea Eliade, *The Myth of the Eternal Return* (Princeton: Princeton University Press, 1991), pp. 3-5. Cf. above n. 5.

[48] See *The Sacred and the Profane*, pp. 106-110.

[49] See *The Notebooks on Primitive Mentality*, pp. 5, 6, 13.

admit that one and the same thing could simultaneously be in two different places. By way of illustration, he referred to an incident between an English missionary, Norman P. Grubb (1895-1993), and a neighbor of his in India. The neighbor accused Mr. Grubb of entering his garden and robbing some pumpkins. In his defense, Mr. Grubb pointed out that he happened to be in a different place, some 150 miles away. What makes this incident particularly instructive is that the neighbor acknowledged that at the time, Mr. Grubb had been 150 miles away. Nonetheless, he could not understand why Mr. Grubb could not have been at the same time in his garden. This is how Lévy-Bruhl described the episode:

> What Grubb did not see is that for the Indian this impossibility—which provides the conclusive force of the alibi—does not exist. Grubb is 150 miles away. The Indian accepts this. But he also admits as no less true that on the same day he entered the garden of his village. How can he allow the two simultaneous presences of Grubb in two places 150 miles apart? This is what Grubb finds unintelligible in an Indian who is not a fool and who reasons normally. But the Indian in vain reasons normally with Grubb: there is between them this difference, which Grubb does not suspect, that in Grubb's view something impossible is not real, whereas in the Indian's eye something felt as real is definitely real, whether it is possible or not.[50]

Mythical time and space are a *sine qua non* for the conveyance of myth. The communication of myth is related to 'simultaneous synthesis.' Although words are experienced successively, in the narration of myth words are experienced 'simultaneously'; as if they were a visual experience, when the various stimuli arriving to the brain are synthesized into a single continuous occurrence, without any time-intervals between them.[51] That is why *ordinary time* and *common knowledge* cannot affect mythical thinking. The following passage by

---

[50] *The Notebooks on Primitive Mentality*, p. 6. Cf. the event mentioned in Silvano Arieti, *The Intrapsychic Self* (New York: Basic Books, 1967), p. 109.

[51] See *Understanding Media*, p. 25. For a full examination of simultaneous and successive syntheses, see *GD,* pp. 30-35.

Jung can help us gain a better understanding of the mythical mind:

> Myths on this level are as a rule tribal history handed down from generation to generation by word of mouth. Primitive mentality differs from the civilized chiefly in that the conscious mind is far less developed in scope and intensity. Functions such as thinking, willing, etc. are not yet differentiated; they are pre-conscious, and in the case of thinking, for instance, this shows itself in the circumstance that the primitive does not think *consciously*, but that thoughts *appear*. The primitive cannot assert that he thinks; it is rather that "something thinks in him." The spontaneity of the act of thinking does not lie, causally, in his conscious mind, but in his unconscious.[52] [Italics in original]

Let us emphasize this pivotal point: "The spontaneity of the act of thinking" is possible because myth has its own autonomous reality—a reality that disallows scrutiny and conceptual analysis.

[6] "Knowledge" of the myth and its corresponding cult bestows the power to make its events 'appear' and 'disappear.' Through the "ceremonial recounting of the myth," explained Eliade, the participant actually, "'lives' the myth, in the sense that one is seized by the sacred, exalting power of the events recollected or re-enacted."[53] The purpose of the ritual is to allow the participants to transcend ordinary time and 'relive' the pristine moment. In this manner, the original protagonists of the myth are made present, and in attendance with the participants of the myth: the audience no longer lives in chronological time, but in the primordial time, when the event *first took place*.[54] [Italics in original]

---

[52] C. G. Jung, "The Psychology of the Child Archetype," in *Essays on a Science of Mythology*, p. 72.

[53] *Myth and Reality*, p. 19. Cf. *Communication and the Human Condition*, p. 126.

[54] *Myth and Reality*, p. 19. I disagree with Professor Arnaldo Momigliano's approach to 'time' in Greek and Jewish thought; see his "El tiempo en la historigrafía Antigua," in *La Historiografía Griega*, tr. José Martínez Gázques (Barcelona: Editorial Crítica), pp. 66-93, which is based on the views and interpretations of writers who are not themselves rabbinic scholars. About this sort of 'Jewish scholar,' see *NC*,

3. Invariant Structures of Mythological Thought

If what distinguishes one culture from another is the medium, rather than the content, then mythological thought and categories did not vanish, as if per 'magic,' from ancient Greece and Rome. According to this premise, the great mantra propounding that Greek philosophy had extinguished mythology, may indeed be just another myth. Before approaching the subject it would be worth considering that claims of hierarchical superiority originate in archetypal structures, immune from tangible reality. Both Greece and Rome were organized along rigid hierarchic lines, whereby those below owe obedience to those above by the fiat of rank. Hierarchic organizations flourish in oedipally-structured families. In this manner, the family served as a model where the third-party absentee, in this case the son, owes submission to the dictates of the first-party father, standing on top of the scale.[55] For our purpose it is important to point out that this type of relationship disallows reciprocity: the son may not turn and address the father as '*you*.' This explains the Oedipal tension characteristic of Greek family life.[56] I am thinking of the father-son conflict in Euripides' *Hippolytos*,[57] which was typical of Classical Greece.

> The peculiar horror with which the Greeks viewed offenses against the father, and the peculiar religious sanctions to which the offender was thought to be exposed, are in themselves suggestive of strong repressions. So are the many stories in which a father's curse produc-

---

Chapter 5.

[55] On the model state/family, see Barry S. Strauss, *Fathers and Sons in Athens* (Princeton, N.J.: Princeton University Press, 1993), pp. 44-45. On the authority of the father in Athenian law, see ibid, pp. 62-72.

[56] See *Fathers and Sons in Athens*, pp.143-153.

[57] For a penetrating analysis of this material, see *Fathers and Sons in Athens*, pp. 166-175.

es terrible consequences—stories like those of Phoenix, of Hyppolytus, of Pelops and his sons, of Oedipus and his sons—all of them, it would seem, products of a relatively late period, when the position of the father was not entirely secure.[58]

The same was with the Roman family. Otto Rank (1884-1939) described the father-son conflict in Roman life, as a conflict between the 'haves' and 'have-nots'; that is, between fathers, enjoying total power, and sons with no power at all. Paradoxically, the fact that the slaves were not expected to have power, whereas the sons did, marked the sons—and not the slaves—as the only 'have-not group.' As argued by Rank:

> Not that the slaves had more, but they had no hope and hence no real desire to demand or take what the 'haves' possessed. It was different with the sons, who, despite their lack of legal rights, were brought up with the idea of promotion—provided they behaved—from the 'have-not' into the 'have' group. Hence, they could easily form the nucleus of a rebellious class striving to overthrow the ruling class of fathers.[59]

Thus, the stark emotions and constant shift of feelings peculiar to Oedipal families.

Hierarchic organization affects the quality and scope of the 'truth.' Greek philosophy, as represented by Socrates, acknowledges the imperative to subject the 'truth' to the State. Probably because of Oedipal considerations, Socrates thought of the State as a kind of *über*-father, in relation to whom a citizen is a "child and slave." Given the hierarchic distance between them, the State can rightly declare that, "you [the citizens] are not on equal terms with us; nor can you think that you have the right to do to us what we are doing to you."[60]

---

[58] E.R. Dodds, *The Greeks and the Irrational* (Berkeley: University of California Press, 1968), p. 46. See the story in *Qiddushin* 31a about a pagan refusing to disturb his father's sleep.

[59] Otto Rank, *Beyond Psychology* (New York: Dover, 1958), p. 126.

[60] *Phaedrus*, in *Collected Works of Plato*, tr. by B. Jowett (New York: Greystone Press, n.d.), vol. 3, p. 152.

In more contemporary times, some distinguished philosophers and pseudo-scientists followed in the footsteps of Socrates, and chose to subordinate their 'precious truth' to the demands of the State. Among those, Heidegger (1889-1976), Paul de Man (1919-1983), and Giovanni Papini (1881-1956), come to mind. But there were scores of similar fellow luminaries, where political accommodation to the State took precedence over everything else, including their professed religious and philosophical ideals.

We have noted previously that myth can only flourish in an oral culture. This is so not only because oral transmission permits the first person to ascertain his hierarchic superiority over the third- party absentee, but more importantly, because the archetypal imagery of the group can only be brought up through oratory, voice manipulation, and staging.[61] We can now understand why, although acknowledging the benefit of writing as a mnemonic tool (to help recall the spoken word), hierarchic societies abhor 'writing' and 'reading.' Socrates offers valuable insights into this matter. The written word is "a reminiscence of what we know" and of what had been previously "taught and communicated orally."[62] This is so because the archetypal imagery can only be elicited orally, when first-party platform invokes the truth to third-party absentee. Given that actual sensory imagery may interfere with archetypal imagery evoked through speech, in Greek literature, "the appeal is always to the ear rather than the eye."[63] Even as a mnemonic tool, writing and reading require careful monitoring because, in an insidious way, they thwart the 'truth.' Socrates provides the reader with an illuminating afterthought. Writing creates,

---

[61] See *HS*, vol. 1, pp. 29-31.

[62] *Phaedrus*, in *Collected Works of Plato*, vol. 3, p. 447. Socrates' 'remembering' has to do with the "primordial memory" that great men, such as Pythagoras and Empedocles, have from the original moment, when began their transmigration and different facets of their "personal histories" on earth; see *Myth and Realities*, pp. 90-91, 123-125.

[63] Moses Hadas, *A History of Greek Literature* (New York: Columbia University Press, 1950), p. 7.

...forgetfulness in the learner's souls, because they will not use their memories; they will trust to the external written characters and not remember of themselves.[64]

Hence the abysmal difference between the class of understanding acquired from reading and the knowledge gained from the word of mouth. Reading only awards "reminiscence," which equals neither "memory" nor true "knowledge."[65] To help avoid the trappings of writing and reading, Simonides of Ceos (ca. 556-468 B.C.E.) invented the "art of memory." It consisted of imprinting a building in the memory of the student, and then associating the words of the composition at hand with the building. His method was adopted by the schools of rhetoric, and was further developed by Giordano Bruno (1548-1600).[66] In this way, the student could avoid the negative influence of reading and writing. The preceding suggests that contrary to what we were taught in school, Greece was not *a primarily literary civilization*. The supremacy of the *logos,* 'word' (standing for 'reason') in Greek intellectual history, reflects Socrates' ideal conception of the oral dimension of knowledge.

Aversion to writing will explain why both Greece and Rome did not care to preserve their national archives. It also explains the joy they found in burning the national archives of other people, among them Persia and Israel. Pagan historians, too, based their account mostly on oral reports, with little reference to written records. Herodotus did not know Persian, and his account of the Persian religion is demonstrably unreliable.[67] Very little of Thucydides (c.460-395

---

[64] *Phaedrus,* in *Collected Works of Plato,* vol. 3, p. 442. For a more modern discussion of the pros and cons of writing, see James W. Carey, *Communication as Culture* (New York: Rutledge, 1992), pp. 164-169.

[65] *Phaedrus,* in *Collected Works of Plato,* vol. 3, pp. 442-443.

[66] Let us note that this methodology formed part of European education until relatively modern times; see *GD,* p. 32.

[67] See Émile Benveniste, *The Persian Religion* (Paris: Libraire Orientaliste Paul Guenther, 1929), pp. 118, 119; and *GD,* p. 155 notes 37-39.

B.C.E.) is based on written sources.[68] Nonetheless, there is nothing to worry. As we were taught countless times, given that these accounts were made by hierarchically superior men, further inquiry is unnecessary.[69]

There is another aspect to Greek philosophical thought. Eliade pointed out that the idea of cyclical time played a key role in Greek philosophy.

> ...the Greek philosophical genius accepted the essence of mythical thought the eternal return of things, the cyclic vision of cosmic and human life...[Greek] philosophical thought could employ and continue the mythical vision of cosmic reality and human existence.[70]

The notion of cyclical time affected the Greek concept of history. Given that linear time is incompatible with the notion of cyclical return of things, the idea of history, unfolding in a linear course, was alien to Greek historiography. Referring to Greek historians, Eliade wrote:

> None of these authors—not even Herodotus, with his passionate interest in exotic Gods and theologies—composed his *History* in the way that the authors of the oldest historical narratives in Israel did: in order to prove the existence of a divine plan and the intervention of the Supreme God in the life of a people. This does not mean that the Greek and Roman historians were necessary unreligious. But their religious conception had no place for the intervention of a single personal God in History; hence they did not give historical events the re-

---

[68] The veracity of his oral reports, too, is dubious; see Arnaldo Momigliano, *The Classical Foundations of Modern Historiography* (Berkeley: The University of California Press, 1990), Chapter 2.

[69] This methodology permitted rabid anti-Semitic historians, such as Tacitus and Cicero, to base their report about Jews and Judaism on oral reports made by other rabid anti-Semites; see *HS*, vol. 1, pp. 92, 191.

[70] *Myth and Reality*, pp. 112-113; cf. ibid, p. 90. For a sustained and informative overview of the main trends and opinions on Herod's historiography, see Arnaldo Momigliano, *Studies in Historiography* (New York: Harper & Row, 1966), Chapter 8; cf. ibid, Chapters 4 and 11.

ligious meaning they had for Jews.⁷¹

The same atemporal thinking characterizes many of the biographies penned in classical times. The life of their subjects does not unfold in gradual phases. These authors "preclude biographical thinking—thinking in periods of life as stages of development." The account they provide "is much more than biography," since "it nevertheless comprehends the periods themselves as *timeless realities*."⁷² [Italics added] A similar view was expressed by Arnaldo Momigliano (1908-1987):

> If anything characterizes the exploration of human life in the fourth century [B.C.E.], is that it often takes biographical and autobiographical forms, but without a constant and clear distinction between reality and imagination.⁷³

This applies even to the *Cyropaedia*, "indeed the most accomplished biography we have in classical Greek literature." Nevertheless, it "was not, and probably never claimed to be, a true account of the life of a real person."⁷⁴

Let us summarize the main points of our discussion. Like the rest of the pagan world, Greece and Rome were organized along hierarchical lines. This mode of organization served to convey the values and institutions invoked by the first-party platform, while simultaneously disallowing the audience from addressing the first-party as '*you*.' Invocation warrants total affirmation; rejection equals insurrection. Hence, the centrality of oedipally-structured families for the successful conveyance of values. In a hierarchic situation, the public can witness a dialogue between the first and second person, as in

---

⁷¹ *Myth and Reality*, pp. 134-135.

⁷² C. Kerényi, *Essays on a Science of Mythology* (Princeton, N.J.: Princeton University Press, 1993), p. 25.

⁷³ Arnaldo Momigliano, *The Development of Greek Biography* (Cambridge, Mass.: Harvard University Press, 1993), p. 110; cf. ibid. Chapter 2.

⁷⁴ *The Development of Greek Biography*, p. 55. As Momigliano remarked, ibid, p. 54, it is highly doubtful that even a writer of the stature of Xenophon "really intended to preserve the memory of the real Socrates." Cf. ibid. pp. 34-35.

poetry and drama, but can never transcend the status of *absentee* and address the first-party platform as '*I*' to '*you*.' The 'words' pronounced by the first-party platform are thus immune from critical analysis; their function is to enchant—not to generate discourse.

4. Myth and Media

The principal thesis of this chapter is that 'myth' is coeval with 'human inequality,' and that it permeates all forms of hierarchic society, past and present. In the past, it led to the development and expansion of slavery and socio-economic inequity.

Often, when singing the beatitudes of Greece and Rome, teachers forget to point out the underlying inequality, including slavery, basic to the hierarchic structure of the ancient *polis*.

> The city-states can thus be defined as a system of institutions which allows a privileged minority (the citizens) exclusive access to landed property within a definite area. In this sense the *polis* was a particular form of land appropriation.[75]

This led to social and political unrest. In modern times it began with the French Revolution (1789-1799), and continued in more or less spectacular forms until our own days. Karl Marx (1818-1883) exploited human inequality, exclusively in terms of political economy, and used it as a pivotal argument against capitalism.

> Greek society was founded upon slavery and had, therefore, for its natural basis, the inequality of men and of their natural labour powers. The secret of the expression of value (namely, that all kinds of labour are equal and equivalent, because, and so far as, they are human labour in general) cannot be deciphered until the notion of human equality has already acquired the fixity of a popular prejudice. This, however, is possible only in a society in which the great mass of the produce of labour takes the form of commodities, in which, con-

---

[75] *Myth and Society in Ancient Greece*, p. 16.

sequently, the dominant relation between man and man is that of owners of commodities. The brilliancy of Aristotle's genius is shown by this alone, that he discovered, in the expression of values of commodities, a relation of equality. The peculiar conditions of society in which he lived alone prevented him from discovering what 'in truth' was at the bottom of this equality.[76]

Myth patterns of thought and valuation are basic to all forms of hierarchic organization—ours included. It is commonly agreed that children live 'in a mythical' world.[77] Myth, however, does not vanish 'suddenly, as per magic'. Adults, too, indulge in 'mythical fantasies,' principally, but not only, for the sake of 'recreation.' As it was argued by Arieti,

> Even western normal adults resort to this type of perceptual thinking when they want to relax and indulge in a state of reverie or daydreaming....We rather go to the movies than to a lecture on a metaphysical subject.[78]

The role of myth goes deeper and wider than 'children's fantasies and entertainment.' It is the core strategy employed to validate the system of structures and configurations employed for the control and maintenance of society. To understand its overwhelming role, we must consider myth in the function of medium, rather than content.

The best example of a medium, taught McLuhan, is the electric light, which is "pure information."[79] There are three aspects to this metaphor, relevant to our discussion. First, the electric light is *not* a neutral conduit. We see what we see, because of, and insofar as the surround has been *affected* by, the electric light. The electric light, not only 'reveals,' but also 'conceals.' If we would use ultraviolet light, we would have perceived the items differently. Second, the *content* of the

---

[76] Karl Marx, *Kapital* (Chicago: Encyclopedia Britanica, 1952), I, A,3, p. 25.

[77] *Myth and Reality*, p. 77. See accompanying footnote.

[78] Sylvano Arieti, "Primitive Intellectual mechanism in Psycho-Pathological Conditions," p. 11.

[79] *Understanding Media*, p. 8.

light is *not* the light.⁸⁰ Seeing the *content* of the light *prevents* us from seeing the light itself. And thirdly, only someone standing outside the light could distinctly see both the light *and* the content of the light. (But then he would need to have another source of light).

Building on this metaphor, I propose that if we would consider myth, not in terms of its content, but as a means of conveyance, then we will have to conclude that the same integral structures and configurations peculiar to myth-conveyance prevail in the modern media. Modern technology is not a bulwark against myth, quite the contrary. "The effects of technology do not occur at the level of opinions or concepts," noted McLuhan, "but alter sense ratios or patterns of perception steadily and without resistance."⁸¹ The fact is that, whether conscious or not, myth penetrates surreptitiously into our lives and shapes it accordingly. As it has been well expressed by McLuhan:

> For myth *is* the instant vision of a complex process that ordinarily extends over a long period. Myth is contraction or implosion of any process, and the instant speed of electricity confers the mythic dimension on ordinary industrial and social action today. We *live* mythically but continue to think fragmentarily and on single planes.⁸² [Italics in original]

With the exception of the exact sciences—that which can actually be expressed in mathematical language and verified in a laboratory—our knowledge of matters pertaining to our daily lives is not fundamentally different than that of the 'primitive' man. We know what we know because somebody—in relation to whom we are relegated to a perennial state of 'absentee'—said so. That is the case, not only in the realm of fashion and entertainment, but also in our social, economic, and political lives. Invariably, the media and popular culture,

---

⁸⁰ See *Understanding Media*, pp. 8-9.

⁸¹ *Understanding Media*, p. 18. In particular, it impacts the content of a person's mind, and how an individual would 'recall' a past event and react to a present stimulus. On this pivotal point, see Susan T. Fiske and Shelley E. Taylor, *Social Cognition* 2ⁿᵈ ed. (New York: McGraw, 1991), Chapter 7.

⁸² *Understanding Media*, p. 25.

invoke their message from the first-party platform, addressing a public that is precluded from addressing the media from the subjective '*I*' to '*you*.' (Have you ever witnessed a member of the general public interviewing a member of the media?) Thus, the message takes on an autonomous existence. Only the first-party platform can ascertain which 'facts' are 'real' and which 'are not': 'truth' is predicated on *who* invokes it.

Before the rise of the electric-speed media, one could argue, together with Eliade, that the written word has finally prevailed over orality.

> There is more here than the triumph of *logos* over *mythos*. The victory is that of *the book* over oral tradition, of the document—especially of the written document—over a living experience whose only means of expression were preliterary.[83] [Italics in the original]

This is no longer the case. Thanks to electric-speed communication, time and space, which served as the minimal categories of 'rationality,' have vanished. "The great paradox of our age," noted a distinguished media scholar, "is that although it is undergoing social and intellectual change of totally unprecedented speed and depth, its thought has become, in the main, unhistorical or ahistorical."[84] In practical terms, it means that the first-person platform is omnipotent, and can make 'tangible reality,' 'apodictic truth,' etc., 'appear' and 'disappear' at will: precisely as with the rituals accompanying the performance of myth. The message has an existence of its own and cannot be scrutinized on the basis of 'facts'—unless those 'facts' had been previously acknowledged by echelons vested with the authority to *invoke* 'facts.' Differences between properly accredited members of the media are expected to be resolved by the fiat of *authority*—not by rational discourse between the first and second person. Surely, free-

---

[83] *Myth and Reality*, p. 157. See *GD*, pp. 158-161.
[84] Ernst Gellner, *Plough, Sword, and Book* (Chicago: Chicago University Press, 1988), p. 12, quoted in *Parchment, Printing and Hypermedia*, p. 41. See *Understanding Media*, pp. 16-17.

dom of thought, creed, and opinion are fully guaranteed, with the *proviso* that members of the third-party absentee duly acknowledge the 'apodictic truth' invoked by the first-person platform.

There is another fact the West inherited from archaic times. In a hierarchic society, *everyone* has the mindset of a third-party absentee, including those 'on top.'[85] I am referring to the mental slavery peculiar to the 'higher echelons,' unable to understand that they, too, are slaves, of the worst class.[86] Jung called attention to the slave mentality peculiar to Roman society.

> Every Roman was surrounded by slaves. The slave and his psychology flooded ancient Italy, and every Roman became inwardly, and of course unwittingly, a slave.[87]

The same phenomenon is found among political leaders, old and new, who fall "slaves of their own fictions." A leader prone to enslave others will become "the victim of his own inflated ego-consciousness, as numerous examples in history show."[88]

A contributing factor to the 'slave mentality' is that communication between the first and third parties excludes a 'linguistic person.' Benveniste made the essential point, that "I use *I* only when I am speaking to someone who will be a *you* in my address." Given that the 'the third-party absentee' cannot designate himself as '*I*' and address the first-party as '*you*,' and given that the first-party platform does not posit himself to a '*you*,' neither of the parties is in fact a *linguistic* person. There are far reaching consequences to this linguistic situation, primary among them is that, "Consciousness of self is only possible if it is experienced by contrast" between the first linguistic person '*I*' and the linguistic second person '*you*.' '*I/you*' implies lin-

---

[85] See *HS*, vol. 1, pp. 105-106.

[86] See José Faur, "Of Cultural Intimidation and Other *Miscellanea*: Bar-Sheshakh *vs.* Raba," *Review of Rabbinic Judaism* 5 (2002), pp. 34-50.

[87] In *Contributions to Analytical Psychology* (London, 1928); quoted in *Understanding the Media*, p. 21.

[88] *The Undiscovered Self*, p. 23; see ibid, pp. 21-22.

guistic parity between the constitutive persons of the dialogue. "I use *I* only when I am speaking to someone who will be a *you* in my address." The horizontality imposed by the '*I/you*' parity is the matrix of the linguistic person.

> It is this condition of dialogue that is constitutive of *person*, for it implies that reciprocally *I* becomes *you* in the address of the one who in his turn designates himself as *I*.[89]

The relationship first-party platform → third-party absentee is germane to the dislocation of the self and—*á la* Socrates—abdication of individual judgment on behalf of *über*-father State.[90] To illuminate those below, society gives rise to political elites, skilled in the management of the national and diplomatic affairs of the state.[91] In turn, the same system will justify the seizure of power by ideologues, excelling in the art of manipulation and the administration of violence.[92] We can well understand how in a situation where man is disallowed to address those invoking the 'truth,' as *you*, "the individual," as pointed out by Jung, will become "more and more a function of society." Eventually, both society and state will become "an abstract idea."

> The State in particular is turned into a quasi-animated personality from whom everything is expected. In reality it is only a camouflage for those individuals who know how to manipulate it. Thus the constitutional State drifts into the situation of a primitive form of society, namely the communism of the primitive tribe where everybody is subject to the autocratic rule of a chief or an oligarchy.[93]

---

[89] *Problems in General Linguistics*, pp. 224-225. See above n. 14 and below Chapter 7.

[90] See C. G. Jung, *The Undiscovered Self* (New York: A Mentor Book, 1957), pp. 22, 50-51, etc.

[91] For a comprehensive analysis of this subject, see Harold D. Lasswell, "Introduction: The Study of Political Elites," in *World Revolutionary Elites*, eds. Harold D. Lasswell and Daniel Lerner (Cambridge, Mass. M.I.T. Press, 1965), pp. 3-28.

[92] See the learned study of Daniel Lerner, "The Coercive Ideologist in Perspective," in *World Revolutionary Elites*, pp. 456-468.

[93] *The Undiscovered Self*, pp. 26-27.

Such a society will produce political leaders who will become prey of their own demagoguery.[94] The end result is a society made up of people totally dependent on *über*-father Leader.

> The individual is increasingly deprived of the moral decision as to how he should live his own life, and instead is ruled, fed, clothed and educated as a social unit, and amused in accordance with the standards that give pleasure and satisfaction to the masses.[95]

This type of society is beautifully portrayed by George Orwell (1903-1950) in *Animal Farm* (1945).

The logic enabling the first-person platform to make 'facts' 'appear' and 'disappear' is grounded on paleologic thinking, whereby identity is established on the basis of predicates, rather than substantives. On the basis of this logic, the media can conclude that *Cat white* is identical to *Dog white*, rather than to *Cat black*, given that both *are* white. If need will arise, the same logic could identify *Cat white/Black cat* on the basis that neither of them barks. Conversely, the identity *Cat black/Dog white* can be established on the basis that both were the victims of *Cat white*. This can be demonstrated on the widely accepted theory that originally, all four legged mammals were black, until *Cat white*—with malice and forethought—bullied good-*Doggie* to forfeit its original blackness and become *white*. We all should unite and condemn *bad-Cat-white*, for the sake of all four-legged mammals, as well as truth and justice. Let us point out in passing that the core strategy of the entire advertisement industry is grounded on this sort of logic: identity is made on the basis of predicates—not substantives. The wisdom of this sort of logic can be best appreciated upon realizing that the principle object of the media is to enchant the public, rather than generate discourse between the linguistic first and second person.[96]

One of the effects of this sort of conveyance is the creation of

---

[94] See above, n. 88.

[95] *The Undiscovered Self*, p. 22.

[96] On the role of magic in Western rhetoric, see *HS*, vol. pp. 29-32.

mythological folk heroes, including the glorification of certain political entities and ideologies and the demonization of others.[97]

The preceding observations bear on the rise and fall of political dictators and mass murderers in modern times. Great orators—not only in Greece and Rome—have been vested with power, not only to invoke *what* took place *when* and *where* in the *past*, but also to ascertain, with uncanny precision, what is taking place in the *present* and what will transpire in the *future* if and/or unless... One can wonder whether mass murderers of the ilk of Hitler, Mussolini, and Stalin, to name just a few, would have been able to carry on their nefarious plans without the aid furnished by the first-person platform media. This does not mean that there were no honorable men in the media—there surely were—but, were they more principled than Socrates who counseled to submit to the *über*-father State as if we were a "child and slave"? Many, I am sure, will readily assure us that indeed they were, and I suppose that they should be believed "because *they* said it is so." The Nobel Prize laureate, Elias Canetti (1905-1994), recounted about a schoolmate, the son of a judge who, unlike his father, believed that Hitler was the man that could save the world from war.

> When I advocated the opposite conviction, he insisted that he had heard Hitler *say so himself.* [Italics in the original] That was the reason he supported him, he said, and no one would ever talk him out of it. I was so flabbergasted that I saw him again for that very reason, continuing the same conversation several times. He would then come out with the same or even lovelier statement about peace. I can see him before me, his glowing face for peace, the countenance of an apostle, and I hope that he did not pay for his faith with his life.[98]

And now a pivotal question: Is there any substantive difference between the student believing that Hitler will bring world peace, because (thanks to the media), "he had heard Hitler *say so himself*," and

---

[97] See *Myth and Reality*, pp. 184-193. An important variation popularized by Hollywood is that the hero usually ends up triumphant; see ibid. p. 199.
[98] *The Torch in my Ear*, p. 257.

the Eskimo who confirms his faith "because it is said that it is so"?[99]

"The grammar of print," wrote McLuhan, "cannot help to construe the message of oral and nonwritten culture and institutions."[100] In fact, we are at the threshold of a new mode of communication, governed by the grammar of "convergence"—a term first coined by Professor Ithiel de Sola Pool (1917-1984). Henry Jenkins defines it as follows:

> By convergence, I mean the flow of content across multiple media platforms, the cooperation between multiple media industries, and the migratory behavior of media audiences who will go almost anywhere in search of the kinds of experiences they want. Convergence is a word that manages to describe technological, industrial, cultural, and social changes depending on who's speaking, and what they think they are talking about.[101]

The new culture shall give "power" to both the consumer and the citizen. Thus, the book concludes in a buoyant tone:

> Welcome to convergence culture, where old and new media collide, where grassroots and corporate media intersect, where the power of the media producer and the power of the media consumer interact in unpredictable ways. Congruence culture is the future, but it is taking shape now. Consumers will be more powerful within convergence culture—but only if they recognize and use that power as both consumers and citizens, as full participants in our culture.[102]

In my view, this "new culture" is what José Ortega y Gasset (1833-1955) called, "the right of vulgarity, or vulgarity as a right."[103] The result is a "New Adam"—a humanoid, possessing a special type of "self-confidence" having to do with the "innate hermetism of his

---

[99] See above n. 4.

[100] *Understanding Media*, p. 15.

[101] Henry Jenkins, *Convergence Culture* (New York: New York University Press, 2006), pp. 2-3.

[102] *Convergence Culture*, p. 270.

[103] José Ortega y Gasset, *The Revolt of the Masses* (New York: W.W. Norton, 1957), p. 70.

soul."[104] Commenting on European society before World War II, Ortega y Gasset noted that, "[a]t least in European history up to the present, the vulgar had never believed itself to have 'ideas' on things."[105] Now, we find the vulgar passing judgment on politics, art, literature, etc.[106] Ortega y Gasset called these sorts of ideas, "intellectual barbarism," and "the absence of standards to which appeal can be made"[107] —a form of 'intellectualism,' which will lead to violence.

> Under the species of Syndicalism and Fascism there appears for first time in Europe a type of man who does not want to give reasons or to be right, but simply shows himself resolved to impose his opinions. This new thing: the right not to be reasonable, the "reason of unreason."[108]

Upon some consideration, "New Adam" is nothing else than the glorification of the third-person absentee, and "the mass-man," wholly dependent on a "transcendent authority" which for all practical purposes "is not of this world." This situation would permit treating the 'individual' as morally irresponsible, while at the same time, regard "the leader or party boss" as some sort of "a demigod beyond good and evil." Compliance must be total, with no room for those "who think differently."[109] (See below Section III, Chapter 37)

In brief, the medium conveying the message, rather than the massage itself, is what counts. To express the same more elegantly,

> Our conventional response to all media, namely that it is how they are used that counts, is the numb stance of the technological idiot. For the 'content' of a medium is like the juicy piece of meat carried by the burglar to distract the watch-dog of the mind. The effect of the medium is made strong and intense just because it is given anoth-

---

[104] *The Revolt of the Masses*, p. 69.

[105] *The Revolt of the Masses*, p. 70.

[106] See *The Revolt of the Masses*, p. 71.

[107] *The Revolt of the Masses*, p. 72, see ibid. n. 1.

[108] *The Revolt of the Masses*, p. 73.

[109] *The Undiscovered Self*, pp. 32-33.

er medium as 'content.'[110]

Ever since Sophocles, we have been taught, "Don't kill the messenger"—the media just report! After all, unlike our parents and grandparents, duped by all kind of fantasies, we have evolved into a "New Adam"—totally liberated and totally coherent. If there is one thing we can all rest assured of it is that the "new convergence media" is immaculate and absolutely neutral (unlike the clergy in the Dark Ages). There are all sorts of mechanisms—a bit difficult to explain to the average Joe—that render the system foolproof. We can be positively certain of that because… it is said that it is so!

5. Israel's Medium: Speaker-'*I*,' Addressee-'*you*'

The medium of myth is communication from the first-person platform to third-person absentee. The medium of Israel is the dialogue 'Subjective-Speaker-God/Addressee-Israel' spoken at Sinai. Its content is the entire value-system, literature, and institutions, developed in six millennia of history. We shall explain.

The *Tora* or Covenantal-Law, freely contracted by the people at the foothills of Sinai, is the alternative to mythical thinking. It is also anathema to the myth-medium culture. The Hebrew people were the first to master the grammar of tyranny. Alone, among the nations of the world, Jews discovered that they were slaves. Only Jews had the mettle to leave the country and culture enslaving them, cross the Desert, and go ahead to establish *a new* type of society *under* a Covenantal-Law. The seminal concept of Judaism is quite simple: every human being is created in the *image* of God. Given that there is a *single* God, it means, not only that all humans are created equal, but that they *are* equal. This concept is an abomination to mythical-value systems, where everyone is either higher or lower than everybody else. The idea of a Covenant contracted *by the people* is an affront to hierar-

---

[110] *Understanding Media*, p. 18.

chical structures. Nothing could be more absurd to the pagan mind than a God coming *down* to speak to a bunch of slaves. The fact that the *Tora* was not *imposed by force*, but *freely contracted*, is an outrage. One needs not be particularly sensitive to pagan values and structures to recognize that the story of runaway slaves succeeding in instituting a governing Law is a challenge to mythical mind and ethos.[111] At the time, Jews were not even a nation, and had neither their own territory nor a ruling monarch. It is ludicrous to think that any 'Law' could be established *without* a mighty state governing with an iron fist. More heinous is the idea of a 'Covenant,' implying that to be binding, a 'Law' requires the consent of the governed!

The Covenant was not invoked from a first-party platform to a third-party absentee. At Sinai, God addressed Israel in the subjective-first-person-singular '*I*' (Hebrew *anokhi*), to an addressee made up of second person singular '*you*' (Hebrew *-kha*).[112] The medium of the covenant is the 'linguistic person,' involving reciprocity between speaking-subject singular *I*/God (Hebrew *ano-khi*) and singular-addressee *you*/individual-Israelite (Hebrew *-kha*). Together, 'God/individual Israelite' constitutes 'the dialectical person of the Covenant.' This means, first and foremost, that Israel can turn and address God in the second person singular '*you*.' Moses, in function

---

[111] It would be even more preposterous to admit that a bunch of Holocaust survivors, together with Jews expelled from Arab lands, could establish a new and vibrant society in the midst of the 'New Babel'—particularly after Europe and Arabia became '*Jüdenrein*,' and succeeded in instituting the Commonwealth of 'Eurabia.' *Avant-Garde* institutions in the States, aspiring to emulate 'Europe' succeeded in turning some of the most prestigious Universities, into 'little Amerabia.' It is only a modest beginning, but one must start up somewhere. Incidentally, before World War II, Jews in the Middle East believed that Arab anti-Jewish feelings were the result of a carefully planned work by France, among Christian Arabs, and England, among Muslim Arabs, so that they could take over the Arab market, and eliminate Jewish competition. On British promotion of anti-Jewish feelings among Arabs in Israel, see Abraham Shalom Yahuda, *Hakotel Hama'arabi* (Jerusalem:5728/1968), "Introduction." Recent developments in Eurabia seem to vindicate the 'Old' Testament's adage of "an eye for an eye." Under the more enlightened and progressive leadership, 'little Amerabia' will surely follow.

[112] For some linguistic background, see *GD*, pp. 41-49.

of the duly appointed spokesman of the people (see *Ex* 20:15; cf. *Ps* 91:15), "would address" God during the Theophany at Sinai, and in turn, "God would reply to him by a voice" (*Ex* 19:19), which was perceptible to the people's ear. In the same way, every Jew is expected to address God in the second person singular *'you'* (*atta*), as part of the ongoing dialogue 'God/Israel.' The second commandment, barring intermediaries (Greek *mesites*) between speaking-subject-people and second-person-singular God, expresses *the same idea in the reverse*. The concept of 'an intermediary' (Greek *mesites*) defies 'the dialectical person God/individual Israelite.' Such 'intermediary' (Greek *mesites*) would then occupy the first-party platform peculiar to myth conveyance, and invoke the apodictic truth to two third-persons absentees: God and Israel. In which case, instead of the ensuing dialogue 'God/Israel,' both parties would know the 'truth' "because the intermediary (Greek *mesites*) said that it is so."

In Israel, neither the people act in terms of a third-person absentee, nor God dictates from a first-party platform. At both, Sinai and Moab, God's proposal to establish a covenant required ratification by the people. The sanctions of the covenant, too, were ratified by a unanimous "Amen!"[113] At the Synagogue, the congregants express approval to the prayers by responding 'Amen!' In Judaism, the precentor leading in the prayers *does not* stand for some sort of 'higher authority' to whom the congregation supposes to submit. Rather, as per its Hebrew designation, he is the *Sheliaḥ Ṣibbur* or 'congregation's envoy.' Accordingly, he requires the *unanimous* consent of the congregants. In practical terms it means that,

---

[113] See *Dt* 27:15-25. In other occasions, when addressed by the political leader, the people gave their consent in a similar manner; see *Neh* 5:13 [cf. *Ps* 106:48; 1*Ch*16:36], 8:6. At the end of his career, when proposing to the people to accept God's Law as the Law of the land, Joshua sought and received the explicit consent of the people; see *Joshua* 24:1-28, specially, vv. 21-28. Even a woman suspected of adultery was required to give her consent to the invocation of the priest, and respond "Amen!" See *Nu* 5:26. More significant is the rule requiring that the congregants respond with an approving "Amen" to the priestly blessings at the Synagogue; see *MT Tefilla* 9:3.

... even a single member of the congregation may prevent his nomination, and state: 'I do not wish that he should be the precentor.'[114]

Would he attempt to lead the services without obtaining their consent, the public is then advised to refrain from answering 'Amen.'[115]

The dialogue 'God/Israel' began at Sinai. The Book of *Genesis* and the portions of *Exodus*, came *after*, and as a *consequence*, of the Covenant: the *pre*-Sinaitic portions of the *Tora* are *post*-Sinaitic.[116]

Myths do not allow for dissention or diverse interpretation. The rabbinic principle, "the *Tora* expresses itself in the language of man," serves to ascertain the linguistic reciprocity 'speaker/addressee.'[117] A major consequence of this principle is that the sense of words is determined by the second-person addressee—not by the speaking '*I*.' This leads to the rabbinic doctrine, first enunciated by R. Joshua (1st and 2nd centuries), a member of Israel's Supreme Court: the "*Tora* is not within the realm of Heaven!" That is, the meaning of God's words is to be determined by Israel (the addressee)—not God.[118] Thus, the 'Oral Law,' standing for the *constitutional* interpretation of the *Tora*, is designated the *perush* or 'interpretation' of the Written *Tora*; i.e., as it was understood by Moses and the collective mind of Israel. To underscore the subjective dimension of the second-person addressee, peculiar to the 'Oral Law,' this expression is rendered in Judeo-Spanish '*Ley mental*' or 'Mental Law'; that is, the Law as under-

---

[114] Maran Joseph Caro, *Shulḥan 'Arukh, Oraḥ Ḥayyim* LIII, 19.

[115] Rama, *Shulḥan 'Arukh, Oraḥ Ḥayyim* DLXXXI, 1; cf. ibid. DCXC, 1.

[116] See Mishna *Ḥolin* 7:6; *Ḥolin* 100a-b; *Yerushalmi Mo'ed Qaṭan* III, 8, 82c; *Perush ha-Mishnayot Ḥolin* 7:6, vol. 5, p. 212; José Faur, *Studies in the Mishne Tora* (Heb.) (Jerusalem: Mossad Harav Kook, 1978), pp. 149-150. Cf. *MT Ebel* 1:1; *Studies in the Mishne Tora*, p. 14 n. 5, pp. 148-151; *HS*, vol. 1, p. 53. This doctrine reflects the rabbinic principle that the *Tora* is not compiled in chronological sequence; see *Pesaḥim* 6a; *Yeushalmi Sheqalim* VI, 1, 49d, etc.

[117] See *Berakhot* 31b; *GD*, p. xxi and corresponding note, pp. 151-152.

[118] See *Baba Meṣi'a* 59b; cf. *GD*, pp. 13-14, 119; *HS*, vol. 1, p. 58.

stood by the mind of God's addressee: Israel.[119]

We can now proceed to consider two fundamental aspects of the 'God/Israel' dialogue. Moses *wrote* the consonantal text of the *Tora*, and then *published* it in a Scroll, which he deposited next to the Ark of the Tablets.[120] Both these aspects are essential to the dialogue 'God/Israel.' The *consonantal* text stands for God First-Person speech, ineffable by human standard. The *publishing* is the formal conveyance of the text onto the domain of the second-person addressee, Israel—thus, permitting the processing of the consonantal text into a vocalized system representing the 'mind of the addressee'. It is through the interaction first-person, consonantal-text/addressee-reader, that the 'dialectical person, God/Israel' is generated every time a member of the Sinaitic Covenant reads the *Tora*. Since it is not possible to convey a pure consonantal text orally, the *Tora*, standing for God's consonantal speech, had to be conveyed in writing (*Tora she-Bikhtab*). The Scroll published by Moses is the archetype of the *Tora* found in the Synagogue.

In a primary oral culture speech is apprehended by the phonetic contour of words. Speech is conditioned to voice manipulation, staging, and the diverse gambits of oratory. 'Meaning' and 'understanding' have to do with extra linguistic factors, such as voice resonance and theatrics. The *Tora*, however, is to be grasped on its own merits. Moses, we all remember, was "slow of speech and of a slow tongue" (*Ex* 4:10)—not an orator. By reducing the dialogue 'God/Israel' to the most basic elements of speech—consonants—the interference of non-linguistic factors is eliminated. Consonantal reading requires the active participation of the reader. He must supply the vowels to the consonantal text and *generate* meaning from the consonantal speech of God. As it were, the second-person addressee responds to God's consonantal speech with a fully vocalized text. Analphabetic cultures, and individuals too dull to generate meaning on their own, will find it

---

[119] See *HS*, vol. 2, Chapter 6.

[120] See *HS*, vol. 1, Chapter 7, and vol. 2, Appendix 1.

difficult to make heads or tails, either of the *Tora* at Sinai or the rest of the *Hebrew Scripture.*

McLuhan's seminal distinction of 'hot' and 'cold' medium can help us understand the difference between the medium of myth and the *Tora*. A 'hot' medium requires minimal input from the public, whereas a 'cool' medium requires an active participation from the public.

> Telephone is a cool medium, or one of low definition, simply because the ear is given a meager amount of information. And speech is a cool medium of low definition, because so little is given and so much has to be filled by the listener. On the other hand, hot media do not leave so much to be filled in or completed by the audience. Hot media are, therefore, low in participation or completion by the audience. Naturally, therefore, a hot medium like radio has very different effects on the user from a cool medium like a telephone.[121]

Unlike myth-narrative, the *Tora*, and indeed the whole of Judaism, is a 'cool medium.'

The God of Scriptures does not communicate to an analphabetic crowd. At Sinai, Israel not only *heard* His words but actually processed them as if, "written in black letters, against the white parchment of the sky."[122] R. 'Aqiba (50-135) explained: "They saw, and they heard what they saw. They saw the word of fire coming out from the mouth of the Almighty being inscribed on the tablets."[123] Later rabbinic tradition, explained this to mean that the people actu-

---

[121] *Understanding Media*, pp. 22-23. This distinction is similar to 'writing' and 'graffiti,' discussed in *GD*, Chapter 1.

[122] *Yerushalmi Sheqalim* VI, 1, 49d.

[123] *Mekhilta de-R. Yishma'el, Yitro*, IX, p. 235. McLuhan's description of the sound waves, just before breaking the medium of the sound barrier, *Understanding Media*, p. 12, can serve as a metaphor to Israel's vision in Sinai:

> Just before an airplane breaks the sound barrier, sound waves become visible on the wings of the plane. The sudden visibility of sound just as sound ends is an apt instance of that great pattern of being that reveals new and opposite forms just as their earliest forms reach their peak performance.

ally *read* the voices as they were enunciating the Decalogue. It was a unique experience. The rabbis used the verse "Golden doves we shall make for you with silver dots" (*Song* 1:11), as a metaphor to illustrate the tension between the speech by *I*-God, and its processing in the mind of *you*-Israel. "*Golden doves...* is the *Tora* in the mind of the Almighty. *With silver dots*—R. Abba b. Kahana said: 'These are the letters.' R. Aḥa said: 'These are the words.'"[124]

Jews divide world civilizations into two: the Civilization of Book and the Civilization of the Sword.[125] That was the main difference between Esau and Jacob. Concerning them, *The Book of Jubilees* (19:14), remarked: "And the youths grew, and Jacob learned to write; but Esau did not learn, for he was a man of the field and a hunter, and he learnt war, and all his deeds were fierce."

6. The Publication of a Vowel-less Text and the Formation of the Hebrew-Self

The *Tora* is the first National Publication known to humankind. It is not mere 'literature' or 'history,' but the defining dimension of every Jew, individually and nationally: *Tora* is to a Jew what *territory* is for pagan nationhood. *Publication* of the *Tora* means that the dialogue 'God/Israel' belongs to *every* Jew. A case in point is the following story, taking place around the 3rd century in Galilee. The protagonists were R. Yannai and a stranger. R. Yannai was one of the most illustrious men of the time. He had served in the Supreme Court of Israel under Chief Justice R. Judah ha-Nasi, who published the *Mishna*—the Jewish legal code of Israel. He was a person of considerable means,

---

[124] *Shir ha-Shirim Rabba* I, 11, in *Midrash Rabba* ['*al ha-Tora ve-Ḥamesh Megillot*], 2 vols (Vilna. Reprinted: Jerusalem, 5735/1975), vol. 2, 11d. For a full discussion of this passage, see *GD*, Chapter 5.

[125] *Sifre* #40, ed. Louis Finkelstein (New York: The Jewish Theological Seminary of America, 1969), p. 84 cf. ibid. p. 83; cf. *'Aboda Zara* 17b, *Sifre* # 323, p. 372. See *HS*, vol. 1, p. 231, and ibid. Chapters 14, 23, 31.

and belonged to one of the most distinguished families of Israel. One of his ancestors served as High Priest at the Temple in Jerusalem. Among his disciples we find the most prominent Talmudic masters. Their teaching served as the basis upon which were developed the Talmud *Yerushalmi* and Babylonian Talmud. Of the stranger we know very little, except that he was a thoroughly illiterate man. Nonetheless, for a reason that we would discover in the course of the story, he wanted to pass himself as a scholar, in order to be invited to the rabbi's home. With this purpose in mind, he wore some sort of attire that called the attention of R. Yannai.[126] Assuming that he was a rabbinic scholar, new in town, he invited him to come home and break bread with him. In the course of the meal, R. Yannai discovered that he had been deceived. The stranger was a total illiterate boor! He could not even *repeat* the grace after-meal! Who was this stranger? Why he wanted to be invited at the rabbi's home under false pretenses? Things started spinning out of control. The rabbi, who was known for his humility and patience, lost his composure. Harsh remarks were exchanged.[127] Hurt by the slur, the guest grabbed the rabbi and said:

—'What?! I came to check my inheritance which I had entrusted with you, and you [dare] confront me'?!

—'Which inheritance have you [entrusted] me with'?—replied the rabbi surprisingly.

—'When I was a child I heard that the *Tora* says: "Moses had instructed us the *Tora*, it is the legacy of the Congregation of Jacob" (*Dt* 33:4). It does not say: "the Congregation of Yannai," but "the Congregation of Jacob!"

The stranger may have been facing some sort of a personal crisis. Perhaps he was sensing that he was a failure, and wanted to take a peek at the home of someone who, unlike himself, dedicated his entire life to the study and teaching of *Tora*. The one single thing that he

---

[126] See R. Samuel Yafe Ashkenazi, *Yefe To'ar, Vayyiqra* (Constantinople, 5408/1648), 57a.

[127] I don't recall such offensive exchange in all the rabbinic literature that I've read!

remembered having learned as a child was that the *Tora* is the legacy of every member of the Jewish community—and not of some sort 'privileged elite.' As a full partner, he wanted to check how *his* assets were fairing, and get to know the people managing *his* legacy. R. Yannai agreed with the stranger. After reconciling, the rabbi discovered that the guest was indeed an honest and compassionate individual, and apologized to him.[128] The position of the stranger is anchored in law. R. Aharon Kotler (1891-1962), pointed out that profits gained by one or some of the heirs of an undivided estate, belong to all the heirs.[129] Equal partnership, however, entails equal responsibilities. Hence the doctrine stipulating that all Jews are "responsible for one another."[130] Given that Jews are responsible for each other, a Jew confesses his sins, not in the singular, but in the first person plural.[131]

Being in the public domain of Israel, the *Tora* is the great equalizer, awarding equal standing even to the "meekest" Jew. Regarding this overwhelming principle, the rabbis taught:

> ...If one hears a word from the mouth of the meekest Israelite (="simple believer"), he must regard it as if he had actually heard it from a great sage...he should not regard it only as if had actually heard it from a single sage, but as if he had actually heard it from all the sages...and not only as if he had actually heard it from all the sages, but as if he had actually heard it from the *Sanhedrin* [Supreme

---

[128] See *Vayyiqra Rabba*, ed. M. Margulies, 6 vols. (Jerusalem: The American Academy for Jewish Research, 1953), vol. 1, IX, 3, pp. 176-179. See the editor's comments ad loc, and *Yefe To'ar, Vayyiqra*, 57b.

[129] R. Aharon Kotler, *Mishnat R. Aharon*, vol. 1 (Jerusalem: Beth Midrash Gavoha-Lakewood, 5744/1984), pp. 36-37. The Talmudic reference is to Mishna *Baba Batra*, 9:3; see *MT Naḥalot* 9: 1. Accordingly, the study of *Tora* is to be classified as a precept affecting the relation between an individual and his fellowman (*ben adam le-ḥabero*), and not solely an individual and His Maker (*ben adam lam-maqom*); see ibid vol. 1, p. 37.

[130] *Sanhedrin* 27b, and *Shebu'ot* 39a. For a learned orientation on this subject, see Samuel Belkin, *In His Image* (New York: Abelard-Schuman, n.d.), pp. 140-143; and the penetrating remarks in *Mishnat R. Aharon*, vol. 1, pp. 243-245.

[131] See Silvano Arieti, *Abraham and the Contemporary Mind* (New York: Basic Books, 1981), p. 125.

Court]…and not only as if he had actually heard it from the *Sanhedrin*, but as if he had actually heard it from Moses the Shepherd…and not only as if he had heard it from Moses the Shepherd, but as if he had actually heard it from the mouth of God, blessed be He![132]

The rules of protocol, fundamental in the relationship between son and father, disciple and teacher, are momentarily suspended when discussing *Tora*. In the heat of an argument, "Father and son, teacher and student, may become adversaries when investigating *Tora*," noticed the rabbis. In the end, however, "they would not leave the place until becoming friends again."[133] To ensure that no hierarchic symbol stands between students and teacher, the rabbis established: "the teacher may not sit on a chair and students on the ground; either all sit on the ground or all sit on chairs."[134]

The dialogue 'God/Israel' is a central factor in the discovery of the self and the development of individuality. Contrary to common belief, the subjective 'I' does not emerge, as if per magic, from an amorphous mass we designate 'society.' We had the opportunity to learn that consciousness of one's self is realized when the subjective 'I' discovers the individual to whom he is addressing as '*you*.'[135] In the words of Benveniste:

> And so the old antinomies of 'I' and 'the other,' of the individual and society, fall. It is a duality which it is illegitimate and erroneous to reduce to a single primordial term, whether this unique term be the 'I,' which must be established in the individual's own consciousness in order to become accessible to that of the fellow human being, or whether it be, on the contrary, society, which as a totality would preexist the individual and from which the individual could only be disengaged gradually, in proportion to his acquisition of self-consciousness. It is in a dialectic reality that will incorporate the two

---

[132] *Sifre* # 41, p. 86; see *GD*, p. 56.

[133] *Qiddushin* 30b.

[134] *MT Talmud Tora* 4:2; *Shulḥan 'Arukh, Yore De'a* CCXLVI, 9. The source is *Megilla* 21a.

[135] See above pp. 43-44.

terms and define them by mutual relationship that the basis of subjectivity is discovered.[136]

A fundamental condition of 'I' and 'you,' within the context of dialogue, is that they "are reversible: the one whom 'I' defines by 'you' thinks of himself as 'I' and can be inverted into 'I,' and 'I' becomes a 'you.'"[137] Properly understood, 'I' and 'you' don't indicate 'concepts' or the idea of 'person' in general, but the *actual* participants in the act of speech.

Given that one cannot discover his own subjective 'I' unless first addressed as a 'you,' how did man first acquire his subjective self? According to the *Hebrew Scripture*, God created Adam in His "image" (*Gn* 1:27), which was understood to stand for the linguistic faculty. To be fully operative, however, it required to be imbued with a special 'spirit.' With this purpose in mind, God "blew" into Adam's nostrils "a breath of life," and he became "a living soul" (*Gn* 2:7). The *Targum* or Aramaic version, which is the traditional interpretation of the *Tora*, rendered this phrase: "a speaking spirit." Translated in our terms, it means that the "breath of life" that God "blew" into Adam, activated God's image within, so that Adam could discovered his subjective self-consciousness. This came in a primordial dialogue, 'God/Adam.' The rabbis explained. At first, (because he was endowed with God's image) Adam realized that he was different from the rest of the animal kingdom, but he had not yet discovered his own subjective self. His own individual self, he discovered later, when he responded to a question that God posed to him. Here is how the rabbis described the primordial dialogue God/Adam. First, God proceeded to parade before him beasts, wild animals, and birds, and asked him:

—'This! What is it called?'

—'This is an ox!'

—'This, what is it called?'

---

[136] *Problems in General Linguistics*, p. 225.

[137] *Problems in General Linguistics*, p. 199.

—'This is a camel!'
—'This, what is it called?'
—'This is a donkey!'
—'This, what is it called?'
—'This is a horse!'...

In this manner it was demonstrated how God's image in Adam awarded him the faculty to describe, linguistically, the world around him.[138] At this stage of human development, Adam could 'speak' and communicate with others; however, he had not yet discovered his subjective self. To discover his subjective self, Adam had to demonstrate two other aptitudes. First, could he look inside himself and depict himself linguistically? God asked him:

—'And you, what is your name?'

—He answered Him: 'To me it would be fit to call Adam, since I was created from *Adama* (earth).'

Adam proved himself far above the rest of the animal kingdom. He demonstrated, not only that he could describe the world around him, but that he could look inwardly into himself. There was one more test: could Adam assume the role of subjective speaker 'I,' and address God as '*you*'; i.e., as someone "completely exterior" to himself? To ascertain this, Adam had to respond to one more question:

—'And what is my name'?

—'To you it would be fit to call *Adon* (Master), since You are the Master of all your creations.'[139]

The Adam of Jewish tradition is an individual, not only conscious of the image of God within, but he also is "a speaking spirit" that could ascertain his '*I*' in syntagmatic opposition to '*you*' God.

Adam's children, too, can gain consciousness of their individual

---

[138] In linguistic terminology, Adam had the faculty to structurally connect the signifier (sound-image) or 'name' with signified (linguistic concept) and create thus a linguistic sign; see *GD*, pp. xix, 71.

[139] *Bereshit Rabba* XVII, 4, eds. J. Theodor and Ch Albeck, 3 vols. (Jerusalem: Wahrman Books, 1965), vol. 1, pp. 155-156. See *HS*, vol. 1, pp. 22-25. See above n. 14.

self by establishing a dialectical relationship with fellow human beings, in an '*I/you*' dialogue. The Hebrew precept urging a person to "love" *re'akha* (= 'the other') "like yourself" (*kamokha*) (*Lev* 19:18)—often quoted, but rarely understood—acquires a very precise sense upon realizing that *re'akha* is not your 'neighbor' or 'friend,' but your "interlocutor": the individual with whom you maintain an '*I/you*' dialogue, and form together a dialectical person. The "love" urged in the Scriptures (Hebrew *ve-ahabta*) has nothing to do with neurosis (see below Section III, Chapter 30). Rather, it is the feeling of empathy, involving awareness and deference, for the wishes and concerns of the '*you*' with whom you maintain a dialogue. The preposition "like yourself" (*kamokha*),[140] insisting on a reciprocal relationship between both parties, makes perfect sense once we bear in mind that both '*I*' and '*you*' discover their respective identities and differences, through dialectical relationship with one another.

A few notes would help up us gain a better grasp of the subject. The imperative "to love" (Hebrew *ve-ahabta*), appears four times in the Scriptures. Twice in *Leviticus*, the first time in 19:18 urging love towards a Jew. The second time it urges the same with "the stranger." The continuation of the verse, "for you were strangers in the land of Egypt" (19:34), clarifies that it is a case of human fellowship, not limited by religion or nationality. It appears two other times in *Deuteronomy* (6:5; 11:1), in relation to God. This means that an individual may forge his own self, both in relation to God and man. As with the God/Adam primordial dialogue, the God of the *Hebrew Scripture* reveals Himself to an individual in accordance to the image of God that the individual had forged within himself. Moses, so tell us the rabbis, could not perceive God as merciful and compassionate until he himself became merciful and compassionate. Hence the rabbinical doctrine: "Just as God is compassionate, you, too, must become compassionate." Which involves the reverse proposition: "Just as you are compassionate, God, too, is (i.e., will reveal Himself to you as) Com-

---

[140] *Kamokha* = preposition *kemo* 'like' + 2nd per sing mass suffix *kha*.

passionate."[141] Building on this thought, the rabbis taught: "Whoever is compassionate with others, Heaven will be compassionate with him."[142] As it were, existentially, both the God and the man of the *Hebrew Scripture* are always 'in the making.'

A consequence of the preceding is the human right to participate in the dialogue 'God/Adam.' Abraham did not hesitate to argue with God on behalf of Sodom and Gomorrah.

> Abraham's attitude shows not only his compassion and desire to help his fellow man but also his feeling of entitlement to argue with God. *Even the authority of God should not be unquestionably accepted.* [143] [Italics in original]

The thrust of this story is that "In all decisions if God has to be considered, man has to be considered, too."[144] This means that God's judgment must be in accord, somehow, with the criteria of the righteous. "I issue a judgment," declared God, "and the righteous annuls it."[145] As a matter of fact, "God yearns for the prayers of the Righteous."[146] Moses, too, argued with God on behalf of Israel, and God pardoned them (see *Nu* 14:20). We can therefore understand the value of prayers and supplications in Judaism: they are an ongoing continuation of the dialogue 'God/Israel.'

7. Masks and the Absentee Society

Given that the self can only be experienced by interaction, first

---

[141] *Shabbat* 133b; see quotation below n. 144, and *HS*, vol. 1, pp. 24-25. Cf. below n. 161.

[142] *Shabbat* 151b.

[143] *Abraham and the Contemporary Mind*, p. 112.

[144] *Abraham and the Contemporary Mind*, p. 110.

[145] *Mo'ed Qatan* 16a; cf. *Shabbat* 63a.

[146] *Yebamot* 64a.

person 'I' → second person '*you*' (and vice versa),¹⁴⁷ consciousness of self is not attainable in environments centered on 'first-party platform → third-party absentee' communication. The 'absentee' condition is facilitated by the "three symmetrical persons" peculiar to Indo-European languages. "Contrary to what our terminology would make us believe," writes Benveniste, "they are not homogeneous."¹⁴⁸ The symmetry "is an anomaly at the very center of the languages," of "an extreme and exceptional nature."¹⁴⁹ It serves, however, an extremely valuable role, by creating the illusion that the third-party absentee is actually a 'person,' just like the 'first' and 'second.' Connected to the "three symmetrical persons" is the verb 'to be,' suggesting the notions of 'being' and 'becoming,' implying the possibility of 'transformation,' 'rebirth,' etc.¹⁵⁰

Myth-centered cultures provide an assortment of masks to help the absentee 'become' *somebody*: an ancestor, a fearsome animal, a hero, etc.¹⁵¹ Masks play an important role in religious ceremonies. There were religious masks for the faithful and the divinities, for ceremonials initiation, for symbolic masquerades; masks that permitted the gods to appear in double persona, as man and as woman, and

---

[147] See *Problems in General Linguistics*, p. 199.

[148] *Problems in General Linguistics*, p. 197.

[149] *Problems in General Linguistics*, p. 199.

[150] On the verb 'to be' and its relation to magic and metaphysic, see *HS*, vol. 1, pp. 13-14. On the idea of re-birth and re-generation in Christian thought, see Paul Tillich, "The Importance of New Being for Christian Theology," in ed. Joseph Campbell, *Man and Transformation* (Princeton, N.J.: 1972), pp. 161-178.

[151] On the role of masks in rituals, see Mircea Eliade, *Symbolism, the Sacred, and the Arts* (New York: Continuum, 1992), pp. 64-71; on puberty-initiation rites, see idem, *Rites and Symbols of Initiation* (New York: Harper Torch Books, 1975), p. 39. Generally, masks are connected with the cult of ancestor; see idem, *Shamanism: Archaic Techniques of Ecstasy* (Princeton, N. J.: Princeton University Press, 1974), pp. 166-168; and assist the spirits to 'transform' the wearer into a ferocious animal, a bird, etc.; see ibid, pp. 88-95, 176-180. In this fashion, the shaman can incarnate a mythical animal and learn its language, see ibid, pp. 93-94. Masks can also help the dead avoid recognition and elude evil spirits, see ibid. p. 166. We should point out at the usage of 'Death Masks' for celebrated figures, among them Mozart (1756-1791) and Joseph Smith (1805-1844).

possess hyper-virility, swinging into bestiality. There also were sexual organs-cum-masks, tragic masks, theatric masks, masks only for gods and gods who were nothing but masks.[152] Special clothing, too, could fill the role of masks and help seize all sorts of spirits and magical powers. So, that some shamans used special garments instead of masks.

> True masks are rather rare among Siberians shamans, but among the Eskimos, especially in Alaska, where the influence of American Indian cultures is strong, the shamans do use masks. However, shamatic dress is in itself and in origin a mask. Mask or dress, the function is the same: to proclaim the incarnation of a mythological figure—a god, ancestor, or mystic animal. The mask effects the transubstantiation of the shaman, transforming him before everyone's eyes into the supernatural being he is impersonating.[153]

Masks not only bestow the wearer the power to be his 'real self,' but also to escape ordinary time and fly into a more beautiful past and or to a glorious hereafter.

> Masks, then, are always, in one way or another, bound up with the idea of time. Whatever sort of mask is worn, the wearer transcends earthly time. Whether ritual, funerary, or for any spectacle, the mask is an instrument of ecstasy. He who wears one is no longer himself, since he is projected beyond his personal identity. He becomes 'other,' even when the mask is his own portrait.[154]

To help the absentee gain a personality of his 'very own,' modern society provides a vast stock of masks to choose from. Some of the most effective masks are military, ecclesiastic, and medical uniforms. Among the most successful designers of masks is the fashion

---

[152] See Jean-Pierre Vernant and Pierre Vidal-Naquet, *Myth and Tragedy in Ancient Greece* (New York: Zone Books, 1990), Chapters IX and XVII. On the use of masks for animism and ancestor-worship, see Wilhelm Koppers, "On the Origins of the Mysteries in the Light of Ethnology and Indology," ed. Joseph Campbell, *The Mystic Vision* (Princeton, N.J.: Princeton University Press, 1982), p. 38.

[153] *Symbolism, the Sacred, & the Arts*, p. 66.

[154] *Symbolism, the Sacred, & the Arts*, pp. 70-71.

industry, in all of its varied and miscellaneous forms. Modern societies provide scores of symbols in function of masks, designed to denote kindness, morality, etc. To assist the spiritually-bent absentee, they sponsor the circulation of archaic beliefs, such transmigration, astrology, mysticism, and all sorts of cults.[155] For the intellectually savvy absentee, there is 'philosophy,' 'psychology,' 'literature,' 'art' and the whole field of the 'humanities,' ready to help answer the existential question: 'Who am I'?

People tend to *become* the mask they wear. In more poetic language: the mask ends up taking over the personality of the wearer. When discussing the sacred costumes among shamans, Eliade noted that a similar symbolism is found "on the robes of the priests and sovereigns in the ancient Orient." Adding:

> This series of facts fall under a 'law' well known to the history of religions: *one becomes what one displays*. The wearers of the masks *are* really the mythical ancestors portrayed by their masks.[156] [Italics in the original]

In general, masks have a dual function. First, they offer a ready-made persona, vesting the absentee with a 'real individuality.' In this manner, the absentee escapes the *present* and dwells in a better and kinder *time* and *place,* somewhere in the glorious past. Masks also offer the possibility to transcend the *present*, passing after death to a *future* and better world. Pictures, testimonials, eulogies, and all kind of symbolic mausoleums give substance to this undeniable fact.[157]

> The mask's capacity for existence on another time level perhaps explains its dual function: alienation of the personality (ritual and theater masks) and preservation of the personality (death masks and portraits). Both cases exemplify a reactivation of past time: primordial

---

[155] This includes 'cultural fashion' as well; see *Symbolism, the Sacred, & the Arts*, p. 20.

[156] *Shamanism*, p. 179.

[157] Jewish traditional practice was *not* to build a monument on the grave of the righteous, because "their words are their memorial," see *Yerushalmi Sheqalim* II, 7, 47a; *MT Ebel* 4:4.

time in the case of ritual and spectacle masks; historic and personal time in the case of death masks and portraits. Primordial mythological time, reactualized by ritual and spectacle masks, can be *lived*, but only by means of changing the personality and becoming 'other.' On the one hand, death mask and portraits reactualize historic time, which is not only past but dead, for no one can relive the inner life of anyone else. In either case, the time implied by the mask is ecstatic time, removed from the here and now. Whatever its type, every mask proclaims the presence of some being who does not belong to the everyday world.[158]

There are psychological masks, too, first examined by Sigmund Freud (1856-1939). They are designed to conceal disorderly behavior. Some intend to help the absentee cast himself as 'somebody else,' for all sorts of purposes: from the wicked and romantic to the altruistic and sublime. As in a kabuki stage, in the absentee society, too, victory requires the skillful manipulation of masks. It is a matter of survival. To thrive, the participants are expected to become Shakespearean actors. In this connection we should not forget that 'person' derives from the Latin *persona* standing for 'mask'—regularly used by performing actors, and best defined by Jung:

> One could say, with a little exaggeration, that the persona is that which in reality one is not, but which oneself as well as others as others think one is.[159]

In the west, proficiency in the manipulation of masks is connected with the art of 'cunning' (*metis* in Greek), where success depends on the ability of portraying the predator as helpless prey, and the prey as an evil, heartless predator.[160] However, unlike primitive societies, in modern times there are well accredited institutions, like the United Nations and the media, supplying the stage and principled justifications, determining who the aggressor 'really' is and who the

---

[158] *Symbolism, the Sacred, and the Arts*, p. 71.

[159] C. G. Jung, *The Archetypes of the Collective Unconscious* (Princeton, N.J.: Princeton University Press, 1981), p. 125.

[160] See *Naked Crowd*, Section II.

'innocent' victim 'really' is.

There is another aspect to the absentee society. Adam gained consciousness of his subjective 'I' when he addressed God as '*you*.' In this manner he was able to establish the distinction Adam/*Adon* (Master). This distinction helped establish the perimeters 'God/man.' Adam recognized that God is *Adon* (Master), with absolute dominion of the universe, upon discovering that he was a creature from *Adama* (earth). "Fear of God" in the *Hebrew Scripture* involves the recognition of the unbridgeable distance separating earthly-Adam from *Adon*-God. Nonetheless—and always within the perimeters 'Adam/*Adon*'—man has the right to exercise his *own* mind, and *argue* with God. Thus, "Whereas other faiths preach utmost submission and unquestioning acceptance of the divinity, Abraham and his descendants claim the right to argue."[161] As with Patriarch Abraham, the right to argue with God must focus on pleading compassion for others. On the basis of this doctrine, the rabbis taught: "Whoever has compassion for others, he is to be recognized a descendant of Patriarch Abraham, and whoever has no compassion for others, cannot be recognized as a descendant of Patriarch Abraham's."[162] The right to argue with God is realized upon discovering God's image within.

> ...in spite of his limitations and even before God, the human being is not requested to surrender his right to be himself, but is encouraged to interpret according to his judgment and to evaluate in his own way. God has given this personal dignity to the individual by creating him according to His own image.[163]

By contrast, in the absentee society,

> The development of the persona is the outcome of a process of adaptation that suppresses all individually significant features and potentialities, disguising and repressing them in favor of collective factors, or those deemed desirable by the collective. Here again, whole-

---

[161] *Abraham and the Contemporary Mind*, p. 112.

[162] *Beṣa* 32b; cf. quotation above n. 142.

[163] *Abraham and the Contemporary Mind*, p. 112.

ness is exchanged for a workable and successful sham personality.[164]

One of the functions of the '*I/you*' dialogue is to activate the image of God within. In an environment where people cannot maintain an '*I/you*' dialogue with either God or a fellow human being, the image of God within remains dormant. For these folks, society provides a wide assortment of masks to 'discover' and 'choose.' In time, the absentee, too, would come to believe in a 'supreme' *Adon* (Master); but it will not be the creator of Heavens and Earth, but the State—*á la* Socrates.[165] "The State has taken the place of God," writes Jung, "that is why…socialist dictatorships are religions and State slavery is a form of worship."[166] Granted that the absentee may carry on '*I/you*' dialogues at the personal level, with friends and family, but unlike the Jew he cannot argue with God—let alone with members of the anointed class. In Jung's own words:

> The policy of the State is exalted to a creed, the leader or party boss becomes a demigod beyond good and evil…. Anyone who thinks differently is a heretic, who, as we know from history, is threatened with all manner of unpleasant things. Only the party boss, who holds the political power in his hands, can interpret the State doctrine, authentically, and he does so just as suits him.[167]

Idols are the quintessence of masks. Like masks, they 'cover up' and 'represent'—nothing! In the end, idols, just like masks, take possession of the worshiper: the worshiper will be as blind and as deaf and as mute as the god behind the icon (see *Ps* 115; cf. 135). And, we may add, as callous and heartless as the piece of wood and stone they pray to.[168]

---

[164] Eric Neumann, *The Origins and History of Consciousness* (Princeton, N. J.: Princeton University Press, 1993), p. 403.

[165] See *HS*, vol. 1, pp. 117-118; cf. above n. 88 and the quotation at n. 95.

[166] *The Undiscovered Self*, p. 35. A good example was the people's attitude to Fredrick II; see *Symbolism, the Sacred, and the Arts*, p. 40; and *Myth and Reality*, pp. 174-178.

[167] *The Undiscovered Self*, p. 35.

[168] Concerning this type of people, the rabbis taught: "the wicked even when alive is dead"; see *Berakhot* 18b; and cf. *Bereshit Rabba*, XXXIX, 6, vol. 1, p. 369; *Qohelet*

Absentees may believe in some sort of a deity, but not in a *personal* God, whom they can address as 'I' to '*you.*' This has nothing to do with theology. The simple truth is that absentees cannot have a *personal* anything with anybody, even with their own kitty or doggy, for the simple reason that there is nothing *personal* about them. They can only maintain a mask to mask all sorts of relationships, as per Kabuki Theater. These are the good folks making up the "masses" of Ortega y Gasset, and the "conglomerations" of Jung. They are essential and perennial absentees, without whom no demagogue could hold power. That is why, they had no idea of the 6,000,000 men, women and children cremated during the Holocaust, or the massacre of Native Americans by the Spanish and Portuguese *Conquistadores*, or the burning and torture of Jews by the Holy Inquisition, or the countless other crimes committed with impunity by the Masters whom they crowned as gods. On their behalf we may argue that at least, unlike Jews, they are *free*. This they can confirm with absolute self-assurance: "It is so because someone from the first-party platform told them that it is so."

Books, documentations, constitutions, etc. can be also used as masks. As we shall see in the next Section (Chapter 20), Christianity appropriated the 'Old' Testament to serve as a mask to a 'New' one.

A marginal note. Jews greatly contributed to the understanding and manufacturing of modern masks. Freud invented psychoanalysis. Jews were highly active in the development of all forms of mass entertainment, culminating in Hollywood. Thus, helping countless absentees, regardless of age, race, and creed, to 'discover, deep within themselves' all sorts of heroes and heroines with whom to identify and find meaning in their lives.[169] Last but not least, we must mention

---

Rabba, IX, 5, in *Midrash Rabba* ['*al ha-Tora ve-Ḥamesh Megillot*], (Vilna, Reprinted: Jerusalem, 5735/1975), vol. 2, 23b; etc. Cf. *Understanding Media*, pp. 45-46.

[169] For a scintillating narrative, see Neal Gabler, *An Empire of their Own: How the Jews Invented Hollywood* (New York: Doubleday, 1988); and Paul Buhle, *From the Lower East Side to Hollywood: Jews in American Popular Culture* (London: Verso, 2004). Another important work is Kati Marton, *The Great Escape: Nine Jews that Fled Hitler and Changed the World* (New York: Simon & Schuster, 2007).

Jewish contribution to fashion, from manufacturing and design, to promotion and distribution.[170]

8. Escape from Myth

Myth enwraps the mind in a world of rhapsodic fantasies and hallucinations, designed to prevent discovering the image of God within. The *Hebrew Scripture* is about the men and women that successfully escaped the realm of myth and pointed out to new directions. The exemplary men in the *Book of Genesis*, noted Philo, "were not scholars or pupils of others, nor did they learn under teachers what was right to say or do: they listened to no voice or instruction but their own."[171] They formulated their views neither to score points against an avowed enemy, nor to gain sympathy from a potential ally.

> The highest admiration, then, is due to those in whom the ruling impulses were of free and noble birth, who accepted the excellent and just for their own selves and not in imitation of or in opposition to others.

Some, although unable to formulate a valuable doctrine, are admired because they had the fortitude to swim against the current and resist evil, like Noah.

> But admiration is also due to him who stood apart from his own generation and conformed himself to none of the aims and aspirations of the many.[172]

The *Tora* compared Egypt to an "iron furnace" (*Dt* 4:20) — enwrapping the people inside in a wall of fire. King Solomon cited this fact in his inaugural speech at the Temple in Jerusalem (1*K* 8:51). Later, Prophet Jeremiah reminded the people of this extraordinary

---

[170] For a fascinating discussion of the subject, see Barbara A. Schreier, *Becoming American Women: Clothing and the Jewish Immigrant Experience, 1880-1920* (1994).

[171] *On Abraham*, I, 6, in *Philo*, vol. 6, p. 7.

[172] *On Abraham*, VI, 38, in *Philo*, vol. 6, p. 23.

event (*Jer* 11:4). It is unparalleled in human history. Elaborating on the "iron furnace" motif, the rabbis compared God taking the Jews out from Egypt, "to a goldsmith that stretched his [bare] hand to take the gold out of the furnace."[173] *Exodus* marks the people of Israel exiting the medium of myth and coming into a medium regulated by Law and rational discourse. According to Philo, the word 'Passover' (*Pascha*), actually means "passing over" from one realm to the other.[174] He seems to have identified the sacrificial lamb offered in this holiday with a sacrifice offered by shepherds before crossing into a yet unknown territory.[175] Indeed, the Passover Holiday celebrates the passing over from the realm of myth to the realm of Law. In the words of the rabbis, the Passover Holiday expresses thanks to God,

> Who took us out from enslavement to liberty, from sadness to joy, from bereavement to feast, from darkness to vast light, from enslavement to salvation.[176]

In metaphorical terms, Jews saw themselves as fish breeding and nurturing in water, while the nations of the world inhabit dry land: their condition for life and survival are radically different.[177] Mythical knowledge is absolute. Mythically centered societies resist growth and advancement.[178] 'Water' provides for a porous environment, permitting further development and progress. Elaborating on Patriarch Jacob's blessing, "And let them multiply like fish in the midst of earth" (*Gen* 48:16), the rabbis taught:

---

[173] *Midrash Tehillim*, ed. Salomon Buber (New York: Om Publishing, 1947), CVII, 4. We find the same metaphor with a slight variation, ibid. CXIV, 6, comparing God, "to someone taking out fire from the furnace without a rag and without pliers."

[174] See *The Preliminary Studies*, 105, *Philo*, vol. 4, p. 511. Cf. *The Migration of Abraham*, 25, *Philo*, vol. 4, p. 147.

[175] See *The Special Laws* II, 145, *Philo*, vol. 7, p. 395, translator's n. a; and *Appendix*, ibid. p. 627.

[176] *Mishna Pesaḥim* 10:5.

[177] See *Berakhot* 61b cf. ibid. 20a; *'Aboda Zara* 3b; *Midrash Tanḥuma, Ki-Tabo*, IV, ed. Buber, vol. 2, 23b-24a.

[178] See above, pp. 53-4.

Just like fish grow up in water, and yet when a drop of rain comes down from above, they greet it thirstily, as if they never had tasted water in their lives. The same is with Israel, they grow up in the water of *Tora*, nonetheless, when they hear something new about *Tora*, they receive it thirstily, as if they had never previously heard a word of *Tora*.[179]

Put in simple terms, the *Tora* is an open system, which permits historical development, "Each generation in accordance to its thinkers, each generation in accordance to its sages, each generation in accordance to its leadership."[180]

In the *Hebrew Scripture*, God inaugurates Creation with the words: "Let there be Light" (*Gn* 1:3). As with McLuhan's electric-light, God's Light is "pure information." With a major difference: the electric-light conceals while it reveals. Given that God's Light precedes the *content* of Creation, it cannot be hindered by it. Therefore, it alone reveals *without* concealing. The rabbis taught that prior to Creation, God had 'written' the *Tora* and then He "glanced at the *Tora* and created the World."[181] As it were, by 'glancing' at the consonantal text, God established structure and organic interrelation between the various 'consonants' making up the Cosmic *Tora*; similar to when a reader establishes meaning by structuring the consonantal text of the *Tora*, by mentally providing vowels. In this respect, God's creative *dabar* ('word'; Aramaic *memra*) proceeds from a *written* text—unlike the Platonic *logos* which is purely oral.[182] A corollary of this doctrine is

---

[179] *Bereshit Rabba* XCVII, 3; vol. 3, pp. 1246-1247. For variant readings and parallels, see editor's notes, ibid. Abigdor, an Israeli professional fisherman, confirmed to me that fish indeed behave this way.

[180] *'Aboda Zara* 5a; cf. *Sanhedrin* 38b; and *Abot de-R. Natan*, d. Salomon Schechter (Vienna, 5647/1887) A, XXXI, 46a.

[181] King Solomon identifies it with the Cosmic Tora (see *Pr* 6:23; cf. *Is* 2:5), which is one and the same with God's Cosmic Wisdom (see *Pr* Chapter 8:23).

[182] For a critical and comprehensive study of the *logos* in Philo, see Harry A. Wolfson, *Philo*, 2 vols. (Cambridge, Mass.: Harvard University Press, 1948), vol. 1, Chapter 6. In my view, however, Philo's *logos* proceed, as per rabbinic tradition, from a 'written' Law. The subject is too complex to be treated here, at this time I would like to call attention to a passage in *On Joseph*, VI, 29, *Philo*, vol. VI, p. 157

that 'knowledge,' 'truth,' etc., even when proceeding from the mouth of God, requires a process of decoding and organization, whereby the reader "synthesizes the consonants by which were created Heaven and Earth."[183] Thus, a Hebrew person knows because he or she so synthesized the fundamental consonants of the system.

The *Hebrew Scripture* presupposes consciousness of linear time. In the first Chapter of *Genesis*, Creation unfolds in, "Day One…second day," etc. Our seven-day week, too, is related to the Jewish Sabbath, which is related to the story of Creation in *linear time*. Only in the Second Chapter of *Genesis* we are told of Creation in *space*. In the *Book of Exodus* we have the intercrossing of *time* and *space*. To be possible, Moses was instructed to establish a calendar (*Ex* 12:1-2), which enabled him to interlock time and space: "In the third month after the children of Israel came out from the land of Egypt, in that very day, they arrived into the Desert of Sinai" (*Ex* 19:1). In Jewish Law, a testimony that is not set in a specific time-space frame is worthless.[184] This will explain why, "Dialogues between God and man, like the dialogue between God and Abraham, continue throughout the Old Testament *in a historical framework*."[185] [Italics added] National salvation and redemption, too, must take place in historical, that is, chronological, time.[186] For some, what is 'good' cannot be made better. Joseph Campbell relates a story about a Zen master. Just as he was about to deliver a sermon, a bird sang. "The sermon has been delivered"—he said.[187] For the Jew, although the world created by God is "very good," it has been, "created to be made" (*Gn* 2:3). This means that man can make "very good" better, even when made

---

where the *logos* is associated with the *nómos*: "For this world is the Megalopolis or 'great city,' and it has a single polity and a single law (*nómo*), and this is the word (*lógos*) or reason of nature."

[183] See *Berakhot* 55a.

[184] See *MT 'Edut* 1:14; 2:1; and *Homo Mysticus*, pp. 142-147.

[185] *Abraham and the Contemporary Mind*, p. 109.

[186] See *Abraham and the Contemporary Mind*, pp. 109,117-8, 119, 123ff.

[187] Joseph Campbell, *The Power of Myth* (New York: Anchor Books, 1988), p. 27.

by God. Hence the rabbinic doctrine, "the doings of man" could be better than "the doings of God."[188]

Eliade made the very important observation that unlike pagan religions where events take place in circular time,

> The situation is altogether different in the case of the monotheistic revelation. This takes place in time, in historical duration: Moses receives the Law at certain place and at certain date.[189]

The "situation," however, is exclusive to Israel. In neither the *Christian* nor *Muslim Scriptures*, dates—let alone the intercrossing of time and space—are referred to.

Many of the precepts of the *Tora* stipulate linear time. The Jewish prayers entail *precise* knowledge of the hourly passing of day and night. The Sabbath demands the organization of days into weeks, each having a *precise* beginning and an end. The observance of each New Month, with a *precise* beginning and an end, involves a more comprehensive organization of daily life. The same is true for the celebration of the New Year. Judaism does not recognize circular time. Rites do not transport the faithful to a 'pristine moment,' as if per magic. Jewish holidays are a "remembrance" or "commemoration" (*zekher*) of a national event that took place in *historical* time—having nothing to do with reversible time.[190] The Sabbath, too, is a "remembrance" or "commemoration" (*zekher*) of the Creation of the World, which was first celebrated by the Jews after crossing the Red Sea on their way to Sinai (see *Ex* 16:11-27). Jewish history does *not* repeat itself. Rather, people keep on making the same mistakes, in the vain hope that *this time* the effect would be different.

Keen awareness of the linear course of time is the earmark of

---

[188] See *Baba Batra* 10a; and *GD*, p. xxiii.

[189] *The Myth of the Eternal Return*, p. 105. Cf. *Homo Mysticus*, pp. 142-147.

[190] Similar to the rabbinic edicts made *zekher la-miqdash*; see Mishna *Sukka* 3:12; *Rosh ha-Shana* 4:3. *Zekher* is a kind of a mnemonic sign, bringing to memory something more or less similar, with nothing of substance in common; see Mishna *Shabbat* 8:7; 9:4; *Sanhedrin* 8:2. Cf. Philo, *The Special Laws*, II, 160, *Philo*, vol. 7, p. 405: "a reminder of the creation."

the rabbinic sage. The following story illustrates our point. At about the time of the Destruction of the Temple, R. Johanan b. Zakkai (1st century) was imprisoned in a solitary confinement, with no access to daylight. Yet he always knew the exact hour of the day and night. "How did R. Johanan b. Zakkai know (that)"?—asked the rabbis. "By virtue of his reviewing"—they replied.[191] That is, he knew *precisely* the length of time that it takes to recite different texts, so that he could measure the hours of the day and night by the amount of texts he was reviewing.

In short, the *Hebrew Scripture* is for people who can think on their own, like Patriarch Abraham, and resist the folly of the many, like Noah. These are men and women that have a linear concept of time, and therefore are aware of the categories of space and time. The same people are capable of addressing God (and others) as a second person '*you*,' and respond to the subjective personal '*I*' by the interlocutor. Their 'individuation'—that is, self-consciousness of one's absolute uniqueness (there never was nor will there ever be somebody like *you*) is the direct result of a continuous '*I/you*' discourse, both with God and fellow humans. A consequence of inhabiting a time-space continuum is responsibility for one's actions and behavior. By contrast, absentee people are immune from any responsibility for their actions. There is always someone else to blame: the government, society, their parents or spouses, the educational system, etc.

Having in mind *Ps* 115, Philo confronted pagan intelligentsia, with these simple questions:

> Come forward now, you who are laden with vanity and gross stupidity and vast pretence, you that are wise in your own conceit and not only declare (in every case) that you perfectly know what each object is, but go so far as to venture in your audacity to add the reasons for its being what it is, as though you had either been standing by at the creation of the world, and had observed how and out of what materials its several parts were fashioned, or had acted as advisers to the Creator regarding the things He was forming—come, I say, and then,

---

[191] *Midrash Ekha* I, 3, ed. Salomon Buber (Vilna, 1899), 34a; see editor's n. 264.

letting go all other things whatever, take knowledge of yourselves, and say clearly, who you are, in body, in soul, in sense-perception, in reason and speech, in each single one, even the most minute, of the subdivisions of your being. Declare what sight is and how you see, what hearing is and how you hear, what taste, touch, smelling are, or what are the springs and sources of these, from which derived their very being. [See *Ps* 115 and 135] For pray do not, O ye senseless ones, spin your airy fables about moon or sun or the other objects in the sky and in the universe so far removed from us and so varied in their natures, until you have scrutinized yourselves. After that, we may perhaps believe you when you hold forth on other subjects; *but before you establish who yourselves are, do not think that you will ever become capable of acting as judges or trustworthy witnesses in the other matters.*[192] [Italics added]

We should not be surprised to discover, therefore, that the teaching and preaching of absentee man are of little interest to Israel, even when coming from the hallowed 'monotheistic' religions and buttressed by the point of the sword.

---

[192] *The Migration of Abraham*, XXIII, 136-138, *Philo*, vol. 4, pp. 209-211; cf. ibid. XXXIII, 185, p. 241; cf. above n. 168. Francisco Sánchez(s) (1550/51-1623), the son of *conversos* and the father of modern skepticism, used the same argument to demonstrate that since man cannot have a perfect knowledge of his intellectual apparatus, he cannot arrogate to himself perfect knowledge of the outside world. Only God, in function of Creator, can have absolute knowledge of His Creation. *Quod nihil scitur*, in ed. Joaquim de Carvalho, *Opera* (Coimbra, 1955), p. 30, our translation:

> Therefore, He alone is wisdom, cognition, and perfect intelligence, He penetrates, knows and understand everything; because He is everything, and everything is Him and in Him. That imperfect and miserable little man, how could he know other things when he cannot know himself, which is in him, and with him? How could he know the obscure nature, where the spiritual things are, and among them our soul, when he cannot understand that which is clear and evident, what he eats, drinks, touches and hears?

For a comprehensive analysis of Sánchez thesis, see José Faur, "Francisco Sanchez's Theory of Cognition and Vico's *verum/factum*," *New Vico Studies* 5 (1987), pp. 131-146; idem "Maimonides' Water-Clock and its Epistemological Implications: Sánchez's *modus sciendi* and Vico's *verum-factum*," *Jewish Responses to Early Modern Science* (The Van Leer Institute, Jerusalem, May 15-18, 1995), pp. 176-185. Cf. *Homo Mysticus*, pp. 104-105.

9. Christianity, Religion of Myth

Christianity is the religion of myth, both in content and medium of transmission. Not one of the Christian rituals can be traced to the *Hebrew Scripture* or Judaism.

> As is well known, Christianity in its triumph had finally appropriated not only Greek philosophy, but the essential of Roman juridical institutions, and the Oriental ideology of the Sovereign Cosmocrator, but also the whole immemorial heritage of Gods and Heroes, of popular rites and customs, especially the cults of the dead and fertility rituals. This wholesale assimilation was due to the very dialectics of Christianity. As a universalistic religion, Christianity was obliged to homologize and find a common denominator for all the religious and cultural 'provincialisms' of the known world. The grandiose unification could be accomplished only by translating into Christian terms all the forms, figures, and values that were to be homologized.[193]

Myth abhors history. The categories of space and time, let alone of a space-time continuum, are not acknowledged by the mythical mind.[194] Mythical man cannot distinguish between what took place in his mind and an experience gained through sensory perception.[195] We had the opportunity to see that in mythical thought the same object can actually be in *two* different *places* at the same *time*.[196] Mythical time, too, is essentially different than regular time. The quintessence of mythical time is its reversibility.

> One essential difference between these two qualities of time strikes us immediately: *by its very nature sacred time is reversible* in the sense that,

---

[193] *Rites and Symbols of Initiation*, p. 121. Cf. *Symbolism, the Sacred, & the Arts*, pp. 37-38; and *Myth and Reality*, Chapter 9. On the role of 'Cosmocrator' in Christianity, see below Chapter 34.

[194] See above p. 41.

[195] See above n. 42.

[196] See above notes 5, 49.

properly speaking, it is a *primordial mythical time made present.* [197][Italics in the original].

Christian time is reversible. The notion of "sacred history" in Christianity is related to the myth of the "eternal return" common in archaic religions, where the same reality is made and unmade in periodic cycles of creation and destruction.[198] In Christianity, too, time is cyclic, albeit with two major differences. In archaic thought the *illo tempo* is the extra-temporal instant when the eternal cycles began; in Christianity, the primeval instant commences with the birth of Jesus. Eliade explained:

> Since God was *incarnated*, that is, since he took on *a historically conditioned human existence,* history acquires the possibility of being sanctified. The *illud tempus* evoked by the Gospels is a clearly defined historical time—the time in which Pontius Pilate was Governor of Judaea—but it was *sanctified by the presence of Christ.* When a Christian of our day participates in liturgical time, he recovers the *illud tempus* in which Christ lived, suffered, and rose again—but it is no longer a mythical time, it is the time when Pontus Pilate governed Judaea. For the Christian, too, the sacred calendar indefinitely rehearses the same events of the existence of Christ—but these events took place in history; they are no longer facts that happened at the *origin of time,* "in the beginning." (But he should add that, for the Christian the time begins anew with the birth of Christ, for the Incarnation establishes a new situation of man in the cosmos). This is as much as to say that history reveals to be a new dimension of the presence of God in the world. History becomes *sacred history* once more—as it was conceived, but in a mythical perspective, in primitive and archaic religion.[199] [Italics in the original]

The ritual of the Eucharist where the faithful eats Jesus' flesh and blood, transforms *illo tempo* into *illud tempus,* banding together

---

[197] *The Sacred & the Profane,* p. 68.
[198] See *The Sacred & the Profane,* pp. 106-110.
[199] *The Sacred & the Profane,* pp. 111-112.

present and past *time*.²⁰⁰ The sacramental ritual performed *here-now* allows the faithful to partake in Jesus' Crucifixion and Resurrection *there-then*. Past and present *time*, as well as spatial *here* and *there* coalesce, binding in Holy Communion, the *worshiper* and *Jesus*. In this manner, every Christian worshiper, too, is a victim of the same perfidious Jews who betrayed Jesus, crucified him, and prevented Universal Salvation—all out of sheer malice. Thus, a natural corollary of Christian liturgy is Jewish hatred. Let us hear what King Abgar, an early convert to Christianity, had to say about Jews:

> I believed in Him [Jesus] so strongly that I wanted to take an army and destroy the Jews who crucified Him [Jesus], if I had not been prevented by the imperial power of Rome from doing so.²⁰¹

Christian faith is transmitted from first-party platform to third-party absentee. Acceptance of Christianity is predicated on the abolition of the categories of time-space on behalf of mythical thought. In the footsteps of Eskimo theology, Christian faith, "It is so because it is said that it is so." For all intents and purposes, Christian theology commands the submission of reason to myth. In more elegant terms, Christian faith: "It is the object of total surrender, demanding also the surrender of our subjectivity while we look at it."²⁰² Thus, to be a good Christian is to be a perennial third-party absentee.

Christianity is *not* a religion of the Book. The Gospels were composed after Jesus' death, on the basis of secondary sources, by people who were culturally and psychologically removed from Jesus' original setting. Even the 'early versions' of the *New Testament* are found only in late manuscripts that were doctored and re-edited countless times. There are no manuscripts of the Christian account of Jesus before the end of the 2nd century. Most scholars date P46, the

---

²⁰⁰ *Myth and Reality*, p. 112

²⁰¹ Eusebius, *The History of the Church*, tr. G.A. Williamson (Middlesex, England: Penguin, 1983), I, 13.12, p. 68.

²⁰² Paul Tillich, *Systematic Theology*, vol. 1 (Chicago: Chicago University Press, 1953), p. 12.

earliest *fragment* of the *Christian Scripture*, at around the year 200—long after Jesus' death. The Great Uncials of the *Christian Scripture*, like Codex Sinaiticus, are in Greek. There is no consensus among scholars about the precise date of their composition, but it seems that they were not written before the end of the 3rd Century. Codex Bezae, in Greek and Latin, is not earlier than the 5th Century (see below Chapter 31). None of these manuscripts, however, are in Aramaic, the language spoken by Jesus and his disciples. (The only verbatim quotation of Jesus in the original Aramaic is preserved in the Talmud.[203]) Therefore, there are no means to know whether these translations—made by anonymous individuals from uncertified texts—are accurate, and that no later additions and subtractions were made. Jesus wrote no books. Admittedly, "his words have been reported by writers who demonstrably distort their accounts of things to persuade us of their own point of view."[204] The problem is aggravated by the fact that his followers were mostly analphabetic and cared little about the written word. *Jn* 8:6 reports that when a group of Scribes and Pharisees submitted a question to Jesus, he "stooped down, and with *his* finger wrote on the ground." What did he write? Undoubtedly, for a Christian these words ought to be the most important words ever written. Yet, nobody cared to preserve them! Given the careless attitude of his followers towards the written word, even when proceeding from the hand of someone whom they deem to be their God and Savior, it would be too dim to attach much credence to records under their care.

There is another aspect of Christianity rarely discussed. As per Greco-Roman ideology, Christianity cares little about a written text. Granted, that there were some, like Benedict of Nursia (480-547), professing veneration for the written word.[205] However, as per pagan ideology, mainstream Christianity regarded 'writing' as debasing and

---

[203] *Shabbat* 116a-b.

[204] A. N. Wilson, *Jesus* (New York: W. W. Norton, 1992), p. 4.

[205] See *Parchment, Printing and Hypermedia*, pp. 53-61.

shameful. That is why, although venerating the God of the *Hebrew Scripture*, Creator of Heavens and Earth, who inscribed the Tablets of the Law with his "finger" (see *Ex* 31:18; *Dt* 9:10) —[206] Thomas Aquinas (ca. 1225-1274) insisted that it would be undignified for Jesus to write. When attempting to explain how come that Jesus wrote no books, he explained:

> I answer by saying that it is fitting that Christ did not commit his teaching to writing. First on account of his own dignity; for the more excellent the teacher, the more excellent his manner of teaching ought to be. And therefore it was fitting that Christ, as the most excellent of teachers, should adopt that manner of teaching whereby his doctrine would be imprinted on the heart of the hearers. For which reason it is said in Matthew vii, 29, that "he was teaching them as one having power." For which reason even among the pagans Pythagoras and Socrates, who were most excellent teachers, did not want to write anything.[207]

An alternative explanation could be that Jesus' public was illiterate; or as described by the Talmud, '*am-ha'areṣ*—that is, not only analphabetic, but also anti-writing![208]

Because those who compiled and transmitted Jesus words were not educated men, they did not succeed in presenting his views in a systematic way. Anyone reading the *Christian Scripture* will soon discover that whatever Jesus ideas may have been, they "have been incoherently pieced together."[209] Christians wishing to apply some critical methodology and discover the historical Jesus, soon find out that "almost everything in the gospels turned out to belong to the 'Christ of faith'; next to nothing was left of 'the Jesus of history.'"[210] A mod-

---

[206] See *HS*, vol. 1, pp. 5-6.

[207] Thomas Aquinas, *Summa Theologica* III, q. 42, quoted in Marshall McLuhan, *The Gutenberg Galaxy* (Toronto: University of Toronto Press, 1997), p. 98. On the notion of "power" in Christian theology, see below Chapter 33.

[208] On the anti-book ideology of these men, see *HS*, vol. 2, Appendix 21.

[209] Wilson, *Jesus*, p. 253.

[210] Morton Smith, *Jesus the Magician* (New York: Harper & Row, 1978), p. 4.

ern Christian writer expressed the anguish that this type of situation arouses in the faithful:

> I knew that many of my fellow Christians shared my doubts and have continued somehow or another to reconcile the practice of the Christian faith with the knowledge that it is founded on a fundamental untruth.[211]

As we hope to show in the following Section there was malice in the editing of these texts.

The preceding could help us come to grips with two fundamentally different versions of Jesus' biography: one Jewish and another Christian. Jews knew Jesus while he was alive and followed his career from birth to death. Therefore the events are processed in terms of linear time: from birth to death. Christians knew Jesus from reports that they received long *after his death*. His earthly life and personal story must be construed post-*mortem*, after accepting as an apodictic truth the Christian account of his crucifixion, resurrection and ascension to heaven. The point of departure of the Christian version of Jesus' biography is the time of his death and resurrection—not of his birth. To give credence to his Messiahship, his biography needs to be developed backwards, from end to beginning. That is why, the story of Jesus told in the *Christian Scripture* belongs to myth-making. Bearing on this critical point, a modern scholar wrote:

> The Jesus Christ of historic Christianity is not the Jesus of history. He is a product of the myth making mind, basing itself upon historical mistakes and misunderstandings, and even upon some falsifications of history, ultimately shaped by a revolutionary and untraditional reading of the Jewish Scriptures. Christianity does not start with Jesus, but with his followers after his death.[212]

In what follows, we hope to show that the *foundational* difference between Judaism and Christianity has nothing to do with 'reli-

---

[211] Wilson, *Jesus*, p. xvi.

[212] William Nicholls, *Christian Antisemitism* (Northvale, New Jersey: Jason Aronson Inc., 1993), p. 83.

gion.' From time immemorial Jews crossed paths with countless religions without eliciting animosity. The only *religious* enemies of Israel have been 'monotheistic' religions whose main intention is to displace Israel: first Christianity and then Islam. The point of departure of Christian faith is the civilization of myth, while in Judaism is that of the Book. Each has a different mode of logic. The conflict could be reduced to the following quiz. Suppose you have A=white horse, B=black horse, C=white chicken—which items resemble each other: A/C or B/A? Christianity holds A/C, whereas Judaism B/A. In following Section we will see that this is the basis for the claim that Christianity is a "faithful heir to Judaism."[213]

---

[213] See *Myth and Reality*, p. 169.

SECTION II

JESUS, HIS LIFE AND MINISTRY

A JEWISH READING OF THE CHRISTIAN VERSION

10. Christianity and the *National Memory* of Israel

The Christian and Jewish versions of Jesus' biography stem from two diverse social and cultural means of transmission. The 'religious' differences are not primary, but the result of two means of conveying the values designed to shape and bring about the cultural and social cohesion of a people. Paraphrasing Marshall McLuhan, the principal thesis of this Section is that "the medium," that is, the means used to communicate cultural and institutional values, conditions "the message" that Judaism and Christianity, respectively, convey. (See above, Chapter 2)

Israel and the Jewish people are a *nation*. The foundational beliefs of Judaism are a matter of *national memory*. The *Hebrew Scripture* designated the foundational events, values, and institutions peculiar to *the nation* of Israel: *morasha* ('heritage'). The *national memory* of Israel began with the covenant at Sinai. As we saw earlier, mythical time is cyclical (see above, Chapter 3). It originates neither at a definite geographical locale nor at a definite chronological date. Therefore, in the mythological mindset, time and space are two different categories independent of each other.[1] The initial moment of Christianity, too, is the extra-temporal instant *illo tempo*, inaugurated with the birth of Jesus, when the eternal cycles began.[2] Jewish time, and therefore Jewish memory, is *linear*. The Jewish calendar originated at a definite place: Egypt; and it was inaugurated at a definite date: the first day of the first month of the Jewish year (see *Ex* 12:1-2). The initial moment of the *nation* of Israel did not originate at a 'mythological timespace.' The *Hebrew Scripture* registered both the place: the Sinai Desert, and date of arrival; the first day of the third month (see *Ex* 19:1-2). God's address to the people, too, took place at a definite place:

---

[1] See above Section I, notes 71-74.

[2] See above Section I n. 197.

the foothill of Mt Sinai; at a definite date: the sixth day of the third month from the Exodus (see *Ex* 19:15-16). The census of the people of Israel, in preparation for the journey towards the Promised Land, was taken in a definite place: the Sinai Desert; at a definite time: the first day, of the second month, from the Exodus from Egypt (see *Nu* 1:1; cf. 9:1; 10:11).[3] The covenant was not transmitted from a first-party platform God, to a third-party audience excluded, in quality of absentee, from addressing the speaking subject God. The medium of transmission of the covenant was from first person 'I' (*anokhi*) to second person singular 'you' (/*kha*), thus addressing directly every single member of Israel. The *medium* of Israel's message is *the dialogue 'God/I' to 'Israel/you,'* whereby in turn every member of 'Israel' can address directly 'God' as '*I*' to '*you*' (see above Chapter 5). The transmission and interpretation of the covenant is transmitted *from* the people of Israel (first person plural 'we') *to* the people of Israel (second person plural 'you'). Being entrusted with the *morasha* of Israel involves the sacred responsibility to transmit it to the next generation in perpetuity.[4] In the course of history, Israel's *morasha* was documented by the *Hebrew Scripture* (='Written Law'), and afterwards, by rabbinic tradition (='Oral Law').[5]

Christianity's demand, as per imperial command, that Jews repudiate their *morasha* because the Christian-*Übermensch* so demanded, ranks as the most dishonorable requisition ever made in the history of religions. It also constitutes the supreme expression of arrogance and prepotency. It rests on the notion that power (=Constantine's Sword, etc.) awards the Church the right to *meddle in the internal affairs of another people*, and impose on them the 'correct' interpretation of their national documents. Now, Jesus was born and died *before the birth of Christianity*. He lived and preached *in the land of Israel*, and believed himself to be Jewish and a member of the Jewish people. Let

---

[3] For a detailed analysis, see *HS*, vol. 1, Chapters 5, 38.

[4] For the precise definition of this term, see *HS*, vol. 1, pp. 215-217; vol. 2, pp. 34-36.

[5] See *HS*, vol. 1, pp. 230-233.

us remember that although under Roman dominion, Jews and the Jewish people were (and are) an autonomous nation. Even after Rome crushed Israel, Israel was not dissolved as a political entity, and continued to behave as an autonomous nation in exile.[6] Therefore, whatever took place between a Jewish citizen—Jesus—and the Jewish nation, is nobody's business: certainly not of an ecclesiastical body established several centuries later (see below Chapter 28).

There is another crucial detail worth considering. Jewish knowledge of Jesus came from direct, personal contact with him and his followers. The Jesus of Jewish tradition is the Jesus of history, who occupied a definite space, the land of Israel, and lived in a definite time, from *circa* 4 BCE till 30 CE. The Jewish account is not derived from secondary sources, but from direct, personal contacts with him and his followers. To believe that Jews would have deliberately rejected their *own* Messiah makes as much sense as to claim that Christians or Muslims would have rejected *their own* Messiah out of sheer malice. It is even more foolish to claim that Jews failed to 'recognize' *their own* Messiah, while a bunch of illiterate pagans did (see 1*Cor* 2:4, concerning the level of literacy of Jesus' followers and disciples, below Chapters 14 and 25).

In many fundamental aspects, the Jesus perceived by Jews, when he was alive and preaching in Israel, coincides with the Jesus known from pagan and ancient magical papyri. Both Jews and pagans saw him as a magician. More importantly, many of the elements of the Jewish version originate in stories transmitted by eyewitnesses; e.g., according to Jewish tradition, he had his entire body tattooed with magical spells.[7] This piece of information appears in a non-

---

[6] See *HS*, vol. 1, Chapters 21-22. For a brief time, Jews were able to restore their national independence under Simeon ben Koseba, 'Prince of Israel.' For some valuable insight for that brief, but inspiring period in Jewish history, see H. L. Ginsberg, "New Light on Tannaitic Jewry and on the State of Israel of the Years 132-135 CE," *The Jewish Expression*, ed. Judah Goldin (New Haven: Yale University Press, 1976), pp.109-118.

[7] *Shabbat* 104b, see quotation below at n. 190. On this prohibition in Jewish law, see Samuel Belikin, *Philo and the Oral Law* (Cambridge, Mass.: Harvard University Press,

polemical source, and was witnessed by people who *actually saw Jesus* while he was alive.

> The Rabbinic report that in Egypt Jesus was tattooed with magical spells does not appear in polemical material, but is cited as a known fact in discussion of a legal question by a rabbi who was probably born about the time of the crucifixion. The antiquity of the source, type of citation, connecting with the report that he was in Egypt, and agreement with Egyptian magical practices, are considerable arguments in its favor.[8]

There are no sources challenging this fact, either in pagan or Christian lore.

The Talmud reports that Jesus was brought to trial for practicing magic—a capital offence for both Jews and Romans—rather than for being a 'false Messiah,' which Jews never considered a criminal offense.[9] Jews were not alone in describing Jesus as a magician; most of his pagan contemporaries did, too. Only a small band of followers considered him to be more than the average magician (see below Chapters 24-25). Concerning this fact, Professor Smith (1915-1991) wrote:

> "Jesus the magician" was the figure seen by most ancient opponents of Jesus; "Jesus the Son of God" was the figure seen by the party of his followers which eventually triumphed; the real Jesus was the man whose words and actions gave rise to these contradictory interpretations. "Jesus the Son of God" is pictured in the gospels; the works that pictured "Jesus the Magician" were destroyed in antiquity after the Christians got control of the Roman Empire.[10]

Ultimately, whether one believes that Jesus himself was a magician or not—to my mind the magical tattoos covering the whole

---

1940), p. 39.

[8] *Jesus the Magician*, pp. 150-151.

[9] *Sanhedrin* 43b. In addition, the Romans charged Jesus with sedition. This, however, may be connected with his activities as a tax-collector; see below, Chapter 22.

[10] *Jesus the Magician*, p. vii.

body are conclusive proof—is beside the point. Later we will see that the Christian version of Jesus *warrants* belief in magic (see below Chapter 19). Jews had no reason to either fabricate or pervert the events at hand. After all, they were not trying either to *impose* a new religion on others, or to justify the *persecution* of anyone, but, simply, to present the facts as *they* saw them.

11. Jesus' Life-Style

Contrary to what Luke tells us, Jesus was *not* a "helpless-baby in the manger" (*Lk* 2:7). The Talmud reports that Jesus, "was close to the ruling circles" (*qarob la-malkhut*).[11] These were men of immense wealth and influence, who paid huge sums of money to the Roman authorities for the right to extort taxes from the small farmer, the shopkeeper, the artisan, and the laborer (see below, Chapter 12). It was noticed that,

> To challenge the practice of a local publican could lead to a confrontation with Rome's most influential citizens. A provincial magistrate might find it difficult to deal firmly with so powerful a business on which his own position of authority relied.[12]

They had direct access to the upper administrative and political echelons of the government, and constituted a true oligarchy, a kind of elite that pandered to the rich and the powerful and sucked the blood of the poor. They were pitiless and vindictive. Mere allusion to them would send chills through the spine of even a hardened criminal. The following metaphor, mentioned casually in rabbinic litera-

---

[11] Mss. *Sanhedrin* 43a, (Yad ha-Rab Herzog; Firenzi, III, 7-9; etc.). See *HS*, vol. 2, p. 143.

[12] Paul W. Walaskay, *'...And so we came to Rome'* (Cambridge: Cambridge University Press, 2005), p. 29. The rabbis reported that among them there were found a few honest men that tried to defend the best interests of the Jewish communities. In recognition of these courageous men, the rabbis made special dispensations for them; see *Soṭa* 49b and *Baba Qamma* 83a.

ture, gives us an idea of their reputation:

> Suppose someone is seated having dinner and [noticed] an enemy that wished to murder him. He could say: 'This food tastes like the food that I ate yesterday at the king's palace.' So that the other [the enemy] would think: 'He is close to the ruling authorities (*qarob la-malkhut*). I will let him alone, in case the king would investigate.'[13]

The Talmud preserved a description of a people "close to the ruling circles" (*qarob la-malkhut*), in Neharde'a (Babylonia). They bore names and garments intended to frighten their victims, and had horses and mules parading before them. These men were in the habit of whipping their victims, and would not hesitate to kill with impunity anyone that refused to comply.[14]

Because publicans were known to pander (*mahanifim*) to the mighty, on the one hand, while crushing the poor and the downtrodden, on the other hand, the rabbis went on to condemn the 'flatterers' (*mahanifim*). Typically, before pointing the finger at others, the rabbis acknowledged their own faults. Earlier, they had flattered King Agrippa I (10 BCE-44 CE), unchaining a series of events that brought suffering on to the Jewish people. Among the injuries that the 'flatterers' (*mahanifim*) bring into the world, the rabbis counted divine "anger." God "will not heed" the prayers of a public that stands for these kinds of people. The rabbis add that "a public that tolerates flattery (*hanuppa*) is polluted." In the end, they "will go into exile," and they will not behold "the Countenance of God's Glory" (*pene Shekhina*), etc.[15]

The Jewish public regarded tax-collectors as plain thieves.[16] The reason, explained the Geonim, was their "pandering. They are con-

---

[13] *Leqah Tob* (*Pesiqta Zotrata*), ed. S. Baber (Jerusalem, 5720/1960), XXXIII, 10, pp. 171-172.

[14] See *Gittin* 14b.

[15] *Sota* 41b-42a. See below notes 45, 56, 85.

[16] See *Mishna Nedarim* 3:4; *Tosefta Nedarim* 2:2, p. 104; *Sanhedrin* 25b. Cf. MT *Gezela* 5:9; *'Edut* 10:4.

siderate with the wealthy, easing their burden, while at the same time, they oppress the poor and make them pay more than what they are supposed to pay."[17] These cold-blooded criminals made Roman occupation of the Holy Land possible. Because they had access to Roman power, they had contempt for common men and women. In turn, Jews treated them as outcasts. As with all oppressive minorities, "tax-collectors" trusted nobody, except for their own family.

> There is no such family where one of its members is a tax-collector and all other family members are not tax-collectors. There is no such family where one of its members is a bandit (*listes*) and all other family members are not bandits (*listes*). How so? —Because they would shield him![18]

The *Christian Scripture* gives supporting evidence to the rabbinic tradition that Jesus' family was, indeed, "close to the ruling circles." Jesus' personal habits—as portrayed in the *Christian Scripture*—reflect the life-style of someone raised in the ambiance of the rich and mighty. He loved good food and good wine. Among the people, he gained a reputation as a drunk and gourmand. "The Son of Man came eating and drinking and they say, 'Look, a glutton and winebibber, a friend of tax-collectors and sinners!'" (*Matt* 11:19; *Lk* 7:34; cf. 19:7).[19] Eating and drinking were very important to Jesus and his disciples. This is why they did not mind breaking Jewish food-taboos. His famous maxim: "Not that which goeth into the mouth defileth a man" (*Matt* 15: 11; see ibid. 12-20; *Mk* 7:15; cf. *Acts* 10:10-16; 1*Cor*

---

[17] Quoted in *Oṣar ha-Geonim, Sanhedrin*, ed. R. Ch. Z. Tobias (Jerusalem: Mossad Harav Kook, 1966), p. 208 n. 49. Cf. *Lk* 3:13.

[18] *Shebu'ot* 39a. On the association *lestes*/tax-collectors, see below Section III, notes 23, 29.

[19] See the valuable comment of Professor Morton Smith, *The Secret Gospel* (New York: Harper & Row, 1973), pp. 93-95. As noted by Timothy Freke and Peter Gandy, *The Jesus Mysteries* (New York: Three Rivers Press, 1999), p. 43:

> Like Jesus, Dionysus comes "eating and drinking," yet brings a profoundly spiritual message to ordinary people. He was a god of divine intoxication and a "god of the people" who was often reviled and feared by religious and secular authorities, just as Jesus was.

8:8), served to justify his insensitivity to Jewish mores and food-taboos. This type of behavior was not only a flagrant transgression of the Law, but inconsiderate. Consumption of food-taboos is 'revolting' (*hata*), not only among Jews, but among *all* people.[20] In contemporary terms, this would be equivalent to an American eating a dog or a cat for lunch because he or she felt like it. On one occasion, when Jesus was hungry, he saw a fig tree from afar and went to pick up some figs. When he discovered that the tree bore no figs, he was disappointed and cursed the tree.

> And when he came to it, he found nothing but leaves; for the time of figs was not *yet*. And Jesus answered and said unto it. No man shall eat fruit of thee hereafter for ever (*Mk* 11:13-14; *Matt* 21:18-19).[21]

It seems that Jesus, soon to displace the Creator of Heavens and Earth, did not know that in the land of Israel no fig tree is in bearing in springtime: "for the time of figs was not *yet*."

In *Matt* 12:1 we read that Jesus defended his disciples who were plucking ears of corn on the Sabbath, because they were "hungry." This clearly shows how important eating was for his followers, as well as their contempt for private property and the sanctity of the Sabbath. Jesus' argument that David, too, ate from the Showbread, is worthless: David was *starving* and his life was in peril.[22] Jesus' disciples were frolicking in the cornfield: at most they had worked up an appetite and were "hungry"! Anyhow, there were plenty of people around,

---

[20] See *Yerushalmi Terumot* VI, 2, 44b; VIII, 1, 45c; *Makkot* III, 12, 32b; *MT Terumot* 10:10. Simple respect for the feelings of others, as well as common civility, would prevent the eating in public of something deemed 'repulsive' to others, regardless of 'religion.' On this principle, I would not allow wine on my table when having a Muslim guest.

[21] See *The Case of the Nazarene Reopened*, pp. 27, 682-683. A similar incident is recounted in *Ta'aniyot* 24a with mixed results. On the one hand, unlike Jesus, the fig tree bore fruits; on the other hand, the individual making the request was punished for 'abusing' his Maker.

[22] Concerning Jesus' unfamiliarity with the *Hebrew Scripture*, see below Chapters 25, 32.

and they would gladly feed them, if so Jesus wanted.[23] Jesus' answer that "the Son of man is Lord (*Kyrios*) even of the Sabbath day" (*Matt* 12:8; cf. *Mk* 2: 24-28), reflected the view of the publican elites that resented the fact that Jews were 'idle' on the Sabbath, and could not collect enough revenue for their Roman masters (see below Chapter 13). We should also note that unlike John the Baptist, Jesus and his disciples ate during Jewish public-fasts, (see *Matt* 9:14; *Mk* 2:18).[24] Jesus' way for salvation, too, is to be gained gastronomically, by ingesting the Eucharist. As put so delicately by Jesus: "Truly, truly, I say to you: Except you eat the flesh of the son of man, and drink his blood you do not have life in yourself" (*Jn* 6:53, cf. ibid. 56).[25] Finally, during the last supper, he tells his disciples that he expected to have wine with them "when I drink it new" in God's "kingdom" (*Matt* 26: 29). Or, according to *Lk* 22:30, "That ye drink and eat at my table in my kingdom, and sit on thrones judging the twelve tribes of Israel."

There is another aspect to Jesus' eating habits that merits explanation: Jesus suffered from an extreme case of anxiety about washing his hands before meal. Consistently, he would refuse to wash his hands when invited to break bread. When the host would inquire for the reason, Jesus would respond with a barrage of insults. In *Lk* 11:37-39, *Pocket Interlinear New Testament*, p. 170, we read:

> And *as he* was speaking, a certain Pharisee asked him that he would to dine with him: and he went in, and sat down to eat. And when going in, he reclined. But watching, the Pharisee marveled that he did not first wash before dinner. But the Lord (*'O Kyrios*) said to him, now you Pharisees cleanse the outside of the cup and of the dish, but your

---

[23] For a full analysis of this episode, see *HS*, vol. 1, Chapter 35. Justice Haim Cohn framed this episode wrongly; see his *The Trial and Death of Jesus* (London: Weidenfeld and Nicolson, 1972), pp. 41-43.

[24] It seems, however, that Jesus fasted on *Yom Kippur*; see Shlomo Pines, "The Jewish Christians...," (Heb.), p. 173 n. 10.

[25] The same ritual was practiced in the Mithras religion; see *The Jesus Mysteries*, p. 49: "He who will not eat of my body and drink my blood, so that he will be made one with me and I with him, the same shall not know salvation."

inside is full of robbery and wickedness.[26]

Even if one would grant, for argument's sake, that "Not that which goeth into the mouth defileth a man" (*Matt* 15:11), still it does not justify Jesus referring to his host as "Fools!" This affront was followed by a series of slurs (see *Lk* 11:40-43, see further down till the end of the chapter). Whatever his views about 'Pharisees' in general may have been, why abuse the hospitality of a stranger who was kind enough to open his house to you? Anyway, since it was a well-known fact that Pharisees and Jews in general were in the habit of washing hands before eating, what was the point in accepting a dinner invitation, and then insulting the host in the presence of his friends and family? If the washing of the hands was so odious, wouldn't it have made more sense to decline the invitation altogether, rather than accept the offer and use the occasion to insult the host?

A similar incident was reported by *Mk* 7:1-5, *Pocket Interlinear New Testament*, p. 97:

> And the Pharisees were assembled to him, also some of the scribes, coming from Jerusalem. And seeing some of his disciples eating bread with unclean hands, that is unwashed hands, they found fault. For the Pharisees and all of the Jews do not eat unless they wash the hands with the fist, holding the tradition of the elders. And coming from the market, they do not eat unless they wash themselves [i.e., their hands]. And there are many other things, which they have received to hold: washing of cups and of utensils, and of bronze, vessels, and couches. Then the Pharisees and scribes questioned him, "Why do your disciples not walk according to the traditions of the elders, but eat bread with unwashed hands?"

Jesus' lack of civility was exceptional in Jewish ambiance (see *Pr* 17:13). Even ungrateful guests were expected to be polite with their host and exhibit good manners. Concerning the 'good' and the 'bad' guests, the rabbis observed:

> A good guest, what does he say: May the host be remembered for his

---

[26] On the significance of the term *'O Kyrios*, see below, Section III, n. 17.

kindness! How many types of wine he brought before us! How many cuts of meat he brought before us! How many delicate loaves of bread he brought before us! Everything he did, he did it for me! Whereas an awful guest what does he say: 'What did I eat of him, a loaf of bread? Did I drink a cup of wine?—whatever he made, he made it for his wife and children'![27]

Now, there is nothing nasty about washing the hands before eating. Why not then go along and wash the hands, rather than offend the sensitivities of the host?

A marginal note. R. Simeon b. Gamliel (1st Century CE), who was eventually executed by the Romans, proposed that in evaluating our fellow man, "The worth is not the sermon (that an individual preaches), but (in his) action."[28] Having this principle in mind, the rabbis taught: "There may be one, who preaches finely, but does not act finely; (or conversely) that acts finely but does not preach finely." The ideal person is someone that "Preaches finely and acts finely."[29] Jesus preached, "Not that which goeth into the mouth defileth a man." In light of the bombardment of insults and curses that "cometh" constantly from Jesus' mouth, against his hosts—not to mention the Pharisees and scribes—how would you measure his conduct in light of the second half of the verse, "but that which cometh out of the mouth, this defileth a man" (*Matt* 15:11)? Would you count Jesus among those that "preach finely and act finely"?

To understand his hostility to washing the hands, we must take note of Jesus' fixation with washing the feet. For reasons that will soon be apparent, Jesus took special pleasure in having his feet massaged in expensive oil (*Lk* 7:36-40). On one occasion, he did not

---

[27] *Tosefta Berakhot*, ed. Saul Lieberman (New York: Jewish Theological Seminary, 1955), 6, 2, p. 34. For additional sources and commentaries, see idem, *Tosefta Ki-Fshutah*, vol. 1 (New York: Jewish Theological Seminary, 1955), pp. 105-106.

[28] Mishna *Abot* 1:16.

[29] See *Tosefta Ḥagiga*, ed. Saul Lieberman (New York: Jewish Theological Seminary, 1955), 2, 1, p. 380. For parallels and further rabbinic sources, see *Tosefta Ki-Fshutah*, vol. 5, p. 1288.

mind having Mary Magdalene "anointing his feet" with "a pound of ointment of pure, costly spikenard." The lady in question "wiped off" his feet "with her hair. And the house was filed with the odor of the ointment." In reply to Judas' objection that 300 *denarii* worth of ointment would best be "given to *the poor*," we are told that Judas did not actually care for the poor, but that he was a thief (*Jn* 12:1-6; cf. a similar story involving Jesus' head and body, in *Mk* 14:3-8). The explanation offered in *Jn* 12:8 "For the poor you have with you always, but me you do not have always," makes it clear that in his mind, these kinds of extravagances supersede charity to the poor![30] One can only wonder why Judas' alleged thievery was not taken in consideration *before* he objected to Jesus' 300 *denarii* foot-massage. To have an idea of what 300 *denarii* meant at the time of Jesus, it would be well to remember that, as we learn from *Matt* 20:2-13, a worker earned only one *denarius* a day. At the time of Domitian (83-84 CE), a legionnaire made 300 *denarii* a year. In simple words, this meant that Jesus was spending a whole year's salary on a single foot-massage! To dismiss Judas' criticism because he allegedly was a thief, does not answer the question: what was the justification for spending a year's salary on such a triviality, instead of distributing it to the poor? The preceding seems to be the basis for the Christian idea that all you need to become a saint is to point an accusing finger at Judas, the proverbial 'other.'

Let us examine another case involving foot-massage. In *Lk* 7:36-40 (*Pocket Interlinear New Testament*, p. 153), we are told about a Pharisee, who invited Jesus to share his Sabbath table. Somehow, a prostitute heard that Jesus was in town, and

> taking an alabaster vial of ointment, and standing at his feet, weeping behind *him*, *she* began to wash his feet with tears. And she was wiping with the hair of her head. And *she* ardently kissed his feet, and was anointing *them* with the ointment. But the Pharisee who invited him spoke *within himself* (our italics), saying, this one if he were a prophet,

---

[30] See *The Case of the Nazarene Reopened*, pp. 252-255.

would have known who and what the woman *is* who touches him, for she is a sinner. And answering [what Jesus thought was in his host's mind],[31] Jesus said to the man, Simon, I have a thing to say to you. And he said, Teacher, say *it*. And turning to the woman, he [Jesus] said to Simon, Do you see this woman? I came into your house. *You did not give me water for my feet* (our italics), but she washed my feet with tears, and wiped off with the hairs of her head. You gave me no kiss, but she from *when* I entered did not stop fervently kissing my feet. You did not anoint my head with oil, but she anointed my feet with ointment. For this reason I say to you, her many sins are forgiven, for she loved much.[32] But to whom little is forgiven, he loves little. And he said to her, your sins are forgiven. (Ibid. vv. 44-48)

I don't know how many of you would deem acceptable the display of affection between a known prostitute and a guest, whom you just invited to share your Sabbath table. There were other guests (see ibid. v. 49), and we must assume that there were women and children present. The poor host did not utter a word, and managed to maintain his composure throughout this awkward episode. Even after Jesus' shocking behavior, the host addressed him respectfully, as "Teacher." Jesus, however, *read* the host's mind about the foot-massaging prostitute, and jumped at the opportunity to embarrass him.[33] Let us pose the same question differently: Why was Jesus not uncomfortable when having his feet washed in the lavish manner of the opulent, but flew into a rage when he was asked to wash his hands? The Pharisees and scribes addressed him respectfully. Jesus exploded with angry words: "you hypocrites" (*Mk* 7:6), fuming insults. Why? And one more question. Concerning the platitude, "your sins are forgiven." How come Jesus did not show the same magnitude towards his host, and forgive him for the monstrous crime of not having anointed his head with oil, or not "fervently kissing" his

---

[31] See below n. 45.

[32] As noted in *The Secret Gospel*, p. 125, the story had been edited. The original text read: "loved me." See *The Case of the Nazarene Reopened*, p. 350.

[33] About Jesus uncanny ability to read minds, see below notes 45, 105.

feet, as "she," the prostitute, "anointed my feet with ointment"?

Before proceeding to unravel the mystery of Jesus' pro-feet/anti-hands washing, there is an important detail concerning Jesus' eating habits. Invariably, Jesus would "recline" to eat and drink. This means that, as per Roman sumptuous *coena* or luxurious supper, he would have his dinner reclining on a special kind of a sofa—used by the upper classes to dine. Since people reclined barefooted, they had their feet washed, so as not to soil the couch. Therefore, Jesus expected his feet to be washed, or at least to be offered water to wash his feet. We have seen earlier that he reproached his host: "You did not give me water for my feet!" (*Lk* 7:44). This explains "the washing of the feet" mentioned in connection to Jesus (*Jn* 12:2-4) and his disciples (*Jn* 13:2-4). The fact that Jesus did not mind that Mary "anointed his feet" with costly oil (*Jn* 12:1-3), indicates that he was not a stranger to these types of amenities. In the case of Jesus (*Jn* 12:2-4) and his disciples (*Jn* 13:3-16), the feet were washed by someone important, as a sign of affection. From the fact that after washing the feet of his disciples in the Last Supper, they reclined, (*Jn* 13:12, as accurately translated in the *Pocket Interlinear*, p. 263: "reclining again"), we learn that the participants in the Last Supper were reclining on a couch.

Jesus' opposition to the washing of the hands was connected to the washing of the feet. How? People belonging to the 'upper echelons' of society, namely, the *qarob la-malkhut*-crowd, who had their meals reclining on a divan, needed to have their *feet* washed, so as not to soil the couch. 'Washing of the feet' was the earmark of the upper class, sucking the blood of the workingmen and women. 'Washing the hands' was the earmark of the 'low class,' workers and artisans, who washed their hands before breaking bread—as per the habits of Pharisees and the common Jew. The *qarob la-malkhut* elite *sneered* at the masses 'below,' needing to wash their *hands* before eating. Hence, taught the rabbis, "Whoever sneers at the washing of the hands, he himself shall become a destitute."³⁴ Given that the *qarob la-malkhut* circles were able to get away with their contemptible behavior towards the poor—they always could summon the Roman sword—the rabbis taught that in the end, they "Will be pulled-up from the world," i.e., violently.³⁵ The contempt with which the *qarob la-malkhut* treated the general public was so offensive, that the rabbis declared that those sneering at the washing of the hands merit excommunication.³⁶ In order to underscore the symbolic importance of washing the hands, R. 'Aqiba, when he was imprisoned by the Romans and eventually tortured to death, refused to eat without washing his hands. When on one occasion the guard threw away half of his daily portion of water (probably bribed to do so by a member of the *Übermensch*-clan), and R. 'Aqiba had to choose between drinking the water or using it for washing the hands, he chose the latter.³⁷ To dismiss the notion that people enjoying sumptuous dinners do not need to wash their hands, the rabbis associated this rule with King Solomon—symbol of luxury and opulence.³⁸

Three details—casually mentioned in the *Christian Scripture*—corroborate the rabbinic tradition that Jesus came from *qarob la-malkhut*-circles. These are: his violent reaction to washing the hands, his fondness for foot-massage at meal-time, and his reclining on a

---

³⁴ *Shabbat* 62b.

³⁵ See *Soṭa* 4b, and '... *And so we came to Rome*', p. 81, n. 77.

³⁶ See *Berakhot* 19a.

³⁷ See *'Erubin* 21b.

³⁸ See *Shabbat* 14b, and *'Erubin* 21b. The rule concerning the washing of the hands was old, certainly *before* Jesus' time. The statement by Haim Cohn, *The Trial and Death of Jesus*, p. 46: "that the washing of the hands before meals was set down as a rule of law by El'azar ben Arakh" [second half of the 1ˢᵗ century] is incorrect. Given that the rabbis associated washing of the hands with King Solomon, they could not possibly have said that R. El'azar ben 'Arakh had instituted that rule! What the Talmud, *Ḥolin* 106a actually said, is that R. El'azar ben 'Arakh "furnished the *justification* for this rule" (*mikan samkhu ḥakhamim*), not that he instituted this ruling! Contrary to what Justice Cohn states, *Ḥagiga* 18b does not say that some authorities disputed the rule of washing the hands, but only that some authorities argued that the rule for washing the hands applies only for eating bread, but not for eating fruits!

couch, as per Roman sumptuous *coena*. There is a fourth detail. Noticeably, when questioned by Pilate, Jesus was coy and reflected common civility. However, when dealing with Pharisees, he was poorly mannered. Invariably, when invited for dinner, Jesus would not fail to offend his host. See for example *Lk* 11:37ff, when a Pharisee invited Jesus for dinner, the episode ended with an anti-Pharisee and anti-scribe diatribe. A similar episode is reported in *Lk* 14:1ff, when Jesus was invited by a Pharisee to share the Sabbath meal. It is difficult to take seriously Jesus' calling the Pharisees "hypocrites," while he was reclining on luxurious couches and having his feet anointed with 300 *denarii* ointment (see *Jn* 12:5). Jesus' angry words had to do with something more than poor manners and hand-hygiene: it is a matter of hierarchic superiority. Members of the upper crust should not have to comply with the mores of those below, even when enjoying their hospitality! As we will see in the following chapter, other facts, including archaeological evidence, back up the rabbinic tradition about Jesus' family background.

12. Jesus, Amicus Publicanis

Support to Jesus came mainly from publicans and their associates. His most famous disciple, Matthew, the author of the first Gospel, was a publican (*Matt* 9:9; *Mk* 2:14), and was known as "Matthew the publican" (*Matt* 10:3). Luke, too, seems to have been a publican or at least a member of a publican family. This explains his familiarity with the Roman system of taxation in the land of Israel. It also explains the fact that, "Luke stands at the beginning of a long line of Christian writers who consciously praise the Romans at the expense of the Jews."[39] Lazarus, too, "was rich," and most probably belonged to a publican family. Another disciple was none other than "Zacchaeus, which was the chief among the publicans" (*Lk* 19:2).

---

[39] '... *And so we came to Rome,*' p. 41. See ibid., p. 30, and cf., pp. 48-49.

Jesus felt quite at ease with him and invited himself to stay at his house (*Lk* 19:5). In *Lk* 5:27-29, *Pocket Interlinear*, p. 146, we read:

> And after these things, he (Jesus) went out and saw a tax-collector named Levi, sitting at the tax office. And *he* said to him, Follow Me! And leaving all, rising up he followed him. And Levi made a great feast for him in his house. And there was a crowd of many tax-collectors reclining and others that were with them.

It is noteworthy that, as it was properly translated in *Pocket Interlinear*, they were "reclining," that is, on a 'couch,' used by the upper classes for the *coena,* or dinner (see below Chapter 13).

Jesus was the darling of publicans and for a good reason. As mentioned earlier, his abolition of the Hebrew Sabbath (*Matt* 12:8; cf. *Mk* 2:24-28; *Lk* 6:5), had to do with the fact that tax-collectors resented that the people were 'idle' on the Sabbath and they could not collect enough revenues for Israel's enemies.[40] His famous doctrine, "Render unto Caesar the things which are Caesar's" (*Matt* 22: 21)—transmitted, ironically, by his most prominent disciple, "Matthew the publican" (*Matt* 10:3)—was designed to provide tax-collectors with a mantle of respectability. It also served to legitimize their practice of dispossessing owners from their property *without* due process. Celsus (3rd century), a pagan, described Jesus' apostles, as "*infamous men, and … the most wicked tax-collectors and sailors.*"[41] [Italics in original] Jesus put in practice this doctrine and confiscated a donkey on his own behalf, without due process (see below Chapter 22). Publicans reciprocated. They regarded Jesus as their spiritual guide, and addressed him as "Teacher." We are told that when "tax-collectors" came to John the Baptist, they saw Jesus and said to him: "Teacher, what shall we do?" (*Lk* 3:12). There was mutual affection and support between them. Although it was readily conceded that in many aspects publicans behaved worse than heathens (see *Matt* 18:17), Jesus consistently favored them, and the harlots they patronized, over the Pharisees (see

---

[40] See *HS*, vol. 1, Chapter 35; vol. 2, pp. 49-50, 141-144.

[41] *Origen: Contra Celsum*, p. 58.

Matt 21:31-32).[42] It was not a matter of whim. Jesus happened to have the uncanny faculty of reading the minds of Pharisees and people whom he happened to dislike.[43] Accordingly, he could directly address them and ask, point-blank: "Why do you think evil in your hearts?" (*Matt* 9:4). Thanks to this gift, Jesus could ascertain, with infallible precision, the supremacy of tax-collectors and the prostitutes they patronized over the Pharisees. "Truly I say to you, the tax-collectors and the harlots go before you into the kingdom of God" (*Matt* 21: 31, *Pocket Interlinear*, p. 54). A simple, illustrative example may help elucidate this wondrous gift, as it was explained in *Lk* 18:10-14 (*Pocket Interlinear*, p. 189):

> Two men went up into the Temple to pray, the one a Pharisee and the other a tax-collector. The Pharisee was standing and praying these things to himself, God I thank You that I am not as the rest of the men, rapacious, unrighteous, adulterer, or even as this tax-collector. I fast twice in the week, I tithe all things, as many as I get.[44] And standing at a distance, the tax-collector would not even lift up *his* eyes to Heaven, but smote on his breast, saying, God be merciful to me, the sinner! I say to you, this one went down to his house justified, rather than that one. For everyone exalting himself will be humbled. And the *one* humbling himself will be exalted.

And what can be a better example of people refraining from self-congratulatory remarks, than Jesus and his followers, then and now?

"Blessed are the pure in heart; for they shall see God" (*Matt* 5:8)—is a reference to publicans, who, although squeezing the blood out of the poor and committing all kind of abominations, have, deep down, a lily-white heart. In conscious opposition to the demonic Pharisees, who "cleanse the outside of the cup and of the dish," but their "inside"—and Jesus knew this because he could look straight

---

[42] See '... *And so we came to Rome*', p. 30.

[43] See below at n. 45.

[44] This includes a special tithe (*ma'aser 'ani*) to be distributed among the poor.

into people's hearts—"is full of robbery and wickedness" (*Lk* 11:39, *Pocket Interlinear*, p. 170). It is on the basis of this unique faculty, that Jesus could claim the right to call the Pharisees and scribes "Fools!" (ibid. 40) and "hypocrites" (see *Mk* 7:6), and abuse them verbally.[45] A close reading of *Matt* 5:43-48, will reveal that Jesus' plea to "love" the enemy was self-serving: the enemy in question was none other than the infamous publicans hated by *all* Jews. It was also one-sided: we won't hear Jesus preaching to publicans to love Pharisees.

The relation Jesus → *qarob la-malkhut*-circles was social, not merely ideological. Jesus and his disciples would regularly fraternize with "tax-collectors." The following is the translation of a passage in *Matt* 9:10-11, as rendered in *Pocket Interlinear*, p. 19:

> And it happened as he [Jesus] reclined in the house, Behold many tax-collectors and sinners coming, *they* were reclining with Jesus and his disciples. And seeing, the Pharisees said to his disciples, why does your teacher eat with tax-collectors and sinners?

From the preceding it is apparent that Jesus and his disciples did not patronize dingy eateries, but places frequented by the infamous publicans. We should bear in mind that these men were heartless criminals, who made Roman occupation of the land of Israel possible. To consort with these sorts of criminals at the time of Jesus was not less offensive to Jews of that era than it was to the French, when their men and women fraternized with the Nazis during the German occupation (1940-1944). In the eyes of Jews, condoning this sort of behavior then was no less immoral than when the clergy applauded men and women who, moved by Christian love, consorted with Gestapo officers and German collaborators. Tax-collectors were greedy and predatory and evil. (The parable in *Lk* 19:12-27 is a good illustration of their rapacious habits.) One need not be particularly ingenious to realize that this sort of gentleman would not share his

---

[45] To counter this promise, the rabbis taught that these people will never "behold the Countenance of God's Glory" (*pene Shekhina*), cited above n. 15. On Jesus' ability to 'read minds,' see above notes 33, 43; and below, notes 105, 188.

couch with penniless preachers and childlike youths. A most telling detail is that *they* came to Jesus and *they* reclined with him. The question asked by the Pharisees, "Why does your teacher eat with tax-collectors and sinners"?—was proper. The Pharisees addressed Jesus' disciples respectfully. As a matter of common courtesy, one would expect a polite answer. Instead, Jesus responded with a series of angry invectives (see *Matt* 9:12-13; cf. 7:6-23; 19:3ff).[46]

Jesus' followers and disciples, known in rabbinic terminology as *minim* or 'sectarians,' were associated with the *qarob la-malkhut*-circles (see below Chapters 15-16). Either were they themselves publicans or had commercial and family ties with publicans.[47] The sumptuous tombs in the Talpiot area, near modern Jerusalem, where Jesus' associates are buried, clearly show that they belonged to the *qarob la-malkhut*-circles.[48]

---

[46] Jesus' reply that only the sick require the attention of a healer (*Matt* 9:12), misses the point. A 'physician' who believes that you can cure a patient just by eating and drinking with him is a charlatan, guilty of malpractice, not a healer. If he was doing something more substantial than that, he should say so, rather than demonize his critics. It is the same with his preaching about "mercy and not sacrifice" (*Matt* 9:13). No Jew, particularly no rabbi, needs to be given a sermon about "mercy" by someone who spends his time eating and drinking with thugs. Taking the metaphor of 'physician-patient' a step further, who do you think has genuine 'mercy': a physician determined to apply the right medicine, although it may be painful, or one who takes the patient for a drink? Incidentally, as we shall see further down, shortly after Jesus' death, Christendom chose Paul—someone who never met the real Jesus—over his disciples (see below Chapters 29-30). This should tell you something about Jesus' educational method. There was, however, 'an esoteric' aspect to this sort of 'healing'; see *The Secret Gospel*, pp. 112-114.

[47] Cf. above n. 41. See the story in *Shabbat* 116 a-b, (*filosof* there stands for 'a Christian magistrate'; cf. *Tosafot s.v. Filosofa*), and Chief Rabbi David Matzger, ed. *Perush R. Ḥanan'el, Shabbat* (Jerusalem: Makhon Leb Sameaḥ, 5755/1995), p. 232 n. 24. They were also in charge of collecting taxes in the land of Israel; see the case mentioned *'Aboda Zara* 4a. It is also known that at least in one of the Jewish districts in Babylonia, they also were in charge of collecting taxes; see above n. 14. A careful review of the episode with Bar-Sheshakh, *'Aboda Zara* 65a, leads me to believe that he was a Judeo-*min*. I hope, some day, to carry the analysis further; meanwhile see my "Of Cultural Intimidation and Other *Miscellanea*: Bar-Sheshakh vs. Raba," *Review of Rabbinic Judaism* 5 (2002), pp. 34-50.

[48] See Simcha Jacobovici and Charles Pellegrino, *The Jesus Family Tomb*. Contrary to what Professor Pines proposed, the language spoken by the *minim* was Aramaic—

The love between Jesus and publicans went deeper than eating and drinking and going for foot-massage together. An illuminating example of their devotion is Joseph of Arimathea. He was a "rich man," and a faithful "disciple of Jesus" (*Matt* 27:57). He, too, belonged to the *qarob la-malkhut*-circles (cf. *Mk* 15:23).[49] Evidence to this is the fact that he had direct access to Pilate, and could walk straight to him and demand "for the body of Jesus." At once, Pilate "commanded the body [of Jesus] to be given to him." People acquainted with the ways of "the ruling circles"—then and now—know that tyrants and bully autocrats are extremely accommodating with those that provide them with sustenance. In our case, Joseph of Arimathea, the publican, was the one deemed worthy of such accommodation. It is highly symbolic that before being moved to his family mausoleum in Talpiot, Jesus was laid to rest in the "new tomb which he (Joseph of Arimathea) had hewn out of the rock" for himself (*Matt* 27:57-60; cf. *Mk* 15:43-47; *Lk* 23:50-53; *Jn* 19:38). In this fashion, Jesus ended up sharing with publicans something much more symbolic than a couch in a fancy eatery.

This last detail could help us understand the conflicting reports about the disappearance of Jesus' body. Matthew reported that when the women came to visit Jesus' tomb, they found it empty. "For the angel of the Lord descended from heaven, and came and rolled back the stone from the door, and sat upon it" (*Matt* 28:2). And told them: "He is not here; for he is risen" (*Matt* 28:6). This is the official version of Christendom. There was another version "commonly reported among the Jews until this day" (*Matt* 28:15), explaining the empty tomb; namely, that Jesus' disciples "came by night, and stole his body" while the guards "slept" (*Matt* 28:13). (This is the version my grandfather used to tell us during '*La Semana Santa*'). There may be a third explanation. It is highly unlikely that the women that came to visit Jesus' grave would have known that Jesus' body had been re-

---

not Hebrew; see "The Jewish Christians..." (Heb.), pp. 175, 184, 193, 215. At that time 'Hebrew' stood for the Judeo-Aramaic language spoken by the Jews.

[49] See *The Jesus Family Tomb*, pp. 27, 29, 71-73.

moved by Joseph of Arimathea to Talpiot. Rather, it would be safe to assume that they went to visit Jesus' original sepulcher, where his body was laid to rest. The women arrived at the sepulcher *after* his body had been moved by Joseph of Arimathea, and taken to the "new tomb which he had hewn" in Talpiot. The same explanation applies to the version reported in *Lk* 24:1ff.[50]

In conclusion, Jesus' humble origin is a myth invented by Luke. Archaeological evidence confirms that as reported by the rabbis, Jesus belonged to a family that was close to *qarob la-malkhut*-circles. From the sumptuous tombs of Jesus' family and early Christians found in the Talpiot area it is evident that these mausoleums belonged to very affluent families, who could not possibly have made their fortunes as shop-keepers or artisans. The archaeologists inspecting these tombs, noted:

> Only the religious, political, and economic elite could afford family crypts or tombs in which to store the ossuaries. The poor were buried in the ground (either by simple placement into little niches cut into the local "chalk stone" or by burial in soft earth, far beyond the city walls).[51]

13. Jesus, *Adversus* Pharisees

Modern scholars continue to debate whether Josephus was a Pharisee.[52] Regardless of whether he *really* was or was not, the fact of the matter is that he did not hesitate to criticize the Pharisees on *policy* matters,[53] while acknowledging, at the same time, that they "are con-

---

[50] See *The Jesus Family Tomb*, pp. 70-74.

[51] *The Jesus Family Tomb*, p. 27. Cf. ibid, p. 28.

[52] For a comprehensive analysis of the sources and standard views on this matter, see Albert I. Baumgarten, "Josephus on Ancient Jewish Groups from a Social Scientific Perspective," eds. S.J.D. Cohen and J. Schwartz, in *Studies on Josephus and the Varieties of Ancient Judaism* (Leiden: E.J. Brill: 2007), pp. 1-13.

[53] In the debate concerning the Pharisees' ability to tell the future, scholars failed to

sidered the most accurate interpreters of the laws." Moreover, and this is a pivotal point for our argument, Josephus acknowledged that the Pharisees "are affectionate to each other and cultivate harmonious relations with the community."[54] Some historians propose that their popularity was due to the fact that "their penal code was milder."[55] This 'explanation' presupposes that those supporting the Pharisees were people involved in illicit activities, seeking to escape the rigor of the criminal justice system. At the same time, contemporary Jewish academicians bend backwards to 'explain' blatant anti-Pharisees and anti-Rabbinic bogus charges in the *Christian Scripture*—unproven and unprovable—while positing as axiomatic the 'unreliability' of rabbinic sources. Their position has nothing to do with 'scholarship,' but with Judeo-self-hatred that these academicians believe is propitious for future promotion, and for gaining grace in the eyes of potential patrons. It is also designed to cover up the fact that they cannot read a single passage of Talmud on their own.[56]

---

distinguish between 'forecasting' the future, in quality of acquired knowledge and wisdom, as forecasting the weather or the market in modern times, and a 'prediction' by virtue of supernatural powers, as with soothsayers and astrologers. About the former, the rabbis (*Tamid* 32a; cf. *Abot* 2:9) taught: "Who is a man of wisdom (*ḥakham*), he who can foresee the impending consequence (*ha-nolad*)" of an action or situation. About the latter, the rabbis (*Baba Batra* 12b) said: "From the day that the Temple was destroyed, prophecy was taken away from the prophets and given to the mentally-unfit (*shoṭim*=Gr. *exeste*; cf. Section III, n. 9). Obviously, the allusion to "Temple" is to the first, not to the second; see *Meharsha ad loc*. Rejecting the value of prophecy in post-Temple times, does not contradict the belief that a righteous person (*ṣaddiq*) could plead to God on behalf of something or someone, as for example, Ḥofni ha-Me'aggel, *Mishna Ta'aniyot* 3:8. Thus, the fundamental difference between 'prophecy' and 'prayers'; otherwise, we would have to abolish the Synagogue altogether.

[54] *Jewish Wars* II, 166; *Josephus*, vol. 2, p. 387.

[55] Steve Mason, "Josephus's Pharisees: the Narratives," in eds. Jacob Neusner and Bruce D. Chilton, *In Quest of the Historical Pharisees* (Waco, Texas: Baylor University Press, 2007), p. 19, see ibid, pp. 20-21.

[56] Professor Lieberman explained that originally, 'Pharisees' (Heb. *parushim*) was applied to *all groups* that for better or for worse deviated from the general standards. Therefore, it could apply to people that out of religious scruples decided to stand apart from the rest, and adopt more stringent measures; or to people who in times of peril "withdrew," or "departed" (*parshu*), from the standard practice of the

Josephus explained that the Pharisees gained popularity among the people because of their lifestyle and the respect they had for tradition.

> The Pharisees simplify their standard of living, making no concession to luxury. They follow the guidance of that which their doctrine has selected and transmitted as good, attaching the chief importance to the observance of those commandments which it has seen fit to dictate to them. They show respect and deference to their elders, nor do they rashly propose to contradict their proposals. Though they postulate that everything is brought about by fate, [see corresponding n. *d* by translator *ad loc.*] still they do not deprive the human will of the pursuit of what is in man's power, [see corresponding n. *e* by translator *ad loc.*] since it was God's good pleasure that there should be a fusion and that the will of man with his virtue and vice should be admitted to the council-chamber of fate [see corresponding n. *a* by translator *ad loc.*] They believe that souls have power to survive death and that there are rewards and punishments under the earth for those who have led lives of virtue or vice: eternal imprisonment is the lot of evil souls, while the good souls receive an easy passage to a new life. Because of these views they are, as a matter of fact, extremely influential among the townsfolk; and all prayers and sacred rites of divine worship are performed according to their exposition. This is the great tribute that the inhabitants of the cities, by practicing the highest ideals both in their way of living and in their discourse, have paid

---

community. In the latter sense, we find *parushim* lumped together with *minim*, 'heretics'; see *Tosefta Ki-Fshuṭah,* vol. 1, pp. 53-54, and cf. Mishna *Soṭa* 3:4. Obviously, the *parushim* of history were men that distinguished themselves by following *a higher standard* than the general public; e.g., in matters of sacramental purity, or by abstaining from fraternizing with dissolute people, such as publicans and informers. There were also bogus *parushim* who were severely criticized by the rabbis. Fake sainthood and phony idealism may be found in all movements, religious or otherwise. What distinguishes the "rabbis" and "Pharisees" from their Christian critics is that they did their utmost to expose their own religious impostors. "The hypocrites must be exposed, even on the Sabbath, because of the outrage they cause"; see *Tosefta Yom ha-Kippurim* 4:12, p. 253; *Yoma* 86b, *Tosefta Ki-Fshuṭah,* vol. 4, p. 828, and *HS*, vol. 2, Appendix #60. Concerning these frauds, the rabbis taught that they will never "behold the Countenance of God's Glory" *(pene Shekhina)*"; see *Soṭa* 42a, *Sanhedrin* 103a. Cf. above n. 15, and below notes 85, 86, 87.

to the excellence of the Pharisees.⁵⁷

Surely, there were groups, like the Sadducees and Essenes, that disagreed with the Pharisees on ideological as well as practical matters. The same was true with individuals like Josephus, who opposed some of their policies. All Jews, however, treated them respectfully. The only exception was Jesus and his followers, who consistently, addressed them with insults. Why?

The Pharisees were men of grit. They alone dared confront the greedy and the opulent that made a living by sucking the blood of the masses. For that reason they were loved by the general public, and for that very reason Matthew—"the publican"—and other members of Jesus' entourage, hated their guts and carried on a smear campaign against them. That is why, first they maligned the Pharisees, and later on the rabbis and eventually *all* Jews, because they—and they alone—dared disturb the habits of men having their feet massaged with 300 *denarii* of perfumed oil, while men with 'soiled hands' were starving for a piece of bread!

The conflict between Jesus and the Pharisees was a clash between two political camps: the oligarchs, made up of publicans and their associates, and the Jewish masses, standing up against enemy-collaborators, self-hating Jews, and informers. Jesus spoke to the Pharisees with contempt, for the same reason that men of 'rank' speak with scorn and derision to 'inferior' people. This explains the notable fact—somehow unnoticed by specialists and historians—that, *as reported in the Christian Scripture*, there never was a publican or a prostitute that Jesus did not treat with deference, nor a Pharisee and rabbi that he did not insult.⁵⁸ We would like to call attention to the fact that although Jesus appears very loving and polite with prostitutes, he was rude with his mother (see *Mk* 3:33-34). She surely resented his behavior because, as registered in *Matt* 28:2, unlike some

---

⁵⁷ *Jewish Antiquities* XVIII, 11-13, *Josephus*, vol. 9, pp. 11-13.

⁵⁸ Concerning Jesus' association with disreputable women, see *The Case of the Nazarene Reopened*, pp. 696-697, n. 228.

of the prostitutes that came to visit Jesus' tomb, his mother did *not*. Let us note, in passing, that the ladies that loved Jesus dearly and massaged his feet for free, must have been sponsored by gentlemen of means, who could reward them accordingly. Otherwise, how can you explain that one such lady could afford to give Jesus a massage worth 300 *denarii* of oil for free?

14. Who was the 'Good Samaritan'?

Christianity is *not* the religion of the Book. As it has been well expressed by Eusebius (ca. 263-339), Jesus' followers were not literary men:

> Those inspired and wonderful men, Christ's apostles, had completely purified their lives and cultivated every spiritual virtue, but their speech was that of every day. The divine wonder-working power bestowed on them by the Savior filled them with confidence; and having neither the ability nor the desire to present the teachings of the Master with rhetorical subtlety or literary skill, they relied only on demonstrating the divine Spirit working with them, and on the miraculous power of Christ fully operative in them.[59]

This will explain why even a man of Paul's stature was not a prolific writer.

> We may instance Paul, who though he surpassed all others in the marshalling of his arguments and in the abundance of his ideas, committed to writing nothing but his very short epistles; and yet he had countless unutterable things to say, for he had reached the vision of the third heaven, had been caught up to the divine paradise itself, and had been privileged to hear their unspeakable words.[60]

Therefore, we should not be surprised to find out that the idea

---

[59] *The History of the Church*, I, 24.5, p. 131. See ibid, n. 1 and 1*Cor* 2:4.

[60] *The History of the Church*, I, 24.5, p. 131. On the "unspeakable words," see 2*Cor* 12:2-4. On these sorts of 'words,' see *The Secret Gospel*, pp. 99, 102, 116-118, and below n. 161.

of a strictly controlled text, as in Hebrew scribal tradition, was alien to early Christians. Christians did not view the *Christian Scripture* as a historical document that must be rigorously guarded, letter-by-letter, as in Jewish tradition, but as an *inspirational work*, full of allegorical lessons that could be applied and refined in the course of time—precisely as in pagan tradition!

> The pagan sages did not regard the myths of Osiris-Dionysus as histories that must never be changed or adapted, by allegorical myths, which could be syncretized with each and revoked. The Gnostic Christians, likewise, did not regard their gospels as historical records, but works of allegorical literature encoding eternal truths that could be creatively developed and refined.[61]

A condition for the authenticity of the *Christian Scripture* is the suppression of historical rationality and critical judgment in favor of mythical reasoning and validation. The *Gospels* were composed after Jesus' death, on the basis of secondary sources, by people that were culturally and psychologically removed from the original setting. Even the 'early versions' of the *Christian Scripture* are to be found only in late manuscripts that were doctored and re-edited countless times. (See above Chapter 9). Jesus' apostles, too, were not men of letters (see below, Chapter 25). Eusebius explained:

> The divine wonder-working power bestowed on them by the Savior filled them with confidence; and having neither the ability nor the desire to present the teachings of the Master with rhetorical subtlety or literary skill, they relied only on demonstrating the divine Spirit working with them, and on the miraculous power of Christ operative in them.[62]

Because those who compiled and transmitted Jesus words were not men of letters, they did not succeed in presenting his views in a systematic way. Anyone reading the *Christian Scripture* will soon discover that whatever Jesus' ideas may have been, they "have been

---

[61] *The Jesus Mysteries*, p. 111.
[62] *History of the Church* III, 24, p. 130.

incoherently pieced together."[63] Christians wishing to apply some critical methodology and discover the *historical* Jesus will soon find out that, "almost everything in the gospels turned out to belong to the 'Christ of faith'; next to nothing was left of 'the Jesus of history.'"[64] A modern Christian writer expressed the anguish that this type of situation arouses in the intelligent believer:

> I knew that many of my fellow Christians shared my doubts and have continued somehow or another to reconcile the practice of the Christian faith with the knowledge that it is founded on a fundamental untruth.[65]

Sometimes it is patently clear that there was malice in the editing of these texts. A case in point is the story of the Good Samaritan (*Lk* 10:30-35). Joseph Halévy (1827-1917) showed that the text was deliberately doctored in order to conceal that occasionally, there were respectful relationships between Jesus and the rabbis. In the original story, the man who assisted the injured person on the road was an Israelite, not a Samaritan.[66] As it stands, it could only make sense to people unaccustomed to critical reading. The story told in *Luke* is about an injured man, lying helplessly on the road. A Priest and then a Levite on the way to Jerusalem passed by and did not stop to help him. Then passed someone, who *Lk* 10:33 identifies as "a certain Samaritan" on a journey, who stopped to assist the injured man. There are a few inconsistencies in the story. At the time of Jesus, Jews referred to Samaritans as "Cutheans." Only pagans referred to them as "Samaritans."[67] Moreover, Samaritans and Jews regarded each other as mortal enemies. The same was true with Jesus and his disciples: they, too, regarded the Samaritans as enemies. Jesus warned

---

[63] Wilson, *Jesus*, p. 253.

[64] *Jesus the Magician*, p. 4.

[65] Wilson, *Jesus*, p. xvi.

[66] See Joseph Halévy, "Nótes et Mélanges," *Revue des Études Juives*, 4 (1882), pp. 249-255.

[67] See "Nótes et Mélanges," p. 253. Cf. Josephus, "General Index," *s.v.* 'Cuthea,' vol. 20.

his disciples, "Go not into the way of the Gentiles, and into *any* of city of Samaritans enter not. But go rather to the lost sheep of the house of Israel" (*Matt* 10:5-6; cf. 15:24).

Let us consider another point. In the story, the supposed 'Samaritan' was on his way to Jerusalem. But Samaritans, as recorded in the *Christian Scripture*, refused to receive Jesus into their city, "because his face was as though he would go to Jerusalem" (*Lk* 9:53). And yet, are we to believe that the individual assisting the injured man was a Samaritan, who happened to be on such good terms with the innkeeper, that he would wait for him to "come again" and "repay" for his expenses (*Lk* 10:35)? No Samaritan could come and go freely from Jericho to Jerusalem, and even if he did, the innkeeper would not have trusted him to "come again" and pay for the expenses. Rather, as shown by Halévy, the original version must have referred to a Priest, a Levite, and an *Israelite*. The first two did not attend the injured man *because* they were on the way to discharge their *sacramental responsibilities* at the Temple, and needed to maintain their ritual purity. On the other hand, a common Israelite, since he had no *sacramental duties* to perform, was not required to maintain ritual purity. Thus, he preferred to help the injured man, rather than go to the Temple. Otherwise, it would make little sense to mention first the Priest and then the Levite. The moral of the story is that by attending the injured man, the common pilgrim showed more concern for human welfare (kindness-*raḥamim*) than the Priest and the Levite—a point about which both Jesus and the rabbis agreed![68] Luke, however, changed the story, because he intended to produce,

> an *apologia pro imperio*, which would help the Christian community live effectively with the social, political, and religious realities of the present situation until the advent of God's reign.[69]

Jews were hated by Luke, the Romans, and the Samaritans. At

---

[68] See "Nótes et Mélanges," p. 251. Cf. Joseph Jacobs, *Jesus as others saw him*, p. 226, n. 83; and above "Introduction," n. 50.

[69] "...*And so we came to Rome*," p. 67.

the time of Luke, but not during Jesus' life, the Samaritans had firmly allied themselves with Rome. It would be much more expedient to put "Samaritan" in place of "Israelite," than let the people discover that there was some common ground between the rabbis and Jesus. Let us note, in passing, that Luke was in the habit of 'editing' stories that may appear to be favorable to Jews.[70] After all, who is going to notice the change?

15. The Sin of *Minut*

In general, *minim* 'sectarians' (sin. *min*) were individuals "that have rejected (one) of the principles" (*kofer be-'iqqar*) of the Jewish faith.[71] In particular, the term was applied to the *Jewish* followers of Jesus.[72] They were the most heinous type of 'heretics'—more wretched and evil than even the infamous epicurean (the *apiqoros* of rabbinic literature).[73] What made Judeo-*minim* particularly odious was their cunning. They used the *Hebrew Scripture* not to teach, but to trap the dull-minded. Their 'faith' and ostentatious 'piety' were baits designed to entrap the gullible (cf. *Pr* 14:15). In spite of their pretentious religiosity, they were cynics, using 'salvation' and other such terms to acquire power. Accordingly, R. Ṭarfon (1ˢᵗ CE) proposed that a Scroll of the *Tora* written by *minim* should be incinerated along with any occurrences therein of the Tetragrammaton—the Name standing for the God of Israel, Creator of Heaven and Earth. His

---

[70] See, for instance, *Lk* 7:36-50, and *The Secret Gospel*, pp. 125-126.

[71] See R. Ḥanan'el and Rashi on *Shabbat* 75a; *'Arukh s.v.* GDF, and Rashi on *Dt* 1:12. Similarly, Maimonides, *Teshubot ha-Rambam*, #263, vol. 2, p. 499, defined *min* "as someone that rejects one of the principles of the *Tora*." There are five such principles; see *MT Teshuba* 3:7; *HS*, vol. 1, Chapter 25.

[72] See *Mekhilta de-R. Yishma'el*, p. 220, and R. Meir Abul'afya, *Ḥiddushe ha-Rama...*, *Giṭṭin*, ed. R. A. Shoshana, vol. 1 (Jerusalem: 5745/1985), p. 326a.

[73] Who sins for the sake of pleasure, not theology.

opinion became law.[74] It is important to note that we are talking about educated *minim*, capable of writing a Scroll of the *Tora* correctly—not an easy task. Jewish law prohibits desecrating the Tetragrammaton. Accordingly, what is the justification for what seems to be a sacrilege? To answer this question, we will have to come to a lucid understanding of *minut*, the 'religion' of the *minim*. Here is what R. Ṭarfon said on the matter:

> If they [Scrolls written by *minim*] would come to my hands, I will burn them together with the Names (=Tetragrammaton) inscribed in them. In like manner, if someone is chasing another to kill him, or if a snake would be running after him to bite him, it would be more preferable to enter into the abode of idols than into their abode. Because they [the *minim*] know [God] and profane [Him], but they [the idolaters] don't know [God] and profane [Him]. About them [the *minim*] it is written: "And also behind the door and the doorpost (Heb. *mezuza*) you have set up your remembrance: [for you have uncovered *yourself* to a different one than me, and are gone up from Me; you have enlarged your bed, and made a *covenant* with them (alien deities); whose bed you loved, whose hand you saw]" (*Is* 57:8).[75]

R. Jacob ibn Forna (17th century) explained. In his exegesis, R. Ṭarfon was not taking the word *mezuza* in the general sense of 'doorpost,' but in the specific sense of a 'mezuzah' (a small case containing a parchment with the first two sections of the *Shemaʿ*), attached to one of the doorposts of the house. What made the sinners at the time of Prophet Isaiah contemptible was their deceitfulness. By appending a mezuzah to their doorpost, they intended to display their veneration for the *Tora*, while in reality, they despised it: inside the mezuzah

---

[74] See *Giṭṭin* 45b. R. Naḥman conveyed this ruling with the technical term *naqeṭinnan* 'we hold,' indicating that it was 'the practice of the court' (*halakha le-maʿase*). Concerning this term, see R. Nissim Gerondi on R. Isaac Alfasi, *Giṭṭin* 27b, s.v. *naqeṭinnan*. On this ruling, see *MT Yesode ha-Tora* 6:8. The standard version 'אפיקורס' is wrong; instead read: 'מין ישראל'.

[75] *Shabbat* 116a.

they concealed the names of idolatrous deities.⁷⁶

The *minim*, too, practiced the same sort of duplicity, using Jewish sacred symbols as a cover to conceal their creepy practices (see above Chapter 7, and below). These men would not hesitate to use the Tetragrammaton—the Holiest of Holies of the Jewish Faith—to masquerade their obscene 'mysteries.'⁷⁷ That is why the Judeo-*minim* are viler than heathens. Pagans are not fraudulent. They do not pretend to 'observe' the Law or to speak in the name of the God of Israel! Incinerating their Scroll of the *Tora* (including the Tetragrammaton written by them) is the supreme responsibility of a genuine leader. It proclaims that there is nothing in common between Israel and the *minim*. Jews do not venerate the Scroll of the *Tora* as if it were a totem. Its sanctity does not depend solely on *what* it is written in it, but on *who* wrote it.⁷⁸ The same applies to the Tetragrammaton. It, too, could be made into an instrument of evil in the hands of *minim*. It is the supreme responsibility of the teachers of Israel, not only to transmit the values and institutions of the Law, but also to expose those *who use* the Law to abuse the credulous. Incinerating the Scroll of the *Tora* written by *minim*, together with the Tetragrammaton it contains, is an extreme form of expressing revulsion for their 'religion' and what they represent. Because Judaism was blessed with daring leaders like R. Ṭarfon, 'religion' never attained the bad name it acquired thanks to Christianity.

The rabbis compared the religion practiced by *minim* (=*minut*) to "toxic waters" (*ha-mayim ha-ra'im*), which appear crystalline and placid,

---

[76] Cited by R. Ḥayyim Algazi, *Bene Ḥayye* (Orta-Kivvae, 5479/1719), 64a. This is somehow similar to the advice given in *Abot* 4:20; cf. the story of R. Joshua and Caesar's daughter, *Ta'aniyot* 7a.

[77] In my view, the Judeo-*minim*'s concept of "the Mystery of the Kingdom" was linked with the idea that the Tetragrammaton/ 'O *Kyrios* stood for "legal master," rather than "God, Creator of Heaven and earth"; see below Chapter 22. For a somehow similar form of desecrating the Tetragrammaton, see *Sanhedrin* 102b.

[78] Accordingly, the commentaries and works written by rabbis, although they are not of the same stature as the Tora, must be treated with the same type of reverence; see *MT Yesode ha-Tora* 6:8.

but are fatal to any and all who would drink from them.[79] The *minim* were convinced that "there is only a single world," this one.[80] As with the classical epicurean, they, too, believed that it is possible to experience 'true, pure pleasure,' free from pain and apprehension (*eudaimonia*) in *this* world.[81] In the following chapter we will see that the *minim* maintained that those who had experienced Jesus in his true glory achieve this sort pleasure; i.e., "that have eaten his flesh and drunk his blood." An absolute condition to enjoy Epicurean bliss is for the individual to be "released" from all mundane "troubles" and responsibilities. In this manner, taught Diogenes (412/404 BCE-323), it would be possible to maintain "a continual remembrance of the highest and most important truths."[82] Similarly, the 'chosen few' admitted into "the Mystery of the Kingdom" *in this world*, must be free from all the restrictions of the Law (see following chapter). We can now understand why Maimonides regarded *minim* as utter cynics, men void of core-values, using 'salvation,' 'sin,' 'redemption,' etc., to manipulate the general public and gain power. Referring to *minut*, the 'religion' practiced by the *minim*, Maimonides wrote:

> ...*Minut* is more heinous than idolatry, because the *minim*—may God cut them off— poke fun at (all) religions, and they say: 'Those who propose them [religions] are wicked. Those who study them [religions, that is, they take them seriously] are crazy.' In fact, they deny prophecy altogether.[83]

Because hypocrisy is fundamental to their mental apparatus,

---

[79] *Abot* 1:11. It is important to distinguish between the expression *ha-mayyim ha-ra'im*, with the article *h*-, which is an allegorical reference to *minut*, see *Perush ha-Mishnayot*, vol. 4, p. 414, and cf. *Perush ha-Mishnayot*, vol. 3, p. 153; and the expression *mayyim ha-ra'im*, without the article *h*-, which means 'polluted' (*Beṣa* 18a) or 'infected' water (*Yerushalmi Sanhedrin* IX, 2, 27a).

[80] See Mishna *Berakhot* 9:5; *Berakhot* 54a.

[81] See Leo Strauss, *Spinoza's Critique of Religion* (New York: Schocken Books, 1965), Chapter 1.

[82] *Diogenes Laertius*, X, 82 (Loeb Classical Library), vol. 2, p. 611; cf. ibid.129, pp 653-655.

[83] *Iggeret ha-Shmad*, in *Iggerot ha-Rambam*, vol. 1, p. 37.

minim are worse than atheists. Maimonides used the Arabic term *zindiq*—standing for 'a hypocrite, using religious conventionalities to cover-up his heretical practices'—to describe the *minim*.[84] The ploy used by *minim* was 'religious devotion'—a common scam used by charlatans to bait the criminal and naïve, looking for shortcuts to salvation. It was on account of their endemic flattery that the rabbis referred to the *minim* as hypocrites (*ḥanifim*). Alluding to the verse, "For the congregation of hypocrites (*ḥanifim*) shall be desolate," the rabbis taught that they will be in perennial solitude, and will not behold "the Countenance of God's Glory" (*Jb* 15:34).[85] Having the flattery and pandering of *minim* in mind, R. Jonathan (2nd century) declared, "Every time that 'hypocrites' (*ḥannafim*) are mentioned in Scripture, it is a statement about *minim*, both Jewish and gentile."[86] Therefore, their prayers will go unanswered.[87] In sharp contrast, the Prophets of Israel believed "that their God is truthful and they would not flatter (*maḥanifin*) Him."[88] Consequently, whereas every sinner may be accepted back into the fold, "*Minim* are not Jews in any sense whatsoever, and can never be accepted as repentant."[89] Maimonides clarified that if their contrition is sincere, God will surely forgive them, just as He forgives every penitent. However, since *minut* is grounded on deceit, only God can know whether the *min* had actually repented or he is showing signs of contrition as bait to ensnare the naïve. Plain humans, however, cannot be sure that "the piety that

---

[84] See *Perush ha-Mishnayot*, *Ḥolin* 1:2, vol. 5, p. 175: *zindiq*, *zandaqa*, and the note of R. Joseph Qafiḥ *ad loc.*

[85] *Soṭa* 41b-42a; i.e., they will not be rewarded for their 'religiosity'; see R. Baḥye ibn Faquda, *Ḥobot ha-Lebabot*, ed. and tr. R. Joseph Qafiḥ, (Jerusalem, 5733/1973), V, 3-4, pp. 244-246. Cf. above notes 15, 45.

[86] *Bereshit Rabba* XLVIII, 4, *s.v. paḥadu*, vol. 2, p. 480. Cf. *Is* 32:6; *Jb* 8:13; 13:16; 15:34; 20:5; 27:8, etc.

[87] *Mishnah of R. Eliezer*, (Heb.) ed. H.G. Enelow (New York: Bloch Publishing Company, 1933), XII, p. 225.

[88] *Yerushalmi Berakhot*, VII, 3, 11c; cf. *Yerushalmi Megilla* III, 7, 74c; *Yoma* 69b, etc.

[89] MT *'Aboda Zara* 2:5. See MT *Teshuba* 3:7, 14.

they [the *minim*] display is not because of fear or to take in the people."⁹⁰

In short, the *minim* used the *exterior* of the Tora as bait, as when according to *Lk* 5:10 [I don't believe it to be true], Jesus advised Simon, the fisherman: "from henceforth thou shall catch men."⁹¹ Their usual catch, however, was made up of the criminal and naïve, men and women looking for a quick-fix of 'salvation,' like the infamous publicans and pitiable harlots making up Jesus' entourage: thus, the imperative to distinguish between Hebrew piety, and the phony religiosity of *minim*. Let us summarize the main rulings concerning *minim*.

First, given that they have no moral scruples, they are "beyond healing," and cannot regain their full status in the eyes of Israel.⁹²

Second, addressing the Karaite communities of his time, Maimonides distinguished between the original ideologues, who broke away from the Congregation of Israel, and those following *minut* because of their upbringing; in which case "we should endeavor to bring (them) back into the fold, and draw them with expressions of peace, so that they would return to the foundations of the *Tora*."⁹³

Third, the rabbinic rulings about *minim* apply to Jewish-*minim* alone. Non-Jewish *minim* are not subject to the same regulations. Therefore, although a Scroll of the *Tora* written by a heathen cannot to be used for liturgical services, it may not be desecrated.⁹⁴ Significantly, in the paragraph in which Maimonides writes the regulations against Jewish-*minim* and other undesirables, he emphasized that these regulations do not apply to heathens, adding: "and their men of virtue (*ḥasidehem*) have a portion in the World to Come"; i.e., they

---

⁹⁰ *Teshubot ha-Rambam*, vol. 2, pp. 501-502. Cf. *Mishnah of R. Eliezer*, XIX, p. 351. Because they are inveterate liars, trying to hunt 'the other,' mere humans can never be sure that their 'repentance' is not one of their psychological games.

⁹¹ About the 'sailors' in Jesus entourage, see above, n. 41.

⁹² *Perush ha-Mishnayot*, *Abot* 2:17, vol. 4, p. 429.

⁹³ *MT Mamrim* 3:3. This ruling was accepted by other legal authorities.

⁹⁴ *MT Yesode ha-Tora* 6:8.

shall be saved.[95]

We have explored the outside of the *minim*'s mezuzah. And now a foundational question: what was concealed inside their mezuzah? Answering this question would require us taking a peek at the "mysteries of the Kingdom."

16. Taking Pleasure in the Mystery of the Kingdom

The preceding may help us come to grips with the nomistic and antinomian elements crisscrossing throughout the *Christian Scripture*. In general, scholars tend to dismiss these contradictions as 'obscure' technicalities in Jesus' legal teachings. The contradictions, however, are structural, and pertain to the core of Christian teachings. Here is what Professor Smith had to say on this subject:

> But as a matter of fact the traditions about Jesus' legal teaching are not merely obscure, they are openly contradictory, and this is not merely from one Gospel to another, but even within the same Gospel.

Take, for instance, *Matt* 23:1-3:

> Then spake Jesus to the multitude, and to his disciples, Saying, The scribes and the Pharisees sit in Moses' seat. All therefore whatsoever they bid you observe, *that* observe and do; but do ye after their works: for they say, and do not.

Properly understood, this is

> —a direct command to his followers to keep not only the entire Mosaic Law, but also the oral law as taught by the Pharisees. And again we find him saying, "That which goes into the mouth does not make a man impure" [*Matt* 15:11]—a ruling which wipes out at one stroke almost the entire body of laws, both oral and written, concerning the purity of food. And this contradiction is by no means isolated; the Gospels contain many similar pairs of sayings, one supposing the

---

[95] *MT 'Edut* 11:10.

Mosaic Law still in force and its observance necessary for salvation, the other invalidating some legal requirements or promising salvation on other grounds without any concern for legal observance.

In fact,

> the nomistic and the antinomian elements in the Gospels are so extensive that no attempt to eliminate either can be convincing. And anyhow, such elimination misses the main difficulty, which is, not to account for either one of the rulings, but to account for the fact that *we have both* of them.[96] [Italics in original]

Professor Smith proposed that Jesus had in mind two groups of followers. One was made up of the general public, who although subject to the Law in general, were exempted "from certain everyday obligations, such as that of fasting." The other group consisted of the chosen few that had access to "the mystery of the Kingdom... and whose initiates were free as the winds."[97] He further developed a similar thesis in another study, where he asserted that there was,

> a secret initiation by which he [Jesus] admitted his intimates to the Kingdom of God and thereby enabled them to escape from the authority of the Law (*Lk* 16:16; *Matt* 11:11).[98]

Accordingly, Jesus had two messages, one for the general public, and another for those found worthy of partaking in the delights *inside* the *minim*'s mezuzah:

> Many stories and sayings in the Gospels represent Jesus as free of the law and declaring or defending the freedom of his disciples. "The law and the prophets were [only] until John [the Baptist], from then on the kingdom of God is proclaimed." And is available to those who

---

[96] Morton Smith, "Jesus' Attitude towards the Law," *Fourth World Congress of Jewish Studies*, vol. 1 (Jerusalem: World Union of Jewish Studies, 1967), p. 242. For a list of these contradictions, see ibid. n. 22.

[97] "Jesus' Attitude towards the Law," p. 244.

[98] Morton Smith, "The Reason for the Persecution of Paul and the Obscurity of Acts," in *Studies in Mysticism and Religion presented to Gershom G. Scholem* (Jerusalem: Magness Press, 1967), p. 261.

will use violence. The new message is the new wine, not to be put in the old skin of Judaism; it is the new garment not to be mutilated to patch up the old. Therefore the Son of Man (Jesus) is the lord of the Sabbath, can forgive sins, and does not come, like the Baptist, in "the way of righteousness," but "eating and drinking." He is a friend of publicans (Jews who cooperated with the Roman government) and sinners. His yoke, by contrast to that of the law, is light. The law came by Moses, but grace by Jesus. He alone has revealed the hitherto unknown Father. His followers shall know the truth and the truth will make them free.[99]

This explains the widespread reference to libertine practices throughout the early Christian communities—they were *not* the result of an 'unfortunate mix-up.' They came directly from the teachings of Jesus and his disciples.

And now we know from whom that position derived: a figure earlier and even more influential than Paul, and a figure notorious for his libertine teaching and practice. He broke the Sabbath, he neglected the purity rules, he refused to fast, made friends with publicans and sinners, and was known as "a gluttonous man and a winebibber." He not only taught his disciples that the law had come to an end with the Baptist, but he also administered a baptism of his own—"the mystery of the kingdom of God"—by which he enabled some of his disciples, united with himself, to enter the kingdom and to enjoy his own freedom of the law.[100]

Thus, the 'Father' is revealed to the faithful via cannibalistic rituals, where the 'flesh' and 'blood' of the 'Son' is consumed. In this fashion, "the kingdom can be taken by violence," and all twelve of Jesus' disciples, *become* Jesus, because,

They have seen Jesus in his true glory, have eaten his flesh and drunk his blood. The least of those who is now in the kingdom is greater

---

[99] *The Secret Gospel*, p. 112. Concerning "violence," see ibid, p. 95. This may be related to a ritual involving a sin performed *le-hakh'is*; see below n. 104, cf. n. 162.

[100] *The Secret Gospel*, p. 130. His followers too, through "the work of the spirit," are identified with him and can enjoy the same type of freedom; see ibid. pp. 103-104.

that the Baptist. The prodigal son has been admitted at once to the feast.[101]

The 'legalistic' teachings of Jesus are for "those outside," to them the exterior of the mezuzah will suffice. However, for those who had been "baptized with the spirit," the restrictions of the law no longer apply.[102] In this spiritual mood, we find some celebrating "orgiastic communion meals which they said gave them access to the kingdom of God."[103] Some Christian congregations practiced "fornication," which included "that one should have his father's wife" (1 *Cor* 5:1).[104]

Professor Smith's investigations illustrate R. Ṭarfon's metaphor: underneath the nomistic elements of the *Gospels*, lurks the antinomian 'Mystery of the Kingdom.' Dismissal of the Jewish-*minim* from the bosom of Israel had nothing to do with 'theology'— theology is a *Christian* invention, designed to justify the persecution of undesirables. Rather, the expulsion of Judeo-*minim* from the bosom of Israel had to do with a type of behavior that could not be tolerated

---

[101] *The Secret Gospel*, p. 95. On cannibalistic orgies, see James George Frazer, *The Golden Bough, Spirits of the Corn*, 2 vols. (London: Macmillan and Co., 1919), vol. 1, pp. 18-19.

[102] *The Secret Gospel*, pp. 112-113.

[103] *The Secret Gospel*, p. 136.

[104] For more examples, see *The Secret Gospel*, pp. 126-130. I propose that this type of ritual corresponds to a category of transgression that the rabbis designate *le-hakh'is*; that is, that they are performed in order "to anger" God. Usually, rabbinic commentators interpret this as referring to an individual who, having the choice to eat a kosher piece of meat, would eat non-kosher meat out of wantonness; see Rashi, *'Aboda Zara* 26b *s.v. le-te'abon*. However, the Talmud, *Mo'ed Qaṭan* 18b, makes it clear that in a *le-hakh'is*-transgression, the individual intends not merely to 'sin' but to 'affront' God, imputing "unto the Lord their God things that were not right" (2 *Kings* 17:9); e.g., as when Paul depicts the God of Israel as a sadomasochist deity, deceiving Israel by giving them the *Tora*, a legal system impossible to fulfill; see *Rom* 3:19-20, and *HS*, vol. 1, Chapter 30. Some of *le-hakh'is*-activities involved sexual promiscuity and incestuous relations; see *Sanhedrin* 103b. In this manner the individual would succeed in extinguishing all traces of spirituality within, and become totally absorbed by the material world; see below, n. 162. This will explain why an individual in a *le-hakh'is*-mindset, has forfeited his "brotherhood" with Israel; see *'Aboda Zara* 26b and *MT 'Aboda Zara* 2:5. Cf. *MT Gezela* 11:2; *Roṣeaḥ* 4:10.

in any community. Concerning "the persecutions" of Christians, Professor Smith wrote:

> The persecutions cannot be explained solely by reference to the peculiarities of Messianic beliefs of the Christians, since peculiarities of Messianic belief seem to have been matters of comparative indifference in the first century, *provided* (italics in the original) they did not lead to peculiarities of practice. What we must find, therefore, is some peculiarity of primitive Christian practice sufficient to explain the persecution. This peculiarity, I argued, was Jesus' teaching of freedom from the Law and *the libertine consequences which he and his followers drew from it*.[105] [Italics added]

It is a matter of the highest importance to note that both the 'exoteric' and 'esoteric' teachings circulating among early Christians, "went back to Jesus himself."[106] The one was applicable to the ordinary convert, and the other to those that,

> had been possessed by Jesus; he lived in them, they were part of his body, they were 'in' him, so they must be in the kingdom and free

---

[105] "The Reason for the Persecution of Paul and the Obscurity of Acts," p. 262. I disagree with Professor Smith concerning the so-called 'persecution' of Christians. Indeed, the rabbis *expelled* the Jewish-*minim* from the bosom of Israel (see next Chapter), but there is no documentary evidence that Jews persecuted Christian-*minim* or Christians in general. The sole source for these allegations comes from Christian sources that used these allegations as a pretext to persecute Jews. This strategy was first designed by Pharaoh, who accused the Jews of wanting to plot against Egypt to justify the enslavement of Israel (see *Ex* 1:9-11). Caligula and other anti-Semites applied a similar method. An important factor to consider is that because of his own anxiety, Jesus felt that 'Jews' wanted to harm him. When he asked some Jews, "Why do you lust to kill me," they responded: "You have a demon (*Daimonion exeis*) —who lusts to kill you?" (*Jn* 7:19-20). Translated into contemporary language, they were saying to him: 'It's all in your mind, Brother Jesus.' His anxiety and feelings of persecution were aggravated by the fact that Jesus felt that he could 'read' other's people's minds, and ask: "Why do you think evil in your hearts?" (*Matt* 9:4); thereby ascertaining that their hearts were "full of robbery and wickedness" (*Lk* 11:39). Concerning Jesus' uncanny faculty of reading minds, see above n. 45 and below, n. 188. Obviously, this was nothing more than "an exteriorization of an unconscious process," well known in psychiatric circles; see *Demons of the Inner World*, p. 179.

[106] *The Secret Gospel*, p. 131.

from the law. Here was the basis for a deep and long-lasting dispute as to the liability of ordinary Christians to observe the law.[107]

This once again substantiates R. Ṭarfon's exegesis of *Is* 57:8: underneath the *minim*'s mezuzah lurked rituals having to do with pathological aberrations and behavior. Sephardic Jews preserved a proverb that fit well these 'mysteries': *"Pecado de padre"* ('Sin of a priest').[108]

17. Why were the Judeo-Christians expelled from Christendom?

The Hebrew term *min* (pl. *minim*), 'heretic' in rabbinic literature, is a broad, nonspecific idiom, used to designate an individual that have rejected a fundamental belief of Israel.[109] Mostly, however, it was applied to Judeo-Christians. These were men who had been familiar with Jesus while he was alive in the land of Israel and followed his teachings.[110] Their knowledge of Jesus did not come from preachers and books, but from direct, frontal instruction they received from a man whom they regarded as their supreme tutor. Post-Jesus Christianity, made almost exclusively from converts from pagan humanity, felt uncomfortable with 'Jews,' with any *Jews*—but *particularly* with

---

[107] *The Secret Gospel*, p. 119.

[108] Similarly, concerning the display of 'religiosity,' a proverb in Judeo-Arabic says: *Min barra arkham wu-min-ju'a skham* ("On the outside [it shines like white] marble, but inside [you will find] filth").

[109] For an extensive discussion of this term, see *HS*, vol. 2, Appendix #55; cf. ibid. pp. 95-97.

[110] The best collection of rabbinic sources about the Judeo-Christians in rabbinic literature is *Christianity in Talmud & Midrash*. I am not aware of a systematic study of their legal and theological doctrines. They seem to have denied the possibility of repentance; see *Shemot Rabba, Bo*, XIII, 3, in *Midrash Rabba* [*'al ha-Tora ve-Ḥamesh Megillot*], 2 vols. (Reprinted, Jerusalem, 5735/1975), vol. 1, 24d—hence the need for a special form of atonement provided by Jesus. They also denied bodily resurrection; see *Midrash Tanḥuma, Naso* XXX, ed. S. Buber. 2 vols. (Vilna, 5645/1885), vol. 2, 21a. The view about Levirate-marriage, in *Midrash Sekhel Ṭob*, ed. Buber (Berlin, 5660/1900), *Bereshit* XXXVIII, 4, is probably theirs.

Judeo-Christians, professing to have a direct tradition about Jesus and his teachings, *independent* of the ecclesiastical authorities and the *Christian Scripture*: an 'authority' which was formed about two or three centuries after Jesus. The conflict between the Judeo-Christians and the Christian authorities does not pertain to 'religion.' 'Religion,' 'spirituality,' etc, are consequences of the two media of transmission, one peculiar to pagan humanity and the other to Israel.

We had the opportunity to learn that in Israel the medium of transmission is from the first-person 'I' to the second-person 'you.' We explained that this medium is grounded on the fundamental (linguistic) horizontality, between the speaking persons 'I/you,' where the second-person may turn to the speaker and address him as 'I' to 'you' (see above Chapter 1). A fundamental aspect of linguistic horizontality is that the speakers 'I/you' share the same moment; a moment, ensuing from the intersection time-space. It is only within such a time-space context that the constitutive values of Israel unfold; horizontally, from speaking subject 'I'—God, Moses, prophets, rabbis—to the second-person audience, singular 'you.' By contrast, the medium of Christianity is from a first-party platform, to a third-person platform, which in quality of 'absentee' (*nistar*) or 'non-person', is excluded from addressing the first-party as 'I' to 'you.' Given that the first-party platform is occupied by a *Übermensch,* the facts, doctrines, etc., transmitted to the third-party audience are apodictic truths. Refusal to accept them constitutes rebellion.

A key difference between these media is that in Israel, the dialogue 'I/you' unfolds in the context of a geographic space and a chronological time, as when God spoke at Sinai with Israel. The Christian medium rules out a common frame of reference between the first and the third-party platforms. Properly understood, faith in Jesus' ministry, his Trial, Crucifixion, and eventual Resurrection and Ascension, are the effect of a prior and more elemental belief: the supreme authority of the first-party platform/*Übermensch*. The faithful knows all these to be so, because the *Übermensch* occupying the first-party platform said that it was so. In a precise sense, Jesus' Salvation, etc. are *means* to ascertain the categorical authority of the first-party platform/*Übermensch*: faith is a function of obedience. The problem with the Judeo-Christian communities was that their knowledge of Jesus and his teachings did not warrant faith in the first-party platform/*Übermensch*. Eventually, the Christian authorities—instituted about three centuries after Jesus— expelled the Judeo-Christians for the simple reason that a 'Jesus' that bypasses the first-party platform, renders the first-party platform/*Übermensch* worthless.[111]

Principally, the Judeo-Christian traditions differed from the *Christian Scripture* in two pivotal points. First, the Judeo-Christians did not believe that Jesus was some sort of a 'god.' Concerning the Ebionites, a Judeo-Christian sect, Eusebius wrote:

> They regarded him (Jesus) as plain and ordinary, a man esteemed as righteous through growth of character and nothing more, the child of a normal union between a man and Mary.[112]

The Judeo-Christian perception of Jesus was the view that everyone, Jew and pagan, held of Jesus *while he was alive*. Since they had known Jesus from first-hand contacts with him, and had followed his life carefully, many Judeo-Christians, "did not believe that he was crucified."[113] This happened to coincide with the traditional Jewish position, which saw nothing 'criminal' about Jesus' activities—nothing warranting a 'Trial,' much less a 'Crucifixion' (see below Chapters 22-23). We should note, in passing, that in the Arabian Peninsula, Jews and Christians alike did not believe that Jesus was crucified. Otherwise, the *Koran* would not have omitted this important fact.[114] This may explain why the Judeo-Christians did not recognize

---

[111] On the beliefs of the Judeo-Christians, see "The Jewish Christians...," (Heb.), pp. 170-216. For a fine and well-balanced survey of the different Judeo-Christian sects and their clash with Paul, see J. E. Ménard, "Judeocristianismo," *Enciclopedia de la Biblia*, vol. 4, (Barcelona: Ediciones Garriga, 1969), cols. 758-765.

[112] *The History of the Church*, III, 27, p. 137. See *Origen: Contra Celsum*, pp. 311-312; "The Jewish Christians...," (Heb.), pp. 178-179.

[113] See "The Jewish Christians...," (Heb.), p. 177.

[114] See "The Jewish Christians...," (Heb.), p. 177; cf. ibid, pp. 181 n. 49; 207. This

the cross.¹¹⁵ Moreover, not all of them were willing to admit that Jesus was born of a virgin.¹¹⁶ Some regarded 'Firstborn' to be an honorific title, and not a description of Jesus' conception and birth.¹¹⁷

Second, the Judeo-Christians maintained that the Jewish Law was binding, and that Jesus never taught that the *Tora* was no longer valid. This is what Eusebius wrote about them:

> They did not deny that the Lord was born of a virgin and the Holy Spirit, but nevertheless shared their refusal to acknowledge His pre-existence as God the Word and Wisdom. Thus the impious doctrine of the others was their undoing also, especially as they placed equal emphasis on the outward observance of the Law.... Like the others [Jews], they observed the Sabbath and the whole Jewish system.... It is because of such practices that they have been dubbed with their present name: the name of Ebionites hints at the poverty of their intelligence, for this is the way in which a poor man is referred to by the Hebrews.¹¹⁸

The first point finds some backing in the *Christian Scripture*'s report that the general public, including his own mother and relatives (see *Mk* 3:21, 31-33), believed that Jesus "was insane" (*Jn* 10:20, see below, Chapter 19). It is somehow difficult to envision that a mother having experienced Immaculate Conception, would deem her son anything less than a 'god.' The second point is supported by *Matt* 23:2-3, *Pocket Interlinear,* p. 58, where Jesus reportedly taught: "The scribes and the Pharisees sat on Moses' seat. Then all things whatever they tell you to keep, keep and do. But do not do according to their works; for they say, and do not do." Similarly, in *Matt* 5:19-20, *Pocket*

---

view found new adherents; see for instance, Michael Baigent, *The Jesus Papers* (San Francisco: Harper, 2006).

¹¹⁵ See "The Jewish Christians...," (Heb.), p. 181 n. 48, and p. 190.

¹¹⁶ "The Jewish Christians...," (Heb.), p. 177; cf. ibid, p. 181 n. 49.

¹¹⁷ See S. Pines, "'Israel, My Firstborn' and the Sonship of Jesus," in *Studies in Mysticism and Religion presented to Gershom G. Scholem,* eds. E. E. Urbach *et al* (Jerusalem: Magness Press, 1967), pp. 177-190.

¹¹⁸ *The History of the Church,* III, 27, p. 137. See also *Origen: Contra Celsum,* pp. 66, 311.

Interlinear, p. 9 we read: "Whoever then shall break one of these commandments, the least, and shall teach men so, he shall be called least in the kingdom of Heaven. But whoever does and teaches *them*, this one shall be called great in the kingdom of Heaven. For I say to you, if your righteousness shall not exceed *that* of the scribes and Pharisees, you in no way shall go into the kingdom of Heaven." Clearly, this coincides with the Judeo-*minim* tradition that Jesus upheld the authority of the Law *and* rabbinic teachings, and "that they must observe every detail of the Law."[119] In this connection we should note that no lesser a figure than R. Eli'ezer b. Horqanos (1st and 2nd centuries)—one of the great rabbinic leaders in the generation after the destruction of the Temple—had some contacts with Judeo-*minim*. In one occasion, he "was pleased" by a word passed on to him by "One of the disciples Jesus of Nazareth."[120] In another occasion, the same rabbi was asked if "a certain person"—an allusion to Jesus—"has a portion in the World-to-Come," and he refused to answer.[121] Obviously, if he had believed the reports of the *Christian Scripture* about Jesus' creeds and actions (see above Chapter 11, and below Chapter 24), he would not have hesitated to reply in the negative. Likewise, neither R. Judah ha-Levi nor Maimonides—both of whom were well-acquainted with the *Christian Scripture*—would have credited Jesus for having paved "the road for the King-Messiah" (See "Introduction").

Conclusive evidence that Jesus' earthly followers did not believe that he was some sort of a deity, is to be found in the name *Christianous*, used to identify members of the Christian faith. It first

---

[119] *The History of the Church*, III, 27, p. 137. Cf. "The Jewish Christians...," (Heb.), p. 188.

[120] As in the Spanish ms., *Tractate 'Aboda Zara*, ed. Prof. Shraga Abramson (New York: The Jewish Theological Seminary, 1957), 14b. See *Tosefta Ḥolin* 2:24, *'Aboda Zara* 16b-17a, and the comments in *Christianity in Talmud and Midrash*, pp. 137-146. On the life and teachings of this rabbi, see Y.D. Gilat, *R. Eliezer ben Hyrcanus* (Ramat-Gan: Bar-Ilan University Press, 1984).

[121] *Yoma* 66b. For a well-balanced analysis of this passage, see *Christianity in Talmud & Midrash*, pp. 45-47.

appears in *Acts* 11:26. The English version, *Pocket Interlinear*, p. 307 reads: "And the disciples were first called Christians (*Xristianous*) at Antioch." Commonplace among commentators is to explain that the pagan population of Antioch called Jesus' disciples "Christians." This interpretation is wrong. A close reading of the Greek text will show that it was not the people who invented the name 'Christian,' but Jesus' disciples who "called themselves Christians." Professor Bickerman showed that what the text is saying is that Jesus' *Jewish* followers were the ones that identified themselves to the *pagan* populations in Antioch, as "*Christianous*." (Read *Acts* 11:26: "And the disciples [of Jesus] first called themselves Christians (*Christianous*) [to the pagan population] *at* Antioch").[122] What does this name mean? Obviously, it is somehow connected to Jesus' title *Christus*, 'the Anointed one' or 'Messiah.' However, "the formation of their name," noted by Bickerman, "is exceptional," adding that "in normal Greek the followers of Christ would be designated by an appellative with the suffix -*eioi*."[123] If so, why did the Jews in Antioch use the suffix -*nous*? The answer goes to the heart of the Christian faith. The title *Christianous* meant, "that they"—Jesus' disciples—"were agents, representatives of the Messiah." It is radically different from the appellative "Jesus' slaves" used by Paul (1*Cor* 7:20, 21, 22, 23, *Pocket Interlinear*, pp. 396-397: *doulos*, see below). In Greek, to be a 'slave' (*doulos*) of a god means that you *worship it* as a god, or that you are a slave of, dwelling in a temple of, and or are devoted to the worship of, that god. To dispel the notion that they worshiped Jesus, his *Jewish* followers designed the title *Christianous*, that is, *emissaries, followers*—not *worshipers* or *slaves* (*doulos*)—of Jesus. "[S]peaking to the pagan world," observed Professor Bickerman, Jesus' Jewish followers "could not style themselves: 'slaves of Christ.'" Such a designation, "would have suggested

---

[122] Josephus, in *Jewish Wars*, VII, 43-44, *Josephus*, vol. 3, p. 517, writes that the Jewish population "was particularly numerous in Syria…. But it was at Antioch that they specially congregated."

[123] Elias Bickerman, "The Name of Christians," in his *Studies in Jewish and Christian History*, Part Three (Leiden : E.J. Brill, 1986), p. 145.

the blasphemous idea that they adored the Messiah as their God." At the initial moment of Christian history, the only 'Jesus' was the Jesus that unfolded in the world of the here-now. The Jews of Antioch encoded that moment in the name '*Christianous*'—the very name 'Christian' identifying the faithful until this very day.

> The name which the followers of Jesus gave themselves officially at Antioch, about 40 A.D. is a precious relic which has survived from the short and obscure period between Jesus and Paul, whose preserved letters start a decade later. The name shows that at this date, in the first decade after the end of the glory of Jesus, his followers continued to think of him according to Jewish patterns of thought. They were still a Jewish movement, who believed themselves to be the "third order" called to enter the Kingdom of Heaven, and who, as such, declared to the pagan world that they were officers of the Anointed King in his kingdom, which was a present reality. "The darkness is passing and the real light is already shinning" (1*Jn* 2:9).[124]

Paul perceived Jesus in terms of pagan spirituality. For him, to believe in Jesus meant to be his "slave" (see 1*Cor* 7:20, 21, 22, 23, *Pocket Interlinear,* pp. 396-397: *doulos*), that is, to worship Jesus as a god. Professor Bickerman explained:

> When Paul says that the free man is called the "slave of Christ" (1*Cor* 7:21, 22, 23), he uses not only the non-Greek, but also non-Jewish concept of free persons who became self-devotees of an Oriental divinity.[125]

In short, in the early history of Christianity, there were two distinct concepts of what Jesus expected from his followers. The Judeo-Christians maintained that a follower of Jesus ought to be, first and foremost, '*Christianous,*' that is, an agent or representative of the person whom they regarded as the Messiah of Israel. Paul maintained that to believe in Jesus is to be his 'slave' (*doulos*) and worship him as a god. We can now understand why the Judeo-Christians "held that

---

[124] "The Name of Christians," p. 151.
[125] "The Name of Christians," p. 149.

the epistles of the Apostle [Paul] ought to be rejected altogether, calling him [Paul] a renegade of the Law."[126] Later on, in the footsteps of the Judeo-Christians in Antioch, the ecclesiastic authorities designated the faithful '*Christianous.*' At the same time, they fully accepted Paul's doctrine, and defined '*Christianous*,' not as an emissary or representative of Jesus, but as a 'slave' (*doulos*) of Jesus worshiping him as god. Hence the compelling reason for expelling the Judeo-Christians: their version of Christianity is incompatible with the Pauline version. To protect the faithful from "Judaistic errors," Christian authorities determined that it would be best to expel the Judeo-Christians. Thus, Christianity succeeded in expelling the Jesus of history, replacing him with the Jesus of myth. Put in theological terms:

> Only as the crucified is he [Jesus] 'grace and truth' and not law. Only as he who sacrificed his flesh, that is, his historical existence, is he Spirit or New Creature.

While in human garb, his life did not amount to much. Hence the overwhelming principle, agreed upon by all major branches of Christianity:

> A Christianity which does not assert that Jesus of Nazareth [=the Jesus of History] is sacrificed to Jesus as the Christ [=the Jesus of Myth] is just one more religion among many others. It has no justifiable claim to finality.[127]

Bearing on this critical point, a modern scholar wrote:

> The Jesus Christ of historic Christianity is not the Jesus of history. He is a product of the myth making mind, basing itself upon historical mistakes and misunderstandings, and even upon some falsifications of history, ultimately shaped by a revolutionary and untraditional reading of the Jewish Scriptures. Christianity does not start with Jesus, but with his followers after his death.[128]

---

[126] *The History of the Church*, III, 27, p. 137.
[127] *Systematic Theology*, vol. 1, pp. 134, 135.
[128] *Christian Antisemitism*, p. 83. See *HS*, vol. 1, pp. 175-176. See below Appendix # 1.

Origen (c. 185-254)—one of the great Christian scholars and theologians—acknowledged that although the God of the Christians is the same for the Jews, the God of the Jews is not the same for the Christians.

> But let us grant that there are some among us who do not say that God is the same God as that of the Jews. Yet that is no reason why they are to be criticized who prove from the same scriptures that there is one and the same God for Jews and Gentiles. So also Paul, who came to Christianity from the Jews, says clearly: 'I thank my God whom I serve from my forefathers in a pure conscience.' [2 *Tim* 1:3][129]

Paul was the son of converts. He was uncircumcised, and personally repudiated Jewish circumcision (see below Chapter 18). He could not read a word of the *Hebrew Scripture*, and only quoted from the Greek version. Unlike the Judeo-Christians, Paul never met Jesus. Rather, he tells us that post-*mortem* Jesus met him, when he was on the road to Damascus. Suddenly: "a light from heaven, above the brightness of the sun, shining round about me and them which they journeyed with me" (*Acts* 26:13). At this supreme moment of illumination, post-*mortem* Jesus revealed to Paul that the faithful must worship him in quality of 'slaves.' The faithful knows these facts to be absolutely true, "because it was said that it was so" by *Übermensch*-Paul. This fact had been so confirmed by the anonymous editors of the *Christian Scripture*, and although the earliest manuscripts date to the 3rd century at the earliest, their authenticity is nonetheless incontrovertible, since the first-party platform declared it to be so.

In sum, Christendom accepted Paul's doctrine that, a "slave of Christ" is truly "a freed man" and not "a slave of man" (1 *Cor* 7:21, 22, 23). Of this, the faithful can be certain, given that the hierarchy, standing upon the first-party platform, declared it to be so.

---

[129] *Origen: Contra Celsum*, p. 311.

18. Paul, Saint *and* Mimic Actor

Who was Paul? He was either a professional mimic actor, or a keen observer of the mimic theater.[130] Therefore, when examining his words and actions, it is of primary importance to determine whether what he was reporting was a real-life experience, or parts of the many repertoires that he learned from comic scenarios. Let us note that the mimic theater was popular in Syria and other regions visited by Paul.[131] One of the most popular roles played by mimic actors was that of the classical 'fool.'[132] The fool (*morós, stupidus*) was a familiar figure in the cities of the Roman Empire where the mime was so popular that it "practically monopolized the stage."

> The fool was the secondary actor in the mime (*mimos deúteros, actor secundarum partium*): that is, he aped the performance of the archimime, comically misinterpreting and reacting to him.... The fool typically had a shaven head, and might be endowed with a prominent phallus.[133]

A key motif recurring in Paul's narrative is the "foolishness" of his discourse.[134] It has been shown "that Paul's discourse in 2*Cor* 11 and 12 was modeled "on the performances of the mimic fools that populated the ancient stage."[135] An analysis of Paul's foolish dis-

---

[130] See Laurence L. Wellborn, "Runaway Paul," *Harvard Theological Review* 92 (1999), pp. 123 n. 64; 127 n. 99, and pp. 157-158. Wellborn suggests that Paul could have learned about mimes from literary sources; see ibid, pp. 128-129.

[131] See Allardyce Nicoli, *Masks Mimes and Miracles* (New York: Cooper Square Publishing, 1963), pp. 38, 94. A mime song was inscribed on the door of a pagan Temple in Marissa, Southern Israel; see "Runaway Paul," p. 124; and cf. ibid, p. 128.

[132] On the "Mimic Actors" in general, see *Masks Mimes and Miracles*, pp. 83-109. On the "Mimic Fool" in particular, see ibid, pp. 47-50.

[133] "Runaway Paul," p. 124. For sources and bibliography, see the footnotes accompanying the text. For portraits of mimic fools in terra-cotta, see ibid, pp. 162-163; for a description of these figures, see ibid, pp. 125-126; and *Masks Mimes and Miracles*, pp. 47-49.

[134] See Runaway Paul," pp. 122-126.

[135] "Runaway Paul," p. 123; see ibid, pp. 137-151.

course in *2Cor* 11:21b-12:10 shows that he had combined elements of different types of fools in his performance at 11:24-27; evoking the "anxious old man" in 11:28-29, and portraying the "learned impostor" in 12:1b-4 and 12:7-9. The combination of several types of fools was widespread throughout the ancient theater.[136] In the prologue to the speech in *2Cor* 11:1b-21a, Paul took pain to show that he was actually playing the role of the fool. He characterized his discourse as "foolishness" (11:1, 17), and repeatedly referred to himself as a "fool" (11:16, 19). These self-references are the linguistic counterpart of the dress and manners by which the fool was identified in the mimic theater.[137] "Like a fool, Paul boasts of his 'accomplishments'" (see *2Cor* 11:24-27). Some of his boasting "is modeled upon the exploits of the *miles gloriosus* ['the boastful soldier'], a stock character of comedy and mime."[138] Paul's catalogue of the hardships he claimed to have endured (*2Cor* 11: 24-27) resembles that of Alcibiades regarding the hardships suffered by Socrates.[139] His "journey to heaven," (*2Cor* 12: 2-4), his "visions," and "revelations," are common features "of foolish discourses in antiquity."[140] Likewise, the account of his illness, "a thorn in the flesh" (*2Cor* 12:7), "for which he thrice sought a miraculous cure through prayer," is "a motif that appears in portrait of the learned impostor."[141]

And what about Paul's trip to Damascus, upon which his very apostleship rests? Here, too, "Paul had shaped the account of his flight in accordance with the convention of the mimic stage."[142] Many features of the passage in *2Cor* 11:32-33 (cf. *Acts* 9:23-25), which have puzzled students and commentators, can be explained upon realizing

---

[136] "Runaway Paul," p. 137.

[137] "Runaway Paul," pp. 137-138.

[138] "Runaway Paul," p. 143.

[139] "Runaway Paul," p. 141; cf. ibid, p. 123.

[140] "Runaway Paul," p. 147. For similar examples and sources, see ibid, pp. 148-149.

[141] "Runaway Paul," p. 150.

[142] "Runaway Paul," p. 157. pp. 115-163.

that Paul's escape from Damascus was patterned according to one of the most popular characters of the mimic stage: the Runaway Fool.[143]

> Many of the particular features of passage 2Cor 11:32-33 are illuminated by the recognition that Paul has shaped the account of his flight in accordance with the convention of the mimic stage.[144]

Because scholars failed to consider Paul's theatrical background, "many aspects of Paul's most powerful compositions are poorly understood, above all the flight from Damascus."[145]

Let us conclude with two notes, concerning Paul's attacks against the circumcision. His main purpose was to delegitimize Jesus' disciples. They all were circumcised (see *Acts* 21:20-25) and regarded Paul to be a fake. There is something else. In his attack against circumcision, Paul pronounced some troubling words (*Gal* 5:12). Translators tried to cover up the language. The *King James Version* reads: "I would they were even cut off which trouble you." The correct translation was given by Hyam Maccoby: "I wish they would have their penises chopped off completely."[146] We have noticed earlier that the fool usually appeared with a shaven head and a prominent phallus.[147] May I make a suggestion, without any serious claim to legitimacy, that the words "...their penises chopped off completely," come from one of the live-performance given by the Apostle? It must surely have commanded a big laughter![148]

The entire apparatus of the Christian faith rests on Paul's al-

---

[143] See "Runaway Paul," pp. 152-159. It has been noted that although Paul *plays* the role of the fool, his performance differs from a genuine *mimus* in one important respect: Paul plays the role "in bitter earnest," see ibid, p. 159.

[144] "Runaway Paul," p. 157.

[145] "Runaway Paul," p. 123.

[146] Hyam Maccoby, *Paul and Hellenism* (Philadelphia: Trinity Press, 1991), p. 46.

[147] Cited above n. 82.

[148] On mimic obscenity, see *Masks Mimes and Miracles*, pp. 123-124. For the figure of mimic-fool with a prominent phallus, see ibid, figure 82, p. 89; and "Runaway Paul," terra-cotta 6. Paul was associated with the more libertine branch of Christianity; see *The Secret Gospel*, pp. 121-143.

leged epiphany on his road to Damascus. Suddenly, "At midday," reports Paul, "I saw in the way a light from heaven, above the brightness of the sun, shining round about me and them which journeyed with me." Overwhelmed by the splendor of the vision, and barely able to speak, he asked: "Who art thou, Lord"? And the voice responded: "I am Jesus whom thou persecuted" (*Acts* 26:13, 15).[149] It was at this sublime moment that he was vested with the authority to introduce himself, as "Paul, a slave (*doulos*) of Jesus Christ, called *to be* an apostle, separated unto the gospel of God" (*Rom* 1:1). It is on the basis of this message that the Judeo-Christian disciples were removed from the bosom of Christendom, and with them, the Jesus of history. The legitimate "slave" (*doulos*) of Jesus could then freely speak up in the name of "The Son of God with power, according to the spirit of holiness, by the resurrection of the death" (*Rom* 1:4).

With Paul, Jesus' biography commences at the time of his death. To give credence to his Messianship, his biography must be developed backwards, from end to start. The story of Jesus told in the *Christian Scripture* belongs to myth, not because it is unproven, but because it is and it must be unprovable. In Christianity, faith in Jesus is not a primary belief, but an upshot of faith in the supreme authority of the first-party platform. A modern theologian explained, with clarity and finesse, the subtleties underlying this overwhelming principle.

> Authority for the Christian is therefore not so much a privilege as it is a responsibility. When it is vested in the Church, it becomes not a mark of superiority but the source of a mission. Christians do not claim to have the truth. *They are claimed by it, and communicate the truth in the expectation that it will claim others as they are claimed.*[150] [Our italics]

Because Paul's vision is absolutely lucid—leaving no room for doubts whatsoever—one should not hesitate to ascertain that any

---

[149] On the character of this 'persecution,' see above notes 98, 105.

[150] Carl Michelson, "Authority," in *A Handbook of Christian Theology* (New York: Meridian Books, 1958), p. 27.

form of criticism is rank obstinacy. Addressing this fundamental issue, one of the foremost theologians of our time taught: "...an attack on theology *as such* in the name of reason is a symptom of rationalistic shallowness or rationalistic *hybris*."[151] Building on this premise we may conclude: "Christian doctrine is what the church declares it to be through its official authorities."[152] Let us note, in passing, that the same "rationalistic *hybris*" was evident in Abraham, the first Patriarch of Israel, who dared say 'No!' to *Übermensch*-Nimrod, not on the basis of some sort of 'epiphany,' but because of "his own precise intelligence."[153] The Prophets and teachers of Israel persisted in Abraham's folly. In fact, Jews of all persuasions and backgrounds still persist in the same type of obstinacy as Patriarch Abraham. Hence, the traditional support of the ecclesiastic authorities for the Nimrods of the world (see below, Chapter 35).

19. Jesus as Jews and Pagans saw him

Jesus looked, spoke, and acted like a magician. To begin with, Jesus had his *entire body* tattooed with magical spells. This fact was reported by people who *saw* Jesus while he was *alive*. The information was brought up casually, to illustrate a legal point, having nothing to do with either Jesus personally or with Christianity.[154] There is archeological evidence confirming this tradition. A bowl (end 1st century BCE-2nd century CE) was found bearing a Greek inscription: "DIA CHRSTOU O GOISTAIS," meaning either "by Christ the magician," or "the magician by Christ."[155] Images depicting Jesus today would not have been recognized by his contemporaries: early

---

[151] *Systematic Theology*, vol. 1, p. 47.

[152] *Systematic Theology*, vol. 1, p. 83.

[153] See above, "Introduction," n. 52.

[154] *Shabbat* 104b.

[155] See Appendix # 2.

images of Jesus portray him as a magician holding a magic-wand, like a common sorcerer.[156] The *Christian Scripture*, too, depicts him a magician—not as a rabbi, and least of all as *the* 'Messiah.' As noted by Professor Morton Smith:

> All these claims and stories and rites are those of a magician, not of a rabbi or a Messiah. Who ever heard of the Messiah being an exorcist, let alone being eaten?[157]

The preceding considerations permit the correct interpretation of a figure of Jesus holding a magic-wand, raising Lazarus, found in a gold-glass plate (ca. 4th century).[158] Similarly, a painting from the Roman catacombs (4th to 5th centuries) has Jesus resurrecting Lazarus with a magic-wand.[159] These pictures illustrate, quite vividly, a key passage in the "Secret Gospel of Mark" discovered by Professor Smith. It reads: "he [Jesus] stretched forth his hand and raised him, seizing his hand." The significance of the wand is compelling, once

---

[156] This explains why the rabbis used 'Balaam'—the paradigmatic 'sorcerer' of the Hebrew Scripture (see *Josh* 13:22)—as code-name for 'Jesus.' See *Sanhedrin* 106b, where a Judeo-*min* asked a rabbi if he had any idea about how old 'Balaam' was when he was executed, and he responded that he was "between thirty-two and thirty-three" years old; adding that on his tomb-stone was engraved that he was executed by *"Pineḥas Lisṭa'a"* ('Phinehas the brigand')—a code-name for 'Pilate'; cf. *Christianity in Talmud & Midrash*, p. 73, and below Section III, n. 165. The title 'brigand' has to do with the fact that he was in charge of collecting taxes; see below Section III, notes 29 and 165; the nick-name 'Phinehas' is an allusion to the fact that the name 'Pilate' came from the Latin *pilus* 'javelin,' the weapon used by the Biblical Phinehas, see *Nu* 25:7; cf. below Section III, n. 163. See also Rashi on *Abot* 5:19, s.v. *Lo*; R. Elie Benamozegh, *Em la-Miqra*, vol. 5, 171b; below, n. 162; and above, "Introduction," n. 49.

[157] *The Secret Gospel*, pp. 106-107.

[158] See Appendix #2.

[159] See *The Jesus Mysteries*, figure 9, between pp. 152-153. The high priest of pagan mysteries, too, used a wand to guide the spirits; see ibid. figure 8. The wand is the identifying symbol of the 'sorcerer' (*qosem*); see *Sifre* (*Debarim*), #171, p. 218; hence the connection between the "magic-wand" (*'eṣo, maqlo*), and "the spirit of whoredom" in *Hos* 4:12, guiding the sinners. The wand formed an integral part of sexual-magical rituals; see *Hos* 4:7-19. On the "mystical quality" of fornication, see below n. 162.

we realize that in sex-magic it represents the penis.[160] The entire text reads as follow:

> And they [Jesus and his disciples] come into Bethany. And a certain woman whose brother [Lazarus] had died was there. And, coming, she prostrated herself before Jesus and said to him, 'Son of David, have mercy on me.' But the disciples rebuked her. And Jesus, being angered, went off with her into the garden where the tomb was, and straightway a great cry was heard from the tomb. And going near Jesus rolled away the stone from the door of the tomb. And straightway, going in where the youth was, he stretched forth his hand and raised him, seizing his hand. But the youth, looking upon him, loved him and began to beseech him that he might be with him. And going out of the tomb they came into the house of the youth, for he was rich. And after six days Jesus told him what to do and in the evening the youth came to him, wearing a linen cloth over his naked body. And he remained with him that night, for Jesus taught him the mystery of the kingdom of God. And thence, arising, he returned to the other side of the Jordan.[161]

The figure in the gold-plate and in the Roman catacombs, shows that when Jesus "stretched forth his hand and raised him," he touched him with his magic-wand. Bearing in mind that in sex-magic the wand is the magical extension of the penis, the meaning of the symbolism is obvious. A similar incident, involving Jesus and a young man "wearing a linen cloth over his naked body" is mentioned in conjunction with another episode, when Jesus was about to be apprehended. His disciples fled, but he was followed by "a certain young man, having a linen cloth cast about his naked body; and the young man laid hold on him [Jesus]. And he left the linen cloth, and fled from them naked" (*Mk* 14:51-52). A naked body covered with

---

[160] Also the Greek *thyrsus*, a staff crowned with vine and leaves, commonly used in Dionysus rites, had erotic powers. For some illustrations, see *Eros in Antiquity*, photographs by A. Mulas (New York: The Erotic Art Book Society, 1978), pp. 22, 48, 92.

[161] *The Secret Gospel*, pp. 49-52. Probably, the "great cry" mentioned above is related to the "unspeakable words," etc. mentioned above, n. 60.

linen is reminiscent of the paradisiacal nudity, which "was the condition of Adam and Eve in the garden of Eden." Some regarded nudity "obligatory at their meetings." It was explained:

> Nudity was a form of revelation and truth. In some sects the preacher preached naked to a naked congregation. Such occasions usually ended with a feast followed by indiscriminate sexuality. Uninhibited sexual intercourse was regarded as an expression of spiritual freedom raising one to 'the delight of Paradise.' Fornication has a mystical quality that can transform it into a sacrament. Approached in the right spirit it can be likened to a prayer in the sight of God.[162]

Significantly, the *Christian Scripture* acknowledged that sexual rituals were commonly practiced in some Christian communities (see 1*Cor* 5:1-2; cf. 6:9, 11-19).

Magical technique played an important role in sexual rites. Referring to the writings of some Renaissance authors on this subject, a modern scholar explained:

> The use of transitive magic directed at animate beings constitutes an overlap with practical psychology; such magic is meant to control and direct other people's emotions by altering their imagination in a specific and permanent way. There is a marked tendency for such magical techniques to be centered on sexual feelings, both because they were probably recognized to be especially powerful and fundamental, and because they are in fact more closely linked with the imagination than other sensual appetites. Treatises on witchcraft came near to being a pornographic *genre*; and Bruno made a remarkable attempt to outline a technique for controlling all emotions which is explicitly

---

[162] Benjamin Walker, *Gnosticism*, p. 177. In this respect, the Law would impede a total union, as noted in *The Secret Gospel*, p. 114:

> Freedom from the law may have resulted in completion of the spiritual union by physical union. This certainly occurred in many forms of Gnostic Christianity; how early it began there is no telling.

See above n. 104 and the illuminating note in R. Elie Benamozegh, *Em la-Miqra*, vol. 4, 113b-114a. The conspicuous case reported in *Jn* 13: 23 (cf. 25) concerning a disciple "leaning on Jesus' bosom, who Jesus loved," lasting throughout the entire meal, may have involved one of these rituals.

based on sexual attraction.[163]

Astrological considerations, too, were an important factor in the ritual and performance of sex-magic:

> But then come directions for obtaining, not only celestial, 'but even intellectual and divine' benefits, and this is accomplished by using these planetary things, herbs, incense, lights, sounds, to attract good demons into statues....[164] These directions are given without a word of caution, and moreover are said to be exactly parallel to the attraction of evil demons by obscene rites.[165]

There were special words, manual gestures, and voices used in sex-magic that "derive their operative power" from the stars.[166]

There is another aspect to Jesus' ministry related to magic. From Gorgias (ca. 485-380 BCE) on, but even before him, oratory—whether in the form of poetry, spells, or rhetoric—was related to magic: in both cases, the objective was to *suspend ordinary rationality* and *charm* the audience.[167] When succeeding, the public is 'enthralled,' and 'captivated' by the 'magnetic power' of the orator/magician. Thus the intimate relation between magic and faith; in both cases, 'belief' is predicated on the suspension of common rationality. In this specific sense, Christianity and Judaism stand at two opposite poles. The main concern of the *Tora* and the rabbis is to *instruct*; the objective of Jesus and later on Christianity is to *seduce* and *enthrall* the faithful. Jesus' apostles, too, were known for the power they had to bring the mind of the faithful under control and, as it were, compel him to

---

[163] D. F. Walker, *Spiritual and Demonic Magic* (Notre Dame: University of Notre Dame, 1975), pp. 82-83.

[164] See ed. Walter Scott, *Hermetica* (Oxford: Oxford University Press, 1925), vol. 1, p. 359.

[165] *Spiritual and Demonic Magic*, p. 92. Obviously, this has to do with the concept of circular time, discussed above, Section I.

[166] See *Spiritual and Demonic Magic*, p. 150. On the use of hands; see ibid, p. 113. On 'words' and 'voices' used in sexual magic, cf. above notes 60 and 162.

[167] For a well-researched work on this subject, see Jacqueline de Romilly, *Magic and Rhetoric in Ancient Greece* (Cambridge, Mass.: Harvard University Press, 1975).

believe.[168] Consider, for example, the case of the youngster "of excellent physique, attractive appearance, and ardent spirit" that John left under the care of a bishop. Later, the youth went astray. When John discovered what happened, he was able to get a hold of the youth and bring him back to the fold. The following is a description of how John was able to accomplish this feat.

> Then he brought him back to the church, interceded for him with many prayers, shared with him the ordeal of continuous fasting, *brought his mind under the control by all the enchanting power of words*, (our italics) and did not leave him, we are told, till he had restored him to the Church.[169]

Whether or not, and to what extent, Jesus and his entourage practiced magic, is beside the point. The fact of the matter is that his ministry is predicated on the validity of magic and demonology. His authority is confirmed by the fact that demonic forces acknowledged his authority: "And unclean spirits, when they saw him [Jesus], fell down before him, and cried saying, Thou art the Son of God" (*Mk* 3:11; cf. *Lk* 4:41). The "power to heal sicknesses, and to cast out devils" (*Mk* 3:15) attests to his Messianship: "For this purpose the Son of God was manifested, that he might destroy the works of the devil" (I *Jn* 3:8). Outside the realm of the demonic and paranormal, his miracles are pointless. Therefore, a pre-requisite to acknowledging Jesus is belief in demons and demonology. Jesus offered a lucid and intellectually gripping argument on behalf of this thesis. "But if I cast out devils by the Spirit of God, then the kingdom of God is come to you"; i.e., he himself. Otherwise, you would have to admit a patently absurd hypothesis: "Or else how can one enter into a strong man's house, and spoil his goods, except he first bind the strong man? And then he will spoil his house" (*Matt* 12:28-29). Notably, when invoking his supernatural powers, Jesus used *the very same terminology* used by Egyptians sorcerers in the Scripture: "the finger of God" (*Ex* 8:15).

---

[168] See *The Secret Gospel*, p. 119.

[169] *The History of the Church*, III, 23, pp. 130-131.

On the basis of this argument, he thoughtfully concluded that his exorcism proves that "the finger of God" was acting through him. "But if I with the finger of God cast out devils, no doubt the kingdom of God," in the sense that he himself, "is come upon you" (*Lk* 11:20).[170] It has been noted that, "The early church placed its own exorcist in every community who had his own status in the lower hierarchy."[171] Modern Catholic authorities tell us that, "it was precisely with reference to Jesus' exorcism that theologians confirm their belief in his ministry."[172] That is why Christian "saints need their demons to become saints, and the demons owed their existence to the one-sidedness of the saints."[173]

The reason that the Church condemned magic is because, "the Church has her own magic" —the mass—and "there is no room for any other." The Christian liturgy, with all of its paraphernalia, is the greatest magic-act ever: "the mass, with its music, words of consecration, incense, lights, wine, and the supreme magical effect—transubstantiation."[174] To grasp the subtlety of this doctrine, one needs to distinguish between Christian magic, which is 'good,' and the magic of others, which is 'bad.' Renaissance thinkers provided clear criteria for this distinction:

> There was general agreement on the criteria for distinguishing the magics: bad magic was to do with the devil and demons; good magic was 'natural'—though one could of course argue endlessly about the application of these criteria and few people thought that all magic

---

[170] See *Demons of the Inner World*, p. 25. For a historical analysis of this subject, see the studies of F. C. Conybeare, "Demonology of the New Testament," *Jewish Quarterly Review* 8 (1896), pp. 576-608; and *idem*, "Christian Demonology," *Jewish Quarterly Review* 9 (1897), pp. 59-114.

[171] *Demons of the Inner World*, p. 26. See corresponding note, *ad loc* and the author's reference to *James* 2:19.

[172] "Christian Faith and Demonology," p. 472, and pp. 459-460.

[173] *Demons of the Inner World*, p. 41.

[174] *Spiritual and Demonic Magic*, p. 36. On the magical character of the Eucharist, see *Jesus the Magician*, pp. 122-123.

was demonic.[175]

Regrettably, the proofs confirming Jesus' ministry are not demonstrable to someone who associates the demonic with mental illness. Indeed, many of his contemporaries thought that Jesus was a "madman" (*existe*) (*Mk* 3:21, *Pocket Interlinear*, p. 96).[176] A telling expression of that madness was his paranoiac feelings: he was convinced that there were people who wanted to 'kill' him. The "earmark of the demons," wrote a renowned psychologist, is "that flicker of uncertainty over whether something is happening outside or is an inner image."[177] *Jn* 7:19-20 had preserved a revealing exchange between Jesus and a group of Jews. Fearful that they wanted to kill him, Jesus asked them: "Why do you lust to kill me." On cue they responded: "You have a demon (*Daimonion exeis*), who lusts to kill you?" Rabbinic law distinguishes between someone who suffers occasionally from a delusionary disorder, and someone not of a sound mind (*non compos mentis*) who is not legally competent.[178] To ascertain whether he had control over his mind, Jews confronted Jesus, and politely asked him whether he had "a demon" (*daimonion*), something that he denied (*Jn* 8:48-49).[179] In the next Section we will see that the reason that he was regarded as '*existe/shoṭe*' was not because they wished to disgrace him, quite the contrary. In Jewish law, a "madman" (*shoṭe*) is not legally responsible for any of his acts and cannot be prosecuted in a court of law (see below, Chapter 21). The general public was convinced that he was mad, "Now we know that you have

---

[175] *Spiritual and Demonic Magic*, pp. 54-55.

[176] See *Jesus the Magician*, pp. 47, 48. See below, Section III, n. 5.

[177] *Demons of the Inner World*, p. 2.

[178] For a comprehensive and penetrating analysis of this legal doctrine in modern rabbinic law, see Yuval Sinai, "Neṭel...," www. Netanya. Ac. Il. Com. The reason why Jesus was asked whether or not he was a 'madman,' was to establish his *legal* status. If he would have answered in the affirmative, it could have been taken as evidence that he was only occasionally insane and could stand trial. See following note.

[179] See *Shabbat* 104b. This report is presented as a matter of fact, having to do with a legal question; cf. *Jesus the Magician*, pp. 150-151 and above notes 8, 154.

a demon (*daimonion*)" (*John* 8:52; cf. *Mk* 3: 11-12)—they said to him. His mother and relatives, too, believed that he was "madman" (*exeste*; see *Mk* 3:21, *Pocket Interlinear*, p. 96. see *Mk* 3:31-32)—that is, 'legally insane.' That was the general view: "And many of them said, he has a demon (*daimonion*) and is insane" (*Jn* 10:20).

The Messiah of Israel will be the supreme communicator, so that "he shall smite the earth with the rod of his mouth, and with the breath of his lips shall he slay the wicked" (*Is* 11:4). What can be positively learned from Jesus' earthly ministry is his abysmal *failure to communicate* to his *own* people. Having forfeited any claim to be the Messiah of Israel, Christianity conceived of Messiah/Jesus as a *Übermensch* that will establish his kingdom, not by "the rod of his mouth, and with the breath of his lips," but by the might of his sword—as pagan Cosmocrator (see below, Chapter 34).[180]

20. The Perception Issue

In the *Hebrew Scripture*, Adam, and with him the rest of humanity, have not only an 'outward' but also an 'inner' self as well: "the image of God" within, accessible only to himself and His Maker. This means that in addition to his internal self, as an individual perceives himself, he has an outward existence, as others perceive him. Both aspects are interrelated, and one should nourish and develop both his inner as well as his outer self. In this respect, it would be important to bear in mind that we do not necessarily appear to others as we appear to ourselves. Concerning this point, Prophet Samuel said: "For a man looks on towards the eyes, but God looks on towards the heart" (1*Sam* 16:7). R. Joel ibn Shu'eb (15th century), explained: "A person grasps the inner [reality of another human being or a thing] via its exterior and material features. The opposite is with God."[181] In

---

[180] For further analysis, see *HS*, vol. 1, Chapter 34.
[181] R. Joel ibn Shu'eb, '*Olat Shabbat* (Venice, 5337/1577), 112d.

simple terms, it means that only God can see you as you *really* are; others will judge you according to the image you project, your actions, words, and outer *persona* in general. According to the *Hebrew Scripture*, it is an individual's responsibility to cultivate a "good name" (see *Ec* 7:1). "He who had acquired a good name," taught the rabbis, "had acquired it for himself" (*Abot* 2:7). Therefore, what the public thinks of you *does* matter. That is why a rabbinic-sage should be sensitive to the social canons and the mores of the society in which he lives. For example, "A rabbinic-sage on whose garment a stain is found deserves death," for the simple reason that he may cause the people to think ill of him, and consequently of the *Tora*, which he supposedly represents.[182] In particular, someone occupying a high a position should not dismiss what the general public thinks of him. "For it is not a good report which I hear the Lord's people murmur about you"—told Eli to his sons (1.*Sam* 2:24). Even a priest serving at the Temple should not think himself so high as to be 'above suspicion.' Consider, for example, the following rule. Priests entering the chambers at the Temple, where money was deposited, may not wear anything in which a coin may be hidden, so that the people should not suspect them of theft (Mishna *Sheqalim* 3:2). The rabbis explained the rationale of this rule:

> An individual must fulfill his obligation towards the people, just as he must fulfill his obligations towards God. As it is written: "And you shall be clear before the Lord and before Israel" (*Nu* 32:22). Furthermore, it was said: "So that you should find grace and good favor [1] in the sight of God [2] and man" (*Pr* 3:4).

Accordingly, everyone, big and small, owes "respect to the public" (*kebod ha-ṣibbur*). Out of deference to the public, the priests must pronounce their blessing *facing* the congregation, while giving their back to the Ark of the Tora (*Hekhal*).[183] The Scroll of the *Tora* may

---

[182] *Shabbat* 114a. On the moral standards incumbent on a rabbinic-sage, see *MT De'ot*, Chapter 5.

[183] *Soṭa* 40a.

not be rolled in public, because the public would have to remain inactive within the process.[184] For that reason, the rabbis legislated a series of rules concerning proper deference to the public (*kebod ha-ṣibbur*).[185] Respect cannot be *demanded* from the public or awarded by someone: it must be gained. Once a young rabbinic scholar asked his father to recommend him to his colleagues, the father refused, explaining: "Your actions will bring you closer, (or) your actions will push you further away" (Mishna *'Eduyot* 5:7). Ancestry, too, is not a factor. Hence the rabbinic principle, "A bastard rabbinic-sage," that is, someone with no family pedigree, "has precedence over a High-Priest"—representing the oldest ancestry—"that happened to be illiterate" (Mishna *Horayot* 3:8). What counts in the Hebrew mind are your actions, not *who* you are.[186]

Jesus' demeanor was *not* of a well-bred individual, let alone a rabbi. Whatever Jesus was or supposed to be, the fact of the matter is that—with the exception of publicans and prostitutes—he displayed a total disconnect with the general public. Rather than launching baseless accusations and vilifying the opposition, he should have taken care of his reputation. In case of doubts and false rumors, it was incumbent upon him to provide details and clear up the air.[187] We

---

[184] *Yoma* 70a. See Rashi ad loc. s.v. *mi-pene*.

[185] For a detailed analysis of these rules, see R. Jacob Israel Algazi, *Shalme Ṣibbur* (Salonika, 5550/1790), 1a-4a. In this regard, we should point out that trying to be holier or more punctilious in public than the standard practice is regarded as an act of "arrogance" (*yohara*); cf. *Baba Qamma* 59b, and *Shalme Ṣibbur* 4a-7c.

[186] This ruling was registered by Maimonides, *MT Talmud Tora* 3:2; and Maran Joseph Caro, *Yore De'a* CCLI, 9. It is a key concept affecting Jewish social life: status is to be *gained*, and not awarded! It directly affected the Jewish concept of 'honor' in Christian Spain, preventing the full integration of *conversos* ('newly converted Jews') and *cristianos viejos* ('old-Christians'); see *In the Shadow of History*, pp. 34-37, and cf. pp. 66-70, 111-112. The same is with Jewish integration in other societies, past and present, including those that are purely secular and atheistic.

[187] On the importance of "finding grace" in the eyes of our fellowmen, that is, to be in good relation with society, and to be sensitive on the impact it has on our own intellectual and spiritual welfare, see *Sifre Bemidbar*, #41, s.v. *vi-Ḥunneka*, pp. 44-45. Obviously, all the items mentioned in that passage are interrelated.

have noted earlier that Jesus had his entire body tattooed with magical spells, showing thus contempt for both the *Hebrew Scripture* (*Lev* 19:28) and Jewish law (Mishna *Makkot* 3:6); similarly, by eating taboo-foods, both forbidden by *Scripture* and revolting to Jews, he showed that he cared little for either. People regarded him as, "a glutton and winebibber, a friend of tax-collectors and sinners!'" (*Matt* 11:19). He was uncivil and condescending with his hosts, calling them: "Fools!" (*Lk* 11:39). He used coarse language with Pharisees and scribes, referring to them as "hypocrites" (*Mk* 7:6). When the Sadducees submitted a question to him (*Matt* 22:23), Jesus answered: "You are mistaken, not knowing the Scriptures not the power of God" (*Matt* 22:29). He was disrespectful with his own mother, and addressed her as "woman." In one occasion, when his mother noted that they were short of wine, he answered: "What is that to me and to you, woman?" (*Jn* 2:4). When his mother called him, he refused to come:

> Then his mother and brothers came. And standing outside *they* sent to him, calling him. And a crowd sat around him, and they said to him, behold, your mother and your brothers seek you outside. And he answered them, saying, who is my mother or my brothers? And having looked around *on* those sitting around him in a circle, he said: Behold my mother and my brothers. For whoever does the will of God, this one is my brother, and my sister, and my mother. (*Mk* 3:31-35, *Pocket Interlinear,* p. 86; cf. *Matt* 12:46-52).

At the end of his life, Jesus addressed his mother for last time as, "Woman, behold you son!" (*Jn* 19:26). In glaring contrast, we find him polite and considerate with publicans and prostitutes. Would you consent to have your child study under a teacher with a similar portfolio? Jews would not!

Jesus believed that he could read minds and assumed that others, too, could look directly into his inner self, and see him as he saw himself. [188] This is why he did not pay much attention to the world

---

[188] See above n. 105.

around him, and failed to assess the negative impression that he produced on others. A fact never discussed by teachers of the *Christian Scripture* is that in general, people who knew Jesus did not love him, and believed that he was a fraud. "And there was much murmuring about him [Jesus] in the crowds. Some said, he is good, but some others said no, but he deceives the crowd" (*Jn* 7:12, *Pocket Interlinear*, p. 233; see *Jn* 6:66; *Lk* 4:28-29, and below Chapter 24). Those who knew Jesus and did *not* love him were in the majority—including his disciples: "<u>many</u> of his disciples went back and walked with him no more" (*Jn* 6:66). Among the people who did not believe in Jesus *were members of his own family*. "For neither did his brethren believe in him" (*Jn* 7:5). It is important to take note that those who loved him dearly *were people that never met him*. According to Eusebius, Jesus acknowledged this fact. In a letter of Jesus to Topach Abgar, he wrote:

> Happy are you who believed in me without having seen me! For it is written of me that those who have seen me will not believe in me, and those who have not seen will believe and live.[189]

However, those, "having seen" him, perceived Jesus as,

> The son of a soldier named Panthera and a peasant woman married to a carpenter. Jesus was brought up in Nazareth as a carpenter, but left his home town and, after unknown adventures, arrived in Egypt where he became expert in magic and was tattooed in magical symbols and spells. Returning to Galilee he made himself famous by his magical feats, miracles he did by his control of demons. He thereby persuaded the masses that he was the Jewish Messiah and/or the son of a god. Although he pretended to follow Jewish customs, he formed a circle of intimate disciples whom he taught to despise the Jewish Law and to practice magic. These he bound together and to himself by ties of "love," meaning sexual promiscuity, and the participation in the most awful magical rites, including cannibalism—they had some sort of ritual meal in which they ate human flesh and drank blood. Surrounded by this circle he traveled from town to town de-

---

[189] *History of the Church* I, 13.12, p. 67. See *John* 20:29. Jesus 'disciples,' too, did not think much of him; see *Jn* 6:65, and below Chapter 25.

ceiving many and leading them into sin. But he was not always successful. The members of his own family did not believe him; when he went back to Nazareth his townspeople rejected him and he could do no miracle there. Stories of his libertine teaching and practice leaked out and began to circulate. The scribes everywhere opposed him and challenged his claims. Finally, when he went to Jerusalem the high priests had him arrested and turned him over to Pilate, charging him with the practice of magic and with sedition. Pilate had him crucified, but this did not put an end to the evil. His followers stole his body from the grave, claimed he had risen from the dead, and, as a secret society, perpetuated his practices.[190]

When the God came down to Mt Sinai, He spoke to Israel in the language of man, so that they could understand Him. Jesus, who according to Christianity eventually displaced the 'Father,' could have learned a lesson or two from the God of the '*Old* Testament' about proper speech and good manners.

Admittedly, one can shrug-off all of the above on the ground that "It is *not* so because the first-party platform has said that it is *not* so." By implication, this postulates that being a 'good Christian,' necessitates hating somebody. By sharp contrast, one can be a good Jew, without having to hate anybody, even the Christians and Muslims who had been slaughtering us for centuries. On the contrary, we Jews, hope for the day when men and women of all faith, could put their shoulders to the wheel, and help make this a better, kinder world. (See below Chapter 40)

Post-script. I personally do not believe that the improper conduct that the *Christian Scripture* ascribed to Jesus is grounded on historical facts; otherwise how can you explain the Jewish hope that Jews and Christians would be "standing shoulder to shoulder"—to welcome the Messiah (see above "Introduction")? Rather, I believe that in their efforts to 'shield' Christians with a pagan background from "Judaic infections," the editors of the *Christian Scripture* attributed to Jesus and his *authentic* disciples, cultic practices and opinions current

---

[190] *Jesus the Magician*, p. 67.

among the Gnostic communities—thus ensuring that no friendly contacts could be maintained between the Jewish and the Christian faithful.

SECTION III

JESUS' TRIAL

A PASSION PLAY

21. Jesus' Earthly Life and Death

By centering their faith around Jewish culpability, Christianity established what may be properly described as 'a religion of hatred.' Christianity flaunted her sainthood negatively, not by showing her sanctity in acts of goodness and kindness, but by imputing on Israel all kinds of sins. Beginning with the most absurd crime in legal history: the murdering of 'a god,' creator and master of everything! Without the condemnation of Judaism and hatred of Jews, Christianity loses its *raison d'être*. In the words of a serious investigator of Christian history: "*Christian anti-Judaism is not a later distortion of an original pure religion. It is embedded in the foundation documents of the faith.*"[1] [Italics in original]

The purpose of this Section is *not* to present an historical analysis of what *really* happened: whether or not Jesus was actually tried and executed (I am not convinced that he was), but to show that the story of Jesus' Trial, as it appears in the *Christian Scripture*, belongs to the realm of fiction. Specifically, that the aim of the Christian narrative is not to present an account of Jesus' Trial, based on verifiable data, but to incite hatred against Jews. Rome promoted *political* anti-Semitism; Christianity invented *religious* anti-Semitism: without hatred of Jews and Judaism, Christian 'love' has no validation.

In what follows we propose that 'the Trial of Jesus' as portrayed in the *Christian Scripture,* is in fact a passion play, not different than any of the numerous passion plays performed throughout Christendom, for the purpose of inciting hatred against Jews (see below Chapters 28-29). Acceptance of the *Gospel*'s narrative about Jesus' arrest, his Trial and Crucifixion, demands not only forfeiting common rationality on behalf of mythological thought, but also a high

---

[1] *Christian Antisemitism*, p. 168.

dose of gullibility, coupled with an equal measure of anti-Semitism.[2] It requires a certain level of mental stupor to believe that the story of Jesus, as presented in the *Christian Scripture*, is an honest report. This applies even to the most important event in Christian history: the account of Jesus' arrest and his supposed Trial. After examining the Christian account, a careful reader of the *Christian Scripture* remarked:

> The processes which led to Jesus' arrest and what went on at his trial—whether in the strict sense he had a trial at all—are matters which will remain forever hidden from the historian. The followers of Jesus, from whose testimony, presumably, the early traditions arose which led in turn to the formation of the Gospels, were, by their own confession, in hiding from the moment of Jesus' arrest, though one or two of them followed him at a sheepish distance. None of Jesus' family or followers was present while he was being interrogated, and we are not told that any of them spoke to Jesus again until he was crucified. It follows that all the Gospels must have invented the trial scenes, and that there is very little in them which could be treated historically.[3]

An unbiased reader of the Christian account of Jesus' trial would have to conclude that what we have, are

> incredible inventions to show that Christianity and its founder were really innocent in the eyes of the Roman judge: Jesus was not a deservedly condemned criminal, but the victim of a political deal.[4]

In the course of this Section we intend to show that the Christian portrayal of Jesus' trial was written for the idle mobs (*plethos, oxlous*), roaming through the streets of Alexandria and other cities in the region, looking for a pretext to vandalize a community they profoundly envied: the Jews. No one knowing anything about Jewish or Roman law could actually believe that the *Gospels'* narratives have any basis on facts. The legal proceedings against Jesus are impossible in

---

[2] See *Why I am not a Christian*, p. 203, cited below Section IV, n. 71.

[3] Wilson, *Jesus*, p. 210.

[4] Wilson, *Jesus*, p. 38.

any court of justice. Rather, as we will see in the course of this Section (Chapter 28), it was one of the numerous 'mock-trials' designed to amuse idle mobs (*plethos, oxlous*).

Let us begin with the fact that it was commonly believed that Jesus was a "madman" (*shoṭe*). Therefore, he was legally incompetent to stand trial and could not have been deemed responsible for his actions.[5] The report about Jesus' state of mind does not appear in a polemical context, but was mentioned casually as a known fact, pursuing a legal question, having nothing to do with either Jesus or Christianity.[6] The *Christian Scripture* confirms this fact. *Mk* 3:21 reports that Jesus' relatives believed that he was "mad" (*existe*). The same information is recorded in *Jn* 7:20: a "demon possessed him" (*Daimonion exeis*), a belief that was shared by many pagans.[7] Politely, Jews confronted Jesus and asked him whether he had "a demon" (*daimonion*), something that he denied (*Jn* 8:48-49). We have mentioned earlier that Jewish law distinguishes between 'sporadic incompetence' and 'consistent incompetence.' The latter applies to someone who because of retardation or some acute psychological disorder is permanently unstable. The fact that Jesus was unable to recognize that he occasionally had "a demon" (*daimonion*), convinced the Jews that he was a permanent *shoṭe*, and could not be held responsible for his actions (see *Jn* 8:52; 10:20).[8] The reason that the rabbis declared him "mad" (Heb *shoṭe*; Gr. *existe*) was to *protect* Jesus, so that the Roman authorities could not summon him. The *Christian Scripture* backs this point. When news spread that Herod sought to apprehend Jesus, the Pharisees alerted him of the impending danger. "On that very day some Pharisees came, saying to him (Jesus), 'Get out and depart from here, for Herod wants to kill you'" (*Lk* 13:31). Elsewhere, we are told that Pilate sent Jesus to be judged by Herod, but Herod refused (*Lk*

---

[5] See *Shabbat* 104b, and Section II, notes 176, 179.

[6] See Smith, *Jesus the Magician*, pp. 150-151.

[7] See *Origen: Contra Celsum*, p. 480, and Smith, *Jesus the Magician*, pp. 47, 48.

[8] See above Section II, notes 178-179.

23:6-16). The reason that he refused to try Jesus was that he would not try someone that the Jewish authorities and the general public regarded as "mad" (Heb. *shote*; Gr. *exeste*).[9]

The allegation that Jesus' claim to be a Messiah constituted blasphemy in Jewish law could make sense only to post-Jesus Christianity, believing that the Messiah is the Son of God. Then, and only then, could a bogus Messiah be charged with blasphemy, since his claim would imply that he was divine.

> Only in Christian eyes would be an unfounded claim to be the Messiah blasphemous, since only Christians regard the Messiah as divine. The accounts of the trial in Mark and Matthew therefore presuppose, and require for their intelligibility, a substantial development of Christian theology. Such a development could only have occurred outside the original Jewish environment of Christianity and would have been inconceivable at the time of the circumstances of Jesus' trial.[10]

We will see that the model for such a 'Trial' came from Alexandria, not Israel (see below Chapter 28).

In Judaism the Messiah is a man. Therefore, there are no possible grounds to charge a bogus Messiah with blasphemy. Christian scholars familiar with this subject concluded, "It is not a religious offense at all in Jewish law to claim to be the Messiah.... So far, all the claimants have proved to be mistaken, but they have not been accused of blasphemy."[11] If one were to attribute a divine dimension to Jesus' Messianic claim, then only the Roman emperor–claiming divinity—could be offended. Because,

> the Roman king and emperor becomes, ex officio so to speak, God himself. It is not that, for their deification, the emperors needed any

---

[9] See *The Case of the Nazarene*, pp. 214, 750-751, and notes 167-168. Cf. above, Section II, notes 53, 178. Josephus, *Antiquities* XIV, 168, (4), vol. 7, pp. 537-545, tells us that Herod had been summoned by the Jewish *Sanhedrin* accused of murder; see notes ibid; cf. *Sanhedrin* 19a-b.

[10] *Christian Antisemitism*, p. 106.

[11] *Christian Antisemitism*, p. 106.

divine origin or revelation or authorization by deities other than themselves: they were experts at self-deification, and for that pretentious accolade could rely on precedents going back to Julius Caesar. Practically speaking, the purpose of deification was to secure absolute submission and obedience and the popular veneration that would normally be accorded only to gods. Throughout their great law codes, emperors are referred to, or refer to themselves, as "immortals," their palaces and bedchambers are spoken of as "sacred," their acts of legislation and codification as "consecrations" by their "most sacred names." Not only offenses directed at their persons or at their rule and sovereignty, but also those against their private property, were classified as *sacrilegia*, people who spoke in derision of the emperor were dubbed "irreligious," and to slander him was decried an impiety. Yet real sacrilege, such as the slandering of the gods, was not a punishable offense: the gods be trusted to deal adequately with their own slanderers unaided. The laws enacted by the emperors were their weapons for the vindication of their own divinity. A claim by any mortal within the empire to a competitive, and a fortiori an exclusive, divine title, could not be entertained or suffered by the emperor: he was the divine ruler to the exclusion of all others.[12]

Referring to the proceedings related in the *Gospels*, it was noted:

From the point of view of Jewish law the proceedings are impossible—claiming to be the Messiah does not constitute blasphemy; a condemnation for blasphemy would have to be punished by the penalty legally prescribed (stoning), not by handing the offender over to the Romans; etc., etc. Such considerations, with historical difficulties of the sort already mentioned, leave no doubt that the stories are fictitious; their true function seems polemic—to make Jesus' death result from the Jewish authorities rejection, as blasphemous, of the formal statement of his true nature and rank.[13]

Cynically, it is on the basis of *Matt* 23: 16-22, a known Jew-hater that anti-Judaic scholars, without a shred of evidence, make the contemptible claim that, "To blaspheme the Temple of God was,

---

[12] *The Trial and Death of Jesus*, p. 176. See corresponding notes 92-96, in p. 374.

[13] *Jesus the Magician*, p. 39.

according to the Jewish Law, to blaspheme God himself."[14] Finally we must consider the fact that throughout Jewish history,

> To turn over a fellow-Jew to the authorities of a hated alien government was informing, and informing against his own was one of the worst crimes that a member of an oppressed people could commit. Even in the Middle Ages, when Jewish courts had no power to impose the death penalty upon any offender, an exception was made in countries like Spain in the case of informers. A special plea for divine punishment of informers was added shortly after the destruction of the second temple to the fundamental prayer of the synagogue, the *Amidah*.[15]

Mysteriously, the minutes of Jesus' trial disappeared; somehow, no authentic copies of any of the *Four Gospels* were preserved. The earliest known manuscripts of the *Gospels* were written at least two hundred years after Jesus' death. More seriously, the alleged authors of the *Gospels* were not present at the trial, and none of them could render an eyewitness' testimony. Their report of the trial would not stand up in a common court of justice. After a careful consideration of the material in the *Christian Scripture*, a distinguished scholar concluded, "that the accounts of the trial in the synoptic Gospels are false to history." Following with a most pertinent question: "Why do the Gospels Falsify History?" The answer is appallingly simple: Christians wished to ingratiate themselves with the Romans.[16] There is another reason: to disseminate hatred against the Jews. In this manner, the faithful can deflect his life, and say to himself: 'Yes I am evil, but not as evil as them Jews.' Let us repeat this point over and over again: without hatred of Jews, Christianity and Christian 'love' would be intolerable.

---

[14] Ernest Renan, *The Life of Jesus* (Boston: Little, Brown and Company, 1915), p. 373.

[15] Samuel Rosenblatt, "The Crucifixion of Jesus from the Standpoint of Pharisaic Law," *Journal of Biblical Literature* 75 (1956), p. 319. For references, see ibid, accompanying footnotes.

[16] *Christian Antisemitism*, p. 107.

22. *Kyrios* Jesus, Tax Collector

Jesus' trial and crucifixion may have nothing to do with religion or his Messianic aspirations. Rather, *if* it at all occurred, then it may have had to do with Jesus assuming the authority of *Kyrios* ('Lord'), with the right to forcibly dispossess the owner of a she-ass and her colt. Men challenging the central government, claiming the right to levy taxes and seize property, were a problem plaguing the ancient world. 'Sovereignty' among rulers involves the exclusive right to collect taxes. We had the opportunity to see that Jesus came from a publican family that was "close to the ruling circles" (*qarob la-malkhut*). And, furthermore, that his supporters and some of his disciples came from the same circle (see above Chapter 11). In this chapter we propose that Jesus may have been tried and executed by the Roman authorities for seizing property illegally, under the self-assumed title of *Kyrios* 'the Lord.' A close reading of the *Christian Scripture* will substantiate this view. Jesus assumed the title of, and he was regularly referred to, as *'O Kyrios'* ('the Lord'). This term has two distinct meanings. In Greek—and that was the way it was used by Greek-speaking heathens— *Kyrios* is "a legal term meaning the legitimate master of someone or something, a word which as a substantive was not used in Greek religious language." Jews, however, used it exclusively to translate "the awe-inspiring Tetragrammaton," or God, Creator of Heaven and Earth.[17]

It is not known how Jesus and his entourage supported themselves. What is known for sure is that at least in one occasion, the *Christian Scripture* reports that *Kyrios* Jesus seized somebody's property for his personal usage. What follows is the translation of *Matt* 21: 1-3, *Pocket Interlinear*, p. 52:

---

[17] Elias Bickerman, *From Ezra to the Last of the Maccabees* (New York: Schocken Books, 1962), p. 66. This semantic distinction was overlooked by Wolfson, *Philo*, vol. 1, p. 136.

And when they came near to Jerusalem and came to Bethphage, toward the Mount of Olives, then Jesus sent two disciples, saying to them, Go into the village opposite you, and immediately, you will find an ass tied, and a colt with her. Loosen (*lúsantes*) *them and lead them* to me. And if anyone says anything to you, you shall say, The Lord ('*O Kyrios*') has need of them. And he will send them at once. (See *Mk* 11:1-10)

For an adequate understanding of this passage we would have to take notice that Jesus instructed his disciples to "loosen" (*lúsantes*) the she-ass. Obviously, since the beast was tied, the disciples could not have brought it to Jesus without untying it first. What, then, was the purpose of this instruction? I propose that we are dealing with a technical term coming from Judeo-Aramaic, the language spoken by Jesus and his disciples. The term appears in the Aramaic translation of the *Tora*, *Nu* 16:15, when Moses declared that he had not seized a single donkey, even when he was performing an assignment ordered by God (cf. 1*Sam* 12:3). The rabbis explained that when God sent Moses to Egypt, Moses did not seize a donkey to discharge his mission.[18] In a similar vein, the Aramaic version of the *Tora* rendered the Hebrew, "I have not confiscated (*nasati*) a single ass from any of them," as "I have not *sheharit* a single ass from any of them."[19] The Aramaic *sheharit* for 'confiscated' is related to 'loosen' or 'detaching' a property from its legal owner and seizing it on behalf of the government. Accordingly, Jewish lexicographers associate *sheharit* with 'cutting off' (a property from the legitimate owner) and 'confiscating' it (on behalf of the government).[20] We should point out that this term

---

[18] Quoted by Rashi on *Nu* 16:15, *s.v. Lo hamor*. The basis for this interpretation is that the Hebrew verb *nasati*, and the noun *nasi* 'king' or 'prince,' implying 'sovereignty,' 'authority,' derive from the root NS'. Accordingly, the plain meaning of the verse is 'I did not exercise the authority of a *nasi* or government officer and went on to appropriate a single donkey, even when carrying on a mission in the name of God.'

[19] *Targum* Anqelos (commonly mispronounced 'Onqelos), *ad loc* and *Targum* Pseudo-Jonathan. See Samuel David Luzzato, *Oheb Ger* (Cracow, 1895), p. 123.

[20] See *Baba Batra* 47a. For further references and analysis, see R. Nathan b. Yehi'el,

is related to *shehir* "a small scissor."²¹ Marcus Jastrow (1829-1903) pointed out that *sheharit* means "to declare a thing or a man free, ownerless property, to confiscate, press into public service."²² From the Judeo-Aramaic, this term penetrated the Arabic lexicon in the form *'iskhar*.²³ The Greek "loosen" (*lúsantes*) (root *lío* 'to loosen,' 'to unbind') is a literal translation of the Aramaic *sheharit*; that is, 'to confiscate.' (It is useful to remember that the Greek version of *Matthew* was composed by an Aramaic-speaking writer). The continuation of *Matt* 21:3, "And if anyone says anything to you, you shall say, The Lord (*'O Kyrios*) has need of them"—gives the justification for confiscating the donkey: Jesus, in quality of *Kyrios* or "legitimate master," has absolute dominion over everyone's property.²⁴

Thomas Hobbes (1588-1679) cited this episode as evidence that the sovereign has the right to impose taxes over his subjects and seize their properties:

Lastly, our Saviour himselfe acknowledges, that men ought to pay

---

'Arukh, Aruch Completum, ed. Alexander Kohut. 8 vols. (Vienna and Berlin: Menora, 1926), vol. 8, *s.v.* Shehar, p. 58a.

²¹ This is the reading in *Mishna Kelim* 13:1, preserved in the texts of the Geonim, *Perush ha-Geonim 'al Tahorot*, ed. J. N. Epstein, (Berlin: Mekize Nirdamim, 1924), p. 28; and Maimonides, *Perush ha-Mishnayot*, vol. 6, p. 128. See *Beṣa* 35b and *Perush Rabbenu Ḥanan'el, Beṣa* (Jerusalem, Vashgal Publishing, 5756/1996), 73b (the exchange *r/l* is common in Hebrew and Aramaic; see, for example *Job* 38:32; *Ḥagiga* 15b, etc.). The Hebrew term *shiḥrur* for the 'emancipation' of slaves comes from the same root and has a similar connotation.

²² Marcus Jastrow, *A Dictionary...* (New York: The Judaica Press, 1992), *s.v.* Shehar IV, p. 1551.

²³ R. Se'adya Gaon used this term in his Arabic translation of *Nu* 16:15, *Sharah*, ed. J. Derenbourg, *Version Arabe du Pentateuque* (Paris: Ernest Leroux, 1893), p. 218. This is one of the many Judeo-Aramaic terms incorporated into the Arabic lexicon; see *HS*, vol. 2, p. 7. Jewish law regards self-appointed 'tax-collectors' as common brigands; see Mishna *Nedarim* 3:4; *Baba Qamma* 113a; *MT Gezela* 5:11; *'Edut* 10:4. Cf. *Tosefta Shebu'ot* 2:14, p. 448; *MT Shebu'ot* 3:1, 2; see below n. 29, and above Section II, n. 18.

²⁴ See the "delightful" interpretation of this incident, cited in Ernst H. Kantorowicz, *The King's Two Bodies* (Princeton, N.J. Princeton University Press, 1957), pp. 84-85.

such taxes as are by Kings imposed, where he sayes, *Give to Caesar that which is Caesar*, and payed such taxes himselfe. And that the Kings word, is sufficient to take anything from any Subject, when there is need; and that the King is the Judge of that need: For he himselfe, as King of the Jewes, commanded his Disciples to take the Asse, and Asses Colt to carry him into *Jerusalem*, saying *Go into the Village over against you, and you shall find a shee Asse tyed, and her Colt with her, unty them, and bring them to me. And if any man asks you, what you mean by it, Say the Lord hath need of them: And they will let them go.* They will not ask whether his necessity be a sufficient title; nor whether he be judge of that necessity; but acquiesce in the will of the Lord.[25] [Italics in original]

Probably, this was not the first time that Jesus seized property in anticipation of his soon to be established kingdom of justice and peace on earth. Among the people singing, "Blessed be he that cometh in the name of the Lord" (*Matt* 21:9, *Mk* 11:10), some must have complained to the Roman authorities that *Kyrios* Jesus, was riding a purloined she-ass. Therefore, it is quite possible that Jesus was crucified because he confiscated a she-ass from her legal owner, under the title 'the Lord' (*'O Kyrios*). A claim to the title 'the Lord' (*'O Kyrios*), with authority to dispossess property from its legal owner, constituted a formal challenge to Roman authority.

Romans were very strict with official titles. To address a government officer with the wrong title was a grievous offence punishable by death. When R. Johanan b. Zakkai addressed Titus Flavius Vespasianus (39-81) as 'O King!' before he had been formally appointed as such, he was told that he had committed a capital offense, "Because I am not a king and you addressed me as 'O King'!"[26] Concerning the illegal claim to authority under the Roman legal system, Justice Cohn observed:

> Under Roman law, a claim to be king of a province under Roman rule was tantamount to insurrection and high treason: it was, by the

---

[25] Thomas Hobbes, *Leviathan* (Penguin Classics), XX [106], p. 259.
[26] See *Giṭṭin* 56a.

Lex Julia maiestatis originally enacted by Caesar in 46 BC[E], and re-enacted by August in 8 BC[E], a capital offense known as *crimen laesae maiestatis*, the crime of causing injury to the majesty of the emperor. This injury comprised not only treason proper but also insurrections and uprisings against Roman rule, desertion from Roman forces, usurpation of power reserved to the emperor or his nominees, and all acts calculated to prejudice the security of Rome or the emperor of Rome or of Roman governments in the provinces. The definition of the offense, if indeed it can be called a 'definition,' is so wide as to include practically everything that the emperor or governor might consider harmful to the interests of Rome or of himself.[27]

Lending support to our thesis is the report that "two robbers (*lestai*) were crucified" with Jesus (*Matt* 27:38, *Pocket Interlinear*, p. 76). Rome *did not* crucify common bandits.[28] May I suggest that these outlaws, too, were guilty of collecting taxes under the banner of *Kyrios*?[29] Further evidence to this theory may be found in a curious passage in *Lk* 23:1-2, about "the whole multitude" bringing Jesus to be tried before Pilate. "And they began to accuse him (Jesus), saying, 'We found this *fellow* perverting the nation, and forbidding to pay taxes to Caesar, saying that he himself is Christ, a King (*Basiléa*).'" *Luke* merely 'upgraded' *John*'s story in two marginal details. First, instead of having Jesus being accused of seizing taxes himself—something not very classy for a Messiah, soon to be displacing God, Creator of Heaven and Earth— he is accused of inciting *not* to pay taxes to Cae-

---

[27] *The Trial and Death of Jesus*, pp. 171-172.

[28] See *The Case of the Nazarene Reopened*, p. 699 n. 260, and following note.

[29] According to *Lk* 23:40 all three were, as per *Pocket Interlinear*, p. 207: "under the same judgment"; i.e., condemned for a similar crime. The Greek term *lestés* is common in rabbinic literature, and it is associated with tax-collectors, see the quotation, above Section II, n. 18. For an overview of this term in rabbinic literature, see Daniel Sperber, *A Dictionary of Greek & Latin Legal Terms* (Ramat-Gan: Bar Ilan University Press, 1984), pp. 106-110. On the crucifixion of 'brigands' (*lista'a*) by the Roman authorities, see *Tosefta Sanhedrin* (ed. M. S. Zuckermandel, Jerusalem: Wahrman Books, 5035/1975), 9, 7, p. 429. In support of our thesis that Jesus' Trial had to do with taxes, let us remember that Pilate, as the prefect of Judea, was responsible for the collection of imperial taxes, whereas in other matters his judicial authority was limited. See below, n. 165.

sar. Obviously, *Luke*'s version is impossible in light of Jesus' doctrine to "Render unto Caesar the things which are Caesar's" (*Matt* 22: 21). The change, however, was necessary in order to veil the tax-collector aspect from Jesus' ministry. Second, instead of operating under the title 'the Lord' (*'Kyrios'*), *Luke* upgraded Jesus from 'the Lord' (*'Kyrios'*)—a term that Greek-speaking pagans would interpret as an individual whose authority derives than from a superior—to King (*Basiléa*).

Who was the "multitude" that brought Jesus before Pilate and accused him to forbid paying taxes? They could not be Jews— whether Pharisees or Sadducees. As argued by Justice Cohn,

> neither the Pharisees nor Sadducees, neither priests nor elders, neither scribes nor any Jews, had any reasonable cause to seek the death of Jesus or his removal. Without such, it will be submitted, the reports that they sought to destroy him (*Matt* 12:14; *Lk* 19:47) or that they counseled together "for to put him to death" (*Jn* 11:53; *Lk* 22:2; *Mk* 14:1) are stripped of all plausibility.[30]

If there were Jews counseling Pilate at all, as suggested by *Jn* 19:12, they must have been men 'close to the ruling circles'; i.e., publicans belonging to the same social clique as Jesus' family, wanting to pander to their Roman masters. They, rather than Pharisees and priests, would have good reason to object to '*Kyrios*'-Jesus encroaching on 'their' territory.

A marginal note. Post-Jesus Christianity, wishing to eradicate the publican aspect from Jesus biography, chose to emphasize the *Jewish* usage of '*Kyrios*'/God. Given that Jesus' Jewish followers were marginalized and eventually expelled from Christendom (see above, Chapter 17), the 'godly' aspect of the Greek '*Kyrios*' would not be easily grasped by pagan converts. Nonetheless, it was a wise decision with prodigious consequences, particularly in the realm of theology. Much, if not all of Christian spirituality, including the 'Mystery of the Holy Trinity,' is a spin-off of this choice. In the polytheistic world of

---

[30] *The Trial and Death of Jesus*, p. 38.

the Greek-speaking humanity, having *Kyrios*/God turn Messiah is not such a big deal, whereas *Kyrios*/bogus-tax-collector turned Messiah, feels more like a bad, tasteless, joke.

23. The Christian Account of Jesus' Trial

To maintain that Jesus was tried in a Jewish court, on either the Eve of Passover or on the Seder Night, as related in the *Christian Scripture*, is similar to claiming that the Supreme Court of the USA convened on the 4th of July, to try somebody for a 'crime' not justifiable by American law. An individual, we may add, regarded by the judicial authorities, the general population, and his own relatives, as mentally unfit to stand trial. At the same time, we must assume that thousands of men abandoned their barbeques and family dinner to witness such a 'trial.' The streets were not illuminated, and going in the heart of night towards the court of justice, involved climbing hills and avoiding crevices in pitch-darkness. How could the "chief priests and elders and all the council" (*Matt* 25:29; cf. *Mk* 14:53 and *Lk* 22:66), including the seventy members of the Sanhedrin, abandon their homes on the most solemn night of the Jewish calendar and gather to sit in judgment?[31] We must assume that some of the "priests and elders," were frail and old. How could they have made their way to the council, in the heart of night? And yet, we are told that "*all* the council" (our italics) was present. How were they summoned, and by whom? And what about the "Jewish crowds"? How could the people know about an event allegedly held in the spur of the moment, in secret, at midnight? Who notified them, while the streets were shrouded in darkness? As argued by Justice Cohn:

> If that is true of any ordinary night, it must be all the truer on this particular night: whether it was, as the Synoptic Gospels have it, the very night of the great feast of Passover or, as John reports, only the

---

[31] See *The Trial and Death of Jesus*, pp. 26, 116, 199, 211, 719 n. 115.

night of Passover eve, every Jewish householder was busy at home either celebrating the Seder or preparing for the feast and its sacrifices. It is inconceivable that on such a night he could be lured out into the hills to share in a police expedition.[32]

There is another point to ponder upon. Roman authorities would never have surrendered their jurisdiction to the Jewish court, particularly in a matter of state, having to do with treason and the usurpation of imperial power.

> Respecting general criminal jurisdiction, two further points must be noted. One is that no Sanhedrin could ever have exercised any jurisdiction at all save in accordance with Jewish law: it could take cognizance only of offenses known to and defined in that law and could adopt only such criminal procedures as that the law allowed. And the other is that, with the advent of Rome, there was established in Judaea a second—the Roman—criminal jurisdiction, which means that the Jewish courts could no longer monopolize it. The two points are closely interconnected, because what actually transpired was that the Jewish courts exercised exclusive criminal jurisdiction in respect of acts which were offenses only against Jewish law, and the Roman governor's court exercised exclusive criminal jurisdiction in respect of acts which were offenses only against Roman law. For example, the offense of desecrating the Sabbath, or idolatry, either an offense solely by Jewish law, would be within the exclusive jurisdiction of the Jewish courts, and the Roman governor would never claim jurisdiction over it; he could not, because Roman law did not regard either act as a criminal offense.[33]

Are we to believe that "all the people," that is, *all* Jews, attended a 'trial' that does not conform to Jewish law and Jewish procedure, and said: "His blood *be* on us and on our children" (*Matt* 27:25)? Would you have abandoned your 4th of July barbeque or your Christmas dinner to attend a similar event?

I believe that what had actually taken place with Jesus was the

---

[32] *The Trial and Death of Jesus*, p. 73.

[33] *The Trial and Death of Jesus*, p. 33.

opposite of what was reported in the *Gospels*. Pilate was a bloodthirsty ruler with no conscience; eventually the Roman authorities removed him for his excessive brutality. To claim, as the *Christian Scripture* does, that he tried to defend Jesus against the Jews, is so "improbable as to border on the ludicrous."[34] It is a well-known fact that in a moment of crisis, Jews would rally up and support another Jew, no matter the circumstances. Especially one standing trial before Rome, "the Kingdom of Evil." Listen to what Justice Cohn said:

> Moreover, the whole theory is historically and psychologically misconceived: any Jew who had to stand trial before the Roman governor, irrespective of who he was and what the charge, would automatically have elicited the sympathy of the people, and nobody would have turned against him in any way; and the poorer his prospects of acquittal and the graver the peril of his death, the greater and stronger would that sympathy be. And if the man standing trial was a popular figure, beloved by the masses, the fact alone of his being arraigned by the Roman governor would make him a holy martyr in the eyes of the people, and all the hatred that they could muster would be centered on the odious alien.[35]

With this background in mind, the most likely scenario is one in which the Jewish authorities came to Pilate to intercede on behalf of a fellow Jew, Jesus. They must have claimed that he was a "madman" (*shoṭe*), and therefore not legally responsible for his actions.[36] In fact, this was the defense offered by his relatives (see *Mk* 3:21). The Jewish authorities failed in their mission. In gratitude for their efforts, Christianity exonerated the Romans and condemned the Jews. A distinguished Christian scholar noted that Pilate's handling of the case, particularly as registered in *Luke*, makes it patently clear that what we have is nothing less than an apology to the officials of the Roman Empire on behalf of the Christian Church.[37]

---

[34] *Christian Antisemitism*, p. 107.

[35] *The Trial and Death of Jesus*, p. 159.

[36] See above notes 7-9.

[37] See Paul W. Walaskay, '... *And so we came to Rome*', p. 40.

24. Consuming Jesus Flesh and Drinking his Blood

There is an epic moment in Jesus' ministry. It took place in a Synagogue at Capernaum, by the Sea of Galilee, where Jesus delivered a foundational doctrine. It runs as follows:

> Then Jesus said to them, "Most assuredly, I say to you, unless you eat the flesh of the son of man, and drink his blood, you have no life in you. Whoever eats my flesh, and drinks my blood, has eternal life, and I will raise him up at the last day. For my flesh is meat indeed, and my blood is drink indeed. He who eats my flesh and drinks my blood abides in me, and I in him. As the living Father sent me, and I live because of the Father, so he who eats me, even he shall live because of me. This is that bread which came down from heaven—not as your fathers ate the manna, and are dead. He that eats this bread will live forever. (*Jn* 6:53-58; cf. *Matt* 26:26-29; *Mk* 14:22-24; 1*Cor* 11:24-34).

The consumption of human flesh was not alien to pagan humanity.[38] To save his son Dionysus, Zeus, turned him into a goat. A central rite in the worshiping of Dionysus was tearing a live goat into pieces, and eating it raw. As Sir James Frazer (1854-1941) put it, "they must have believed that they were eating the body and blood of

---

[38] See Herodotus, *Histories*, I, 73 (Penguin Classics), p. 41, where to take revenge from King Cyaxares of Media for having insulted them, the Scythians "decided to kill one of their young pupils, chop him, dress the pieces in the ordinary way like meat, serve them to Cyaxares as a dish of game." Similarly, in *Histories* I, 119-120 (Penguin Classics), p. 63, we are told about King Astyages of Media that to punish one of his subjects, had his son, "butchered, cut up into joints and cooked, roasting some, boiling the rest," and then had him served to the father for dinner. For some interesting notes, see François Hartog, "Self-cooking Beef and the Drinks of Ares," in Marcel Detienne and Jean-Pierre Vernant eds., *The Cuisine of Sacrifice among the Greeks* (Chicago: Chicago University Press, 1989), p. 179; and Marcel Detienne and Jean-Pierre Vernant *Myth and Tragedy* (New York: Zone Books, 1990), p. 447. See also, *The Golden Bough, Spirits of the Corn and of the Wild,* vol. 1, pp. 240, 244, 251. The Aztecs in Mexico had cannibalistic banquets; see Sir James George Frazer, *The Golden Bough, The Scapegoat* (London: Macmillan and Co., 1919), p. 279 n. 1.

the god."³⁹ In Europe, "witches preserved an archaic tradition in which human sacrifice and more or less symbolic cannibalism" was practiced.⁴⁰ Cannibalism, wrote Eliade, "is cultural behavior, based on a religious vision of life."⁴¹ In psychoanalysis, "The cannibalistic act thus becomes comprehensible as an attempt to assure one's identification with the father by incorporating a part of him."⁴²

Drinking human blood, too, was an important feature of pagan religion. It had magical power, and was required for rituals connected with the power of divination. The spirit of Teiresias begged Homer to move away from the pit and let him drink the blood: "Move from the pit and pull away your sword, so I may drink the blood and speak the truth."⁴³ Drinking blood was "good for summoning demons."⁴⁴ It has been noted that, "Greek figured vases show no repugnance at representing human blood spurting from a slit throat [of a human being] to water the god's altar in a horrible sacrifice."⁴⁵ Sacrificial blood was associated with catharsis and spirituality. Linguistically, the term 'blessing' stems from the word 'blood' of the sacrifice sprinkled

---

³⁹ *The Golden Bough, Spirits of the Corn and of the Wild*, vol. 1, p. 18. See Marcel Detienne, *The Garden of Adonis* (Princeton, N.J.: Princeton University Press, 1994), p. 112.

⁴⁰ Mircea Eliade, "Mystery and Spiritual Regeneration," in ed. Joseph Campbell, *Man and Transformation* (Princeton, N. J.: Princeton University Press, 1972), p. 27. See ibid, p. 11.

⁴¹*The Sacred & the Profane*, p. 103. See ibid, pp. 100-102

⁴² Sigmund Freud, *Moses and Monotheism* (New York: Vintage Book, 1955), p. 103.

⁴³ Homer, *Odyssey* II. 96. See Ken Dowden, *European Paganism* (London: Rutledge, 2000), p. 169. Cf. Martin P. Nilsson, *A History of Greek Religion* (New York: W.W. Norton & Company, 1964), p. 141. *Ez* 33:25-26, registered the pagan ritual involving the consumption of blood and "standing on the sword"; see the learned note by R. Elie Benamozegh, *Em la-Miqra*, vol. 3, 46b.

⁴⁴ *European Paganism*, p. 314, n. 10.

⁴⁵ Jean-Louis Durand, "Greek Animals," in Marcel Detienne and Jean-Pierre Vernant eds., *The Cuisine of Sacrifice among the Greeks* (Chicago: Chicago University Press, 1989), p. 91. Cf. ibid, figure #7, between pp. 105-118. Cf. Eric Fromm, *The Anatomy of Human Destructiveness* (New York: Holt, Rinehart and Winston, 1973), pp. 268-269.

on a person.⁴⁶ Far from being thought of as something nauseating and foul, blood was actually savored as a delicacy.

> Some are literally blood-thirsty. The Scordisci...supposedly drank blood from skulls, and Celts and others certainly used skulls as drinking cups. In a Norse temple you drank [the blood] as you feasted on the meat.⁴⁷

The notion that drinking blood brings about communion between the participating parties is old and widespread.

> To drink blood together, or to drink blood drawn from the arm of another person and to offer him one's own in the same manner, are sacred rites of alliance. These rites are very ancient, and are to be found among other races as well as among the Tartars; their object is to establish artificially what we may still call 'blood-brotherhood.'⁴⁸

The third day of the ritual of Attis was known as the Day of Blood. In that day,

> the Archigallus or high-priest drew blood from his arms and presented it as an offering. Nor was he alone in making this bloody sacrifice. Stirred by the wild and barbaric music of clashing cymbals, rumbling drums, droning horns, and screaming flutes, the inferior clergy whirled about in the dance with waggling excitement and insensible to pain, they gashed their bodies with potsherds or slashed them with knives in order to bespatter the altar and the sacred tree with their

---

⁴⁶ See *European Paganism*, pp. 168, 175.

⁴⁷ *European Paganism*, p. 168. Drinking from skulls was practiced by some Amerindians; see *The Golden Bough, Spirits of the Corn and of the Wild*, vol. 2, p. 150. It was also practiced by the Luritcha tribe in Australia, see ibid., p. 260. Eliade, *Yoga*, p. 298, cites someone boasting, "My necklace and ornaments are of human bones; I dwell among the ashes of the dead and eat my food in human skulls." Cf. ibid, p. 300, and *Shamanism*, p. 434 n. 29. For further references, see idem, *A History of Religious Ideas*, vol. 2 (Chicago: Chicago University Press, 1984), pp. 138-139.

⁴⁸ Solomon Reinach, *Orpheus* (New York: Horace Liveright, 1930), p. 163. Eating the flesh and/or drinking the blood of the victim can turn even a foe into a blood brother; see *The Golden Bough, Spirits of the Corn and of the Wild*, vol. 2, pp. 154-156. In 16th century Spain we find "the Brotherhood of the Blood of Jesus"; see William A. Christian, Jr. *Local Religion in Sixteenth Century Spain* (Princeton, N.J.: 1989), p. 151; cf. ibid, pp.187-189.

flowing blood.[49]

Finally, we would like to call attention to a magical text from the time of Paul,

> in which Osiris gives to Isis and Horus his blood to drink in a cup of wine, so that after his death they will not forget him, but must search for him with longing and lamentation, until, brought to life, he is reunited with them.[50]

Communion with Jesus, too, involved the consumption of human flesh and blood. "He who eats my flesh and drinks my blood," taught Jesus, "abides in me, and I in him"; and: "so he that eateth me, even he shall live by me" (*Jn* 6:56-57). It is on the basis of this creed that Jesus and his disciples attained a most perfect communion. In this fashion, it was explained, his disciples "have seen Jesus in his true glory, [and] have eaten his flesh and drunk his blood."[51] Therefore, as Jesus taught his disciples, "He that heareth you heareth me; and he that despiseth you, despiseth me; and he that despiseth me despiseth him that sent me" (*Lk* 10:16). Accordingly, a disciple of Jesus would have the "power to tread on serpents and scorpions, and over all the power of the enemy: and nothing shall by any means hurt you" (*Lk* 10:19; cf. 17:21). That is why, "the least of those who is now in the kingdom," i.e., that ate Jesus' flesh and drunk his blood, "is greater than he" (*Lk* 7:28), John the Baptist.[52]

Therefore, we should not be surprised to discover that the Eucharist is much more than an abstract symbolism. The *Catechism of the*

---

[49] Sir James George Frazer, *The Golden Bough, Adonis, Attis, Osiris,* 2 vols. (London: Macmillan and Co., 1919), vol. 1, p. 368. Cf. 1*K* 18:28

[50] Richard Reizenstein, *Hellenistic Mystery-Religions* (Pittsburgh, Pa.: The Pickwick Press, 1978), pp. 77-78. From the corresponding note 112, pp. 105-106 we learn that drinking the blood would "cause her to feel a love for him in her heart, the love that Isis felt for Osiris..." Cf. *The Anatomy of Human Destructiveness*, p. 179 n. 42.

[51] *The Secret Gospel*, p. 95. Cf. Morton Smith, *Studies in the Cult of Y...*, 2 vols., ed. Shaye J. D. Cohen (Leiden: E. J. Brill, 1996), vol. 2, pp. 101-102.

[52] See *The Secret Gospel*, p. 95; cf. ibid. pp. 102, 107.

Catholic Church, promulgated by Pope John Paul II (1920-2005), teaches that Jesus is *actually* present—not merely symbolically— in the Eucharist.

> The mode of Christ's presence under the Eucharistic species is unique. It raises the Eucharist above all sacraments as "the perfection of the spiritual life and the end to which all sacraments end." In the most blessed sacrament of the Eucharist "the body and blood, together with the soul and divinity, of our Lord Jesus Christ and, therefore, *the whole Christ is truly, really, and substantially* (italics in original) contained."[53] This presence is called 'real'—by which is not intended to exclude the other types of presence as if they could not be 'real' too, but because it is the presence in the fullest sense: that is to say, it is a *substantial* (italics in original) presence by which Christ, God and man, makes himself wholly and entirely present.[54]

It is "by the conversion of the bread and wine into Christ's body and blood that Christ becomes present in the sacrament."[55] The miracle of transubstantiation, whereby the bread and wine consecrated in the Mass are actually—not symbolically—transformed into the

---

[53] The association of wine with blood is natural, especially around the Mediterranean Sea where red wine predominates. Drinking wine became sacred, thanks to a complex ritual whereby the blood of the sacrifice was transferred to the wine (as per the Eucharist); see Walter Burkert, *Homo Necans* (Berkeley: University of California Press, 1983), p. 224, and corresponding notes 38-39. The close relationship between blood and wine is best illustrated in a story from Ancient Greece, from the 3rd century BCE, about a man who "killed the daughter of the king and, having mixed her blood with wine in a mixing bowl, offered to the king to drink on his arrival;" ibid, p. 246. Eliade, *A History of Religious Ideas,* vol. 2, p. 323 cites a text telling how from the dying body of the Mythriaic bull, "its blood [generated] the wine, which produces the sacred drink of the mysteries."

[54] *Catechism of the Catholic Church*, promulgated by Pope John Paul II (Cittá del Vaticano: Libreria Editrice Vaticana, 1994), #1374, p. 340. The quotations correspond, respectively, to *Council of Trent* (1551) DS (=Denzinger-Schonmetzer, *Enchiridion*...) 1651; and Paul VI, MF (=*Mysterium fidei*) 39. For an in-depth interpretation of this mystery, see Pope John Paul, "On the Mystery and Worship of the Eucharist," in *Vatican Council* II, ed. Austin Flannery, O.P. (Collegeville, MN: The Liturgical Press, 1982), pp. 64-92.

[55] *Catechism of the Catholic Church*, #1374, p. 346; cf. ibid. #1375, p. 346. See, *Gnosticism*, pp. 103-104.

flesh and blood of the Christian Savior, is the greatest of all miracles.

> By the consecration of the bread and wine there takes place a change of the whole substance of the bread into the substance of the body of Christ…and the whole substance of the wine into the substance of his blood. The change the holy Catholic Church has fittingly and properly called transubstantiation.[56]

John taught this foundational doctrine in Jesus' name: "Labor not for the meat which perisheth, but for that meat which endureth unto everlasting life" (*Lk* 6:27). In Jesus' own words: "I am the bread of life" (*Lk* 6:35; 48, etc.). In this manner the faithful can integrate cannibalistically with the deity. As Freud explained,

> By absorbing parts of the body of a person through the act of eating we also come to possess the properties which belong to that person.[57]

The cannibalistic consumption of Jesus flesh and blood permits the faithful to overpower Death and the Devil Himself. Paul explained this foundational doctrine, with his unusual grace and sophistication:

> Since then, the children have partaken of flesh and blood, in like manner he himself [=Jesus] also shared the same things [=flesh and blood], that through death he [=Jesus] might cause to cease the *one* having the power (*kratos*) of death, that is, the Devil (*Heb* 2:15, *Pocket Interlinear*, p. 506).[58]

---

[56] *Catechism of the Catholic Church*, #1376, p. 347. The rabbis were familiar with the Eucharist and the "miracle of transubstantiation." See Appendix 3.

[57] Sigmund Freud, *Totem and Taboo* (New York: Vintage Books, 1946), p. 107. See *The Golden Bough, The Scapegoat*, vol. 1, pp. 20-21.

[58] The term *kratos* ('power') that Paul applied to the 'Devil/Angel of Death,' has several meanings. It has the sense of 'superiority,' "whether in battle or in the assembly." In the form *krateros*, it "means 'without equal,' especially in combat." However, in other forms, it could stand for 'hard,' 'cruel,' and 'violent.' It is also connected to the Indo-European-Iranian *kratu-* "which designate the (magical) power of the warrior." See Émile Benveniste, *Indo-European Languages and Society* (Coral Gables, Florida: University of Miami Press, 1973), p. 357. For a full analysis of the term *kratos*, see ibid, pp. 357-367.

This can help us understand how the cannibalistic consumption of Jesus flesh and blood would defeat the dual aspects of 'Devil/Angel of Death' found in Satan. It also fully explains how 'faith,' as manifested by those participating in the Eucharist, renders the *Hebrew Scripture* useless. In what follows we will see that those failing to grasp the subtleties of Christian salvation, could not possibly understand what 'deliverance through Jesus' means.

The *Christian Scripture* relates that after hearing Jesus' foundational doctrine, about consuming his flesh and drinking his blood, many of his disciples were shocked. "Then many of his disciples having heard, *they* said, 'This word is hard, who is able to hear it'" (*Jn* 6:60, *Pocket Interlinear*, p. 231). The expression 'to hear,' as per the Hebrew *shema'* and Aramaic *qabbel*, stands for 'accepting,' and not merely 'hearing.' Surprised at their reaction, Jesus asked them, "Does this offend you?" (*Jn* 6:61). For reasons that we will soon discover, they were dissatisfied with Jesus' explanation, "From that *time* many of his disciples went back, and walked no more with him" (*Jn* 6:65). Apologetically, the *Christian Scripture* discounted the students' question, "For Jesus knew from the beginning who they were who did not believe, and who would betray him" (*Jn* 6:64). Only twelve disciples did not abandon Jesus. Turning to them, Jesus asked: "Will ye also go away?" (*Jn* 6:68). Whatever offended the other disciples, did not trouble them. How come? This episode requires an intelligent interpretation.

The Jewish disciples abandoned Jesus. The remaining disciples were either pagans or came from a pagan background. We have previously noticed that Jesus was insensitive to Jewish dietary laws.[59] To a Jew, the consumption of blood is an abomination. In the *Hebrew Scripture*,

> The blood must be poured into the ground and not eaten under any circumstances. The taboo against blood has to do with the sanctity of life; and the sparing of blood must be connected to the continuity of

---

[59] See above Chapter 11.

the soul after death.[60]

In the Jewish mind, the consumption of human flesh and blood is not only a 'prohibition': it is an abomination.

> But one of the strongest traits of Israelite tradition is the tabu against blood; blood in food was strictly forbidden (*Gn* 9:4, and often). That the blood of the sacrifice of the covenant should be drunk (!) is by traditional Jewish standards an atrocity that can have been conceived only by a circle bent on demonstrating its freedom from the Law.... "This is my body; this is my blood," suggest that some of Jesus' earliest followers went even further than he did in rejection of the Law— or, at least, that they adapted his magical rite of union so as to make it also a ritual expression of his libertine teaching.[61]

The doctrine, "He who eats my flesh and drinks my blood abides in me, and I in him," is a mockery of everything sacred in Judaism: from God and Sinai to Abraham and Moses and every Jewish mother and father that ever lived.

The preceding may explain an episode recorded in *Lk* 4:28-29: "And all they in the synagogue, when they heard these things, were filled with wrath. And they rose up, and thrust him [Jesus] out of the city, and led him unto the brow of the hill, whereon their city was built, that they might cast him down headlong." I propose that Jesus was preaching his doctrine about eating human "flesh" and "drinking" human "blood." This explains why many people, and not only his disciples, believed that he was a fraud, "And there was much murmuring about him [Jesus] in the crowds. Some said, he is good, but some others said no, but he deceives the crowd" (*Jn* 7:12, *Pocket Interlinear,* p. 233). Those who knew Jesus and did *not* love him were in the majority.[62] Including his disciples: "many of his disciples went back and walked with him no more" (*Jn* 6:66). Among the people

---

[60] Cyrus H. Gordon, *The Common Background of Greek and Hebrew Civilizations* (New York: W. W. Norton, 1965), p. 274.

[61] *Jesus the Magician*, p. 123.

[62] Cf. the quotation from Eusebius in Section II at n. 189.

that were repelled by his teaching and did not believe in Jesus *were members of his own family*. "For neither did his brethren believe in him" (*Jn* 7:5).

In short, the *Christian Scripture* reports that according to Jesus, eating his flesh and drinking his blood will ensure the faithful to enter the "kingdom" down here on earth, because "They have seen Jesus in his true glory, [and] have eaten his flesh and drunk his blood."[63] However, to a Jew, the proposal, "He who eats my flesh and drinks my blood abides in me, and I in him," is an abomination. We must point out that this sort of ritual was associated with erotic magic, helping achieve a more effective communion between the participants.

> Finally, he [Jesus] added another rite, derived from ancient erotic magic, by which his followers were enabled, they believe, to eat his body and drink his blood and be joined with him, not only because possessed by his spirit, but also in physical union.[64]

In confirmation of this thesis, one may cite 1*Jn* 3:9, *Pocket Interlinear*, p. 552: "Everyone having been begotten of God does not sin, because His seed (*spérma*) abides in him, and he is not able to sin, because he has been born of God."[65]

---

[63] *The Secret Gospel*, p. 95. Cf. *Studies in the Cult of Y...*, vol. 2, pp. 101-102.

[64] *The Secret Gospel*, p. 140. It is worth quoting the following passage ibid, p. 141:
> Jesus' libertine message and practice were carried to both Jews and gentiles outside Palestine by the original disciples, after they were driven out of Jerusalem, and also by later converts, some of whom had received the full initiation or believed themselves to have had equivalent experiences. Among these latter was Paul.

[65] See *Occultism, Witchcraft, and Cultural Fashions*, pp. 111-112. Of course, in Greek this term means also 'seed' in its botanical sense. On the double sense of this term in the cult of Adonis, see *The Garden of Adonis*, pp. 116, 118, 127. Concerning Paul's opposition to the libertine practices of some of Jesus' followers, Professor Smith, *The Secret Gospel*, p. 130, wrote:
> Paul complains that his name and his sayings are being misused by the libertines. He does not complain of misunderstanding, but of deliberate misrepresentation, and he does not write as if the persons concerned were his former disciples. But if the misrepresentation was deliberate it was pre-

The story of Jesus added nothing new to pagan spirituality. Simply, it comes to confirm its basic tenets and beliefs, including the resurrection of the gods, common throughout the heathen world.[66] Anybody that studied the subject will concur that both in spirit and detail, Jesus' Passion is quite similar to the story of Mythras.

> The story of the Savior was itself, in many particulars, adapted to a pattern. Many gods of the ancient world had been the offspring of Immaculate Conceptions, had had a childhood of danger, and had undertaken a mission which culminated in sacrifice for their people. They had died and risen again (in some cases as a cultivation rite related to the rebirth of the year) and promised their followers salvation through their blood. The most obvious contemporary parallel [to Christianity] was Mithras, from whose story most of the blood symbolism of early Christianity was derived—washed in the blood of the Lamb, and so on. There is practically no blood in the histories of the evangelists. The Mithraic cult also included the 'Eating of the God,' and the belief in a second coming.[67]

The blood of Jesus must be drunk for the very reason that the sacrificial blood is drunk in the mystery ceremonies of Mithraic initiation.[68]

---

sumably in the interest of some already existing position. And now we know from whom that position derived: a figure earlier and even more influential than Paul, and a figure notorious for his libertine teaching and practice. He broke the Sabbath, he neglected the purity rules, he refused to fast, made friends with publicans and sinners, and was known as "a gluttonous man and a winebibber." He not only taught his disciples that the law had come to an end with the Baptist, but he also administered baptism of his own—"the mystery of the kingdom of God"—by which he enabled some disciples, *united with himself* (our italics), to enter the kingdom and to enjoy his own freedom from the law.

Cf. ibid, p. 131.

[66] See *The Golden Bough, Spirits of the Corn and of the Wild*, vol. 1, pp. 12-14.

[67] Pennethorne Hughes, *Witchcraft* (Pelican Book), p. 48. Evidence that the cult of Mithra was practiced by pagans in the Holy Land, is the fact that the *Mishna 'Aboda Zara* II, 3 alludes to it; see W.A.L. Elmslie, *The Mishna on Idolatry 'Aboda Zara* (Cambridge: Cambridge University Press, 1911), p. 31.

[68] See *Shamanism*, p. 121. Cf. "Mystery and Spiritual Regeneration," p. 5.

The mere fact that the Christian apologists vigorously denounced them as diabolical imitation of the Eucharist testifies to their sacred character. As for initiatory baptism, it was also practiced by other cults. But for the Christian theologians of the second and third centuries, the similarity with Mithranism here is even more disquieting, for the sign marked on the forehead with a hot iron reminded them of the *signatio*, the rite that completed the sacrament of baptism; in addition, from the second century on, the two religions celebrated the nativity of their God on the same day (December 25) and shared the similar beliefs concerning the end of the world, the Last judgment, and the resurrection of the bodies.[69]

The only 'new and bold idea' provided by Christianity is unqualified hatred of Jews and Judaism as a pre-condition to Salvation. Every time that the faithful eats the Eucharist, he confirms that Jews committed the most heinous crime ever: the murder of their Savior. The Gnostics, who were best acquainted with the ins and outs of paganism, understood quite well the Christian message. Rather than offering salvation to humanity, "Christ came to destroy the God of the Jews."[70]

I would like to conclude with a question. In view of the repulsion about the consumption of human blood and flesh, universal among Jews, Jewish revulsion to a salvation acquired by 'eating and drinking' the flesh and blood of Jesus is quite understandable. What I find puzzling is Jesus' reply: "Does this offend you?" (*Jn* 6:61).[71] Are we talking about alternative worlds?[72]

25. The Remaining Twelve

---

[69] *A History of Religious Ideas*, vol. 2, p. 328.

[70] Hans Jonas, *The Gnostic Religion* (Boston: Beacon Press, 1963), p. 132.

[71] See Hyam Maccoby, *Judas Iscariot and the Myth of Jewish Evil* (New York: The Free Press, 1992), p. 68.

[72] Cf. below n. 141.

Only twelve (eleven?) disciples remained faithful to Jesus (see *Jn* 6:67). One thing is known about them for sure: they were not repelled by the consumption of human flesh and blood. Therefore, we can positively ascertain that *they were not Jewish*. This explains the fact that they did not know Hebrew.

[1] According to *Mk* 14:61, the High Priest asked Jesus: "Are you the Christ, the Son of the Blessed?" Someone ignorant of Hebrew invented this formula. In Hebrew, "blessed" (*barukh*) *does* not refer specifically to God, but to *any* object upon which a blessing was pronounced, including a morsel of bread. Thus, after pronouncing the blessing on the bread, the host would invite the guest to partake in the meal, with the formula, "Take (the) *barukh*"; i.e., a morsel of bread.[73]

[2] Jesus was referred to as "the son of man" (*Matt* 26: 2, 4, 24, 64; *Mk* 9:12, 31; 14:21, 41; *Lk* 21: 36; 22:22, 48, 69; etc), as if it meant some sort of supernatural being. Actually, in Hebrew it means a 'human being' and nothing more.[74]

[3] While at the cross, "Jesus cried out with a loud voice, saying: 'Eli, Eli, lama sabachthani?' That is, 'My God, My God, why have you forsaken me?' Some of those who stood there, when they heard *that*, said, 'This man is calling for Elijah'" (*Matt* 27:46-47). The Hebrew "sabachthani" (=זבחתני) does not mean "forsaken," but "slaughtered," and is a corruption of *Ps* 22:1[2]. Those 'reporting' the incident must have been pagans, who knew not a word of Hebrew, and were unable to distinguish between the phonetic-sound *'azabtani*

---

[73] *Berakhot* 40a; cf. Rashi, *ad loc*. See *The Case of the Nazarene Reopened*, pp. 120-121, 123, 720, n. 126.

[74] See *The Case of the Nazarene Reopened*, pp. 369-370, 480-481. Concerning the passage in *Dan* 7:13, see ibid. pp. 497-499. It is worth noting that in *Mk* 3:28 "sons of men" stands for a common human being. For a lively discussion of this expression, see Joseph Halévy, *Études Evangeliques,* Premier Fascicule, (Paris: Ernest Leroux, 1903), pp. 97-115, 195-210.

(עזבתני) and the phonetic-sound *sabachthani* (זבחתני).[75]

[4] Those who thought that when Jesus cried "Eli," meant Prophet Elijah, too, were pagans. No Jew would have confused 'Eli/God' with 'Eli/Eliahu-Elijah.'[76]

[5] Jews, even when illiterate, don't misquote the *Scripture*, but Jesus did. When the Sadducees submitted a question to Jesus (*Matt* 22:23), he replied: "You are mistaken, not knowing the Scriptures, nor knowing the power of God" (*Matt* 22:29).

As we will see, Jesus himself, as reported by his disciples, did not know the *Scripture*.

[1] *Lk* 23:46 quotes Jesus saying, "into your hands I commit my spirit." Obviously, this is a reference to *Ps* 31:6. However, in the original it says "your hand" in the singular, not "hands" in the plural.[77]

[2] The same holds true with the quotation from *Zech* 13:7 (*Matt* 26:31; *Mk* 24:27); it is in the past, not in the future tense.[78]

[3] *Matt* 27:9-10 quoted "Jeremiah the prophet saying, 'And they took the thirty pieces of silver, the value of him who was priced, and gave them for the potter's field, as the Lord directed me.'" No such verse is to be found in *Jeremiah*. Some claim that he meant to say '*Zechariah*' (11:12-13). However, that passage does not correspond to the above

---

[75] "The Jewish Christians...," (Heb.), p. 194. It is possible that the original text was '*azabtani*, "forsaken me," as per the *Hebrew Scripture*, and was changed to *zebachtani*, because the whole idea of God "forsaken" Jesus contradicts the Christian Trinity; see R. Saul Levi Mortera, *Preguntas*, (in *Obstaculos y Oposiciones*, Ms. EH 48 D 38, Hebrew University, Jerusalem), #66, 125a-b.

[76] See *The Case of the Nazarene Reopened*, pp. 505-508; cf. ibid, pp. 71, 676-677 n. 82, 701 n. 275.

[77] See *The Case of the Nazarene Reopened*, pp. 508-509.

[78] See *The Case of the Nazarene Reopened*, pp. 489-493.

quotation.[79]

[4] In *Matt* 26:24 and *Mk* 4:21 we read that Jesus, "The son of man goeth as it is written of him." Invariably, the expression "as it is written" refers to the *Hebrew Scripture*. Yet, no such a verse exists.[80]

[5] The same is with *Matt* 26:54, etc, etc.[81]

His disciples were Jewishly clueless.

[1] *Matt* 26:17 reports that on "the first *day* of the *feast of* unleavened bread the disciples came to Jesus, saying unto him, Where wilt thou that we prepare for thee the Passover?" Similarly, we read in *Mk* 14:12: "on the first day of the Unleavened Bread, when they killed the Passover *lamb*." Even a totally boorish Jew knows that the Passover sacrifice *is not* offered on the first day of the Unleavened Bread (=ḥag ha-maṣṣot), but a *day earlier*, on the Passover Festival (=ḥag ha-pesaḥ). Furthermore, the sacrifice is not 'killed' as per pagan ritual, but 'slaughtered.'

[2] *Mk* 14:22 reports that "as they were eating" the Paschal meal, "Jesus took bread, and broke *it*, and gave *it* to the disciples, and said, 'Take, eat; this is my body'" (Cf. *Matt* 26:26). Even the most ignorant Jew knows that blessing on the bread is pronounced at the *beginning*, and not in the *middle* of the meal (cf. *Lk* 9:16). By the way, in the Passover night, Jesus could not have taken a *loaf* (of *bread*, Gr. *hárton*), but a *maṣṣa* (Gr. *axímon*; cf. *Matt* 26:17); i.e., *unleavened* bread.

[3] According to *Matt* 28:1, the Crucifixion took place on a Friday (cf. 23:54, 56). "Now when evening had come" (*Matt* 27:57) a faithful

---

[79] See *The Case of the Nazarene Reopened*, pp. 505-508; cf. 71, 701 n. 275.

[80] See *The Case of the Nazarene Reopened*, pp. 482-486.

[81] See *The Case of the Nazarene Reopened*, pp. 487-488; cf. 482-485.

disciple of Jesus, Joseph of Arimathea came to remove Jesus' body, and took him to the tomb that he "had hewn out of the rock" for himself (*Matt* 27:57-60). The tomb is located in the outskirts of Jerusalem, modern Talpiot.[82] Obviously, once the "evening had come" the Sabbath begins and it would be strictly prohibited to transport Jesus' body.[83] Only a pagan, ignorant of the fact that the Jewish Sabbath begins in the evening, could have concocted such an absurdity.

[4] *Matt* 27:33 (see *Mk* 15:22) states that Jesus was crucified in a "Place of a Skull" (*Golgotha*).[84] At the same time we read about, "the chief priests also" that were "mocking with the scribes and elders" (*Matt* 27:42; *Mk* 15:31, *Jn* 19:17). A priest is categorically forbidden to come even to a place where a human skull or bones were lost![85] The prohibition is particularly severe in the case of the High Priest who must officiate daily at the Temple. While an Israelite is not required to be in a state of levitical-purity on a regular day, he must remain in a state of levitical-purity during the holidays since he has to visit the Temple. Only a pagan, with no idea of the laws of purity governing Israel, could have fabricated this sort of idiocy.

[5] No Jew at the time of Jesus would have thought that the Jewish High Priest was appointed annually. Yet, in *Jn* 18:13, as accurately translated in *Pocket Interlinear*, p. 265, we read: "And they led him (Jesus) away first to Annas, for he was *the* father-in-law of Caiaphas, who was *the* High Priest of that year."[86]

Jesus had no disciples. A careful reading of the *Christian Scripture* will lead us to conclude that rather than 'disciples' in the Jewish or Greek sense of the term, Jesus counted with 'followers' and 'devo-

---

[82] See *The Jesus Family Tomb*, Chapters 2-4.

[83] See *The Case of the Nazarene Reopened*, pp. 703-704, notes 289-290.

[84] See below n. 102.

[85] See Mishna *Ohalot* 17:2, 3.

[86] See *The Case of the Nazarene Reopened*, p. 782 n. 136.

tees.' They were not too bright. When Jesus said to them, "Let these words sink down into your ears, for the son of man is about to be betrayed into the hands of men," they were unable to understand. "But they did not understand this saying, and it was hidden from them so that they did not perceive it." Disregarding the rabbis' advice, "the timid, will not learn" (*Abot* 2:5), "they were afraid to ask him about this saying" (*Lk* 9:44-45). When Jesus announced to them that he will be betrayed by one of them, they were clueless as to what he meant, and "one by one" responded: "*Is* it I?" (*Mk* 14:19). More grievously, they were incapable of feeling empathy for anyone, including Jesus, their mentor and spiritual guide. Prior to the trial, at the most dramatic moment of his life, Jesus was "sorrowful and deeply distressed" (*Matt* 26:37; *Mk* 14:33-34), and asked God: "if it is possible, let this cup pass from me" (*Matt* 26:39, 42; *Mk* 14:36). Amusingly, rather than offering him emotional support, "a dispute arose among them [the disciples] as to which of them would be greatest" (*Lk* 9:46; cf. *Matt* 20:26-28). After finishing quarrelling, they went to take a nap (*Matt* 26:40, 43, 45)—unconcerned with the crisis facing Jesus.[87] In *Mk* 14: 32-41 we read:

> Then they [Jesus and his disciples] came to a place which was named Gethsemane; and he said to his disciples, 'Sit here while I pray.' And he took Peter, James, and John with him, and he began to be troubled and deeply distressed. Then he said to them, 'My soul is exceedingly sorrowful, *even* to death. Stay here and watch.' He went a little further, and fell on the ground, and prayed that if were possible, the hour might pass from him. And he said, 'Abba, Father, all things *are* possible for you. Take this cup away from me; nevertheless, not what I will, but what you *will*.' Then he came and found them sleeping, and said to Peter, 'Simon, are you sleeping? Could you not watch one hour? Watch and pray, lest you enter into temptation. The spirit indeed *is* willing, but the flesh *is* weak.' Again he went away and prayed, and spoke the same words. And when he returned, he found them asleep again, for their eyes were heavy; and they did not know what

---

[87] See *The Case of the Nazarene Reopened*, pp. 33, 101, 193-194, 196-197, 204.

to answer him. Then he came the third time and said to them, 'Are you still sleeping and resting? It is enough!'

It seems that among the many virtues adorning Jesus' disciples, daring was not one of them. When they were confronted with danger, they acted as plain cowards. "Then they all forsook him and fled" (*Mk* 14:50).[88] Renan (1823-1892), who found it obligatory to defend Jesus' disciples at all cost, was compelled this time to admit that their behavior was "skulking cowardice" and "base to the last degree."[89]

We shall now focus on two of his most important disciples, Matthew and Peter. Jesus was *not* a Jew-hater, "Whoever attempts to harm them," that is the Jews, "is as if he were harming the pupils of his own eyes"—reported the rabbis in Jesus' name.[90] Matthew was a Jew-hater.[91] He had been a tax-collector all of his life, and was known as "the publican" (*Matt* 10:3; *Mk* 15:34. See above Chapter 12). Let us point out that there is nothing in the text of the *Christian Scripture* stating that he was Jewish.[92] Most probably, he belonged to one of those pagan families, offspring of Roman soldiers, "close to the ruling circles" (*qarob la-malkhut*). The *Christian Scripture* refers to him as "Matthew the publican" (*Matt* 10:3). In general, tax collectors were despicable men. Philo reported about an individual close to the time of Matthew, who was

> the tax collector for Judaea and cherishes a spite against the population. When he came there he was a poor man but by his rapacity and peculation he has amassed much wealth in various forms. Then fearing that some accusation might be brought against him he devised a scheme to elude the charges by slandering those whom he had

---

[88] See *The Case of the Nazarene Reopened*, pp. 113, 186, 188, 368-369, 723 n. 158.

[89] *The Life of Jesus*, p. 372.

[90] *Gittin* 57a. See Appendix 3.

[91] See *The Case of the Nazarene Reopened*, pp. 57, 62, 77, 81; cf. pp. 678 n. 88; 705-706 n. 307; 725 n. 185; 750 n. 163.

[92] There is no evidence to support the Christian claim that 'Levi' in *Mk* 2:14 and *Lk* 5:27 is one and the same with 'Matthew.'

wronged.[93]

There is no evidence that publican Matthew held a higher moral standard than the above-mentioned publican.

Matthew's contacts with Jews and Judaism were the result of his activities as tax-collector. This may explain his deep anti-Jewish feelings. In his *Gospel* he introduced a new element, designed to 'prove' the guilt of Jewish men, women, and *children*. According to him, but not according to Peter, when Pilate declared himself "innocent," i.e., not responsible "of the blood of this just person," meaning Jesus, "*all* Jews, answered and said: "His blood *be* on us and on our children" (*Matt* 27:25).[94] The 'oath' is an anti-Semitic invention. Never—either before or after—Jews used such a formula. From the point of view of law, both Roman and Jewish, such an oath has no place in a trial. Now, Matthew was *not* present during the trial and could not possibly have heard such a non-sense. There is only one reason for concocting this lie: to justify the spilling of Jewish blood, including "the children."[95]

The same may be said about his statement that Judas "kissed" Jesus, and Jesus greeted Judas as "Friend" (*Matt* 26:49-50; *Mk* 14:8-10). In Judaism a *student* does not kiss his teacher. Furthermore, according to *Matt* 26:55, Jesus was a well-known figure and there was no need for 'Judas' or anyone else to identify him with a 'kiss.' Indeed, when they came to arrest Jesus, he confronted them saying: "I sat daily with you, teaching in the Temple, and you did not seize me." Finally, according to *Matt* 21:8-11, when Jesus entered Jerusalem,

> a very great multitude spread their clothes on the road; others cut down branches from trees and spread *them* on the road. Then the multitudes who went before and those who followed cried out, saying: 'Hosanna to the son of David! Blessed *is* he who comes in the name of the Lord!' Hosanna is the highest!' And when he had come

---

[93] "The Embassy to Gaius," 199-200, *Philo*, vol. 10, p. 108.
[94] See *The Case of the Nazarene Reopened*, p. 674 n. 70.
[95] See *The Case of the Nazarene Reopened*, p. 812 n. 25; cf. ibid. pp. 62-63.

to Jerusalem, all the city was moved, saying, 'Who is this? ' So the multitudes said, 'This is Jesus, the prophet from Nazareth of Galilee' (see *Mk* 11:8-10).

Clearly, according to this report, Jesus was well known in the Temple's quarters and through the streets of Jerusalem where, according to Matthew himself, he had been acclaimed 'Messiah,' a scion of David and a prophet. The only rational for 'bribing' Judas and having him 'identify' Jesus with 'a kiss'—at the very moment that Jesus called him 'friend!'—was to paint 'Judas'—the paradigmatic 'Jew'—as wretched and treacherous. One needs to suffer from a high-level of credulity, to believe that such an individual had access to a discussion held in chambers by the High Priest and members of the Supreme Court. The same is with his statement, "all the chief priests and elders of the people plotted against Jesus to put him to death?" (*Matt* 27:1)—it was motivated by his anti-Jewish feelings, not by fact. In short, Matthew's portrayal, as described in the *Christian Scripture,* reminds us of the proverbial Haman in the *Purim* story, who never met a Jew whom he did not hate (see *Est* 9:24).

What about Peter? Unlike Matthew, he was not a Jew-hater, and never said that the Jews declared that Jesus' blood "*be* on us and on our children" (*Matt* 27:25).[96] However, he was not a learned man. Having Peter in mind, Celsus described Jesus' apostles, as "*infamous men… and sailors* [=fisherman]."[97] Similarly, the *Christian Scripture* described him (and John) as "uneducated and untrained" (*Acts* 4:13). More specifically, either he himself was a pagan or came from a pagan background. Evidence to this is that on the night of Passover, he "drew a sword, and smote a servant of the high priest, and cut off his ear" (*Mk* 14:47; cf. *Jn* 18:10-11). Only a pagan—not a Jew—would carry a weapon on a holiday. Similarly, he spoke of a Jew from Cyrene as "coming from the field" (*Mk* 15:21, *Pocket Interlinear*, p. 125), that

---

[96] See *The Case of the Nazarene Reopened*, p. 137.

[97] *Origen: Contra Celsum*, p. 58. See above, Section II, n. 41. He might have kept some "Jewish customs," as many gentiles in the land of Israel did; see *Origen: Contra Celsum,* pp. 66-68.

is, from work, on the day of the Crucifixion. Only a pagan would not know that on the first day of Passover it is forbidden to work.

We don't propose that in fact, Jesus' twelve disciples were clueless and dishonest. However, *given that the Christian authorities destroyed all the original documentation,* we have no recourse, but to rely on the information provided by the *Christian Scripture*. Admittedly, in real life, Jesus' disciples may have been quite different.

26. 'Gospel-Truth'—Truly?

In English, the expression 'Gospel-truth' came to mean something like 'unimpeachable and absolute truth'—as factual and accurate as the accounts found in the *Gospels*. It is assumed, as a matter of faith that the information provided is like a deposition made by expert witnesses before an officer of the court, which could be taken as evidence in a criminal procedure. On the basis of that 'truth,' countless Jewish men, women, and children were murdered, and their homes and places of business ransacked. In this and the following chapter we intend to question the veracity of the information provided by the *Gospels*. Specifically, we intend to show that rather than a vindication of Jesus, their purpose was to proclaim the guilt of the Jewish people.

Let us begin by pointing out that Christian knowledge of Jesus' trial and death depends on hearsay.

> None of Jesus' family or followers was present while he was being interrogated, and we are not told that any of them spoke to Jesus again until he was crucified. It follows that all the gospels must have invented the trial scenes, and that there is very little in them, which could be treated as historical.[98]

The same was the case with his disciples; none of them attend-

---

[98] Wilson, *Jesus*, p. 210. Unlike Roman law, Jewish law prohibits the judiciary to admit hearsay as evidence; see *Philo and the Oral Law*, pp. 179-181.

ed the trial.⁹⁹ Matthew could not have been present when the Jewish leaders gathered "unto the palace of the high priest," allegedly to "kill" Jesus (*Matt* 26:3-4).¹⁰⁰ Neither could he have been a witness to the 'negotiations' taking place between Judas and the priests (*Matt* 26:14-15).¹⁰¹ Peter sat "below in the courtyard" (*Mk* 14:66). As we will see in the course of this chapter, the accounts provided by these texts do not stand critical analysis.

An examination of some 'details' furnished by the *Christian Scripture* will clearly show that they were fabricated to make an impossible story appear factual.

[1] We are told that Jesus was crucified "in a place called Golgotha, that is to say, Place of a Skull" (*Matt* 27:33). No such place ever existed in or around Jerusalem (cf. *Jn* 19:20).¹⁰²

[2] "Joseph" is identified as a "counselor member, a good and just man…from Arimathaea, a city of the Jews" (*Lk* 23:50-51). If such a person ever existed, he must have been a publican "close to the ruling circles"—not a member of a rabbinic court.¹⁰³ More significant, there was no such city, Jewish or pagan, named "Arimathaea."¹⁰⁴

[3] To emphasize the 'Jewishness' of Judah, who allegedly betrayed Jesus, *he alone* is addressed with the title "Rabbi" (*Matt* 26:25; *Mk* 14:45). Yet, "The title 'Rabbi'…was not conferred upon any sage before the destruction of the Temple, 70 C.E."¹⁰⁵ The same is true of the title 'rabbi' given to Jesus (see *Jn* 3:2, 26; 6:25, etc.). It was a *post-*

---

⁹⁹ See *The Trial and Death of Jesus*, pp. 67-68, 700 n. 263.
¹⁰⁰ See *The Trial and Death of Jesus*, pp. 23-24.
¹⁰¹ See *The Trial and Death of Jesus*, p. 21.
¹⁰² See *The Case of the Nazarene Reopened*, pp. 343-344, 602, 675 n. 77; 698-699 n. 255.
¹⁰³ See above Section II, n. 49.
¹⁰⁴ See *The Case of the Nazarene Reopened*, pp. 344-345.
¹⁰⁵ See *The Case of the Nazarene Reopened*, pp. 151, 154, 729-730 n. 223; 731 n. 238.

humous title awarded retroactively to Jesus by the redactors of the *Christian Scripture, honoris causa.*[106]

[4] To give some credence to an impossible story, a phony 'detail' is provided. However, it is so vague, as to be meaningless. Consider the case of "Salome" who supposedly "brought spices, that they might and anoint" (*Mk* 16:1; cf. 15:40) the body of Jesus *after his burial!* Nothing is known about such "Salome"! She was not identified by the *Christian Scripture*, and would be equivalent to saying that someone by the name 'Jane' or 'Maggie' brought the spices. The sole purpose for furnishing a name was to make an absurd story—the anointing of a corpse *after burial*—appear credible.[107]

[5] The allegation that the High Priest said to Jesus, "tell us whether thou be the Christ, the Son of God" (*Matt* 26:63, cf. *Jn* 20:31)—could only have been made by a pagan.[108] Only a pagan would think that the claim to divine ancestry invested him with the right to assume the throne. As Octavian, who signed himself "*divi filius*, son of a god" so that no one would "forget his connection with Caesar and with Caesar's divine ancestors."[109] In the Jewish mindset, however, not only the 'Messiah,' but every single Jew *is* the 'the son of God' (see *Dt* 14:1). Significantly, this was the topic of a dispute between Turnus Rufus (Tinneius Rufus, the Roman Governor of Judea) and R. 'Aqiba. Contrary to the view of the pagan Governor, who regarded the Jews, particularly after vanquished by Rome, as "slaves," R. 'Aqiba insisted that even when defeated, Jews are the "sons of God."[110] The notion that 'Son of God' is a title exclusive to the Messiah reflects the mind of pagan Turnus Rufus, rather than R. 'Aqiba's

---

[106] See *Catechism of the Catholic Church*, # 581, p. 149.

[107] See *The Case of the Nazarene Reopened*, p. 330.

[108] Cf. *The Case of the Nazarene Reopened*, pp. 364-368.

[109] See Lily Ross Taylor, *The Divinity of the Roman Emperor* (Middletown, Connecticut, 1931), p. 106.

[110] *Baba Batra* 10a. Cf. *GD*, p. xxii-xxiii.

mind.

In a legal proceeding, the character of the witness is of the essence. In the preceding chapter we examined some details mentioned in the *Christian Scripture* concerning the character of Jesus' disciples. Matthew had been a publican, consistently espousing extreme anti-Jewish positions. We have noted that in Judaism, publicans are regarded as brigands.[111] Peter was described as being "uneducated and untrained" (*Acts* 4:13). Nonetheless, he had the distinction of being the first person to have awarded Jesus the title of "Christ, the son of the living God" (*Mt* 16: 16). Jesus reciprocated. Pointing at Peter, he said: "on this rock I will build my church" (*Mt* 16: 18). Moreover, he entrusted him with "the keys of the kingdom of heaven," etc.[112] (*Mt* 16: 19). Yet Peter lied not once, but three times; the last two times making a false oath.[113] First, "Now Peter sat outside in the courtyard. And a servant girl came to him, saying, 'You also were with Jesus of Galilee.' But he denied it before *them* all, saying, 'I do not know what you are saying.'" A few moments later, he lied again, "another *girl* saw him and said to those *who were* there, 'This *fellow* also was with Jesus of Nazareth.'" At this time, Peter added an oath to his lie, thus being guilty of false swearing. So, that when he was charged with knowing Jesus, "he denied with an oath, 'I do not know the man.'" Lastly, when he was confronted for the third time, he lied again and "began to curse and swear, 'I do not know this man of whom you speak!'" (See *Mt* 26: 69-74; *Mk* 14: 71-72).[114] Accordingly, the "rock" upon which Jesus' "church" will be built (*Mt* 16: 18), committed perjury twice under oath. Noting these facts, a distinguished lawyer and first rate Talmudist, wrote:

Yet, Peter remains the Saint upon whom the Christian Church was

---

[111] See quotation above, n. 23. Cf. the quotation at n. 93, and Section II, n. 18.

[112] 'Heaven,' however, was down here on earth; see *The Secret Gospel*, p. 95.

[113] On the gravity of false swearing, see *Zechariah* 5:4. In Jewish law 'perjury' applies even in a non-judicial procedure.

[114] See *The Case of the Nazarene Reopened*, pp. 127, 129, 166, 204.

built, and the memory of those unfortunate Jewish martyrs is disgraced by the Church to this very day.[115]

A person with such a record would not qualify to testify in a municipal court about a traffic violation. Yet, on the basis of a report given by a known perjurer, that is, a repeated liar, guilty of false swearing, not once but twice, Christendom carried on an unremitting campaign of Jewish demonization, often ending in mass murder and pillage.

Jesus' Trial, as portrayed in the *Christian Scripture*, ranks as the most bizarre trial in legal history. More or less, the *Four Gospels* charge that the Great *Sanhedrin* or Supreme Court of Israel unjustly condemned Jesus of blasphemy and delivered him to the Roman Procurator to have him crucified. An 'arrest,' in both Jewish and Roman law, requires 'charging' the accused with *a criminal offense*. In both systems, charging the accused with a crime calls for a clear description of the offence, *as well as citation of the law or statute by which the alleged act may be deemed criminal*. The allegation that claiming to be the Messiah, or of being "able to destroy the temple of God, and to build it in three days" (*Matt* 26:61) constitute 'blasphemy,' is a malicious fabrication gestated in the mind of Matthew, a Jew-hater and a publican, who collaborated with the Roman occupying forces. The 'account' he furnished is a lie. It could only have been hatched by a malevolent person, perversely ignoring Jewish struggle for law and justice throughout history. His description of Jesus' 'arrest' and 'trial,' turns to be a long meandering yarn, sharply at odds with everything known about Jewish and Roman law. The 'testimony' of the 'witnesses' is outright false, excluding relevant information, according to the accepted standards of Jewish and Roman law. It has been properly asked:

> Of what did the chief priests and elders accuse the Nazarene [=Jesus]? What was the nature of their charge against him? All answers to these questions the writer prefers to leave to the imagination

---

[115] See *The Case of the Nazarene Reopened*, p.693, n. 204.

of the reader, so that each and every student may place any interpretation thereon that he chooses. (By the way, one must admit that the Gospel-writer signally achieved his purpose. The imagination of the Christian commentators has been boundless in their effort to clarify the innumerable obscurities in the Gospels.) It is, of course, possible that not choice but ignorance was the writer's source of obscurity. Perhaps he did not possess enough knowledge of any system of law and procedure, either Jewish or Roman, to trump up a charge that could be sustained on the principles of law of either nation. It is hard to understand why any further complaints had to be lodged against the prisoner [Jesus], as he had already admitted to the Roman official that he was guilty of treason, the greatest offense in Roman law.[116]

Referring to Jesus' trial, *Mk* 14:56 remarked, "For many bore false witness against him, but the testimony did not agree" (*Mk* 14:59). The same is true of the testimonies given by Jesus' disciples. They are sharply at odds with each other and deliberately vague and inaccurate.[117] Consider the following cases:

[1] According to *Mk* 15:25, Jesus was crucified at "the third hour"; but according to *Jn* 19:14, he was crucified at "about the sixth hour."[118]

[2] According to *Matt* 26:63-64, *Pocket Interlinear*, p. 72, when the High Priest asked Jesus "if you are the Christ (=Messiah), the son of God? Jesus said to him: "you said *it*"; i.e., you say so, but I remain silent—an evasive answer. However, according to Peter, Jesus replied in the affirmative: "I am" (*Mk* 14:62).

---

[116] *The Case of the Nazarene Reopened*, pp. 694-695.

[117] For a meticulous analysis of these contradictions, see *The Case of the Nazarene Reopened*, pp. 545-563.

[118] See R. Saul Mortera, *Preguntas* #75, 128b-129a. Let me point out at one, among the many contradictions between *Mark* and *John*. In *Mk* 15: 7 Barabbas was supposed to have been "chained with his fellow rebels; they had committed murder in the rebellion" (Cf. *Lk* 23:19, 25). But according to *Jn* 18:40, Barabbas was not a rebel but "a robber," etc., etc.

[3] According to *Jn* 18:24, Jesus was delivered "bound to Caiaphas the high priest," by the former high priest "Annas."[119] But according to *Matt* 26:57, the ones "who had laid hold of Jesus" and led him "away to Caiaphas the high priest" were the officers that arrested him in Gethsemane, and not the former high priest Annas.

[4] According to *Matt* 27:32, *Mk* 15:21 and 23:26, Simon of Cyrene bore the cross at Golgotha. According to *Jn* 19:17 "he (Jesus) bearing his cross went forth into a place called *the place* of a skull, which is called in the Hebrew Golgotha."[120]

[5] According to *Matt* 26:57 and *Mk* 14:53 Jesus was taken at night to the house of the High Priest "where the scribes and the elders were assembled." But according to *Lk* 22:66, p. 204: "And when day came, the body of elders of the people, the chief priests and scribes, were gathered and *they* led him away into the Sanhedrin."

The allegation that at the Feast of Passover, Pilate "was wont to release unto the people a prisoner, whom they would" (Matt. 27:15; cf. *Mk* 15:6; *Lk* 23:17; *Jn* 18:39), is another fabrication without any basis in history. Never in the judicial history of the Roman Empire was there a custom to "release" a prisoner for Passover or for any other Jewish holiday. The whole story is an invention by a known Jew-hater, Matthew the publican, to further malign the Jews and gain favor in the eyes of the Roman authorities.[121]

The charges against Jesus 'reported' in the *Christian Scripture* are meaningless in Jewish, Roman or any other legal system. Jesus became the *Christian* Savior *after* the crucifixion, as a *consequence* of his resurrection. Prior to his death and resurrection, while in human

---

[119] It is deliberately vague, so that it is impossible to ascertain whether this happened before the Jewish court began the investigation or afterwards; see *The Case of the Nazarene Reopened*, pp. 278-279.

[120] See *The Case of the Nazarene Reopened*, p. 600.

[121] See *The Case of the Nazarene Reopened*, pp. 342-343.

garb, he was *not* the Christian Savior. At best, it may be argued that he was the *Jewish* Savior, in which case it is nobody's business except the Jews. In law, you cannot charge someone with injuring the king, before he had been crowned king. One of the first things that the Christian authorities did when they took over the Roman Empire was to destroy *all* the documentation pertaining to Jesus' Trial.[122] None of the Christian manuscripts are in Aramaic, the language spoken by Jesus and his disciples. The current text of the *Gospels* derives from manuscripts written several centuries after the events. Not a word spoken either by Jesus or his disciples was preserved, so that not a single line of the account found in the *Christian Scripture* can be supported by record. The 'words' allegedly spoken by the protagonists are 'translations' by anonymous men of texts that have vanished without leaving a trace. In this respect, the *Gospels* are not dissimilar than the pre-Trojan journal, ascribed to Dictys of Crete. Actually, it was written in Greek. However, in order to enhance its standing, it was said that it had been originally written in 'Phoenician' and *then* 'translated' into Greek.[123] The same is with the text of the *Gospels*. It is *not* a Greek translation, simply *because there never was an original 'Aramaic' text*.

A note on the style of the *Gospels*. A close reading of these texts clearly show that they have been revised countless times, by single-minded advocates, bent on promoting mainstream-viewpoints and doctrines, essential to post-Jesus Christianity. Christian knowledge of Jesus' trial and death depends, in no way, on Jesus and his ministry, but on the 'report' offered by 'disciples,' 'registered' by an 'editorial board' that was and will remain anonymous for all time to come. In fact, there may be good reasons to question whether the Christian

---

[122] Christian knowledge of Jesus is not grounded on Jesus' writings. In quality of a Christian deity, he may have foreseen his arrest and written about it, in the fashion of Prophets Isaiah and Jeremiah, who wrote about events to be unfolding in the future. However, because of Christian anti-writing bias, the few words to have been known that were written by Jesus *were not preserved*; see *HS*, vol. 1, pp. 166-167.

[123] See G. W. Bowersock, *Fiction as History* (Berkeley, University of California Press, 1997), p. 24.

version is an honest and unbiased report, or were there ulterior motives impugning its credibility. Consider the following four points.

First, suppose Jesus would not have been crucified at all, as his Jewish followers maintained (and so it appears from the *Muslim Scripture*). Then we are left with an assortment of patchy sayings, most of which are found in the *Hebrew Scripture* and rabbinic sources. Then, only a very small public would be attracted to his message, mainly tax-collectors and marginal Jews, looking for an excuse for not complying with the requirements of Law. It could also have attracted some people wishing to partake in the delights of "the Mystery of the Kingdom." In which case, Jesus' ministry would have amounted to zero, or pretty close to zero.

Second, suppose Jesus would have been crucified by the Roman authorities for claiming to be *Kyrios* with the authority to seize property, and he was found guilty or innocent of all charges. Then, for all practical purposes, his ministry would have amounted to zero, or pretty close to zero.

Third, suppose that Jesus would have been tried in a Jewish court for claiming to be *Kyrios*, in the sense of 'God' [Tetragrammaton], as per its usage among Greek-speaking Jews. Then the Jewish court would have dismissed the chargers, on the basis that within this specific context, it meant "the legitimate master of someone or something"—and not the actual Tetragrammaton![124] Suppose, for argument's sake, that it could have been proven beyond any reasonable doubt, that by *Kyrios* Jesus, the actual Tetragrammaton was meant, then the charges would have been dismissed on the grounds that within the Jewish community at large, Jesus was regarded as a "madman" (*shoṭe*), and not legally responsible for his words and actions.[125] Therefore any charges brought against Jesus in a Jewish court, would have been dismissed. In which case, his ministry would have amounted to zero, or pretty close to zero.

---

[124] See above, n. 17.

[125] See above notes 7, 8, 9.

Fourth, the only way to make something out of Jesus, was to transform him by virtue of his tragic *death*. Suppose, that Jesus would have been executed by *anybody except the Jews*, then, for all practical purposes, his *life* and *death* would have amounted to zero or pretty close to zero.

The story of Jesus' Passion was not conveyed by a disinterested party. The 'testimony' offered by the *Gospels* was not furnished by competent witnesses, capable of reporting *a judicial process*—not only of a central figure, like Jesus, involving criminal procedure— but even of a common civil case, like a malpractice suit against a certified anesthesiologist. The accounts of the arrest, trial, and execution of Jesus, reflect total ignorance of both Jewish and Roman law. There is nothing in the 'reports' they provide, indicating that they were written by people having any *knowledge* or *interest* in legal matters.

The general assumption that the *Gospels* equal a judicial record, drawn for the purpose of furnishing a precise and unbiased account of the charges, procedures, and conclusion of a trial, is without merits. Rather than an actual trial, the *Christian Scripture* depicts "a mock-trial conducted by imbeciles."[126] The members of the Jewish Supreme Court are portrayed as chronically stupid, to the point of mental retardation. They are reminiscent of the classical 'fool' (*morós*, *stupidus*)—the favorite laughing-stock of the Roman stage. On the one hand, given the enormous 'popularity' enjoyed by Jesus, the Jewish authorities decided *not* to try him during the Passover Holidays, "lest there be an uproar among the people" (*Matt* 26:5). On the other hand, although they wanted to prevent the ire of the huge masses believing that Jesus was the Messiah, they came to arrest him during the holiday, "with a great multitude with swords and clubs" (*Matt* 26:47). More idiotically, "they had bound him" (*Matt* 27:2) and then "led" him through the streets of Jerusalem to deliver him to Pilate.[127] Similarly, *Mk* 14:2 reports that the Jewish authorities decided *not* to

---

[126] See *The Trial and Death of Jesus*, p. 42. Cf. ibid, pp. 35, 41, 42.

[127] See *The Case of the Nazarene Reopened*, pp. 48-49.

try Jesus during the holiday "lest there be an uproar by the people." Yet, imbeciles as they were, they came to arrest Jesus with "a great multitude with swords and clubs," and delivered him to "the chief priests and scribes and the elders" (*Mk* 14:43). On the one hand, evil as they were, the Jewish authorities connived to bring "false witnesses." On the other hand, mindless as they were, "Even though many false witnesses came forward, they found none" (*Matt* 26:60). Similarly, Peter tells us that although many false witnesses came to testify against Jesus, punctilious as the Jewish authorities were, they could not charge him, because "their testimonies did not agree." On the other hand, fraudulent as they were, when a pair of witnesses arose, they relied on their testimony, although "not even then did their testimony agree" (*Mk* 14:55-59). On the one hand, corrupt as they were, they accepted Judas' testimony, although he had admitted, "I have sinned by betraying innocent blood." On the other hand, cynical as they were, they publicly declared, "What *is that* to us?" (*Matt* 27:4); meaning, 'who cares about the Law'? On the one hand, hypocritical as they were, they charged Jesus with breaking the Law, on the other hand, contemptuous as they were, "the trial of Jesus as described in the New Testament was in direct opposition to the express stipulations of the law that was esteemed so highly by the Pharisees."[128] On the one hand, the High Priest Caiaphas, crooked as he was, defied the Law *in the presence of all Israel*, and decided to convict Jesus *without* the valid testimony of two witnesses, as required by the Law (*Dt* 17:6; 19:15). On the other hand, brainless as he was, he "rent his clothes" in accordance to the Law, to express his sorrow for the alleged 'blasphemy' uttered by Jesus (*Matt* 26:65).[129]

Not only the Jewish Court, but also Pilate and Herod acted like the typical 'fool' (*morós*, *stupidus*) of the mimic theater. When Pilate asked Jesus whether he was "the King of the Jews," he answered:

---

[128] "The Crucifixion of Jesus from the Standpoint of Pharisaic Law," p. 318.

[129] See *The Case of the Nazarene Reopened*, pp. 44-45. For similar inconsistencies denoting judicial idiocy on the part of the Jewish authorities, see ibid, pp. 97, 136-137, 210-213, 279.

"Thou sayest *it*" (*Mk* 15:2). Pilate took his evasive answer to mean that indeed he was the "the King of the Jews" (*Mk* 15:9).[130] In support of Pilate's interpretation, we may recall that according to the *Christian Scripture* the Jewish people, "called" Jesus, "the King of the Jews" (*Mk* 15:12). This admission constituted treason against Rome. Nonetheless, brainless as Pilate was, he asked: "Why, what evil hath he done?" (*Mk* 15:14).[131] Similarly, compassionate as Pilate was, he wanted to free Jesus because he was convinced that he was innocent. However, brutal as he was, he *personally* "flogged" Jesus before he delivered him to be crucified (*Mk* 15:15, as per the Greek *fragellósos*, *Pocket Interlinear*, p. 124). Herod, too, acted like a 'fool' (*morós*, *stupidus*). On the one hand, he wanted to "kill" Jesus (*Lk* 13:31) for no apparent reason, just for the fun of it. However, when Pilate delivered Jesus to him, stupid as he was, he "arrayed him in a gorgeous robe, and sent him again to Pilate" (*Lk* 23:11).

The only way that his followers could make something out of Jesus' life was to transform his death into a collective Jewish sin. Bearing this in mind, the purpose of the *Gospels* is threefold: to pander to Roman interest, particularly by switching the responsibility from them on to the Jews; to appeal to heathens looking for an alternative to paganism and Judaism; and to attract anti-Semites–and there were plenty of them, specially throughout Egypt, and Syria— who resented the fact that Jews, although crushed by the Romans, enjoyed a higher and more orderly life-style than their pagan neighbors.

It is high time to point out that thanks to the *Tora*-education, the average Jew was able to reach a level of internal maturation, impossible in the pagan world. To be a Jew (then and now), is to have the faculty to internalize one's duties towards God and man, and if necessary die, rather than forfeit these duties. Countless Jewish men and women chose exile, death, and agonizing torture, rather than

---

[130] *Jn* 18:36 explained that Jesus meant to say, "My kingdom is not of this world."

[131] See *The Case of the Nazarene Reopened*, pp. 64, 66-67, 134-136.

transgress a single *iota* of the Sacred Law. As pointed out by Josephus:

> We have given practical proof of our reverence for our own Scriptures. For, although such long ages have now passed, no one has ventured either to add, or to remove, or to alter a syllable; and it is an instinct with every Jew, from the day of his birth, to regard them as the decrees of God, to abide by them, and, if need be, cheerfully to die for them. Time and again ere now the sight has been witnessed of [Jewish] prisoners enduring tortures and death in every form in the [Roman] theaters, rather than utter a single word against the laws and the allied documents.[132]

Jewish readiness to die for the Sanctity of the Law is well attested throughout history,

> had not the facts made all men aware that many of our countrymen have on many occasions ere now preferred to brave all manner of suffering rather than to utter a single word against the Law.[133]

The Jew was unique in another aspect. Given that he had internalized his duties, he needed not a police or ecclesiastic enforcers 'to have him do the right thing.' Essential to Jewish education is to inculcate in the individual to rely, like Patriarch Abraham, "out of his own precise intelligence." Therefore, a Jew

> is firmly persuaded that to those who observe the laws and, if they must needs die for them, willingly meet death, God has granted a renewed existence and in the revolution of the ages the gift of a better life.[134]

This belief afforded the Jew the ability to face his foes peacefully and without trepidation. When Jews were asked if they were prepared to defy the Roman Emperor, they responded: "On no account would we fight, but we will die sooner than violate our laws." And

---

[132] *Against Apion*, I, 42, vol. 1, pp. 179-181.

[133] *Against Apion*, II, 219, vol. 1, p. 381.

[134] *Against Apion*, II, 218, vol. 1, p. 381. See "Introduction," n. 52.

declared to be ready to be slain, rather than transgress the Law.[135] Thus, "Jews seem to have effectively applied Gandhi's principle of non-violent resistance."[136]

The allegation made in *Matt* 27:25 that "all the [Jewish] people" were ready to forsake the *Tora* and falsely accuse Jesus, ranks as the most villainous accusation ever made in the history of infamy. It is nothing less than spitting in the face of every Jewish martyr in history, including the countless women and men, old and young, tortured and then burnt alive by the Holy Inquisition, rather than to contravene a single letter of the *Tora*. Having the ecclesiastical authorities in mind, the Talmud tells that in reply to the gentiles' accusation that the Jews have failed to fulfill the Law, God will call forth the torturers and murderers of Jews to testify on behalf of their victims. This certainly applies to Christendom. On the one hand, Christians claimed that God had abandoned the Jews because they don't observe the Law, and on the other hand, they kept on persecuting and murdering the Jews because they refuse to transgress the Law![137]

27. Alexandria, Cradle of the First Pogrom

The first pogrom in history was inaugurated in Alexandria.[138] A

---

[135] Josephus, *Jewish Antiquities*, XVIII, 271, vol. 9, p. 161.

[136] Vamberto Morais, *A Short History of Anti-Semitism* (New York: W.W. Norton, 1976), p. 29.

[137] See *'Aboda Zara* 3a.

[138] At the time, Alexandrian Jewry was the most important Jewry outside the land of Israel. In addition to their numbers and wealth, they counted with a large number of highly educated Jews. There were differences of opinion among them, but these differences did not lead to sectarianism. Here is how Professor Harry A. Wolfson, *The Philosophy of the Church Fathers* vol. 1 (Cambridge, Mass.: Harvard University Press, 1956), p. 99, describes them:

> In Alexandrian Judaism, there were renegades, but no heretics. There were indeed individual differences of opinion as to the use of philosophical allegorization of Scripture, and as to the extent of its use, but these never led to sectarianism.

pogrom takes place when a *mob* attacks a designated *minority*, as in the infamous *Kristalnacht* (November 9-10, 1938). It consists of a group of people —militant, boorish, and unanalytical— killing, pillaging, and ransacking a helpless target. The 'masses' are the same people as those of the 'mob,' with one difference: instead of using physical violence, they discriminate, socially, economically, and politically against members of 'the' minority. 'Mob-masses/minority' are not quantitative entities. They are syntagmatic concepts, defined in diametrical opposition to one another. As Ortega y Gasset taught, 'minority' designates men and women demanding personal *excellence* from themselves, in contradistinction to the 'masses,' made up of a homogeneous people (=*plethos, oxlous*), where everyone is and wants to be like everyone else.

> For there is no doubt that the most radical division that it is possible to make of humanity is that which splits it into two classes of creatures: those who make great demands on themselves, piling difficulties and duties; and those who demand nothing special of themselves, but for whom to live is to be every moment what they already are, without imposing on themselves any effort towards perfection; mere buoys that float on the waves.[139]

Individuation and the pursuit of excellence—a corollary of the 'image of God' within—constitute a formal challenge to the masses. The masses not only abhor individuation; it is their sacred duty to persecute, annihilate, and destroy 'anybody' who is not like 'everybody':

> The mass crushes beneath it everything that is different, everything that is excellent, individual, qualified and select. Anybody who is not like everybody, who does not think like everybody, runs the risk of being eliminated. And it is clear, of course, that this 'everybody' is not 'everybody.'[140]

---

[139] *The Revolt of the Masses*, p. 15.

[140] *The Revolt of the Masses*, p. 18. The subject had been previously introduced by

To the pagan masses, Alexandrian Jewry—as well as Jews everywhere—represent the 'other,' and they were persecuted because they dared to be *different*. It is not sufficient to destroy the 'other.' He must be humiliated, dehumanized and then *devoured*: cannibalistically (cf. *Revelation* 19:18).[141] Jews are/were 'the other'; nay, they *are* 'otherness.'[142]

An important tactic in the Roman occupation of the land of Israel was the establishment of pagan colonies, consisting mainly of displaced people from neighboring countries, as well as members of the military and administrative personnel that decided to take up residence in the occupied territory. The intention was to cause friction and destabilize the Jewish population. Nonetheless, the relations between Jews and heathens seem to have been adequate. A careful study of the rabbinic literature shows that the 'antipathy' between Jew and heathen *in the land of Israel* has been grossly exaggerated. Here is what a great Christian Hebraist wrote on the subject:

> Attention may be called to the interesting examples of social and commercial cooperation between Jews and heathens, which are afforded by this chapter [Mishna *'Aboda Zara*, Chapter V]. Certainly the antipathy on both sides cannot have been so deep as has often been suspected.[143]

True, there have been isolated cases when a pagan did something intended to affront Jews. We are told of a Roman soldier, "finding in one village a copy of the sacred law," who tore it "in pieces and flung it into the fire."[144] The Roman authorities punished the soldier and there were no further consequences. A most serious inci-

---

Maimonides; see *Homo Mysticus*, pp. xi, 16-17, 163-164, 174-175.

[141] E.g., Christian violent appropriation of the *Hebrew Scripture*, followed by the school of Biblical criticism; dismembering it piece by piece, digesting it into inconsequential platitudes; and finally, ejecting the rest out, as injurious and destructive.

[142] For a definition of 'the other' and 'otherness,' see *In the Shadow of History*, pp. 4, 8.

[143] *The Mishna on Idolatry 'Aboda Zara*, p. 79.

[144] *Jewish War*, II, 229, *Josephus*, vol. 2, p. 413.

dent took place in the Temple during the Passover Holiday.

> The usual crowd had assembled at Jerusalem for the feast of unleavened bread, and the Roman cohort had taken up its position on the roof of the portico of the temple; for a body of men in arms invariably mounts guard at the feasts, to prevent disorders arising from such a concourse of people. Thereupon one of the soldiers, raising his robe, stooped in an indecent attitude, so as to turn his backside to the Jews, and made a noise in keeping with his posture.

Consequently, "upward of thirty thousand [Jews] perished, and the feast was turned into mourning for the whole nation and for every household into lamentation."[145]

And yet, as grievous as these acts were, they were not orchestrated by a 'mob,' but by a man or a group of men acting on their own. The persecution of Jews under King Antiochus Epiphanes (215-164 BCE) was *not* an indiscriminate attack on Jews in general, but only against Jews who adhered to the *Tora*—the first religious martyrs in history—and refused to bow down to Hellenistic syncretism.[146]

Pogroms against the Jewish population in general, and genuine, venomous anti-Semitism, are an Egyptian invention. "Alexandria," wrote a sharp student of history, is "the cradle of Anti-Semitism."[147] Indeed, in no other place in the Hellenistic world can we find such a deep-rooted hatred against everything Jewish—from the Law of Moses down to the simplest Jew. There arose men like Manetho (3rd century BCE) and Apion (ca. 20 BCE-ca. 45 CE) that produced the first truly anti-Semitic treatises. Thus providing the arguments and tactics that served as models for future anti-Semitic propaganda (e.g., blood libel), including the Nazis and post-Nazis eras. What was truly unique about the massacre of Jews, burning Synagogues, and looting Jewish properties in Alexandria (=*Kristalnacht*), was that they were

---

[145] *Jewish War*, II, 224-227, *Josephus*, vol. 2, pp. 410-413.

[146] See *A Short History of Anti-Semitism*, pp. 17-18, and above, "Introduction," n. 33.

[147] *A Short History of Anti-Semitism*, p. 11.

perpetrated by mobs. These riots had to do with the innate Egyptian jealousy of anything 'foreigner.' "But jealousy is part of the Egyptian nature," explained Philo, "and the citizens were bursting with envy and considered that any good luck to others," i.e., 'foreigners,' "was misfortune to themselves."[148]

The first pogrom came about when the Jewish King Agrippa (10 BCE-44 CE), stopped in Alexandria on his way to Judea. Historians speculate about the 'reasons' motivating these riots (there always must be a 'reason' for 'causing' *good folks* to do something evil, particularly when the victim is a Jew). Philo, who was an eyewitness to these riots, offered the following explanation: the people in Alexandria could not tolerate the fact that 'a Jewish King' passed through their territory.

> [I]n their [the Egyptian] ancient, and we might say innate hostility to the Jews, they resented a Jew [King Agrippa] having been made a king, just as much as if each of them had thereby been deprived of an ancestral throne.[149]

Bursting with envy, they attacked the Jewish population; burning Synagogues and ransacking Jewish property. Philo referred to the rioters as "the lazy and unoccupied mob, a multitude well practiced in idle talk, who devote their leisure to slandering and evil speaking." They were an "undisciplined mob."[150] After expelling the Jews from their own homes,

> Some of the habitual idlers and loungers, would make a circle round the Jews who, as I have said, had been driven and thrust together into a small part of the extremity of the city, and sit there watching them as though they were in a besieged fortress lest anyone should escape unseen.[151]

---

[148] *Flaccus*, 29, *Philo*, vol. 9, p. 319. Cf. *Against Apion*, I 25, *Philo*, vol. 1, p. 253.

[149] *Flaccus*, 29, *Philo*, vol. 9, p. 319. Curiously, many of the same people 'resent' the establishment of the Sate of Israel.

[150] *Flaccus*, 33 and 35, *Philo*, vol. 9, p. 321.

[151] *The Embassy to Gaius*, 198, *Philo*, vol. 10, p. 103.

If they would discover that there were some heathen women among the prisoners, they would let them go free.

> But if they were found to be of our nation [i.e., Jews] then these onlookers at a show turned into despotic tyrants and gave orders to fetch swine's flesh and give it to the women. Then all the women who in fear of punishment tasted the meat were dismissed and did not bear any further maltreatment. But the more resolute were delivered to the tormentors to suffer desperate ill-usage, which is the clearest proof of their entire innocence of wrongdoing.[152]

Setting an example for future anti-Semitic politicians, Flaccus, who was the prefect of Egypt, took advantage of these pogroms, and

> ...hurried and pressed on the matter to conciliate the mob, who were opposed to the Jews, thinking that this would help to bring them to make his policy their own.[153]

In classical pogrom-fashion, instead of punishing the aggressors, Flaccus punished the victims. Large numbers of Jews were flagellated and tortured before they were crucified.[154] Not only that did he not issue "orders to take down [the bodies of Jews] those who had died on the cross," but he also "ordered the crucifixion of the living." This, Flaccus did "after maltreating them with the lash in the *middle of the theater* (our italics) and torturing them with fire and the sword." It is important to take note that the killing of Jews was presented as *a theatrical show*.[155]

> The first spectacle lasting from dawn till the third or fourth hour consisted of Jews being scourged, hung up, bound to the wheel, bru-

---

[152] *Flaccus*, 96, *Philo*, vol. 9, p. 321; see *The Embassy to Gaius*, 361, *Philo*, vol. 10, p. 181. In Spain, too, *cristianos viejos* delighted in forcing *cristianos nuevos*, particularly women, to eat pork before burning them at the stake—it is so funny! See above n. 137.

[153] *Flaccus*, 82, *Philo*, vol. 9, p. 347.

[154] See quotation below at n. 184.

[155] See quotations at notes 156, 158, 185, 187, 188, 189, 184, 190, 191, 192, 194, 195, 196, 198. This may explain the rabbinic attitude towards the theater and theatrical performances.

tally mauled and haled for their death march through the middle of the orchestra. After this splendid exhibition came dancers and mimes and flute players and all the other amusements of theatrical competitions.[156]

Following this spectacle, a special contingent was dispatched to the Jewish quarters, killing and looting, on the pretext that they were looking for 'Jewish weapons.'[157] Later, Caligula emulated Flaccus in the treatment of Jews. Jews were corralled into a theater and then subjected to torture and ignominy to the delight of the jeering mob.

> Such was this combination of a theater and a prison in place of a tribunal, theater-like in the cackling of their hisses, their mockery and unbounded jeering, prison-like in the strokes inflicted on our flesh, the torture, the racking of the whole soul through the blasphemies against God and menaces launched upon us by this mighty despot, who resented the affront not to another, since then he might easily have changed his mind, but to himself and his desire of deification to which he supposed the Jews alone did not assent and could not pledge themselves to subscribe.[158]

In what follows we will see that Alexandria was also the source of inspiration for Jesus' Trial, as well as for some of the most important theological doctrines of the Christian Church.

28. The Alexandrian Precursor of Jesus

It is generally agreed that 'legal' cases found in Latin Declamation Literature, do not portray the law as it was actually practiced. "The law of these cases is often such as never stood in Roman statute books, sometime as no code known to antiquity contained..."[159] The

---

[156] *Flaccus*, 83-85, *Philo*, vol. 9, pp. 347-349.
[157] See *Flaccus*, XI, *Philo*, vol. 9, pp. 349-355.
[158] *The Embassy to Gaius*, 368, *Philo*, vol. 10, p. 183.
[159] Walter C. Summer, *The Silver Age of Latin Literature* (London: Methuen, 1920), p. 7.

same is true of Jesus' Trial. One need not be a legal scholar to realize that the Christian versions of Jesus' Passion *are not* the minutes of a court. The style is emotional and anecdotal, and regular court procedures are not followed. The vocabulary and description do not reflect the course of a court of justice, but of a *mock-trial*, in which events unfold according to a mysterious script, manipulated by a master puppeteer, pulling the strings from behind the curtain (see *Acts* 2:23).

The only 'trials' that the authors of the *Christian Scripture* witnessed were the mock-trials carried on by mobs. In this chapter I propose that the setting of Jesus' Passion was gestated in the whirling mass of odium, generated by the anti-Semitic mobs, roaming through the streets of Alexandria. I will explain.

Philo wrote that to show contempt for King Agrippa, the Alexandrian mobs produced a mock-trial designed to deride "the Jewish King," for having the audacity to set foot on Egyptian territory. Philo, who was an eyewitness to the event, wrote:

> There was a certain lunatic named Carabas, whose madness was not of the fierce and savage kind, which is dangerous both to the madmen themselves and those who approach them, but of the easygoing, gentler style. He spent day and night in the street naked, shunning neither heat nor cold, made game of by the children and the lads who were idling about. The rioters drove the poor fellow into the gymnasium and set him up on high to be seen of by all and put on his head a sheet of byblus spread out wide for a diadem, clothed the rest of his body with a rug for royal robe, while someone who had noticed a piece of the native papyrus thrown away in the road gave it to him for his scepter. And when as in some [theatrical] farce he had received the insignia of kingship and had been tricked out as a king, young men carrying rods on their shoulder as spearmen stood on either side of him in imitation of a bodyguard. Then others approached him, some pretending to salute him, others to sue for justice, others to consult him on state affairs. Then from the multitudes standing round him there rang out a tremendous shout hailing him as *Marin* which is said to be the name for "lord" in Syria. For they knew that

Agrippa was both a Syrian by birth and had a great piece of Syria over which he was king.[160]

There are some striking similarities between Jesus' Trial and the Trial of Carabas.[161]

[1] In the case of Carabas, a sheet of byblus was used as a diadem to mock him. In the case of Jesus we have a "crown of thorns" (*Matt* 27:28; *Mk* 15:17; *Jn* 19:5).

[2] In the case of Carabas, his body was clothed with a rug in quality of "royal robe." In the case of Jesus they put on him "a scarlet robe" (*Matt* 27:28; cf. *Mk* 15:17; *Jn* 19:2, 5; *Lk* 23:11).

[3] In the case of Carabas they used a sheet of papyrus as a "scepter." In the case of Jesus they put "a reed in his right hand" (*Matt* 27:29).

[4] In the case of Carabas, he was "tricked" to believe that he was a "king." In the case of Jesus he was mockingly called "king" (*Matt* 27:28, 37; cf. *Mk* 15:17, 26, 32; *Lk* 23: 3, 37, 38; *Jn* 19:14, 15, 19, 21).

[5] In the case of Carabas "young men" stood on either side in jest, as "bodyguards." In the case of Jesus the soldiers, "bowed the knee before him, and mocked him, saying, Hail, King of the Jews" (*Matt* 27:29, 37; cf. *Mk* 15:18-20; *Lk* 23: 36; *Jn* 19:14, 15, 19, 21). In the case of Jesus, "also the chief priests," as well as "the scribes and elders" were "mocking *him*" (see *Matt* 27:41). With Carabas, "Then

---

[160] *Flaccus*, VI, 36-39, *Philo*, vol. 9, pp. 323-325. On the connection of 'Jesus' with 'Egypt,' see *Matt* 2:13-20, and *Contra Celsum*, p. 28. Significantly, *Bekhorot* 8a registers a confrontation between R. Joshua b. Ḥananya (1st and 2nd centuries), who had served as chorister in the Temple, and was on of the leading rabbinic figure of his time, and a *min* or 'Christian,' taken place in Alexandria. For an analysis of this story, see *Christianity in Talmud & Midrash*, pp. 221-226.

[161] See *The Golden Bough, The Scapegoat*, pp. 418-419; the similarity had been noted before, see ibid, p. 418 n. 1.

others approached him, some pretending to salute him, others to sue for justice, others to consult him on state affairs."

[6] In the case of Carabas the mob used the Aramaic term *marin* ("our Lord") to mock King Agrippa. In the case of Jesus the soldiers "mocked him, saying: "Hail, King of the Jews" (*Matt* 27:29, cf. 37; *Mk* 15:18, cf. 26; *Lk* 23: 36-37; *Jn* 19:3). Paul referred to Jesus with the same title, but with the usual pronunciation: *"maran"* (1*Cor* 16:21).[162]

Jesus' Passion is written in the style of mock-trials performed for the delight of the cheering mobs. This explains the active participation of the "crowd" in the 'legal proceedings,' concluding with the grand finale: Jesus' Crucifixion (see *Matt* 27:20, 24; *Mk* 15: 8, etc.) It was "the whole multitude of them" that brought Jesus to stand trial before Pilate (*Lk* 23:1). Strangely, we are told that Pilate was "afraid" of them (*Jn* 19:8). Sheepishly, Pilate answered not only to the Jewish priests but also to "the crowds," and sought their approval (*Lk* 23:4; cf. 13, 20). In fact it is "they," that is the aforementioned "crowd" that demanded "with loud voices" (*Lk* 23:23; *Jn* 18:40; 19:6, 12, 15), to "crucify" Jesus (*Matt* 27:22; *Mk* 15:8, 13, 14; *Lk* 23:5, 21, cf. 23, 25). To clarify the matter further and make sure that no one would think that there were some pagans among them, it was explained that the "crowd" was made up exclusively of "Jews" (*Jn* 18:31). Meekly, Pilate addresses the Jewish crowd (*Matt* 27:22-23) and goes "out unto them" for consultation (*Jn* 18:29; 19:4). This is contrary to everything known about Roman law. There are no precedents for a Roman officer to go out and seek approval from the "crowd" and "multitude," before rendering a decision. The situation is a bit more awkward in the case of 'Pilate,' from the Latin *pilus* 'javelin."[163] He was not a *kind* person, particularly with respect to the Jews. Philo described him as

---

[162] This term appears once in *Yerushalmi Sanhedrin* VI, 10, 24d.

[163] See *The Life of Jesus*, p. 376. See above, Section II, n. 156.

"naturally inflexible, a blend of self-will and relentlessness."[164] He was dishonest, and known for "the briberies, the insults, the robberies, the outrages and wanton injuries, the executions without trial constantly repeated, the ceaseless and supremely grievous cruelty."[165] Only in a mock-trial would 'Pilate' act sympathetically and benevolent with a 'Jewish crowd.'

The foundational beliefs of Christianity, too, came from Emperor Gaius Caligula (37-41), during his stay in Alexandria.

Jesus never claimed to be a god or demanded to be worshiped.[166] In what follows we hope to show the source of this most fundamental of all Christian beliefs was not Jesus, but Emperor Caligula. It was Caligula—not Jesus—who demanded to be "thought a god."[167] It was the gentile population in Alexandria that inflated his ego, and convinced him that he was god. "For the Alexandrians are adepts at flattery and imposture and hypocrisy," explained Philo, "ready enough with fawning words but causing universal disaster with their loose and unbridled lips."[168] Indeed, the majority of those instigating Caligula "were Egyptians." Adding: They are "a seed bed of evil in whose souls both the venom and the temper of the native crocodiles and asps were reproduced."[169]

Anticipating the position of the Church on Jesus, Caligula proposed that he ought to be worshiped, because he had "the nature (*phisin*) of a god."[170] Interestingly, we are told that Caligula,

---

[164] *The Embassy to Gaius*, 38, 301, *Philo*, vol. 10, p. 151.

[165] *The Embassy to Gaius*, 38, 302, *Philo*, vol. 10, p. 153. Accordingly, in Jewish tradition he was known as 'Phinehas the brigand'; see above, Section II, n. 156.

[166] See the references mentioned in *The Case of the Nazarene Reopened*, p. 433, and above Section II, Chapter 17.

[167] *The Embassy to Gaius*, 198, *Philo*, vol. 10, p. 103.

[168] *The Embassy to Gaius*, 162, *Philo*, vol. 10, p. 83. Greater men than him, among them "Caesar and Alexander," succumbed to the entrapments of adulation and ended up believing that they were gods; see *The Divinity of the Roman Emperor*, p. 76.

[169] *The Embassy to Gaius*, 166, *Philo*, vol. 10, p. 85.

[170] *The Embassy to Gaius*, 368, *Philo*, vol. 10, p. 183.

went so far as to dedicate a temple with priests to his own *numen* [spirit, presence] and to put up within the shrine his golden cult statue which was clad daily with the same clothes as were worn, on that day, by the emperor himself.[171]

In this respect, the principal contribution of Christian theologians was to exchange Caligula's "nature" (*phisin*) for its synonym "essence" (*ousia*). Hence Christianity's foundational doctrine that Jesus, the son "is generated of the essence (*ousia*) of the Father."[172]

An important detail found in Christianity–with no parallels in the history of religions—is the fact that it imputes Jesus' Passion, death, etc, etc, on *all* Jews (see *Matt* 27:25); that is, everywhere, for all time to come, children included. This idea, too, comes from Alexandria. Philo reported that when "the virulent sycophant Isidorus" accused the Jewish leadership of refusing to offer sacrifices on behalf of Caligula, he included *all* Jews. Kindly, sycophant Isidorus explained: "And when I say 'they' I include also the other Jews."[173] There is a perfect logical explanation to sycophant Isidorus' conclusion. For members of a mob, there are no *individuals*, but only people who are and want to be like everyone else. Therefore, if you know one Jew you know every Jew, at any time and at any place.

Anticipating future Christian preachers, Caligula upbraided the

---

[171] *The King's Two Bodies*, p. 501.

[172] See George Foot Moore, *History of Religions*, vol. 2 (Edinburgh: T&T Clark, 1965), p. 171; cf. p. 179. The question dealing with the problem of whether the 'son' is the 'actual' essence or only a 'similar' essence (*homoousios*), was much debated, see *ibid*, pp.179-192. See also Wolfson, *Philo*, vol. 1, pp. 102, 210-1, 277; vol. 2, pp. 106, 107; and *The Church Fathers*, vol. 1, pp. 276, 318-9, 321, 334-5. Concerning the precise sense of the "nature" (*phisin*) of a god, it had been the subject of lively controversy among Christian theologians, resulting in various heretical movements. For a survey of the developments of some of these heresies, see J. P. Kirsch, "Eutychianism," *The Catholic Encyclopedia*, vol. 5 (New York: Robert Appelton Company, 1909), pp. 633-638. Cf. Wolfson, *Philo*, vol. 2, p. 106. For the understanding of *ousia* among Arab and Jewish philosophers, see Harry A. Wolfson, *Studies in the History of Philosophy and Religion*, vol. 2 (Cambridge, Mass.: Harvard University Press, 1977), pp. 304-305, n. 84; cf. ibid, pp. 36-37.

[173] *The Embassy to Gaius*, 355, *Philo*, vol. 10, pp. 177-179. Cf. *Against Apion*, Josephus, 100, vol. 1, p. 338.

Jews, for being "foolish in refusing to believe that I have got the nature (*phisin*) of a god."[174] Understandably, he exhibited "extreme hostility" towards "the whole Jewish race,"[175] and regarded Jews as his "worst enemy."[176] Addressing the Jews, he asked:

> Are you the god-haters who do not believe me to be a god, a god acknowledged among all the other nations but not to be named by you?[177]

Obviously, those "god-haters" ought to be eliminated from the face of the earth. However, prefiguring Christian kindness, Caligula forgave the Jews. Explaining, "They seem to me to be people unfortunate rather than wicked."[178] In this aspect, too, Christian 'kindness' comes from Caligula. At first sight, in light of Matthew's assertion that the entire Jewish people declared: "His (Jesus) blood *be* on us and our children" (*Matt* 27:25; cf. *Acts* 18:6; *Heb* 6:6), one would expect that no effort should be spared to eliminate every single Jew from the face of the earth. Nonetheless, as a kind of *noblesse oblige*, Jesus accepted Caligula' doctrine, and begged God to forgive the Jews, "for they know not what they do" (*Lk* 23:34). Let us point out, however, that in the case of Christianity there is an existential reason as well. Without these moronic Jews, Christendom would not have *a* syntagmatic 'other' against whom it could 'measure' itself.

The Alexandrian roots of Jesus' Trial can help us understand an awkward detail. According to Matthew, the Jews charged Jesus with blasphemy for saying: "I am able to destroy the temple of God, and to build it in three days" (*Matt* 26:61, 65). This sort of speech is meaningless in Jewish law.[179] Moreover, in no place does Jesus ex-

---

[174] *The Embassy to Gaius*, 368, *Philo*, vol. 10, p. 183.

[175] *The Embassy to Gaius*, 201, *Philo*, vol. 10, p. 105.

[176] *The Embassy to Gaius*, 256, p. 131.

[177] *The Embassy to Gaius*, 353, *Philo*, vol. 10, p. 177. As mentioned earlier, those instigating Caligula were Egyptians; see quotation above, at n. 169.

[178] *The Embassy to Gaius*, 362, *Philo*, vol. 10, p. 183.

[179] In the Jewish mind, the Temple does not equal God. To emphasize this point, the law establishes that if one were to destroy the Temple or part thereof, he would be

press any antagonism towards the Temple. Not only did he visit the Temple, but he was deeply concerned with its sanctity, and wished to safeguard it from the abuse of the money changers. Therefore, why would he want to destroy the Temple and then rebuild it? Earlier, we had mentioned that unlike Jesus, Matthew was a Jew-hater.[180] Caligula, as well as all pagans, knew that for a Jew there was "no greater injury than the ruin of the sanctity of their temple."[181] This explains why in the pagan mindset, the destruction of the Temple, allegedly threatened by Jesus, equals blasphemy.

The idea that Jesus was crucified, too, came from Alexandria. Early Judeo-Christians did not recognize the cross, *and did not believe that Jesus was crucified*.[182] The same is true with the *Muslim Scripture*; it recognized Jesus, but it does not acknowledge that Jesus was crucified.[183] The crucifixion was used in the Roman, but not in the Jewish penal system. Indeed, never before or after did Jews adopt this form of punishment. Jews were the *victims* of this form of punishment. What, then, was the basis for the claim that Jews demanded that Jesus should be crucified (see *Matt* 27:22; *Mk* 15:8, 13, 14; *Lk* 23:5, 21, cf. 23, 25)? The answer to this puzzle, too, comes from Alexandria. The crucifixion had been Flaccus' favorite form of dealing with Alexandrian Jews. The description of Jesus' agony, too, is in accordance with the manner in which Flaccus would dispose of the Jews: first, he would flagellate and torture them, and then crucify them. It was expected that at a national festival, such as the birthday of the emperor, the bodies of the crucified victims would be delivered to their relatives for burial. However, in the case of the Jewish victims in Alexan-

---

transgressing a prohibition (*lav*), but he would not be incurring a capital offense; see Maimonides, *Sefer ha-Miṣvot*, ed. and tr. R. Joseph Qafiḥ (Jerusalem: Mossad Harav Kook, 1971), prohibition #65, pp. 215-216.

[180] See above, n. 91.

[181] *The Embassy to Gaius*, 198, *Philo*, vol. 10, p. 103.

[182] See Pines, "The Jewish Christians...," p. 181 n. 48 and p. 190. Cf. above, Section II, n. 113.

[183] See Pines, "The Jewish Christians...," pp. 177, 207-209.

dria,

> Flaccus gave no orders to take down those who had died on the cross. Instead he ordered the crucifixion of the living, to whom the season offered a short-lived though not permanent reprieve in order to postpone the punishment though not to remit it altogether. And he did this after maltreating them with the lash in the middle of the theater and torturing them with fire and the sword.[184]

In accordance with pagan thought, it made 'sense' that Jews would demand that Jesus, too, should die at the cross (see *Matt* 27:22, 23).

There are two details mentioned in the preceding passage that have passed onto the *Christian Scripture*. As with Flaccus, Pilate *first* "scourged Jesus" and *then* delivered him to be crucified (*Matt* 27:28). There is another detail that the *Christian Scripture* borrowed from Flaccus. We are told that in honor of Passover, Pilate "was wont to release unto the people a prisoner, whom they would" (*Matt* 27:15; cf. *Mk* 15:6; *Lk* 23:17; *Jn* 18:39). This is a lie. Never in the history of the Roman Empire, were Jewish convicts "released" on Passover or on any other holiday. Rather, the *Christian Scripture* was 'upgrading' Flaccus' story, from releasing 'the bodies of crucified victims' for burial, to 'releasing convicted prisoners'; and from 'a national Roman festival' to 'Passover.'

29. Theater and the New Faith

In late Antiquity, the stage was used for poking fun at Jews, for all to watch and enjoy. Not only in what was an obvious farce, as in the case of Carabas, but also in historical cases.

> Especially in Syria were the Jews made a subject for mockery and ill-usage in the theater or arena. In the theater their religion was constantly scoffed at, and Jewish women were forced to eat swine's flesh

---

[184] *Flaccus*, 84, *Philo*, vol. 9, p. 349.

on the stage.[185]

It was a way in which to provide good, clean fun to the masses. Occasionally, the number of Jewish victims was so large that it was necessary to use a stadium. As when Vespasian "gave the order for the execution of the old and unserviceable" Jews, to the number of twelve hundred.[186] Flaccus made the torturing and killing of Jews a public spectacle for good folks to enjoy. (The same thing happened during the 'Holy Inquisition' in Spain, Portugal, and Latin America. Burning Jews alive served for family diversion—a nice way to spend a Sunday afternoon with the wife and children).

> The first spectacle lasting from dawn till the third or fourth hour consisted of Jews being scourged, hung up, bound to the wheel, brutally mauled and haled for their death march through the middle of the orchestra. After this splendid exhibition came dancers and mimes and flute players and all the other amusements of theatrical competitions.[187]

This, Flaccus did "after maltreating them with the lash in the *middle of the theater* (our italics) and torturing them with fire and the sword." It is important to take note that the killing of Jews was presented as *a theatrical show*. Caligula's 'trial' of Jews has been described as a

> combination of a theater and a prison in place of a tribunal, theater-like in the cackling of their hisses, their hisses, their mockery and unbounded jeering, prison-like in the strokes inflicted on our flesh [Philo and other members of the Jewish delegation], the torture, the racking of the whole soul through the blasphemies against God and menaces launched upon us by this mighty despot, who resented the affront not to another, since he might easily have changed his mind, but to himself and his desire of deification to which he supposed the Jews alone did not assent and could not pledge themselves to sub-

---

[185] Elmslie, *The Mishna on Idolatry*, p. 26.

[186] Josephus, *Jewish War*, III, 540, vol. 2, p. 729.

[187] *Flaccus*, 83-85, *Philo*, vol. 9, pp. 347-349.

scribe.[188]

Christianity is a *performance game*.[189] The Christian account of Jesus' ministry leading to the Passion is an intense, dramatic experience. It resembles a Greek drama, rather than any of the writings of the *Hebrew Scripture*.[190] There were very close, intimate ties, between the mimic theater and the new faith.[191] Actually, the Church is a stage where the greatest theatrical murder of all time is performed. The audiences are the masses of faithful (*fidelis Christianus*). Through the Eucharist, the faithful experiences Jesus' agony—the most loathsome crime in the history of mankind. Christian liturgy is much more than prayer: it is a dramatic performance where the faithful experiences Jesus' Passion and Resurrection. As noted by a serious student of early Christian history, "The liturgy now was transformed into a public spectacle, accessible to all." Adding, "much as the worship of the Olympian pantheon had been."[192] Therefore, we should not be surprised to discover that the Church adopted the architectural features of the civil Basilica.

> The first public Christian buildings thus were some of the most prominent in their cities, for they took over the civil basilica's architectural style, its grand size, and ostentatious display.[193]

The close relationship between the Christian liturgy and a theatrical performance can be seen in the architectural style of the Church,

---

[188] *The Embassy to Gaius*, 368, *Philo*, vol. 10, p. 183.

[189] From the 4th century onward, new forms of art grew out of the Roman Catholic mass, in the form of religious drama, and the musical setting for the suffering and resurrection of Jesus. This resulted in the development of 'Passion Music.'

[190] See B. H. Branscomb, "The Dramatic Instinct of Early Christianity," *Journal of Bible and Religion* 9 (1941), pp. 3-9.

[191] See *Masks Mimes and Miracles*, pp. 17-21, 120-123; cf. 135-150. In the Roman Empire flourished mime, not drama; see *The Silver Age of Latin Literature, From Tiberius to Trajan*, p. 55.

[192] James Riley Strange, *The Emergence of the Christian Basilica in the Fourth Century* (Binghamton, New York: Global Publication, Binghamton University, 2000), p. 3.

[193] *The Emergence of the Christian Basilica in the Fourth Century*, p. 4, n. 8. Cf. ibid, p. 15.

down to the present. "Many church sanctuaries have for some years contained raised platforms resembling theater or auditorium stages."[194] The change is not merely "cosmetic." It reflects "a specific worship style."

> Thus as the aim of worship more and more approximates the aim of public performances of various types, so the architecture of the one mimics the architecture of the other.[195]

The theatrical performance of Christianity can help us understand a detail mentioned in connection with the crucifixion. *Jn* 19: 34 states, "one of the soldiers with a spear pierced his (Jesus) side, and forthwith came there out blood and water." Why was it necessary to emphasize this point? The answer is obvious once we realize that the stage, in its various forms, was the preferred setting not only for torturing and killing Jews, but also for displaying all forms of anti-Judaic sentiments. The theatrical performance of a 'crucifixion,' demanded the 'flow of blood': the public *expected to see the profuse flowing of blood*, as a theatric close up.

> The crucifixion was enacted with a considerable degree of stage realism. Josephus reports that "a great quantity of artificial blood flowed down from the one crucified." Suetonius records a performance on the day of Caligula's assassination, at the close of which "the chief actor falls as he is making his escape and vomits blood." Suetonius notes that the performance was immediately followed by a humorous after piece in which certain mimic fools (*actors secundarum partium*) "so vied with one another in giving evidence of their proficiency at dying that the stage swam in blood."[196]

The stage, whether in the gymnasium, stadium, or theater, was

---

[194] *The Emergence of the Christian Basilica in the Fourth Century*, p. 18.

[195] *The Emergence of the Christian Basilica in the Fourth Century*, pp. 18-19.

[196] "Runaway Paul," p. 155. The reference to Josephus is *Jewish Antiquities*, 19.94, vol. 9, p. 261. The rabbis were acquainted with this form of representation. The 'trial' of Jesus' disciples, *Sanhedrin* 43a is depicted in the mode of a mock-trial; cf. *Christianity in Talmud & Midrash*, p. 92. Mock-trials are common in aggadic literature; see, for example, *'Aboda Zara* 2a-3b.

the preferred medium where the 'multitudes' and 'crowds' actually gained their voices fully, and *made demands*. In this fashion, the Church *became* a dramatic stage, whose main purpose was to replay Jesus' Passion for the faithful Christian.

As in all great theatrical murders, Oedipus, Hamlet, etc, the 'facts' presented on the stage have no legal standing. If there actually were somebody named 'Othello,' he could not be charged with murdering Desdemona on the basis of Shakespeare's play. The 'actions' unfolding in a dramatic play are designed to stir emotions, not to justify murdering and ransacking the property of individuals named 'Mr. Othello.' The exception to this rule is the 'Jew,' in the sensational melodrama, played day in and day out at the Church.

A key lesson that Christianity learned from Alexandria is that when judging Israel, standard legal procedure needs not be followed. Rather, the accuser may act as witness, prosecutor, judge, and executioner. Given that it is 'known' that the accused is wretched and perfidious, it would be pointless to let him speak. Philo wrote that when Caligula summoned the Jewish leadership for refusing to worship him, they soon discovered "that we had come into the presence not of a judge but of an accuser more hostile than those arrayed against us."[197] Indeed, as he was judging them, they would be

> mocked and reviled by our adversaries, as they do in mimes at the theaters. For indeed the business was a sort of mime; the judge had taken the role of accuser, the accuser the role of a bad judge who had eyes only for his enmity and not for the actual truth.[198]

Shamelessly, the editors of the *Christian Scripture* submitted the people that heard the voice of the Living God at Sinai to the same sort of 'trial.' It is a sad commentary that through intimidation, demonization, bullying, and incivility, the veracity of such 'trial' could pass the straight face test of two millennia of history. However, we should not be judgmental. Let us be reasonable, if Caligula could

---

[197] *The Embassy to Gaius*, 349, *Philo*, vol. 10, p. 175.
[198] *The Embassy to Gaius*, 359, *Philo*, vol. 10, p.179.

submit Israel to this sort of 'trial' for refusing to worship him, why would it be improper for Christendom to do the same with Jews for refusing to worship Jesus?

30. Jesus of Alexandria

"Christianity," wrote Professor Nicholls, "does not rest on what Jesus taught himself, still less on what he taught about himself. It rests on what his followers began to teach about him after his death."[199] Accordingly, we propose that there are *two* Jesu*ses*. First, there was the historical Jesus of flesh and blood, who flourished in the land of Israel before the Destruction of the Temple (68 CE). Then, there was the 'Alexandrian' Jesus, depicted *post mortem* by the anonymous editors and redactors of the *Christian Scripture*. There is little about the Alexandrian Jesus having to do either with the land, the people, or the *Scripture* of Israel: he is a *pagan* invention, manufactured by the same people that inspired the 'multitude' and 'crowds' roaming through the streets of Alexandria, to kill Jews and vandalize their property. What I am proposing is that just as the mock-trial of Carabas was used to model the 'Trial of Jesus,' the person of Caligula was used to shape the Alexandrian Jesus. Consider the following six points.

[1] Just as Caligula demanded to be "thought a god," the *Christian Scripture*, too, demands that Jesus should be thought as god.[200]

[2] Just as Caligula demanded to be worshiped by everyone, particularly Jews, the Church, too, demanded that all should worship Jesus, Jews in particular.

---

[199] *Christian Antisemitism*, p. 44.
[200] *The Embassy to Gaius*, 198, *Philo*, vol. 10, p. 103.

[3] Just as Caligula justified his "extreme hostility" towards "the whole Jewish race,"[201] because they alone, "among all the other nations" refused to acknowledge that he was a god,[202] the Church, too, used a similar argument to justify the persecution of Jews. Jews were Caligula's "worst enemy,"[203] the same was with the Church.

[4] Just as Caligula ended up having 'compassion' on the Jews, because they are a "people unfortunate rather than wicked,"[204] Christianity, too, expressed the same largesse of spirit, and for the same reason. Jews, the only people that heard the living voice of God at Sinai, should be forgiven for not believing in Jesus, because "they know not what they do" (*Lk* 23:34).

[5] Just as Caligula claimed to have "the nature (*phisin*) of a god," Christian theologians claimed that Jesus has the "essence" (*ousia*) of a god. However, a vast abyss opens between Caligula and the Alexandrian Jesus, easy for all to grasp: Caligula had "the nature (*phisin*) of a god," whereas Jesus had the "essence" (*ousia*) of a god.[205] Let it be known that the first conflict in Christendom was the result of a split between two priests in Alexandria, Athanasius (ca. 293-373) and Arius, concerning the 'nature/essence' of Jesus. The conflict was finally settled in the council of Nicaea, convened by Emperor Constantine in year 325, when Arius was declared a heretic.[206]

[6] In his war against Israel, Caligula used a two-pronged line of attack. To demoralize the Jewish people, they were submitted to the "mockery" and "jeering" of the crowd. Launching, at the same time,

---

[201] *The Embassy to Gaius*, 201, *Philo*, vol. 10, p. 105.

[202] *The Embassy to Gaius*, 353, *Philo*, vol. 10, p. 177. As Philo informed us, those instigating Caligula were Egyptians; see quotation above, n. 168.

[203] *The Embassy to Gaius*, 256, *Philo*, vol. 10, p. 131.

[204] *The Embassy to Gaius*, 362, *Philo*, vol. 10, p. 183.

[205] See quotation above at n. 172.

[206] See above "Introduction," n. 34.

a psychological war against their beliefs, "racking of the whole soul [of the Jewish victims] through the blasphemies against God."[207] Christianity chose the same two-pronged tactic. On the one hand, instead of sparking a significant dialogue, Christianity opted to demonize Jews, circulating all kind of slanderous charges, based on pseudo-events, (e.g., 'Jews are god-killers') while launching at the same time, a series of mud-slinging attacks against the faith of Israel, the Law of Israel, and the God of Israel. (In Biblical times, too, the enemies of Israel used the same two-pronged tactic; see *Ps* 42).[208] The fact that Jews continue to flourish to the present day exasperates the old establishment, determined to silence the voice of the living God at Sinai.

An important lesson that the ecclesiastical authorities learned from the 'multitudes' and 'crowds' roaming through the streets of Alexandria is that Jewish property is there for all to take—with impunity. In the same spirit, they ransacked the library of Alexandrian Jewry, beginning with the Greek translation of the *Hebrew Scripture* (the *Septuagint*)—pride and glory of Hellenistic Jewry—as well as the works of highly sophisticated members of the same community. The most important of which, were Philo's writings. Professor Wolfson showed how some of the primary theological arguments and ideas found in the *Christian Scripture* and the *Church Fathers*, were built on the basis of the religious philosophy developed by Philo (without acknowledging him).[209] However, whereas Philo developed his themes and ideas to validate Jewish Law and doctrine in the face of pagan philosophy, Christian theologians used Philo's works to undermine Judaism in the eyes of a fundamentally analphabetic public.

---

[207] *The Embassy to Gaius*, 368, *Philo*, vol. 10, p. 183.

[208] For an analysis of this psalm, see *HS*, vol. 1, pp. 218-220. Maimonides called attention to the two-pronged tactic used by anti-Semites against Israel; see *HS*, vol. 1, p. 221.

[209] Harry Wolfson, *Philo*, 2 vols. (1947); *Studies in the History of Religious Philosophy* (1961); and *The Philosophy of the Church Fathers* vol. 1 (1971).

This is in harmony with pagan spirituality, which permits the victor to appropriate the personality of the victim. On this ground the Church assumed the right to appropriate the persona of vanquished Israel, and designate herself *Verus Israel*. There is ample precedent to justify this course of action. If it is acceptable to murder Jews and ransack their property, why it should be improper to do the same with their works and ideas? After all, compassionate stealing shouldn't be more heinous than compassionate murder. The fact that Christian art, as well as Christian liturgy, kept on incorporating imperial symbols and ceremonies of pagan government, indicate the close proximity between the ideologies of both systems.[210]

Alexandria—not Jerusalem or Rome—is "the Cradle" of the *Christian Scripture*. *Codex Alexandrinus*, known as Codex A (late 4th century early 5th century)—'Glory and Pride' of the British Museum—is the first Greek manuscript of the Old and New Testaments. Some believe that *Codex Vaticanus*, known as Codex B, certainly the most important of the great uncials (first half of the 4th century), as well as *Codex Sinaiticus*, was written in Alexandria. The Church of Alexandria, founded by the Apostle Mark, was the first Apostolic See (*sedes apostolica*), and the dominant Church during the opening two centuries of Christianity. Alexandrian theologians also helped shaped some of the most important creeds of the New Faith.

We will conclude this chapter with an important note. According to Greco-Roman historiography, the account given in the *Christian Scripture* may be regarded as 'historically true.' A most significant element in this sort of historiography is that

> the boundaries between creative imagination and willful mendacity, between fiction and lying, often proved impossible to determine.[211]

---

[210] The same was done with the *Hebrew Scripture*. In this connection we should remember that in the eyes of the Church, deception for 'a good purpose' is acceptable, see Garry Will, *Papal Sins* (New York: Image Books, 2001), pp. 277-295. The same is with lying for 'a good cause,' see ibid, pp. 283-288; on intellectual 'honesty,' see ibid, pp. 4-9, and Appendix 4.

[211] *Fiction as History*, p. 2.

In the intellectual environment of pagan humanity, "History was being invented all over again." This attitude affected not only their account of past events, but also when 'reporting' what the narrator had supposedly 'witnessed.' In this fashion,

> the present was awash in so many miracles and marvels that not even the credulous or the pious could swallow them all.[212]

This attitude affected the Greco-Roman concept of 'history.'

> Cicero could proclaim Herodotus with equanimity as the Father of History and then go on to denounce him as the author of innumerable fabulous tales. History had simply become the plot—what happened or what was said to have happened.[213]

To the Hellenistic mindset, there is no contradiction between 'history' and 'fiction.' All that the Greek term *istoria* meant was a "story as it was known and told—the plot."[214] In short,

> Rewriting the past—the intrusion of fiction into what was taken to be history—becomes from this period of Lucillius and Martial an increasingly conspicuous feature of the Graeco-Roman world. Origen strained every nerve in the third century to confute Celsus' elaborate attempt to expose the Gospel narratives as fiction, and yet he had to admit that fabrication had already thrown the objectivity of what he considered the historical past into considerable doubt.[215]

The difference between 'history' and 'fiction' is the *medium*. Fiction depends, exclusively, on invocation; that is, the authority of the first-party platform addressing the audience. To Christians, the Alexandrian Jesus is apodictic truth because it so had been proclaimed from the first-person platform of the Church. By the same token, the Jesus that lived and died in the Holy Land, and interacted with his

---

[212] *Fiction as History*, p. 3.

[213] *Fiction as History*, p. 8. Cf. *Against Apion*, I, 44-46, *Josephus*, vol. 1, p. 181; and 73, p. 192.

[214] *Fiction as History*, p. 9.

[215] *Fiction as History*, p. 10.

contemporaries and the Judeo-*minim*, is a demonic prevarication of the 'real' Jesus. Of this truth the faithful could be absolutely certain since it was so proclaimed from the first-person platform.

SECTION IV

THE ALLIANCE CROSS-SWORD

MEGALOMANIA AND THE CULTURE OF OBEDIENCE-SUBMISSION

31. Defrocking Israel and Dethroning the God of Sinai

The *Christian Scripture* does not portray a trial, but a trial within a trial. 'The facts' presented in Jesus' Trial are *not* designed to exonerate Jesus. Everyone in the audience knows that the charges are phony. The purpose of Jesus' Trial is to serve as the stage for another trial, *where* a Cosmic Puppeteer pulls the strings, orchestrating every movement of the actors, leading to the *grand finale*: defrocking Israel and dethroning the God that spoke at Sinai: simultaneously. Yes, by defrocking Israel, on whose hands God commanded the Law, the Cosmic Puppeteer is in fact dislodging the very God that entrusted to Israel her historic destiny! This is true, not because Jesus said so— Jesus never said such an abomination— nor because some celestial voice spoke face to face with the anonymous writers and editors of the *Christian Scripture*, as when God spoke to Israel in Sinai. It is so, because to a third-party audience, the first-person platform—*any* first-person platform—equals the 'Gospel Truth' and supersedes God's voice at Sinai (see above Chapter 1). Defrocking Israel and dethroning the God of Sinai are two sides of the same coin: you cannot defrock Israel without deposing the God that chose them, and vice versa. Not only is Israel perfidious and ignominious and sinful, but their God, too, is vengeful, implacable and incapable of love. Thus, in a quick, Oedipal maneuver, Christianity replaced the Father and His Law, with his son and love—substituting, at the same time, herself for Israel (=*Verus Israel*).[1]

Because Christian love calls for hatred of the 'other'—be it the 'Devil' or the 'Perfidious Jew'—Christian love is narcissistic: it demands 100% affirmation—if not, you are toxic. Freud made the essential point that those "who do not belong to the community of believers," are not included in Christian love. Adding:

---

[1] See *HS*, vol. 1, pp. 254-258.

Therefore a religion, even if it calls itself the religion of love, must be hard and unloving to those who do not belong to it. Fundamentally indeed every religion is in the same way a religion of love for all those whom it embraces; while cruelty and intolerance toward those who do not belong to it are natural to every religion.

The last statement is true, only if one were to define 'religion' in Christian (and Muslim) terms. Judaism, as we had shown earlier, rejects the very notion of 'religious enemy' (see "Introduction"). Freud alerted the reader to bear in mind that,

> If today that intolerance no longer shows itself so violent and cruel as in former centuries, we can scarcely conclude that there has been a softening in human manners. The cause is rather to be found in the undeniable weakening of religious feelings and the libidinal ties which depend upon them.

Modern political and secular organizations, although overtly non-religious, have their own version of 'the religious enemy.' In this regard, Freud acutely points out that,

> If another group tie takes the place of the religious one—and the socialistic tie [=Nazism, Communism, Labor] seems to be succeeding in doing so—then there will be the same intolerance toward outsiders as in the age of the Wars of Religion; and if differences between scientific opinions could ever attain a similar significance for groups, the same result would again be repeated with this new motivation.[2]

The narcissistic energy created by Christianity in the realm of religion, was used by the emerging European nations to inflate their national ego. Hitler, Mussolini, Stalin, *et al* were successful in their political ideology, *because* Christian society had been conditioned for centuries to narcissistic fantasies. In the Oedipus complex, you hate your father so much that you kill him, and in the process you become him. Because in essence, the Church functioned as the 'Father-figure,'

---

[2] Sigmund Freud, *Group Psychology and the Analysis of the Ego* (New York: Bantam Books, 1960), p. 39.

both intellectual and political secularists fell into the Oedipal trap.³ As modern secularists tried to kill the Church and the Christian religion, they internalized the same structures of thought and methodologies as those of the 'Church/Father.' Marxism, many forms of atheism and liberalism, as well as bogus scientists and political ideologues, are as authoritarian and intolerant of difference as the 'Orwellian Big Brother' they claim to displace. Ultimately, 'It is so, because they claim to be so from some sacrosanct platform.' The same Oedipal archetype continues to dominate Western thought and civilization. C. G. Jung explained:

> No archetype can be reduced to a simple formula. It is a vessel, which we can never empty, and never fill. It has potential existence only, and when it takes shape in matter it is no longer what it was. It persists throughout the ages and requires interpreting ever anew. The archetypes are the imperishable elements of the unconscious, but they change their shape continuously.⁴

We can now proceed to analyze two forms of narcissism: one that Eric Fromm (1900-1980) designates 'benign', and the other that he designates 'malignant.' In the 'benign' case, "the object of narcissism is the result of a person's effort," for instance, the pride that an artisan and a scientist have in their work and creation.

> Inasmuch as the object of his narcissism is something that he has to work for, his exclusive interest in what is *his* work and *his* achievement is constantly balanced by his interest in the process of work itself, and the material he is working with. The dynamics of this benign narcissism thus are self-checking. The energy which propels the work is, to a large extent, of a narcissistic nature, but the very fact that the work itself makes it necessary to be related to reality, constantly curbs the narcissism and keeps it within bounds. This mechanism may ex-

---

³ Although it applied to herself epithets such as 'Mother Church,' 'Ecclesia,' 'Holy Lady,' in the eyes of the general public, the Church acted as a 'despotic father,' rather than as a 'compassionate mother.'

⁴ C. G. Jung, "The Psychology of the Child Archetype," in *Essays on a Science of Mythology* (Princeton, N.J.: Princeton University Press, 1989), p. 98.

plain why we find so many narcissistic people who are at the same time highly creative.⁵ [Italics in original]

'Malignant narcissism' has to do with the verb 'to be'—a verb which does not exist in Semitic languages.⁶ In such case, a person need not produce or accomplish anything. He 'is' intrinsically superior to the 'other' because it has been so proclaimed from some sacrosanct podium (=first-person platform). Personal excellence and accomplishments are of no consequence. What matters, is *who* you 'are,' not *what* you have personally accomplished. This applies not only to individuals, but to social groups as well, as it had been vigorously debated in Spain by *cristianos nuevos* ('new Christians,' that is, Jews that converted to Christianity) and *cristianos viejos* ('old Christians'). The 'new Christians' contended that 'honor' has to do with personal achievement and excellence; whereas the 'old Christians' maintained that it has to do with family status, the *caste* to which 'you belong'— not your personal accomplishments.⁷ That, precisely, is the difference between Judaism and the Christianity of Paul. "Being justified by faith" (*Rom* 5:1; cf. 10:4), and indulging in "grace" (*Rom* 5:2) and the "love of God," has to do with "the Holy Ghost which is given to us" (*Rom* 5:3), i.e., Christians. Accordingly, the faithful "shall be saved by his [Jesus'] life" and "blood" (*Rom* 5:9-10). Thus, the faithful can take refuge in Jesus (*Rom* 7:25), and would no longer be accountable for their actions, since there is "no condemnation to those" in Jesus (*Rom* 8:1). The reason for that is that Christians *are* "free from the law of sin and of death" (*Rom* 8:2). This means that whoever "believes with his heart" will be "justified," regardless of personal behavior (*Rom* 9:30-32; 10:8-9, cf. 1:16; 3:22-28; 5:1-2; *Gal* 5:5; 1*Pet* 5:9-10; *Jn* 6:27-29). A Christian shall be saved because of what he *is*, no matter what. In stark contradiction, according Judaism and the *Hebrew Scripture*, man's salvation depends on the "works" and *personal accomplishments* of

---

⁵ Eric Fromm, *The Heart of Man* (NY: Harper & Row, 1964), p. 92.

⁶ See *HS*, vol. 1, pp. 13-20.

⁷ See *In the Shadow of History*, pp. 34-37; cf. ibid, pp. 66-70, 111-112.

the individual—not on who he *is*.

Malignant narcissism is a peculiar form of megalomania. People indulging in this sort of dynamic, whether at the personal or at the social level, will find it difficult to tolerate the accomplishments of the 'other.' Having the difference between Jews and Christians in mind, Eric Fromm wrote:

> One who has learned to achieve cannot help acknowledging that others have achieved similar things in similar ways—even if his narcissism may persuade him that his own achievement is greater than that of others. One who has achieved nothing will find it difficult to appreciate the achievement of others, and thus he will be forced to isolate himself increasingly in narcissistic splendor.[8]

We had the opportunity to see the centrality that hatred of the 'Jew' plays in Christianity: he is the *existential* 'other.' Without the 'Jew/other' against whom to stand in "narcissistic splendor", it would be impossible to distinguish Christianity from any other pagan religion. The purpose of theology and theological discourse is to rationalize this fundamental doctrine. It is not a terribly difficult task. All that the faithful need to confirm the Christian "narcissistic splendor" is to point an accusing finger at the voiceless Jew. In this fashion, even the idle mobs (*plethos, oxlous*) can attain sainthood; all what is necessary is to point an accusing finger at the Jews, preferably implicating them in some exotic crime. In this sense, Christianity has the distinction of creating a public perennially addicted to hatred. The non-stop rhetoric about 'love,' is a ruse to hide the fact that unless you are terminally keen on hating the 'other,' you would not be able to swallow the "narcissistic splendor" of Christian megalomania. Successful dictators are the learned practitioners of malignant narcissism.

---

[8] *The Heart of Man*, p. 93.

32. Israel's Primordial Struggle

The conflict between Israel and pagan humanity centers on the concept of dominion. In the pagan mind, dominion is synonymous with 'might.' Given that pagan 'might' is fundamental, and not controlled by any primary or elemental law, it is, by definition, a *tyrannical power*. For Israel, dominion is the effect of creation, *ex nihilo*, and therefore exclusive to the God of the *Hebrew Scripture*. These views concern two radically opposed concepts of the world.

Pagan humanity conceives of the universe in anthropocentric terms. Not only do the gods exhibit human traits and characteristics, but *man*, too, in either his mundane form or in some superlative mode, stands at the center of the universe. An anthropocentric universe is hierarchically structured, as a pyramid, on top of which stands a god or a group of gods. These gods exercise dominion because of their might: they have power, albeit limited in time and space, as per polytheistic theology. Entities with power, and the authority they endow on others, are tyrannical, and require no justification for discharging their dominion. This is why, a 'Law' standing above *everyone*, as per the *Hebrew Scripture*, is intolerable, since it would interfere with the 'tyrannical freedom' enjoyed by the gods. Tyrannical freedom constitutes the identifying nature of divinity in a double sense. Not only do gods exercise tyrannical power, but also, tyrants *are* gods: the formula deity=tyrant is reversible. On this basis, absolute rulers claim to be gods: their divinity is generated by the power they posses. "Mine is my river," announced Pharaoh, referring to the Nile, "and I made my own self" (*Ez* 29:3).[9] When rulers such as Alexander and Julius Caesar claimed to be gods and demanded to be worshiped, their claim was a corollary of their absolute form of government—the idea was *political*, not *theological*. "Under the ideal of government which they had in mind, they were themselves the au-

---

[9] Hence the pagan idea of the sovereign as 'Cosmocrator'; see *HS*, vol. 1, pp. 108, 200, 208. In the *Christian Scripture*, too, Jesus is described as a 'Cosmocrator'; see below Chapter 34.

thors of their own divinity."¹⁰

Tyrants flourish in environments where the boundary between the human and the divine is a function of power. It is precisely in such a setting that absolute rulers end up gods. Eric Fromm, who experienced the yoke of tyranny first-hand, offered a description of the mindset of these rulers:

> They have attained absolute power; their word is the ultimate judgment of everything, including life and death; there seems to be no limit to their capacity to do what they want. They are gods, limited only by illness, age and death.¹¹

For the Hebrews, dominion is the effect of creation; specifically, of creation *ex-nihilo*. Unlike pagan divinities, the God of Israel has absolute dominion *because* He *created* everything—*totally and thoroughly*—out of nothing. This principle was formulated with precision and elegance, by R. Isaac Abendana (c. 1640-c. 1710): "Whereas God Almighty is the Lord and Governor of the Universe, as having by Right of Creation the Supreme Dominion over all Creatures."¹² The

---

¹⁰ *The Divinity of the Roman Emperor*, p. 76. The rabbis associate the political "head" (*rosh*) of a pagan government, with "idolatry" (*'aboda zara*); see *Nu* 14:4 and *Mekhilta de-R. Yishma'el, Beshallaḥ, Vayyassa'* I, p. 153. For some comments and background, see *Em la-Miqra*, vol. 4, 43a-b. The fact that the *Christian Scripture, Col* 2:19, refers to Jesus as "the Head" (=*rosh*), clearly shows the close association between the political "head" and Jesus; see *Em la-Miqra*, vol. 1, 82b-83a, and cf. ibid. 1b-2a. Hence the equation: deity=political head, political head=deity. This is the theory underlying pagan governance *before* and *after* Christianity; see *HS*, vol. 1, Chapter 26. Hence the intimate relation between '*political atheism*' and 'religion.' For some provocative analysis of this topic in contemporary politics, see Chris Hedges, *When Atheism Becomes Religion* (New York: Free Press, 2008).

¹¹ *The Heart of Man*, p. 76.

¹² R. Isaac Abendana, *Discourses on the Ecclesiastical and Civil Polity of the Jews* (London, 1706), p. 126. The source is rabbinic; see *Bereshit Rabba*, eds. J. Theodor and Ch. Albeck, vol. 1 (Jerusalem: Wahrman Books, 1965) XLVI, p. 460, where God said to Abraham: "It should suffice to you that I am your God, it should suffice to you that I am your *patron*." Jewish lexicographers interpret Greek "*patron(ous)*" to mean 'advocate, defender'; see *A Dictionary of Greek & Latin Legal Terms*, p. 139. However, I think that here *patron* stands for 'master,' someone with 'dominion' over you. This is the way this term was interpreted by R. Samuel Yafe Ashkenazi, *Yefe To'ar, Bereshit* (Venice, 5357/1595), 271c, *s.v. dayyakh*: "In addition of being 'God,' that is,

God of Israel has indeed power. However, He exercises power according to the norms of justice (see God's dialogue with Abraham, *Gn* 18:17-33). Above all, the God of Israel is the master of dissimulation. Because He created everything, nothing can resist His presence. Therefore, even when He 'crossed' the Sea to intervene on behalf of Israel, His "footsteps are unknown" (*Ps* 77:27); i.e., He leaves no traces.[13] Therefore His power is not—it cannot be—observable. "We do not find the Almighty of great power"—declared Job! (*Job* 34:37).[14] God's voice is *not* power; but, as the Psalmist sung, His voice is "*in* the power...*in* the waters...*in* the thunder." It is "the voice of the Lord" that breaks "the cedars of Lebanon...that makes them jump as a calf...and strips the forests bare" (*Ps* 29:3-9).

Given that in the *Hebrew Scripture* every human being is created in God's image, and given that there is a *single* God, creator of everyone, it follows that every man and woman is fundamentally equal. Therefore, Judaism rejects the notion of human hierarchy, of a superior *anthropos* sharing a common substance with the divine (see below). Power does not award a divinity license to act outside the canons of justice. To a Jew, a tyrant, be he Pharaoh or Caligula, is a wretched individual—not a god or demigod!

These two concepts lead to two radically different forms of religious devotion. In an anthropocentric universe, you *must* worship the deity: to gain atonement, or good fortune, or to avoid pain, disaster, etc. By contrast, the *Hebrew Scripture* proposes a theocentric universe, rotating around the Creator. Rather than 'worshipping' as per

---

'the First Cause,' I also am 'Lord,' a Sovereign that executes His will'"; that is, without any encumbrance. The association 'Creation/Dominion' is explicit in Maimonides, *Guide* I, 61. See my "Newton, Maimonidean," *Review of Rabbinic Judaism* 6 (2003), pp. 232-233. See also R. Saul Levi Mortera, *Gib'at Shaul*, p. 61.

[13] See *HS*, vol. 1, pp. 25-28; cf. ibid, p. 21.

[14] As it has been pointed out by R. Lindo, the English translator of R. Manasseh Ben Israel, *The Conciliator*, 2 vols. (London: 5602-1842), vol. 1, p. 137 n. 1: "This is the exact translation of the Hebrew words, in the English Bible the Hebrew in this (and so many instances) is not exactly adhered to." Let us note that this is how this verse was understood by the sages of the Talmud; see *'Aboda Zara* 4a; *Yerushalmi Berakhot* IX, 1, 12d.

pagan religion, in Israel you *serve* God because you have *chosen* to. Contrary to pagan religion where religion is *imposed* by the might of a god or gods, Hebrew devotion is the effect of *election* (Heb. *beḥira*). The God of Israel does not impose His service. Rather, you *choose* to serve Him and He *chooses* to establish a covenant (Heb. *berit*) with you. Hebrew election (*beḥira*) involves *mutual* consent, where the parties announce *publicly* their *approval* and *commitment* to contract a specific covenant. As when Israel responded to God's request to establish a covenant with Him (see *Ex* 19:3-6), and declared: "We shall act upon [what you propose] and we shall comply with [what you will further propose] (*Ex* 24:7), the prophets and rabbis compared the covenant (Heb. *berit*) to a nuptial contract: it involves a passionate and unconditional love, and will last for all time. It also resembles the love between parents and children: it is dynamic and perpetually growing.[15] Within the context of a covenant (Heb. *berit*), devotion is an expression of what the *Hebrew Scripture* designates *ahaba*, 'pure, unmotivated love,' and the rabbis designate *leshem shamayim* 'for the sake of Heaven'—a devotion not conditioned by interest, earthly or divine. This type of devotion finds expression in Israel's attitude towards her national devastation and personal catastrophe. In this respect, Jews act differently than pagans. As noted by Sigmund Freud:

> The people of Israel believed themselves to be God's favorite child, and when the great Father hurled visitation after visitation upon them, it still never shook them in this belief or caused them to doubt his power and his justice; they proceeded instead to bring their prophets into the world to declare their sinfulness to them and out of their sense of guilt they constructed the stringent commandment of their priestly religion. It is curious how differently a savage behaves! If he has had bad fortune, he does not throw the blame on himself, but on his fetish, who has plainly not done his duty by him, and he belabors it instead of punishing himself.[16]

---

[15] This explains why Judaism is ineffective in Oedipal environments.

[16] Sigmund Freud, *Civilization and its Discontents* (Garden City, N.Y.: Doubleday & Company, 1958), p. 81.

Two thousand years of expulsions, ignominy, and physical and psychological torture inflicted by the 'monotheistic religions' on Israel, illustrate the meaning of Jewish *ahaba* for God.

Jews were first conceiving of the universe in terms of a theocentric system. That is the reason why tyrants are their archenemies. Concerning this pivotal point, Aldous Huxley (1894-1963) observed:

> Totalitarian politicians demand obedience and conformity in every sphere of life, including of course, the religious. Here, their aim is to use religion as an instrument of social consolidation, an increaser of the country's military efficiency. For this reason, the only kind of religion they favor is strictly anthropocentric, exclusive and nationalistic. Theocentric religion, involving the worship of God for his own sake, is inadmissible in a totalitarian state.[17]

We have noted earlier that prior to Christianity, the only enemies of Israel were political. The reason that Christianity and then Islam clashed with Jews and Judaism, is that they attained prominence thanks to the support of Israel's natural enemies: tyrants and political despots: hence, the centrality of 'power' in the theological apparatus of these 'monotheistic religions.'

33. The Theology of Power

Contrary to Judaism and the *Hebrew Scripture*, Christianity proposes an anthropocentric universe, at the center of which stands Jesus. Christianity repudiates the Jesus of history. (There is no doubt in my mind that the same pious hands that burned countless Jews for refusing to worship 'Jesus,' would not have hesitated to burn alive the Jesus of history for refusing to worship the 'Jesus' manufactured by

---

[17] Aldous Huxley, "Politics and Religion," in *Collected Essays* (New York: Harper & Row, 1971), p. 278. The idea, "the worship of God for his own sake" (=*le-shem shamayim*) is a major rabbinic concept; see Mishna *Abot* 2:12; *Mekhilta de-R. Yishma'el, Bo*, VII, p. 21; *Berakot* 17a; *MT De'ot* 3:3; *Judaism*, vol. 2, p. 98, cf. ibid, vol. 3, p. 167.

the ecclesiastical authorities.) The Jesus of Christianity is a *Übermensch* manufactured in Alexandria. (Such a figure continues to keep appearing and reappearing throughout Europe's long spiritual and political history).[18] Unlike the common man, the Christian *Übermensch* has a substance compatible with both man and god (*homoousios*). Accordingly, Jesus is described as the human "incarnation" of the "Word" or divine *logos* by which the world was created (see *Jn* 1:14, *Revelation* 19:13; cf. *Rom* 9:5). For centuries, Christian theologians labored assiduously to elucidate the 'mystery' of this revelation. However, for the common man in the Hellenistic world no explanation was necessary. This was the standard claim made by Roman emperors and kings, who claimed to be the "incarnation" of something; e.g., "of the eternally productive power of the Roman people"; or "the *Maiestas populi Romani* [something akin to the Christian Holy Ghost] of which he [the king] is the incarnation."[19] It is a well-known fact that,

> the duplication of human and divine natures in one man was an idea not at all foreign to classical thought: Herodotus praised those Greek cities "sacrificing to one Heracles as to an immortal and calling him the Olympian, but bringing offerings to the other as to a dead hero." Heracles, of course, was a mythical figure; but there is no dearth of historical equivalents. What, for instance, did it imply when King Philip II of Macedonia took his seat in the theater at Aigai, while in solemn procession the images of the Twelve Gods were carried into the theater with the image of Philip added to their number as that of

---

[18] As with Nietzsche's *Thus Spoke Zarathustra*, Christianity had to first kill the God of Israel, in order to 'free' humanity from the failings of the 'God/Father.' Only then could Christianity establish a 'New-Order,' where the *Übermensch* could thrive. Because in the eyes of Paul, 'salvation' meant the incorporation of the faithful in the *corpus* of an '*Übermensch*,' and given that the Law at Sinai thwarts the designs of such a super-being, Paul declared that the 'Two Tablets' written by the God of Israel, represent "the ministration of death" (*2Cor* 3:7)—thus, anticipating Nietzsche. Obviously, the 'free man' of Paul and Nietzsche, has nothing to do with the idea of '*Vetus Adam/Novus Adam*' discussed by Christian humanists. For a glimpse of their principal ideas, see *The King's Two Bodies*, pp. 464-476.

[19] *The King's Two Bodies*, p. 504.

the Thirteenth?[20]

Because of his dual divine/human natures, a Roman emperor, "in his capacity of *Pontifex Maximum*...could offer sacrifices and also receive them."[21] Caligula, who was the model used to manufacture the Alexandrian Jesus, had a temple dedicated to his cult. In that shrine, he had set "a golden cult statue." To emphasize his dual reality, he had the statue "clad daily with the same clothes as were worn, on that day, by the emperor himself." [22] The mystery of the Christian Trinity, involving belief in One God that is three distinct Persons, is easily grasped once we realize that such a notion was quite common in the pagan world. As we shall see, this leads directly to the 'theology of power' underlying Christianity.

In line with pagan theological thought, the world of the *Christian Scripture* is dominated by superior entities with 'power' (*dinameis*). The God of the *Christian Scripture*, too, is designated 'power' (*dinameis*). The point is *not* to declare that God has power (see *Matt* 6:13), but that power *is* God. Thus *Mk* 14:62 announced that Jesus would appear "sitting on the right hand of power" (*dinamenos*)—in the sense of 'God' (*cf. Heb* 1:3). In addition to entities possessing 'powers,' the pagan world is populated by superior entities that although possessing no power, have 'authority' (*ezousiav*), which they received from the higher entities with 'power' (*dinameis*). So, to show that they were acting by virtue of the 'authority' (*ezousiav*) vested in them by Jesus, his disciples had to invoke his name in order to obtain results. "Even the devils," declared Jesus' disciples enthusiastically, "are subject unto us through thy name" (*Lk* 10:17). The recipients of 'authority' (*ezousiav*) can exercise tyrannical dominion, just as the potter, who, having "authority (*ezousian*) over the clay," is free to make out of a single lump "one vessel unto honor, and another unto dishonor" (see *Rom* 9:21; cf. the charming metaphor in *Matt* 18:21-35). The excep-

---

[20] *The King's Two Bodies*, pp. 500-501. The reference is to *Herodotus* II, 44.
[21] *The King's Two Bodies*, p. 501.
[22] *The King's Two Bodies*, p. 501.

tional standing of Jesus' disciples is due to the fact that he gave them "authority (*ezousian*) over the unclean spirits" (*Matt* 10:1; *Mk* 6:7), as well as "authority (*ezousian*) to heal diseases and to cast out demons" (*Mk* 3:15). The "authority" they received from Jesus is even mightier than Satan's power: "Behold I give you authority (*ezousian*) to tread on serpents and scorpions and over all the power (*dinamin*) of the enemy [Satan] and nothing shall by any means hurt you" (*Lk* 10:19). Jesus confirmed this point visually. And as he was pronouncing these words—lo and behold—all present witnessed, "Satan falling out of Heaven as lightning" (*Lk* 10:18) —Wow!

By virtue of the "power (*dinamin*) and authority (*ezousiav*)" that Jesus vested on his disciples "over all the demons," they have dominion over them and could do with them as they pleased (see *Lk* 9:1, cf. 10:17, 20) —exactly as the potter with the clay mentioned earlier (see *Rom* 9:21). The authority he vested on them rendered them the faithful spokesmen of their master.[23] "The one hearing you [the disciples] *also* hears me, and the one rejecting you *also* rejects me" (*Lk* 10:16). To avoid possible misunderstanding, the authors of the *Christian Scripture* clarified that the "authority" (*ezousiav*) that they received from Jesus cannot be purchased, but has to be gained (see *Acts* 8:18-24).

The Greek word *dinamis* does not stand for something 'spiritual.' It denotes, exclusively, "*physical power, force, might*"; in the form *dinastes*, it means "*a man who rules by force,*" like "*a ruler, potentate,*" or simply a "*courtier, member of the court.*" As in *Acts* 8:27, where "a man of Ethiopia" is described as "an eunuch of great power" (*dinastes*).[24] Early in his ministry, Jesus fought, *mano a mano*, so to speak, with Satan, and crushed him (see *Matt* 4:1-11). Evidence of Jesus' might is that the "unclean spirits… fell down before him, and cried saying, Thou art the Son of God" (*Mk* 3:11). This positively confirms that Jesus is

---

[23] This is a corollary of the semantic doctrine proposing that the signifier equals the signified.

[24] Alexander Souter, *A Pocket Lexicon to the Greek of the New Testament* (Oxford: Clarendon Press, 1917), p. 76.

mightier even than the angels (see *Heb* 1:4-6). Consequently, the "angels," as well as the "authorities (*ezousion*) and powers (*dinamenon*)" of heaven are under Jesus' control (1*Peter* 3:22). Therefore, we should not be surprised to discover that Jesus had the "authority (*ezousiav*) on earth to forgive sins" (*Mtt* 9:2, 6, 8; *Mk* 2:5,10; 3:28; *Lk* 9:7).

A major feature of pagan semantics is the identification of the signifier with the signified (thus an idol, in function of signifier, equals the signified or deity it represents).[25] Accordingly, those witnessing the *manifestation* of 'power' have actually witnessed the *entity* manifesting said 'power.' It follows that the people who had been privileged to witness Jesus' "works of power" (*dinameis*) (*Lk* 10:13; cf. 9:43), and yet refused to believe in him, are the most despicable men on earth, and will "go down to hell" (*Lk* 10:3-15; cf. *Mk* 6:7-11; 16:15-18). This is the reason that Jesus lost his temper with the Pharisees, and said to them: "Ye do err, [1] not knowing the scriptures, [2] nor the power (*dinamin*) of God" (*Matt* 22:29). These two points are interrelated. The fact that the Pharisees do not equate Jesus [=signifier] with "the power" [=signified], exposes their faulty way of thinking. Such people could not possibly know *Scripture*! Therefore, Jesus had to put them down and show them who was 'really' superior.

In Christianity you must first believe in Jesus and then, subsequently and through him, in God. In the case of Israel, the Lord is God and Moses is his servant: thus, the vast difference between the monotheism of the *Hebrew Scripture* and pagan monotheism.[26] Put differently, if "the man, Moses," who in spite of his amazing accomplishment, "was very meek, more than any human on the face of the earth" (*Nu* 12:3), then by comparison, Jesus—as portrayed in the *Christian Scripture*—must be described as the most extreme case of megalomania known to humankind.[27] Rather than in the mode of

---

[25] See Appendix 4. Cf. *HS*, vol. 1, Chapter 2.

[26] On pagan monotheism, see *Pagan Monotheism in Late Antiquity*, eds. Polymnia Athanassiadi and Michael Frede (Oxford: Oxford University Press, 1999).

[27] Pagans, too, thought that Jesus was "arrogant," see *Origen: Contra Celsum*, p. 71.

Moses and the Hebrew Prophets, Jesus appears as someone suffering psychopathological delusions of fantasies, in the mode of Caligula *et al.* For the sake of illustration, consider the following passages:

[1] "I am the way, the truth, and the life: no man cometh unto the Father, but by me" (*Jn* 14:6). God spoke to Moses in the presence of all Israel (*Ex* 19:9). This was further confirmed by all the people: "And it came to pass, as Moses entered into the tabernacle, the pillar of cloud descended, and stood at the door of the tabernacle, and the Lord talked with Moses" (*Ex* 33:9; cf. 10). The wonders he wrought, too, were made "in the presence of all Israel" (*Dt* 34:11-12), i.e., were acknowledged as such by all the people. Yet, he did not believe himself to be 'God' or even *a* 'god.' Explicitly, Moses taught that no man could see God and live (see *Ex* 33:20). In opposition to this, Jesus declared: "If ye had known me, ye should have known my Father also: and from henceforth ye know him, and have seen him" (*Jn* 14:7; cf. 9 and 10:30-33).

[2] Moses and Aaron belittled themselves and said, "what are we" (*Ex* 16:7; 16:11). Compare that with Jesus' statement: "Believe me that I am in the Father, and the Father in me" (*Jn* 14:11). And, "whatsoever ye shall ask in my name, that will I do, that the Father may be glorified in the Son" (*Jn* 14:13). But that is not exactly true. Jesus believed to be *greater* than God. Consider the following two verses in *Mk* 3:28-30, *Pocket Interlinear*, p. 86. Before quoting these verses, let us recall that people around him, including his own relatives, were saying that he was "mad" (Gr. *exeste*).[28] To prove them wrong, he responded:

> Truly I say to you. All the sins will be forgiven to the sons of men, and whatever blasphemies they have blasphemed. But whoever blas-

---

Unfortunately, in his defense of Jesus, Origen overlooked the passages mentioned below.

[28] See above n. 9.

phemes against the Holy Spirit [=Jesus himself] has no forgiveness to eternity, but he is liable to eternal judgment, because they said, he [Jesus] hath an unclean spirit.

Talk of blasphemy!

The *Christian Scripture* assures us that Jesus performed great miracles, such as feeding a large crowd with five loaves of bread and two fishes, and also walking on water (see *Matt* 14:14-33). Supposedly, these are the equivalent to the daily *manna* falling down for forty years in the Desert, and the Splitting of the Red Sea. The problem with these and similar 'reports' is that they appear in documents written several centuries later, omitting the time and place of these occurrences, attested by people that nobody met, and exhibiting a mode of thought that moves beyond the point of what the Jewish mind regards as rational. One may counter that the same may be said about the *Hebrew Scripture*. Granted, but Jews never tried to shove their faith down anybody's throat.

34. A Heavenly *Cosmocrator*

To come to grips with the historical development of Christianity, a proper understanding of the term "power" (*dinamin*) is of the essence. It *does not stand* for a *spiritual* force (as, for example, the Greek term *alke*),[29] but for *physical* power, as per the *Septuagint* in *Dan* 8:24; 11:6, etc. There are no linguistic grounds to assume that when Jesus is identified with God's "power" (*dinameos*) (see *Heb* 1:3), something purely abstract and non-material was intended.[30] Rather, the purpose was to transform the historical Jesus into a pagan Cosmocrator ('Ruler of the World'), like Caligula. *Matt* 10:34-36 attributes the following sentences to Jesus:

---

[29] See *Indo-European Languages and Society*, pp. 358-360.

[30] Proclus (412-485), one of the last great Neo-Platonists, identified 'power' with the Greek *to Hen* 'the One.' It is interesting to note that his philosophical formation came mainly from Alexandria.

Think not that I am come to send peace on earth: I came not to send peace, but a sword. For I am come to set a man at variance against his father, and the daughter against her mother, and the daughter in law against her mother in law. And a man's foe *shall be* they of his own household.

This means that 'Christian Peace' is one and the same with the *Pax Romana*.[31] In both cases, the goal is to establish good will among men by having everyone submit to the absolute control of the Cosmocrator. The arrival of Jesus will take place at the end of days, when "the powers (*dinameis*) of heavens shall be shaken." In this manner, it will be shown to all that his "power" (*dinameos*) is mightier even than heavens (*Matt* 24:29, 39). In line with the theology of power, Christianity conceives of Jesus' Second Coming in terms of military victory (see 1*Cor* 15:57; cf. vv. 54, 55). For those entertaining some qualms, The *Book of Revelation* 19:11-21 offers these comforting details:

> And I saw heaven opened, and behold a white horse; and he that sat upon him was called Faithful and True, and in righteousness he doth judge and make war. His eyes were as a flame of fire, and on his head were many crowns; and he had a name written, that no man knew, but he himself. And he was clothed with a vesture dipped in blood: and his name is called The Word of God. And the armies which were in heaven followed him upon white horses, clothed in fine linen, white and clean. And out of his mouth goeth a sharp sword, that with it he should smite the nations: and he shall rule them with a rod of iron: and he treadeth the winepress of the fierceness and wrath of Almighty God. And he hath on his vesture and on his thigh a name written, KING OF KINGS, AND LORD OF LORDS. And I saw an angel standing in the sun; and he cried with a loud voice, saying to all the fowls that fly in the midst of heaven, Come and gather yourselves together unto the supper of the great God; That ye may eat the flesh of kings, and the flesh of captains, and the flesh of horses, and the flesh of all men, both free and bond, both small and great. And I

---

[31] See Klaus Wengs, *Pax Romana and the Peace of Jesus Christ* (Philadelphia: Fortress Press, 1987). Cf. *HS,* vol. 1, p. 200.

saw the beast, and the kings of the earth, and their armies, gathered together to make war against him that sat on the horse, and against his army. And the beast was taken, and with him the false prophet that wrought miracles before him, with which he deceived them that had received the mark of the beast, and them that worshiped his image. These both were cast alive into a lake of fire burning with brimstone. And the remnants were slain with the sword of him that sat upon the horse, which sword proceeded out of his mouth: and all the fowls were filled with their flesh. (See ibid, Chapters 20-22).

There is a very disturbing detail about the Christian Cosmocrator. Fromm observed that there are two classes of power:

> Power can mean power *over* people, or it can mean power to do things. What the sadist is striving for is power *over* people, precisely because he lacks the power *to be*.[32] [Italics in the original]

Jesus' power, too, is power *over* the whole people of the world. Christian devotion involves *submission* to Jesus as Supreme Cosmocrator—in contrast to Hebrew devotion involving the *fulfillment of one of the precepts of the covenant, freely negotiated by God and the Jewish people*. Jewish devotion presupposes the *freedom* to refuse (see *Josh* 24, especially v. 15). Worshiping Jesus-Cosmocrator *is not* a matter of choice. In quality of Cosmocrator, Jesus is worshiped because of his power. Therefore, he *imposes* his dominion over his subjects. In his own words, "He that is not with me is against me: and he that gathereth not with me scattereth" (*Lk* 11:23). Accordingly, he instructed his disciples,

> But into whatever city ye enter, and they receive you not, go your ways out into the streets of the same, and say, Even the dust of your city, which cleaveth on us, we do wipe off against you: notwithstanding be sure of this, that the kingdom of God is come nigh into you. But I say unto you, that it shall be more tolerable in that day for Sodom, than for that city" (*Lk* 10:10-12).

An important doctrine taught by Caligula is that those refusing

---

[32] The *Anatomy of Human Destructiveness*, p. 296; cf. ibid. pp. 345-346.

to worship the Cosmocrator are his "worst enemy."[33] This is also true of Jesus. He *must be worshiped by the whole world* for the same reason that the subjects of Alexander, Julius Caesar, *et al* must worship their Master. For the very same reason, it is incumbent upon all, both Jews and Greeks, to acknowledge Jesus as God's "power" (*dinamin*) (see 1*Cor* 1:24; cf. 2:4). This is an indisputable fact, since he "had been marked Son of God in power" (*dinamei*) (*Rom* 1:4, *Pocket Interlinear*, p. 357). The 'salvation' that Jesus offers, too, is effected by power. In Paul's own words: his "gospel is power (*dinamis*) to salvation" (*Rom* 1:16). There is a logic to all this. A categorical imperative, common to pagan humanity, is the principle dictating that the vanquished must *submit* to the will of the Conqueror. Only the Jews rejected the claim put forward by Rome (and tyrants everywhere) that together with the battle, the vanquished lose the right to conscience and faith.

In brief, according to the *Christian Scripture,* the purpose of Christianity is to answer the challenge posed by Patriarch Abraham, the *Hebrew Scripture,* and Jewish tradition. Contrary to the Jewish concept of devotion, as an act of *ahaba,* involving choice and election, Jesus must be worshiped as the Supreme Cosmocrator: it is not a matter of choice, but of submission. The model for this sort of worship is to be found, not in the *Hebrew Scripture,* but in Alexandria and the rest of the pagan world, ruled by the formula tyrant=deity. The purpose of abrogating the Jewish Law was not to award 'freedom' to the faithful—we all need to be constrained by a legal system—but to permit tyrants to act with impunity: only despots benefited from Christian 'freedom.' Thanks to the 'freedom' that Christianity awarded them, no despot could be summoned to an earthly tribunal. Chattering aside, could one cite a single case when an ecclesiastical authority summoned a Nimrod for throwing Abraham into a furnace of fire?

In contrast to the Christian Cosmocrator announced in the *Book of Revelation* 19:11-21, consider the *Jewish* Messiah, as envisioned

---

[33] *The Embassy to Gaius*, 256, p. 131. See above Section III, n. 176.

by Prophet Isaiah, 2:2-4:

> And it shall come to pass in the end of days, that the mountain of the Lord's house shall be established as the top of the mountains, and shall be exalted above the hills; and all nations shall flow unto it. And many people shall go and say: 'Come ye, and let us go up to the mountain of the Lord, to the house of the God of Jacob; and He will teach us of His ways, and we will walk in His paths.' For out of Zion shall go forth the law, and the word of the Lord from Jerusalem. And shall decide for many peoples; and they shall beat their swords into plowshares, and their spears into pruning hooks; nation shall not lift up swords against nation, neither shall they learn war any more.

The difference between Judaism and Christianity is not only between Moses and Jesus, but also between *Isaiah* 2:2-4 and *Revelation* 19:11-21.

35. The Divine Right of Tyrants

The Pauline doctrine proclaiming the Divine Right of Kings is an upshot of the Christian Theology of Power. Once the formula power=god is accepted, we must conclude that *political* authority (*ezousia*) is also divine. Hence, the doctrine of the Divine Right of Kings commands absolute submission to political authority in general. As thoughtfully explained by Paul, *Rom* 13: 1-5:

> Let every soul be subject unto the higher authorities (*ezousiais*). For there is no authority (*ezousia*) but of God: the authority (*ezousia*) that are ordained of God. Whosoever therefore resisteth the authority (*ezousia*), resisteth the ordinance of God: and they that resist shall receive to themselves damnation. For the rulers are not a terror to good works, but to evil. Wilt thou then not be afraid of the authority (*ezousian*)? Do that which is good, and thou shalt have praise of the same: For he is the minister of God to thee for good. But if thou do that which is evil, be afraid; for he beareth not the sword in vain: for he is the minister of God, a revenger to execute wrath upon him that doeth evil. Wherefore ye must be subject, not only for wrath, but also

for conscience sake.[34]

The doctrine stipulating submission to the "higher authorities" (*exousiais*) as a matter of "conscience," stems from the formula postulating power=god.[35] It is a categorical imperative, governing not only the relation between subjects and ruler, but in general, between the 'lower' and 'higher' elements of the political and social fabric of Christendom. Quoting Paul:

> Submit yourselves to every ordinance of man for the Lord's sake; whether it be to the king, as supreme; or unto the governors, as unto them that are sent by him for the punishment of evildoers, and for the praise of them that do well. (1*Pet* 2: 13-14)

A parenthetical note. Occasionally, the *Christian Scripture* seems to reject the principle of unconditional submission, urging disrespect to the authorities in charge, see *Acts* 4:19, cf. 5, 6; 5: 21, 29, cf. 5, 6, 17. These, however, refer exclusively to the *Jewish* authority, which,

---

[34] On the basis of a passage in Philo, *Allegorical Interpretation*, III, 80, *Philo*, vol. 1, p. 355, Erwin R. Goodenough, *The Politics of Philo Judaeus* (New Haven: Yale University Press, 1938), p. 99, concluded that Philo recognized "the king's divine nature." His interpretation of the text is faulty; see Wolfson, *Philo*, vol. 2, p. 331. Explicitly, Philo denounced the Greek deification of heroes and kings; see ibid, vol. 1, p. 29.

[35] *The King's Two Bodies*, p. 54, quotes a mediaeval author offering a more original interpretation of Jesus' famous saying, urging to render unto 'Caesar' that which belongs to 'Caesar' (*Matt* 22:21). This author notes that Jesus did not say to render "unto Tiberius the things that are Tiberius." But he said,

> Render to the *power* (*potestas*), not to the person. The person is worth nothing, but the *power* is just. Iniquitous is Tiberius, but good is the Caesar. Render, not unto the person worth nothing, not unto iniquitous Tiberius, but unto the righteous *power* and unto the good Caesar the things that are his... (Our italics)

It is all a matter of power (*potestas*). Power defines the person, not the other way around. That is why, Christianity saw in the suffering of Israel, and particularly the Destruction of the Jewish Temple, an absolute proof of the Divine Origin of Christianity. Contrary to what Christian authors claim, the Islamic idea of 'Holy War' and *ijtihad* comes from the Christian argumentations against Israel; principally, the notion that defeat in war constitutes 'Absolute and Irresistible Proof,' of the worthlessness of Judaism. For a defense of the view that Christianity merely was following in the footsteps of Islam, see Américo Castro, *The Structure of Spanish History* (Princeton, N.J.: Princeton University Press, 1954), pp. 219-221.

unlike dictatorships, is *ipso facto* null and void. It is fine to be disrespectful with the Law given by God at Sinai, however, we all must show proper respect and consideration for the laws promulgated by pagan tyrants and dictators, "for the Lord's sake."[36]

The principle of submission ought to regulate also the relations between the various elements of the working class. Quoting Paul, again:

> Servants, *be* subject to *your* masters with all fear; not only to the good and gentle, but also to the forward. For this *is* thankworthy, if a man for conscience toward God endure grief, suffering wrongfully. (1*Pet* 2: 18-19).

Given that in Paul's eyes, wives are hierarchically inferior, they must be subservient to their husband. The distance between them equals the distance between man and God:

> Wives, submit yourselves unto your own husbands, as unto the Lord (*Kyrios*). For the husband is the head of the wife, even as Christ is the head of the church: and he is the savior of the body. Therefore as the church is subject unto Christ, so *let* the wives *be* in their own husbands in every thing. (*Eph* 5: 22-24; cf. 1*Pet* 3: 1).

We should remind the reader that *Kyrios* ('Lord') was the holiest word in the vocabulary of Greek-speaking Jews, and it was used in the Septuagint to translate the Tetragrammaton, the holiest term in

---

[36] Although the context of these passages makes it clear that they refer exclusively to *Jewish* authorities, the *Catechism of the Catholic Church*, #2256, p. 524, applies this principle to all "directives of civil authorities when they are contrary to the demands of the moral order" (and not only to laws issued by the Jewish authority). Obviously, the "the moral order" does not include the racist legislation of the Holy Inquisition, and the Expulsion and murdering of Jews throughout the centuries, or the extermination of 6,000,000 Jews during the Holocaust. On the lamentable behavior of the Pope during the extermination of Jews in World War II, see *Papal Sins*, pp. 13-16, 57. The same is with the genocide of Native Americas, and the mass murder of Black-Africans by European Nations in the 19th and 20th centuries. For a less aggressive position, but one still vague enough so that it could be manipulated either which way; see *Catechism of the Catholic Church*, ##1897-1904, pp. 463-464.

the Hebrew vocabulary.[37] The identification 'husband/*Kyrios*' speaks volumes about Paul's theological conceptions. It also reveals his inner thoughts about the status of women in general and their relation to men.

The principle of submission serves to regulate the spiritual lives of *every* Christian. An individual Christian expresses his or her faith by submitting, unconditionally, to the ecclesiastical authorities (*fidelis Christianus*). Paul's doctrine of Original Sin (*Rom* 5:14, 19; cf. 1*Cor* 15:21) serves to justify the need for submission.[38] No matter how one wishes to interpret it, it postulates the worthlessness of the individual, and the impossibility of salvation without absolute submission to the ecclesiastical authorities. As we will see in the course of this chapter, there were some worldly implications to this doctrine.

Christian theology provided a model to explain how the earthly king had, "a royal super-body conjoined in some mysterious way to the king's natural and individual body."[39] Or, to put it in more philosophical terms, that the king, although "a mortal being," is "yet immortal with regard to his Dignity and his Body politic."[40] The doctrine of the "King's Two Bodies," proposed that the monarch was a "*persona mixta*," having, like the heavenly Christ, a double-nature substance, compatible with both man and god (*homoousios*).[41] As with the rest of Christianity, this doctrine has nothing to do with the *Hebrew Scripture*. It was first expounded by the Pythagorean Ecphantus (4th Century BCE):

> Man has the highest nature of anything on earth, but more godlike is the king who claims the lion's share in that more exalted part of our common nature. He is like the others with respect to his tabernacle

---

[37] On the significance of the term *'O Kyrios*, see above, Section III, n. 17.

[38] Judaism explicitly denies this doctrine; see the sources cited by Hyam Maccoby, *Paul and Hellenism*, p. 189 n. 6.

[39] *The King's Two Bodies*, p. 46.

[40] *The King's Two Bodies*, p. 294; cf. ibid, p. 497.

[41] *The King's Two Bodies*, p. 45. In the footsteps of Maimonides, Newton rejected the Christian doctrine of Jesus' *homoousios*; see "Newton, Maimonidean," pp. 226-227.

(*skanos*), since he came into being out of the same material; but he was made by the supreme Craftsman, who, in fabricating the king, used Himself as the archetype.[42]

Underlying this and similar ideas was the belief in the apotheosis of kings. There are serious political implications to this belief. Professor Abraham J. Heschel (1907-1972) observed:

> Through the apotheosis of the Roman emperor as *Dominus et Deus* and medieval traditions, down to modern times, one may trace the tendency to deify the king or to garb him with the trapping of divinity.[43]

The monarch was "represented as if it were the image of God upon earth," and "absolute princes, such as the sovereigns of England, were a species of divinity"; kings "represent unto us the person even of God Himself."[44] According to this doctrine, we all should conclude, "that the empire was founded by God directly."[45] Consequently, "Those who wage war against the holy realm of France," for instance, "wage war against King Jesus."[46] Premised on this logic, King James I (1567-1625) of England proclaimed:

> It is atheism and blasphemy to dispute what God can do...so it is presumption and high contempt in a subject to dispute what a king can do, or say that a king cannot do this or that.[47]

Christian theology could help us grasp the double nature of the monarch. It is somehow analogous to the Mystery of the Holy Trinity, which, although the essence of the Christian faith, is impossible to grasp by our finite minds. Kindly, modern historians, however, had pointed out that there is,

---

[42] Quoted in *The Politics of Philo Judaeus*, p. 98.

[43] Abraham J. Heschel, *The Prophets* (New York: The Burning Bush Press, 1962), p. 475.

[44] Cited in *The Prophets*, p. 475.

[45] *The King's Two Bodies*, p. 294; cf. ibid, p. 297.

[46] *The King's Two Bodies*, p. 255.

[47] Quoted in *The Politics of Philo Judaeus*, p. 4. Cf. *HS*, vol. 1, Section III, n. 218.

a single—though essential—difference between the Anointed in Eternity [Jesus] and his terrestrial antitype [the earthly king] anointed in Time: Christ was King and *Christus* [please, duly note capital letter 'K' and 'C'] by his very nature, whereas his deputy on earth was king and *christus* [please, duly note lower case 'k' and 'c'] by grace only.[48]

Christian liturgy helped further consolidate the identification 'earthly king/Jesus.' Originally, images were not used in the Christian liturgy. They were introduced later, in the fourth century, when Christianity became the official religion of the Roman Empire. There may have been a practical reason for that. The worship or 'veneration' of images helped consolidate the link between the earthly monarch and the heavenly Christ. Christian art contributed, "for occasional facial similitude between the deity and the ruler, between Christ and his vicar on earth."[49] We should not be surprised, then, to find an image representing Emperor Constantine as god.[50] In this fashion, an alliance was established between the earthly and the celestial: while Cosmocrator Jesus will appear *at the end of days* and reign *for all time to come*, in the interim, the monarch *now* and *here* is the *Christian Übermensch* ruling temporarily on earth.[51] In this fashion, a nice and robust relationship developed between the temporary *Übermensch* and the Holy See, up to our days. One of the greatest achievements of this sort of relationship is the political treaty, known as Lateran Concordat (*Pax Laetitia*), February 11, 1929. It recognized the Vatican as an Independent City State with full sovereignty; at the same time, extending financial and special privileges to the Church. The treaty was signed by Benito Mussolini, on behalf of King Victor Emmanuel

---

[48] *The King's Two Bodies*, p. 47. Cf. *HS*, vol. 1, Section III, n. 220.

[49] *The King's Two Bodies*, p. 504. Images were introduced in the Christian liturgy *after* it became the religion of the empire. For sources and bibliography on the use of images in the Christian liturgy, as well as the status of Christianity in Jewish law, see *Studies in the Mishne Tora*, pp. 230-234.

[50] See Arnaldo Momigliano, *Essays in Ancient and Modern Historiography* (Middletown, Conn.: Wesleyan University Press, 1982), p. 156.

[51] See Eric Fromm, quoted above at n. 11.

III, and by Cardinal Gasparri, on behalf of Pope Pius XI.[52] It was hailed as a momentous event in Christian history. In 1935 the Vatican celebrated this alliance as "the Day of Faith." It is reminiscent of the first accord with Constantine, declaring Christianity the religion of the Roman Empire. I find the criticism of his successor Pius XII, unfair and disingenuous. Why would it be fine for Pius XI to sign a treaty with Benito Mussolini, Head of the Fascist Blackshirt Party, and inappropriate for Pope Pius XII to collaborate with his racist and anti-Semitic policies? Or to put the same in different words: Why it would be fine to conclude a treaty with Cosmocrator Constantine, and not do the same with Cosmocrator Mussolini?

36. The Alliance Church-Monarch

It is generally taught that the Church contributed little, either to political or to legal philosophy. This view is only superficially true. By blocking the concepts of law and civil government taught in the *Hebrew Scripture*, Christianity *positively* and *deliberately* fostered the idea of absolute authority vested in a *Übermensch* or political leader, who was nothing less than an earthly god. Thus, while overtly speaking in the name of 'God,' Christian theology was used as a tool to suppress the questioning of the political system from within. As Titus was instructed: "Put them in mind to be subject to principalities and powers, to obey magistrates, to be ready to every good work" (*Titus* 3:1). In this fashion was created an alliance, Church-Monarch, that ruled Christendom with an iron-fist for over one and a half millennia. Consequently, the faithful owed, as a church's rule, 'unconditional submission' to the earthly power. Quoting Oscar S. Straus (1850-1926):

> It carried with it as a state doctrine the unconditional submission on the part of the governed to the powers to be, as preached by Nero.

---

[52] Significantly, the alliance was known as *Pax Laetitia*, *Laetitia* being the Roman goddess of joy.

While the establishment in its inception may have had the effect of fostering and spreading the light of the new faith in the pagan world, it proved on the other hand a hindrance to the development of civil liberty for twelve centuries and more, distinct traces of which are yet to be found in the despotic governments of the Old World. Its immediate consequences were the augmentation of the power of the Pope and the subjection of every Christian country, in matters temporal as well as ecclesiastical, to the throne of Peter.[53]

The net result of the alliance Church-Monarch was a society made up of docile, submissive subjects, forbidden to question the wisdom of those standing 'above.' "But avoid foolish questions, and genealogies, and contentions, and striving about the law; for they are unprofitable and vain" (*Titus* 3:9). This leads to the overwhelming principle, regulating the life of the Christian faithful: "That the verdict of the superior—no matter whether just or unjust—had to be obeyed by the inferior subject."[54] Intimately related to this principle is the *inequality* intrinsic to Christian society: to be a Christian means to be superior or inferior to someone else. Hence the principle of "inequality," fundamental to Christian Society, as taught by Professor Ullmann (1910-1983):

> One should never forget that the principle of equality is of fairly recent date; in other words, that the members of society had by virtue of being members of society, equality of standing within the public field was not a doctrine that was known to the high Middle Ages. Here operated inequality before the law.[55]

One may argue that with the secularization of the modern state, beginning with the French Revolution (1787-1799), the negative effects of Christian doctrine on the political and social life of the State came to an end. Not at all. The culture of obedience-submission affected the ethos of Christian folks. At the psychological level, obedi-

---

[53] Oscar Straus, *The Origin of the Republican Form of Government in the United States* (New York: G. P. Putnam's Son, 1885), pp. 88-89.

[54] *The Individual and Society in the Middle Ages*, p. 13.

[55] *The Individual and Society in the Middle Ages*, p. 14.

ence is the ultimate act of faith—the highest form of spiritual *abnegation*—whereby self-individuality is annihilated, as a *sine qua non* condition for salvation. As taught by Paul, 'salvation' is the effect of the very act of *faith* in the intrinsic pre-eminence of those standing 'above.'[56] Within this culture, it is nigh impossible for the average young man and woman to develop the self-confidence necessary to question the rationality and methodologies used by the 'eminent authorities.' If one adds to this, the fierce Christian opposition to anything remotely comparable to critical thinking, one can fully appreciate the enormous struggle facing those who dared look at the truth with their own eyes. Referring to Freud's criticism of religion, Fromm wrote:

> by teaching people to believe in an illusion and by prohibiting critical thinking [Christian] religion is responsible for the impoverishment of intelligence. This charge like the first one was leveled against the Church by the thinkers of the Enlightenment. But in Freud's frame of reference this second charge is even more potent than it was in the eighteenth century. Freud could show in his analytic work that the prohibition of critical thinking at one point leads to an impoverishment of a person's critical ability in other spheres of thought and the power of reason.[57]

It is important to point out that in the lexicon of modern Jewish intellectuals, like Freud and Fromm, 'religion' is a code-term for 'Christianity.'[58] We should also point out that in modern Europe, Jewish intellectuals were under the same peril as Jewish *conversos* were in Spain and Portugal, where a linguistic or intellectual 'indiscretion' could result in persecution, disgrace, and worse. The preceding also explains why 'Talmud,' 'Rabbis,' and 'Pharisees,' occupy the most prominent place in the Christian blacklist of works and authors. Aimé Pallière (1868-1949), quoted the view of a modern Christian apologist

---

[56] See, *The Individual and Society in the Middle Ages*, pp. 10-15.

[57] Eric Fromm, *Psychoanalysis and Religion* (New Haven: Yale University Press, 1950), pp. 12-13.

[58] See *Homo Mysticus*, p. 12-13.

about the 'Talmud':

> "Without the Talmud," he repeated,—and this reflection contains an implicit statement, which deserves to be remembered—"without the Talmud the Jews would have converted long ago."
>
> One might as well say they would no longer continue to exist, and I [Pallière] did not fail to ask him how it came about that the Church, so respectful of the individual rites of diverse peoples, sought to confound the Israelites with the Latin multitude, in stripping them of every religious characteristic.[59]

This explains why 'Christian philosophers,' although occasionally 'inspirational,' are disappointingly shallow. Quoting Aldous Huxley:

> Christian philosophers have found no difficulty in justifying imperialism, war, the capitalistic system, the use of torture, the censorship of the press, and ecclesiastical tyrannies of every sort from the tyranny of Rome to the tyrannies of Geneva and New England. In all these cases they have shown that the meaning of the world was such as to be compatible with, or actually most completely expressed by, the iniquities I have mentioned above—iniquities which happened, of course, to serve the personal or sectarian interests of the philosophers concerned. In due course, there arose philosophers who denied not only the right of these Christian special pleaders to justify iniquity by an appeal to the meaning of the world, but even their right to find any such meaning whatsoever. In the circumstances, the fact was not surprising. One unscrupulous distortion of the truth tends to beget other and opposite distortions. Passions may be satisfied in the process; but the disinterested love of knowledge suffers eclipse.[60]

An important feature associated with Christian obedience is the visual factors designed to identify 'authority', such as the peculiar form of religious buildings; the interior of the place of worship; the attire of those representing the different echelons of ecclesiastical

---

[59] *The Unknown Sanctuary*, p. 43.

[60] Aldous Huxley, "Beliefs," in *Collected Essays* (New York: Harper & Row, 1971), p. 366.

authority; and more besides. Even the visual signs were designed to create "the relevant situational context" for submission to the civil authorities.[61]

37. The Banality of Evil

The phenomenon submission/obedience generated by the alliance 'Church-Monarch' deeply affected the socio-political structure of modern Europe. Totalitarian systems, including fascism and communism, could not have taken root in the heart and mind of Europe, without a population consisting of 'subjects,' for whom submission to authority was in and of itself, an imperative—regardless of content. Properly understood, 'obedience' is nothing less than the annihilation of the individual self as an absolute condition to personal salvation. The Christian imperative to obey a 'superior' is not grounded on expediency or on realistic considerations, but on *faith* in the intrinsic pre-eminence of those standing 'above.'[62] As per tyrannical regimes, it assumes that "obedience under orders can by its very *form*, assume moral virtue."[63] [Italics in original] A consequence of the equation authority=power=divinity is that obedience to tyrants is a *theological imperative*. Paul provided the faithful with a lucid explanation: "Whosoever therefore resisteth the authority (*exousia*), resisteth the ordinance of God: and they that resist shall receive to themselves damna-

---

[61] See Arthur G. Miller, *The Obedience Experiments* (New York: Praeger Special Studies, 1974), pp. 224-255.

[62] Let me quote the words of Professor Ullmann, *The Individual and Society in the Middle Ages*, p. 37, n. 75:
> From the medieval point of view this suppression of the individual's opinion was not by any means seen as a violation of his rights or of his dignity as a Christian, because a Christian attacking established faith forfeited his dignity and could be considered a "bad man." Killing this individual did not violate his dignity, just as killing an animal did not affect anyone's dignity.

[63] *The Obedience Experiments*, p. 227.

tion. For the rulers are not a terror to good works, but to evil" (*Rom* 13:2-3).

The blending of obedience (to the ecclesiastical authorities) and submission (to the governing authorities) was a major factor in the formation of the socio-political culture dominating *modern* Europe. Bertrand Russell (1872-1970) pointed to the relationship between the 'old' ecclesiastical regimes and the 'new' socio-political ideology dominating modern Europe.

> I admit at once that new systems of dogma, such as those of the Nazis and the Communists, are even worse than the old systems, but they could never have acquired a hold over men's mind if orthodox dogmatic habits had not been instilled in youth. Stalin's language is full of reminiscences of the theological seminary in which he received his training.[64]

Christian apology to the contrary, without fifteen hundred years of preaching and teaching the beatitudes of obedience-submission, European society would not have been predisposed to follow the diktat of Hitler, Mussolini, Stalin and their ilk.[65] The indoctrination of obedience-submission, led to the deep-rooted belief that as long as someone was following orders, he could not be held personally responsible for his actions.[66] The "banality of evil" and the "normality thesis," proposing that Nazi war criminals were 'normal' people—are the effect of that belief. Those who had the opportunity to examine Nazi criminals were shocked to discover that they "were neither perverted nor sadistic, that they were, and still are, terribly and terrifying-

---

[64] *Why I am not a Christian*, p. 206.

[65] See, *Papal Sins*, pp. 13-19.

[66] On this point, the rabbis taught the juridical doctrine, "There is no fiduciary relationship involving a transgression of the law"; that is, an agent cannot disclaim responsibility on the grounds that he was acting under orders of a superior authority; see *Baba Meṣi'a* 10b and parallels; *MT Me'ila* 7:2. This principle applies even when receiving a direct order from the king; see *Baba Qamma* 56a; *MT Melakhim* 3:9. In line with this thought, the *Tora* rejects the notion of 'sovereign immunity'; see *HS*, vol. 1, Chapter 13. Consequently, acting 'under orders' does not excuse a subaltern for 'obeying' a 'superior' to commit an illegal act; see ibid. pp. 153-154.

ly normal." Eichmann himself "was found sane by a number of psychiatrists."

> Prior to his role in the Final Solution, he had actually expressed pro-Zionist sentiments. For a time in Vienna he had a Jewish mistress and a Jewish half-cousin whom he protected. In Essence, Eichmann's biography was remarkably free of psychopathology.[67]

Psychologists that examined Nazi criminals such as Hess, Eichmann, Himmler, *et al* concluded that, "these were not monsters in any usual sense of the term."[68]

> All were family men with children...they were above all ordinary—banal.... And banal were their almost inconceivable crimes, if measured in causal and motivational terms. None of them basically hated their victims. None was sadistic. None psychotic. None insane. None of course was criminal by the laws of his society. None, for that matter, apparently ever personally killed any of their victims. [They were] Normal, ordinary men.[69]

In this chapter we will try to answer a question posed by scholars like Leon Bass: "I said to myself, my God, what is this? How could people do this to other people?" And Lucy Dawidowicz: "The annihilation of six million Jews, carried out by the German state under Adolf Hitler during World War II, has resisted understanding. The question persists: How could it have happened?"[70]

The question is a bit unsettling to someone familiar with *Jewish* history. Central to Jewish memory was the awareness of how 'good people' behaved. In modern times, European nations were committing the worst kinds of abominations with total impunity. It is particularly instructive to see what a leading thinker of the time wrote about these 'good people.'

---

[67] *The Obedience Experiments*, p. 184.

[68] *The Obedience Experiments*, pp. 190-191.

[69] *The Obedience Experiments*, p. 191.

[70] Quoted in *The Obedience Experiments*, p. 179.

[1] Anti-Semitism was promoted by Christianity from the moment the Roman Empire became Christian. The religious fervor of the Crusades led to pogroms in Western Europe. It was Christians who unjustly accused Dreyfus and the freethinkers who secured his final rehabilitations. [2] Abominations have in modern times been defended by Christians, not only when Jews were the victims but also in other connections. The abominations perpetrated by King Leopold's government of the Congo were concealed or minimized by the church and were ended only by an agitation conducted mainly by freethinkers. The whole contention that Christianity has had an elevating moral influence can only be maintained by wholesale ignorance or falsification of the historical evidence.[71]

The question posed above by Bass and Dawidowicz involves two fundamental errors: [1] it assumes that *only* during the Nazi period were the Jews victims of despicable crimes, and [2] that Jews were the *only* victims of these 'good people.'

A look at history will clearly reveal that the same 'normal and ordinary men' did not see anything wrong with *wiping out the entire native population of Jamaica, Bermuda, St. Thomas, Puerto Rico, Panama, and Cuba*—where not even a single soul of the *original native population survived*. In the course of only fifty years, the Spaniards managed to reduce the population of Native Americans from 80 million to 10 million. By the year 1600, the original population of Mexico was reduced from 25 million to 1 million. This is the greatest genocide in recorded history, both in absolute and relative terms.[72] Consider, in the name of sanity, the common practice of snatching children from their mother's arms and throwing them to be devoured alive by dogs, or smashing them against the rocks and throwing them to die in the

---

[71] *Why I am not a Christian*, p. 203. Professor Nicholls, *Christian Antisemitism*, pp. 249-259, suggested that there might be a link between the instinctual renunciation demanded by Christianity, and anti-Semitism. Since the anger could not be directed against the religious authority, it is projected in paranoid hostility against members of other religions.

[72] See Tzevetan Todorov, *La conquête de l'Amérique* (Paris: Editions du Soleil, 1982), pp. 138-139.

mountains. The usual way to kill indigenous leaders was in groups of thirteen, in honor of Jesus and the twelve apostles. To prolong their agony, they would burn them in a slow fire. Occasionally, the executioner would insert sticks in their mouths to prevent their screams from disturbing the *siesta* of a captain. Their sexual mores deserve special attention. It was a common practice to tie the hands and feet of the husband *under* the bed, while raping the wife *in* bed. When a young Native American wife explained to a Spanish captain that she could not have sex with him because she had promised her husband to be faithful, the captain unleashed his dogs and had them devour her alive.[73] Miguel de Monsalve (16th century) reported that it was common for the Spaniards, to

> take not only the properties of these wretched [native Americans], but also their daughters, taking them by force and raping them; if they do not give consent of their own will, they tie them, and torture them, lash them and punish them with great cruelty.... if they [the Spaniards] would find out that someone [a Native American] husband had had relations with her [the Native American woman that they grabbed] they burn them, mistreat and torture them, lash them and bring them before their eyes in irons, stripped, exposed, abused, dog-bitten and very hurt.[74]

Spaniards in Chile "unleashed their dogs against some [Native Americans], burnt others, in addition to mutilating them, cutting their noses, arms, or breasts, and inventing a thousand other ways how to tear them into pieces."[75] It was customary that for reasons of work distribution, a few Spaniards would parcel a native family among themselves. Thus, one would take the wife, another the husband, and a third one the children, "in the same manner as if they would have been pigs."[76] In addition to those dying of sickness, exhaustion, ill

---

[73] See *In the Shadow of History*, pp. 4-5.

[74] Quoted in Henry Méchoulan, *El Honor de Dios* (Barcelona: Editorial Argos Vergara, 1981), p. 49.

[75] Quoted in *El Honor de Dios*, p. 41.

[76] Quoted in *El Honor de Dios*, p. 51.

treatment, and abuse, we must consider those who simply "are buried alive in the mines."[77]

Christian thinkers and theologians debated whether Native Americans were humans or beasts. It was Pope Paul III (1534-1549), the first of the 'reform popes,' who issued a decision in 1537 declaring that Native Americans have a 'soul.' The decision was self-serving on two accounts. It was designed to absolve the Spanish sexual deviants and rapists from the sin of bestiality, and to legitimize Spanish oppressive behavior against the indigenous population, as a necessary means to bring them into the fold. It would be instructive to examine how this labor of love was carried on. A report from June 1756, recounts,

> how the Father priest orders that the Indians lie on the floor and without being tied except for the respect that they have for him they get twenty five lashes and right away they stand up, and go to give thanks to him [the priest] and kiss his hands.[78]

An Italian, Pedro Mártir (1459-1525), author of the first chronicle of the Americas, wrote:

> In the midst of such an abundant plenty, there is something that gives me no small anguish. These men so simple and naked, they are used to work so little; now many perish as a result of the great exhaustion in the mines, and they are desperate to the point that many kill themselves and do not care to raise children. They tell that the pregnant mothers take medicine to abort, seeing that they would give birth to slaves for the Christians. Although a royal decree had declared that they are free, nonetheless, there are forced to serve more than what would please a free man. The number of these wretches had diminished immensely; many say that once a census was take of one million two hundred thousand, how many there are today, it causes me horror to say. Let us change the subject.[79]

---

[77] Quoted in *El Honor de Dios*, p. 53.

[78] Cited in Martha B. Etchart, *Documentos de Historia Americana* (Buenos Aires: Cesarini Hnos., 1971), p. 70.

[79] Pedro Mártir de Anglería, *Libros de las Décadas del Nuevo Mundo* (Buenos Aires:

The method of bringing in the Native Americans to the religion of love was rather simple. All the natives need, "is bread and whipping." An enlightened priest explained, "Without the whip," the natives "are lost like children." Priests had their own jails, with pillories and other instruments of torture, to torment the natives and teach them the meaning of Christian spirituality.[80]

The same strategy of bad-mouthing the victims, practiced by anti-Semites in the Iberian Peninsula, was pursued in the New World. A series of 'blood-libels,' designed to exculpate Spanish crimes against Native Americans, were fabricated to excuse their savagery: the natives "worshiped idols" (unlike the "images" in the Christian Church),[81] and used human sacrifices.[82] However, as Jews pointed out, Christians, too, used human sacrifices. What was the incineration of old and young, men and women, but *Autos de Fé,* i.e., 'acts of faith,' in honor of the Christian deity?[83] Is there any other way to classify the slow burning of Native Americans in groups of thirteen, in honor of Jesus and the twelve apostles? King Charles V (1500-1558) justified his brutal persecution of Moors in Valencia (1525-1526), "as a sacrificial thank-offering for his miraculous preservation."[84] The same sort of 'blood-libel' underlies the Spanish condemnation of natives' sexual mores. Early Spanish chroniclers saw nothing deviant in the mores of Native Americans. Some went on to describe their life-style

---

Editorial Bajel, 1944), Dec. III, Lib. VIII, chap. I, p. 273.

[80] See *El honor de Dios,* p. 43.

[81] On the worship of images in Christianity, see Edwin Bevan, *Holy Images* (London: George Allen, 1940). On the input of the *conversos* in this debate, see *In the Shadow of History,* p. 40. For the *converso* charge against *cristianos viejos* of the crime of idolatry, see Lucía García Proodian, *Los Judíos en América* (Madrid: Instituto Arias Montano, 1966), p. 148.

[82] The accusation seems to be based on fact; see Alberto M. Salas, *Tres Cronistas de Indias: Pedro Mártir de Anglería, Gonzalo Fernández de Oviedo, Fray Bartolomé de las Casas* (Mexico: Fondo de Cultura Económica, 1959), p. 48.

[83] See Américo Castro, *De la España que aun no conocía,* vol. 1 (Mexico: Finisterre, 1972), pp. 18-19, 20-21.

[84] Michael de Ferdinandy, "Charles V," *Encyclopaedia Britannica,* 14th Edition, vol. 5, p. 269.

in paradisiacal terms. It is only *after* the Spaniards committed the most horrendous sexual crimes against the indigenous population that they accused the Native Americans of sexual perversion. Similarly, Spaniards justified the brutal treatment of Native Americans by claiming that they were lazy and unproductive. There were other accusations, concerning for instance the natives' personal hygiene and honesty, that Spaniards used in order to justify their treating of the Native Americans as sub-humans. Does this remind anybody about anything? Germans? Polish? Jews?

In the end, all's well that ends well! The slaughtering and raping of Native Americans, as well as the plundering of their precious metals, the robbing of their land, and the extermination of their people were for a good cause! The following explanation was offered by one of those noble souls, expressing the highest form of kindness and spirituality that it can only grow in the Garden of Obedience. It runs as follows:

> The white race and the Indian race are like two sisters that their father wanted to marry off. The first one is very beautiful and intelligent; her marriage presents no difficulties, since she lacks no suitors. But the other is very ugly, lazy, stupid and dumb. In order to get married she would need a valuable dowry, a rich trousseau, and also something else. The dowry of the ugly daughter is the precious metals in the American soil.[85]

How lovely!

It may be of some interest to note that the Supreme Court of the United States, too, seems to have regarded the Native Americans as "very ugly, lazy, stupid and dumb" —more or less. In 1955, the Supreme Court ruling, *The Tee-Hit-Ton Indians v. United States* 348 U.S. 272, 75 S. Ct. 313, 99 L. Ed. 314 (1955), at 293, we read that "Permissive Indian occupancy may be extinguished by Congress in its own discretion without compensation." However, "Generous provision has been willingly made to allow tribes to recover for wrong, as a

---

[85] Quoted in *El Honor de Dios,* p. 39.

matter of grace, not because of legal liability." Continuing:

> It is to be presumed that in this matter the United States would be governed by such considerations of justice as would control a Christian people in their treatment of an ignorant (="very ugly") and dependent race (="lazy, stupid and dumb").[86]

A parenthetical note. Rather than "very ugly, lazy, stupid and dumb," the first Jews that came in contact with Native Americans, regarded them as "brethren from the Ten Lost Tribes"—as indeed they and all the victims of the culture obedience-submission are.[87]

In short, the same people that expelled the Jews out of the Iberian Peninsula, pillaged their property, massacred their children, women and men, old and young, and went on to burn them alive as a holocaust in homage to the religion of love, were responsible for the extermination of a large segment of the native population of Latin America. Spain has the distinction of having promulgated the first set of regulations designed to discriminate against Christians, with even partial Jewish blood. It has been shown that the infamous Nuremberg legislation was modeled according to the racist policies legislated in Spain several centuries earlier.[88]

And now a question addressed to those who raised the above question: what are the grounds to assume that 'good folks,' nourished

---

[86] See *HS,* vol. 2, Appendix #16.

[87] See in the *Shadow of History,* p. 7.

[88] See Israel Salvador Revah, "Les Marranes," *Revue des Études Juives* 118 (1959-60), pp. 32-33; cf. ibid. pp. 38-39, 50, and 55-56. The preceding is essential to understand the system of casts (*castas*) upon which Spanish society rested. Américo Castro (1885-1972) was the first scholar to note that Spanish society is structured on the basis of "[c]astes, rather than [c]lasses," *The Structure of Spanish History,* p. 607. 'Class' is radically different than a 'cast.' A social class bases its rank on what it does; the rank of the caste depends on the mere existence of the person: in the last analysis, all the Hispano-Christians ended up feeling themselves a superior caste by virtue of the fact that they were Christians and not Moors or Jews; see ibid, p. 609. 'Cast' is a racist term. Originally, *castas* applied to the races of animals; see idem, *La Realidad Histórica de Espana* (Mexico City: Editorial Porrua, 1975), p. 25. Concerning the relationship between the Nuremberg legislation and Spanish racist policies, see *In the Shadow of History,* p. 232 note 12, and cf. ibid. pp. 233-234, note 41.

in the culture of obedience-submission, would care about the 'good people'—*here* and *now*—more than what they cared about Jews and Native Americans *there* and *then*? Was there any evidence that the ecclesiastical and secular authorities would care about the extermination of Jews any more than about the extermination of natives in Africa by Belgians, Italians, *et al*? And why should they? Christian religious leadership did not object to mass murder of Jews by the Cossacks in the 17th Century, or the murder of a million of black men, women, and children in the Congo by King Leopold II (1835-1909). Why should it be different a few years later with *Jews*?

38. *Nova creatura* and *Humanitas*

The problem with Jewish scholars dealing with the above question is that they did not seem to care much about their grandmothers. If they would, they would have known that not all 'good people' could be trusted regarding the safety of 'other' good people, Jews in particular. According to Christian doctrine, Jews have the legal status of 'slaves.' Hagar, the slave, represents the Synagogue; while Sara, the mistress, represents the Church. This is basic Christian dogma, as it was so gracefully expressed by Paul, *Gal* 4:21-26 and 30-31:

> Tell me, you that desire to be under the Law, don't you listen to the Law? For it is written that Abraham had two sons, one by the bondmaid, and one by the free woman. However, the son by the bondmaid was born according to the flesh, but the son by the free woman was born through promise. These things contain an allegory, for these are two covenants. One is from Mount Sinai, bearing children to bondage, which is Hagar. For this Hagar is Mount Sinai in Arabia, and answers to the Jerusalem that exists now, for she is in bondage with her children. But the Jerusalem that is above is free, which is the mother of us all.... Nevertheless what said the scripture? Cast out the bondwoman and her son: for the son of the bondwoman shall not be heir with the son of the freewoman. So then, brethren, we are not children of the bondwoman, but of the free.

There is a profound reason for that. To be incorporated in Jesus, it means to be a *nova creatura* or 'new creature': "Therefore if any man *be* in Christ, *he is* a new creature: old things are passed away" (2*Cor* 5:17; see *Gal* 6:15). As a *nova creatura*, the faithful is *renatus,* 'born again' as an integral part of Jesus. This is fundamental to the very notion of baptism:

> The sacramental act of baptism was also endowed with effects in the public field since as a baptized Christian the individual was said to have become a new creature, was said to have undergone a metamorphosis—he ceased a mere man; he ceased to be, to use Pauline language, a man of nature, a man of flesh, an "animalic man." [Footnotes by the author: 1*Cor* 2:14 and 3:33; *Gal* 5:24; *Col* 2:12.] As a result of the working of divine grace, he had divested himself of his natural humanity, his *humanitas*, and has become a participant of the divine attributes themselves.[89]

Building on this belief, it should be apparent why, in quality of a *nova creatura*, every Christian is a *Übermensch*, in reference to the Jews. Let us remember that as taught by Paul, since Jews *refused to betray the covenant* that they contracted *with God at Sinai*, they proved to be wretched and unworthy. The logic is self-evident. The subjects of a vanquished or demised ruler *must* pledge faith to their new ruler. By refusing to comply with this imperial canon, Jews have the status of slaves. There are some practical consequences to this doctrine; principally, that there could not be any moral objection to plundering and despoiling Jewish property. This doctrine had been enunciated, with kindness and sympathy, by Thomas Aquinas, one of the most brilliant and, we may add, ethical minds to grace the face of Christendom. Briefly and to the point he wrote: "Since Jews are the slaves of the Church, the Church may take disposition of their property."[90]

---

[89] *The Individual and Society in the Middle Ages*, pp. 7-8. See ibid, p. 101. See above Chapter 4.

[90] *Summa Theologica* II, 2, 10, 10. Cited in *The Structure of Spanish History*, p. 471 n. 10, in the name of the illustrious Rosa Lida. Since the original could prove a bit unsettling, the English version in ed. Timothy Mc Dermot, *Summa Theologiæ* (London: Eyre and Spottiswoode, 1989), p. 341, mistranslates: "The church has the right to

The same status applies to Jewish lives and limbs. Only according to the *Hebrew Scripture* is a 'slave' *a full human being*, and if killed by his master, the master will be tried for murder and face the death penalty. How successful would a search be for any other case, in any polity, wherein someone was summoned to a court of justice to answer for killing his slave? In Europe? In America?

The preceding will explain why, after butchering and or expelling the Jews, there should be no objection to 'upgrading' their Synagogues by turning them into Christian places of worship. King David *purchased* the site where the Jewish Temple was built (see *2 Sam* 24:18-25), but, as we all know, the Church need not abide by such a mundane, worldly standard. The famous Church at Jerash, Israel, had been a Synagogue. At about the years 530-531 it was appropriated and 'converted' into a Church. There is a very reliable tradition that in the year 325, Constantine's mother built a Church at the site of the Jewish Temple. In the 7th century, during the Sassanid period, Jews regained control of the site for a few years and began to rebuild the Temple. When Christians took over the site, they destroyed the building and turned it into a garbage dump. Finally, the Muslims took over the site (691) and built on it the Dome of the Rock. Early in the 12th century, the Crusaders seized the site, where they built the "Templum Domini," and placed the Cross on top of the Dome (the site of the Mosque was used as a Royal stable). The place was recaptured by Saladin (1187).

This was not an aberration. Seizing Jewish places of worship, and 'converting' them into Churches, was standard practice in the Christian Roman Empire. The same was true in Medieval Europe. E.g., the four Synagogues in Trani, Italy, were forcibly confiscated and then 'upgraded,' respectively, to Santa Maria in Scolanova, San Leonardo Abate, San Pietro Martire, and Sante Quirico e Giovita. Another example is the Maribor Synagogue, in Slovenia. And last, but not least, the Ibn Shushan Synagogue in Toledo, Spain—probably the

---

dispose of the Jew's property since he is the subject of the church."

oldest Jewish house of worship in Europe—was transformed into "Santa María la Blanca" (it is still 'owned' by the Church). In this fashion, countless of Synagogues were 'upgraded' to Christian places of worship. Justification for this practice may be found in the fact that Jesus confiscated a she-ass for his triumphant entrance to Jerusalem (see *Matt* 21:2-3, and above Chapter 22).

The Christian attitude towards the *Jewish Temple* served as a model for her attitude towards the *Hebrew Scripture*. Let me begin by pointing out that following the destruction of the Jewish Temple (68 CE), the *Hebrew Scripture* was Israel's *virtual Temple*. The text is designated *Kitbe ha-Qodesh*. It means, *not* 'Holy Scripture,' but the *Scripture at the Sanctuary*. Upon opening the *Scripture*, the Jew finds himself/herself at the gate of the Jewish Temple. Perusing the text means exiting the realm of the mundane, and advancing in a sacred procession through the hallways of the *Hebrew Sanctuary*, until coming face-to-face with the God of Israel and the People of Israel.[91] By *appropriating* the *Hebrew Scripture*, Christianity was desecrating the *virtual Temple of Israel*; by *imposing* on it her Christological interpretations, the ecclesiastical authorities were vandalizing the *Tora*, the *Prophets*, and the *Hagiography* of *Israel*. 'Reconstructing' these texts to fit the needs of Christian theologians, is not different than if someone would raid a Church, take the Crucifix and similar religious symbols apart, and use the pieces to manufacture artifacts for his own cult. Attaching the *Hebrew Scripture* to the *Christian Scripture*, as an ancillary text in case of a 'crisis'—as perennially used by the Church—is no different than if Islam or any other religion would do the same with the *Christian Scripture*. By naming the *Hebrew Scripture*, the '*Old* Testament,' the Christian authorities were in fact deposing the God of Abraham, Isaac, and Jacob; as when an earthy ruler, who once dead or deposed, is replaced by a *New* one. On behalf of the Christian authorities one may point out that Emperor Titus (70-81), as reported by the rabbis, performed a most obscene act in the Holy of Holies—an act intended to

---

[91] See *HS,* vol. 2, Appendix #58, especially pp. 129-133.

desecrate, simultaneously: the Temple of Israel, the Law of Israel, and the God of Israel.[92] Now, if the Roman Emperor could desecrate the Jewish Temple and the Jewish Law and the Jewish God, why would it be improper for the ecclesiastical authorities to do the same? The Church saw nothing objectionable with Titus' behavior. Evidence to this is Constantine's Arch, dedicated in 315. It consists of three arches in one—symbolic of the Holy Trinity. In token of admiration, Constantine placed his triumphal arch next to Titus' Arch. In the construction of the arch, spoils were taken from the monuments dedicated to Trajan (98-117) and Hadrian (117-138), both of whom being celebrated for their massacre of Jews.

In brief, a Christian is a *nova creatura*. Therefore, there could be no logical justification to charge a Christian—any Christian—with 'crimes' against *humanitas*! By the same sort of logic, it would be cynical to criticize Pope Pius XII (*et al*) for his anti-Semitic policies.

We can now understand the theological principle underlying the behavior of the *Conquistadores* and the modern *Übermensch*. Given that as members of the Christian faith, they had divested themselves from *humanitas*, it would be improper to fault them for the genocide of Native Americans and other members of *humanitas*. People censuring them do not understand that to be a member of the *mystic body of Jesus* means that you have been absorbed,

> by the Church, which itself, however, was governed on the monarchic principle, according to which original power was located in one supreme authority, from which all power in the public sphere was derived—a system which, for want of a better name, I call the descending or theocratic theme of government and law.[93]

Therefore, any charge against an individual *nova creatura* is in

---

[92] On Titus obscene act of desecration, see *Giṭṭin* 56b, and *HS,* vol. 1, pp. 92-93; on Constantine's Arch, see ibid, pp. 248-249. For some background on Constantine, see Walter Kaufmann, *Religions in Four Dimensions* (New York: Reader's Digest Press, 1976), pp. 141-143.

[93] *The Individual and Society in the Middle Ages*, p. 9, see corresponding note ibid. On the *Jewish* concept of theocracy, see *HS*, vol. 1, pp. 130-134.

fact a charge against the Supreme Authority governing the *nova creatura*. Simply put, lower men and women, obeying orders, are not responsible for their actions: a Christian is, first and foremost, a "*subditus*, who, by virtue of his baptism and the consequential incorporation into the Church, had no autonomous character." It was "that obedience to the command of the superior authority was his hallmark."[94]

Scholars that have examined Nazi atrocities maintained that certain acts should be deemed not only criminal but also inhuman, for example "*throwing children alive into crematoria.*"[95] [Italics in original]. Now, Christendom at large never condemned "snatching children from their mother's arms and throwing them to be devoured alive by dogs, or smashing them against the rocks and throwing them to die in the mountains." What could then be the rationale to expect Pope Pius XII to condemn throwing Jewish babies into a crematorium? The reason that, "The annihilation of six million Jews…has resisted understanding," is because those investigating the subject failed to ask their grandmothers about these 'good people.' If they would, they could have learnt that in a culture of obedience-submission [1] you do what you are told, [2] therefore, you only have a subordinate role and bear no personal responsibility for your actions. In a culture of obedience, people need not hate the enemy to kill him: one just follows orders. "Never in history have more people been killed with less real hatred than during World War II."[96]

In short, a culture of obedience is ruled by the formula: authority = power = god. Let us repeat once more the *theological imperative* taught by Paul: "Whosoever therefore resisteth the authority (*exousia*), resisteth the ordinance of God: and they that resist shall receive to themselves damnation. For the rulers are not a terror to good works, but to evil" (*Rom* 13: 2-3). The function of religion is to inculcate in

---

[94] *The Individual and Society in the Middle Ages*, p. 12, see corresponding n.
[95] Hans Askenasy, *Are We All Nazis?* (Secaucus, N.J.: Lyle Stuart Inc., 1978), p. 104.
[96] *Are We All Nazis?* p. 101.

the faithful that obedience to authority is not merely a matter of compliance, but "also for conscience sake" (*Rom* 13:4). Therefore, we should not be surprised to discover that in the footsteps of the Pauline doctrine of obedience, Nazi criminals believed that they were innocent.

> *Most individuals believe that they owe obedience to authorities, and are in turn absolved from responsibility for their destructive behavior because it was committed in the name of such authorities.*[97] [Italics in original]

I wish to end this chapter with a question. It seems that there is a huge difference between Nazis and the lily-white souls teaching Native Americans about love. Nazi criminals were described as "normal, ordinary men." The situation is somehow different with Christian saints. Writing about Christian saints, my friend, the late Professor William Nicholls, wrote: "Even saints are not always psychologically healthy, and their ardent devotion can mask severe unconscious problems."[98] The same culture of obedience-submission produced both. Hence my question: Who is worse, the Nazi criminal or the crazy saint? Think carefully before answering.

39. The *Tora*—an Evolutionary Gift to Humankind

The *Tora* is an all-encompassing *political* system.[99] The basic idea of Judaism is that freedom is unattainable under the pagan system of governance, where a man or a group of men are the supreme authority, with the power to interpret, legislate, and abrogate the Law. Even when having the finest constitution made by men, like that of the

---

[97] *Are We All Nazis?* p. 102, see ibid. pp. 104-105. Concerning the issue of obedience in military law, there is a wonderfully reasoned and detailed study by Mark J. Osiel, *Obeying Orders: Atrocity, Military, Discipline, and the Law of War* (New Brunswick and London: Transaction Publishers, 1999).

[98] William Nicholls, "Saints and Fanatics: The problematic connection between religion and spirituality," *Judaism* 46 (1996), p. 451.

[99] See *HS*, vol. 1, Chapter 24.

United States—given the absolute discretionary power of the Supreme Court, "the people," as it was eloquently expressed by Thomas Jefferson, "will have ceased to be their own rulers, having to that extent practically resigned their government in the hands of that eminent tribunal."[100] The alternative proposed by the *Tora* is a Constitution based on a mutual *berit* or 'covenant,' contracted by God and Israel at the foot of Mt Sinai. The result of this alliance is the Law serving as the *Constitution of Israel*. In this manner, the Law, rather than a man or a group of men, is the supreme authority of the Jews. There is wisdom in the Jewish covenant.

Having 'God' as a party to the covenant, not only means that God, rather than man, is the guarantor of the alliance, but, above all, that He Himself accepts the ultimate authority of the Law. Two revolutionary principles follow. First, given that God is a party to the covenant, even if He (or a 'prophet' or 'divine spokesman') would voice a view contrary to the Law, it would be declared void and null. The rationale is simple. By concluding a covenant with the people of Israel, Heaven had in fact acceded to conform to the interpretations and understanding of the people of Israel.[101] The second principle would apply in case a man or group of men will claim to have power *over* the Law, and wish to change or to abrogate it. As such, the *Tora* stands for an evolutionary stage, wherein humanity will not be governed by 'obedience' and 'submission,' but by a supreme Law, binding equally man and God, governor and governed. In this stage of human development, a local 'court of justice,' *without a police force,* would suffice, as illustrated by the local Rabbinic Court of Justice (*Bet Din*), throughout the long history of Jewish exile (*galut*).

The *Tora* is an evolutionary gift, permitting human organization without the liabilities involved in the rule of might. To be effective, the Law needs to be *internalized* by the people. As Moses taught: "The Lord had entrusted us with the Law, it is the inheritance of the com-

---

[100] Letter Sep 28, 1820 to William C. Jarvis.
[101] See *HS*, vol. 1, Chapter 5.

munity of Jacob" (*Dt* 33:4). Hence the supreme relevance of education: Hebrew freedom warrants firsthand knowledge of the national Constitution of the people. This means that the people—not the governing authorities—are the depositary of the Law. Consequently, if the Supreme Court of Israel, together with the Priests at the Temple and the civil authorities, would depart from the terms of the Law, as it happened under King Antiochus, the people *will not obey*. The Festival of Hanukah commemorates this glorious moment in human history.[102] There are no parallels to Hanukah, where a people revolted against their judicial, ecclesiastical, and civil authorities in support of their constitution. We can thus understand why Jews believed that the *Tora* is the best constitution.[103]

In short, the Jewish view is that 'liberty' without a Law contracted in a solemn covenant with God, is an invitation to political tyrants, religious demagogues, and intellectual charlatans, to manipulate the people.

The Church's claim that when Jesus allegedly said, "Do not think that I come to abolish and destroy the Law or the Prophets I did not come to do away, but to fulfill" (*Matt* 5:17, *Pocket Interlinear*, p. 9), he meant to abolish the Law, is tantamount to the claim that when an individual comes to make a deposit in a bank in fulfillment of a payment, he intends to put an end to the bank's authority, and abrogate banking altogether.[104] Judaism rejects Paul's notion of 'liberty'

---

[102] The Mishna *Horayot*, together with the corresponding Babylonian and *Yerushalmi* Talmud, explore the boundaries of the Supreme Court of Israel, the Temple and the King, and where their authority ends. Were any of these institutions to trespass the boundaries stipulated by the Law, their authority would be *ipso facto* null and void; see *HS*, vol. 1 Chapter 19. To emphasize that the monarch is *under* the Law, the Jewish monarch must have a copy of the *Tora* attached around his arm at all times, as the "ensign of sovereignty." Thus, displaying publicly the principle that the ruler is *under* the Law—not the other way around; see *The Special Laws*, IV, 164, *Philo*, vol. 8, p. 111.

[103] See *Against Apion*, II, 184-186, *Josephus*, vol. 1, p. 367. Cf. quotations above, Section III at notes 133-137.

[104] I haven't found a single case in which "to fulfill the Constitution," actually means that the Constitution has been abrogated, and is henceforth not binding.. To a Jew, the *Christian interpretation* of this statement, sounds like an armed robber

without a Law. His plea: "Stand fast therefore in the liberty wherewith Christ had made us free, and be not entangled again with the yoke of bondage" (*Gal* 5:1), is not a plea on behalf of the people. Rather, it is a plea for the people to *submit* to the bestial freedom that Christianity awarded to the worst tyrants known to humankind. The same is with the "truth" offered by *Jn* 8:32: "And ye shall know the truth, and the truth shall make you free." It is a truth predicated on "the obedience of faith" (*Rom* 16:26; cf. *Jn* 4:14), defined by the Vatican Council II as: "full obedience of the intellect and will to God," in accordance to the teachings of the Church.[105] In this sense, Christian 'freedom' is more restrictive than *submission* to tyrannical government. *Submission* to tyrants enchains the subject from without; *obedience* to the Church's magistrates enchains the subject from within.

When evaluating Christian claims against the Law of Israel, it is important to bear in mind that Jews view the *Tora* as a *national* document, where theological and historical considerations are unacceptable. This is true for the same reason that theological reasoning is unacceptable to expressions such as "God" in the Declaration of Independence, and "act of God" in the law of torts. More to the point, Christian theological argumentation designed to debunk the *Tora* are worthless and intrusive, for the simple reason that it is none of the business of Christian divines to tell Jews what is the correct interpretation of their *Sacred Scripture*, anymore that is their business to tell

---

telling the bank teller: 'think not of me as a bank-robber, I came not to rob, but to deposit!' I personally believe that the authors of the *Gospels* have maliciously perverted the actual behavior and teachings of Jesus. There is much we can learn about his faith and ethics from the *Epistle* written by his brother James. There is not a single word in it that can be construed as non- or un- or anti-Jewish. His exhortation to moral virtues, and emphasis on works (rather than on Pauline 'faith'), goes hand and hand with the teachings of the rabbis. This may explain why the canonicity of this work was contested down to the 16th century. This also may explain the dichotomy between ethics, as *actually* practiced in Christian society, and the ethics *taught* by James. As noted by Bertrand Russell, *Why I am not a Christian*, p. 25: "the teaching of Christ, as it appears in the Gospels, has had extraordinarily little to do with the ethics of Christians."

[105] *Vatican Council II*, ed. Austin Flannery, O.P. (Collegeville, MN: 1983), p. 432.

Muslims or Buddhists how to interpret *their Sacred Scriptures*. That Constantine's Sword permitted Christianity to purloin the *Hebrew Scripture* with impunity, awards such usurpation no more legitimacy than to kidnappers assuming the right to inherit the child they just abducted under the claim that *they* are his *verus* parents.

And now a question: why did the Christianity of Paul, combat so fiercely the *Jewish* Law? Specifically, why did it choose not to debate but to demonize? What was the strategy behind the promotion of a whole series of unfounded accusations, beginning with the nonsensical charge of "deicide"—a charge repeated over and over, including during the Nazi period? Before replying, let us remind the reader that this strategy was pursued by no lesser a figure than Pope Pius XI. It is an undisputable fact, that

> Pius XI said in a 1937 encyclical that "Jesus received his human nature from a people who crucified him"—not some Jews, but the Jewish *people*. And the same Pope suppressed a Catholic organization, the Friends of Israel, that tried to discontinue the charge of deicide. Furthermore, Catholic preachers over the centuries have continually made the deicide charge, and seminaries taught it, and biblical commentaries explained it, and persecutions were based on it. In finally rejecting this claim, the Second Vatican Council [1962-65] said nothing about the church's past record. It did not express penitence for official encouragement of such a view, or for pogroms and other actions taken on the basis of it. The price of getting the statement through the Council's sessions was that it *not* admit that the church had ever said or done anything wrong.[106] [Italics in original]

Christianity failed to treat the above questions critically. Why? Here is my take on this matter.

Suppressing the Law permitted the kings to claim unlimited sovereignty over the people they ruled. In retribution for this errand, the ecclesiastical authorities were remunerated with the right to demand absolute obedience from the faithful. Paradoxically, this resulted in the fact that Jews enjoyed more freedom in their Ghettos, than

---

[106] *Papal Sins*, p. 19; for further elucidation, see ibid, pp. 19-28.

Christians under the axis obedience-submission. Hence the need for an unremitting chain of self-congratulatory remarks, *ad nauseam*, on the part of Christian prelates, designed to camouflage deep feelings of *guilt* and *inferiority*. The insatiable need for anti-Semitic and anti-Judaic propaganda, (recently upgraded to 'anti-Israel'), is motivated by envy—envy of a people, chosen by God to have the sacred responsibility of pointing to the world the next stage in the evolutionary development of humankind.

Israel is hated for another reason. To survive Imperial Rome, Israel could have bowed down to Caligula and other dictators. It certainly had the linguistic and cerebral ability to rationalize and validate cowering to the mighty. But Israel didn't. To survive *Galut* or 'political exile', one must have grit. Cowards hate people with daring, and people trafficking in hatred abhor people of grit.

40. Thinking *Shalom*

Judaism does not recognize 'religious enemies.' The Scripture acknowledges the spirituality of pagan humanity (see *Malachi* 1:11; cf. *Jer* 10:7-8), and the God of Israel cares about the well-being of *all* people (see the book of *Jonah* and *Ps* 145:9). Accordingly, the rabbis declared that pious gentiles are saved.[107] Prior to Christianity, Israel never encountered a 'religious enemy' for the simple reason that there were none. The idea of a 'religious enemy' is a Christian invention, for the sole purpose of targeting Jews and Judaism. Christian authorities could have chosen a path in which members of other religions are tolerated and differences acknowledged, without haranguing, incessantly, on Jews and Judaism.

It seems to me that in addition to the 'theological imperatives,' it was expedient to bad-mouth Jews and Judaism. In this manner the ecclesiastical authorities could cement the alliance 'Church-Monarch'

---

[107] See *HS*, vol. 2, Appendix #11, and above, "Introduction," notes 23 and 44.

and harvest the earthly benefit that such a partnership provides. I will explain. By publicly renouncing all political aspirations, Christianity was in fact granting *carte blanche* to the ruling authorities. At the same time, by 'taking-over' the *Hebrew Scripture* and silencing the Jews and Judaism, Christianity was depriving humanity of an alternative to political and intellectual oppression.

The philosophers of the Enlightenment developed a similar tactic. In the footsteps of the ecclesiastical authorities, whom they replaced, these philosophers were terribly hostile to anything remotely 'Jewish.' Especial care was taken *not* to mention anything that could be construed as something positive about Judaism, particularly in the realm of law and political organization. There were, however, notable exceptions. One of these was Joseph de Maistre (1753-1821), who came to appreciate the uniqueness of the Jewish Law.[108] Although he was a strong supporter of the Catholic Church (and therefore an advocate of monarchial and hierarchic authority), he maintained that the Law of Moses was an exceptional document. On the one hand, he was convinced that, *"Man cannot create a constitution, and no legitimate constitution can be written."* [Italics in original] To be effective, a constitution would have to be written *after* the nation was formed. "The collection of fundamental laws which necessarily constitute a civil or religious society never has been or will be written *a priori.*"[109] Naturally, in such a situation, the input of special interests would be a determining factor, conditioning the tenor and orientation of the Constitution. That is why man-made constitutions demand continuous adjustments and reorganization, with all the political, social, and economic unrest that these changes entail. On the other hand, de Maistre acknowledged that there was an exception to this rule.

---

[108] Another great thinker was Giambattista Vico (1688-1774), the father of modern humanism; see my "The Splitting of the *Logos*: Some Remarks on Vico and Rabbinic Tradition." *New Vico Studies* 3 (1985), pp. 85-103; "Francisco Sánchez's Theory of Cognition and Vico's *verum/factum*," *New Vico Studies* 5 (1987), pp. 83-99; "Imagination and Religious Pluralism: Maimonides, ibn Verga, and Vico," *New Vico Studies* 10 (1992), pp. 85-103.

[109] Joseph de Maistre, *On God and Society* (Chicago: Henry Regnery, 1967), p. 40.

To this general rule, that *no constitution may be written or made a priori*, we know but one exception: the legislation of Moses. This alone was *cast*, so to speak, like a statue and written even to the smallest details by an extraordinary man who said, FIAT! Without this work ever after needing corrections, additions, or modifications by himself or anyone else. This alone has withstood time, from which it borrowed and expected nothing. It survived fifteen hundred years [before Christianity], and even after eighteen more centuries have passed the great anathema which it struck it on the fated day [the destruction of the Temple, 9th of Ab, 68 CE], we see it enjoying a second life and still binding, with some nameless and mysterious bond, the various scattered families of a people dispersed but not disunited [Jews throughout the Diaspora]. Like magnetism, and with a similar force, it operates at a distance, making one whole of many separated parts. Evidently, to intelligent minds, this legislation surpasses the limits of human capability and is a magnificent exception to a general law which has yielded only once, and then to its Author [i.e., God].[110] [Italics in original]

Christians in general came to appreciate the exceptionality of the Jewish Law, through an unexpected source: the establishment of a new kind of polity. Before exploring this subject, it would be important to remind the reader that for Jews, the problem never was with Christianity or Christians (or with Islam and Muslims, or members of *any* religion). Rather, the problem was with the alliance 'Church-Monarch,' whereby religion became an instrument to choke the voice of Israel. Concerning this alliance, Oscar S. Straus observed:

> The public establishment of Christianity by Constantine in the beginning of the fourth century had the effect of placing the altar on the throne, and the ultimate result was the desecration of the one and the degradation of the other.[111]

This alliance was shattered in the New World. The first steps

---

[110] Joseph de Maistre, *On God and Society*, pp. 41-42. For some background, see *The Works of Joseph de Maistre* (New York: Schocken Books, 1971), pp. 77-80, 95-98.

[111] *The Origin of the Republican Form of Government in the United States*, pp. 88-89.

were taken in Puritan England. Thanks to the English translation of the *Scriptures*, the faithful were able to read the *Hebrew Scripture* without the encumbrance of the ecclesiastical authorities for the first time.

> "No greater moral change ever passed over a nation than passed over England during the years which parted the middle of the reign of Elizabeth from the meeting of the Long Parliament. England became the people of a book, and that book was the Bible. It was as yet one English book which was familiar to every Englishman: it was read in the churches and read at home and everywhere its words, as they on ears which custom had not deadened, kindled a startling enthusiasm." What the revival of classical learning had done on the Continent was done in England in a far profounder fashion by the translations of the Scriptures.[112]

Still, while in England, the first colonial settlers were not free to worship according to their conscience; it was only in *New* England where, for the first time, Christians were truly free to read the *Scriptures,* without the supervision of ecclesiastical authorities.

> With the rise of the Puritans, and their struggle for independence and freedom from ecclesiastical tyranny, came a revival of the study of the Old Testament, of Hebrew and Hebraic learning. With the American Puritans especially, the Mosaic code and the Hebrew commonwealth were living realities, so intense was their interest, so earnest was their religious life. No architect drew his plans with more fidelity of purpose to reconstruct a building after an ancient model, than did the Puritans study this Biblical code and the Hebraic form of government which they endeavored to apply literally to their New Canaan.[113]

Thus began a quiet revolution, with monumental consequences:

---

[112] The extract in quotation marks comes from Green's *Short History of the English People,* cited in W. B. Selbie, "The Influence of the Old Testament on Puritanism," in eds. I. Abrahams *et al, The Legacy of Israel* (Oxford: Clarendon Press, 1928), p. 407. The rest of the quotation is from Selbie himself.

[113] Oscar S. Straus, "The First Settlement of the Jews in the United States," in *The American Spirit* (New York: The Century Co., 1918), pp. 279-280.

the new settlers chose the *Hebrew*, rather than the *Christian Scripture*, as their guide for political and legal inspiration.

> Puritan theology was arrayed against the politico-theological tenets of the Established Church. The divine supremacy of the Law, as embodied in, and illustrated by, the Hebrew Commonwealth, was brought in conflict with the 'Divine Right' of kings, as exhibited in the absolutism of George III, and out of the struggle came to life American liberty.[114]

It is a historical fact that the ideals upon which the United States was founded came from the *Jewish*—not the *Christian*—Scripture.

> The Bible was to them not only their guide in religion, but their textbook in politics. They studied the Old Testament and applied its teaching with thoroughness and literal devotion that no people, excepting only the Jews, and perhaps the Scotch, had ever exemplified, for they seemed to recognize a striking similarity between their own hardships, history, and condition and those of the children of Israel under Moses and Joshua.[115]

The focus of the Christian reader of the *Hebrew Scripture* never had been this or that ritual (it is abundantly clear to an unbiased reader, that Jewish rituals are not binding on gentiles), but on the *people of Israel,* as a model and inspiration to men and women enslaved by absolute rulers.

> They [the colonists] quoted its texts [the *Hebrew Scripture*] with a literal application. Their condition they characterized as "Egyptian Bondage," James I they styled "Pharaoh," the ocean whose dangers and hardships their ancestors were driven to encounter they spoke of as the "Red Sea." They likened their own numbers to that of the children of Israel, "three million souls," America in whose wilds they had come was their "Wilderness," and in after days Washington and Ad-

---

[114] *The Origin of the Republican Form of Government*, pp. 99-100.

[115] *The Origin of the Republican Form of Government*, pp. 70-71.

ams were frequently referred to as their Moses and Joshua.[116]

The early colonists were not only inspired by Israel, but they ended identifying with them.

> They even baptized their children no longer by the names of Christian saints but by those of the Hebrew prophets and patriarchs.[117]

Regardless of whatever 'errors' may one attribute to the colonists, the 'Hebrew inspiration' culminated in *the foundation of the first truly democratic republic in modern times.*

> The spirit of Judaism became the mother spirit of Puritanism in Old England; and the history of Israel and its democratic model under the Judges inspired the Pilgrims and Puritans in their wandering hither and in laying the foundations of their commonwealths in New England. The piety and learning of the Jews bridged the chasm of the middle ages; and the torch they bore amidst trials and sufferings lighted the pathway from the ancient to the modern world.[118]

It is worth repeating this point, over and over again: the inspiration came exclusively from the *Hebrew Scripture*. The *Christian Scripture* was cited to give support to those that *rejected the principles of civil liberty*, and advocated *submission* to King George III.

> It is, at least, an historical fact, that in the great majority of instances the early Protestant defenders of civil liberty derived their political principles chiefly from the Old Testament, and the defenders of despotism from the New. The rebellions that were so frequent in Jewish history formed the favorite topic of the one—the unreserved submission inculcated by St. Paul, of the other. When, therefore, all the principles of right and wrong were derived from theology, and when by the rejection of traditions and ecclesiastical authority, Scripture became the sole arbiter of theological difficulties, it was a matter of manifest importance, in ascertaining the political tendencies of any sect, to discover which Testament was most congenial to the tone

---

[116] *The Origin of the Republican Form of Government*, p. 71.

[117] *The Origin of the Republican Form of Government*, p. 73.

[118] Oscar S. Straus, "American Judaism," in *The American Spirit*, p. 291.

and complexion of its theology.[119]

The non-Christian dimension of the U.S.A. was explicitly proclaimed by the Founding Fathers, beginning with its first President. In the Treaty of Tripoli, approved by the U.S. Senate in 1797, we read: "The government of the United States is not, in any sense, founded on Christian religion."[120] The so-called 'Judeo-Christian' values upon which the *United States* was founded is an *invention* by people refusing to acknowledge what George Washington freely declared, and the U.S. Senate confirmed: "The government of the United States is not, *in any sense*, founded on Christian religion." [Our italics] Similarly, in a letter to Thomas Cooper (1804), President Thomas Jefferson wrote: "We may safely affirm that Christianity neither is, nor ever was, a part of the common law."[121]

By freeing religion from the clutch of the alliance 'Church-Monarchy,' the Founding Fathers permitted 'religion' to be kinder and more responsive to human needs. This, I believe, is the greatest contribution to religion in modern times. Therefore, the Church in America did not allow itself to become a political tool on behalf of intolerance. Not only did it not preach hatred against Jews, but it had been a strong voice against anti-Semitism. For those that may be

---

[119] Quoted in *The Origin of the Republican Form of Government*, n. 2, pp. 19-20, from Lecky, *Rationalism in Europe*, vol. 2, p.168.

[120] *Treaty of Peace and Friendship between the United States of America and the Bey and Subjects of Tripoli of Barbary*, November 4, 1796-January 3, 1797, art. XI, 1796 U.S.T. Lexis 4; *See Treaties and other International Acts of the United States of America, Volume 2, Documents 1-40; 1776-1818*, ed. Hunter Miller (United States Government Printing Office, Washington: 1931), pp 364-366. On the specific non-Christian aspect of American religiosity, see *The Origin of the Republican Form of Government*, pp. 67-69.

[121] Quoted in *The Origin of the Republican Form of Government*, pp. 67-68. The term 'church' in the famous clause establishing the separation of "church and state" meant to exclude institutions and organizations established for the purpose of promoting and protecting a particular religion, i.e., the *Church*, to meddle in matters of the State. Not, as currently argued, to exclude *religion* altogether! Principally, separation of "church and state" is a repudiation of the union cross/sword promoted by the ecclesiastical authorities. It means, not only freedom to worship or not to worship, but, above all, rejection on the part of the civil authorities of using religion or religious institutions to either promote or attack matters of the state.

somehow skeptical, let me repeat the words of the American Cardinal Joseph L. Bernardin (1928-1986):

> It is no secret that many of our past [theological] formulations have seriously distorted the role of the Jewish people in human salvation. These distortions undoubtedly played a role in the persecution borne by Jewish communities in so many parts of the world and tragically helped provide a seedbed for Christian collaboration with the fundamentally antireligious philosophy of Nazism.[122]

The new spirit affected Christianity globally. I am thinking of Pope John Paul XXIII (1881-1963) in particular, and his encyclical *Pacem in Terris*. This allowed for a less constricted relationship between Jews and Christians, ending by promoting greater respect and cooperation between members of all faiths and persuasions.

We are witnessing a new evolutionary stage in the development of religion. The efforts to silence the *Hebrew Scripture* and to disallow Judaism have been mostly abandoned. The Puritan reading of the *Hebrew Scripture* is now integral to the American ethos and intellectual history. The concepts concerning individual liberty, the supremacy of law, the sanctity of conscience, and other foundational principles that the colonists gathered from the *Hebrew Scripture*, serve as an alternative to the classical post-revolutionary governments in Europe, where one set of rulers, enjoying unlimited sovereignty, replaces another set of the same type. Thus, the first colonists began a process of transformation that effectively challenged the old political and social structures, of what had been an imperial universe. Referring to the sociopolitical ideals of the early colonists, Oscar Straus wrote:

---

[122] Quoted by Carol Ann Morrow, *St. Anthony Messenger*, March 1989, p. 30. He was a staunch supporter of the State of Israel and Modern Zionism; see his letter criticizing the United Nations General Assembly, for having classified Zionism as 'racism,' published by Meir Mendes, *Ha-Vatican ve-Yisrael* (Jerusalem: The Hebrew University, The Leonard Davis Institute for International Relations, 1983) pp. 167-168. Of course, anti-Semitism has not disappeared from America, and could emerge resurgent at any time. For a well-documented and well-reasoned work on the subject, see Spencer Blakeslee, *The Death of American Antisemitism* (Westport, Connecticut: Praeger, 2000).

On the other hand, their form of government [of the New England settlers] was constructed upon laws of universal humanity, upon the broad principles that all men are equal, that God alone is King; which were as true when the Declaration of Independence was adopted as in the times of Moses and Joshua, and as true in New England as they were in Canaan.[123]

What is truly amazing is that in the course of time America became a *Kosher* Nation.

Today one-third to one-half of the food for sale in the typical American supermarket is kosher. That means more than $200 billion of the country's estimated $500 billion in annual food sales is kosher certified, a remarkable statistic considering that less than 2 percent of the population is Jewish, and only a minority of them keep kosher.[124]

We can now proceed to explain Maimonides' vision of the *Jewish* Messianic era. Once freed from the clutches of idiotic governments, the voice spoken at Sinai would resound loud and clear, thus preparing the ground for a new evolutionary stage, wherein teamwork and mutual aid among people will replace contention and conflict. It has to do with the idea of *Shalom,* or *Pax Hebraica*, which Jews believe will take place in the Messianic era. According to the rabbis, *other religions and ideologies would persist in the post-Messianic age*.[125] The purpose of *Shalom* is not to eradicate human individuality, so that everyone would be a perfect clone of everyone else, but to bring about cooperation among all peoples, religions, and cultures, working together with "one shoulder," to make this a better world. Thus, in the last chapter of the *Mishne Tora*, Maimonides penned these golden lines:

All these matters (of Jesus), [omitted from standard printed texts for

---

[123] *The Origin of the Republican Form of Government in the United States*, p. 74; cf. ibid. p. 115.

[124] Sue Fishkoff, *Kosher Nation* (New York: Schocken Books, 2010), p. 4.

[125] See *Yebamot* 24b where the Talmud declares that new converts to Judaism *will not be accepted* in the Messianic Age.

fear of Christian censorship!], and of the Ishmaelite (i.e. Muhammad) coming after him (Jesus), came to pave the road for the King-Messiah; and prepare the whole world to worship God *jointly* [italics added]. As it is written, "Because then I shall bestow upon the nations a clear speech, summoning all in the name of God, to worship Him with one shoulder" (*Zeph* 3:9).[126]

We should remind the reader that the world of the *Hebrew Scripture* "was created by God to be made (*la'asot*)" (*Gn* 2:1). This means that it *warrants further development and the pursuit of excellence*.[127] For this, human cooperation is of the essence. A note on two Hebrew terms will help us grasp the close, intimate relationship, between the survival of humanity and the ecology of our planet. In Hebrew, *adam* 'man' and *adama* 'earth' stem from the same root: ADM. *Adam* designates the first man created by God, as well as *all* of his descendants. *Adama* stands for the land inhabited by *adam*. Together, *adam-adama* forms a single organic complex, in which each term of the equation depends on the wellbeing of the other.[128] Simply put, the survival of earth-*adama* warrants the *cooperation* of all of *Adam*'s children, regardless of race, creed and religion. This involves the planning and coordination of specific activities—not of faith. As per the *Hebrew Scripture*, people are defined by their *actions*. And what about matters of *faith*? They are exceedingly valuable and personal. That is why they should be left to the individual and his or her Maker. After all, 'unbelievers,' too, are Adam's children, endowed with the same image of God within.

---

[126] *MT Melakhim* 12:4. The association "one shoulder" in *Zeph* 3:9 with the Messianic Age, comes from R. Abraham ibn 'Ezra, *Commentary to Psalms*, CXLIX, 7. See above "Introduction," n. 40.

[127] See *GD*, pp. 22, 138, and *Shabbat* 119b.

[128] This theme has been first introduced and properly analyzed by R. Elie Benamozegh, *Israel et l'Humanité* (Paris: Ernest Leroux, 1914), pp. 336-338.

EPILOGUE

Judaism gave birth to something that no other religious or political system has: a joyous crowd. Some political systems have produced beautiful constitutions, lasting for centuries. Christianity and Islam have spectacular places of worship, imposing rituals and ceremonies, and inspiring ethical and theological doctrines. But if you want to understand Jews and Judaism, think of *Simḥat Tora* ("The Joyfulness of the Law"). Then, you will realize that Judaism is actually a love story: the story of the love of a people for a book, the Scroll of the Law with which the folks march on *Simḥat Tora*—as if the *Tora* were a bride. Imagine a group of English or American jurists or law professors and their students, so seized with the beauty of their subject, that they march in joyous procession around the Supreme Court holding books of legislation in their arms. There is much that other religious and political systems want to teach the world, particularly regarding their superiority over the Jewish Law. May I suggest that a most effective first-step in that direction would be by having their own people parade, bursting with joy, with their Sacred Books, *Simḥat Tora* style? Secularists, too, may try. Having "so many" devotees, they could surely get a *minyan* to march joyfully, perhaps with Kant's *Metaphysics of Morals*, or Marx's *Das Kapital*?

(The above was inspired by a paper written by Chief Rabbi Lord Jonathan Sachs, *Covenant & Conversation*, *Simchat Torah* 5772).

APPENDICES

Appendix 1
Section II, n. 128

To conceal the Jesus of history, Christianity invented the Jesus of myth.[1] In classical pagan fashion, Christianity used the '*Old* Testament' to manufacture a series of kabuki-masks to communicate with a perennially third-party audience, rapidly exchanging masks according to the occasion at hand (see above, Chapter 7). With this purpose in mind, Christianity appropriated various terms and ideas from the *Hebrew Scripture*, and upgraded the Jewish-*minim* mezuzah to a series of full-blown kabuki-masks. However, the 'mezuzah/masks' were poorly made, with plenty of cracks all over, permitting every Jew, not to speak of the 'rabbis' and wretched 'Pharisees,' to take a peek inside. To safeguard the faithful Christian from "Judaic infections," Christianity invented the *religious enemy*. It was done with good intentions: without hatred of Jews and Judaism, the faithful may fall into "Judaistic errors." Thus, a condition *sine qua non* for Christian love is Jewish hatred.[2]

Within this context, anti-Semitism, and the vilification of the wretched 'Pharisees' and diabolic 'rabbis' play a pivotal role: they excuse Christianity from common civility, when speaking about Jews

---

[1] See *The Jesus Mysteries*, Chapters 1-3.
[2] See *HS*, vol. 1, Chapter 40.

and Judaism. To make certain that the rupture with historical Jesus would be total, not *a single Jewish rite* was admitted in the Church: the 'Law' is not only dead, but deadly. Christian rites must come, exclusively, from the pagan world. E.g., the mysteries of Demeter and Orpheus: "most obviously in the myths and rites of the Virgin and the Mass."[3] The stories about the mythical Jesus, his birth, childhood, and adult life, reflect the mindset of pagan lore—having nothing 'Jewish' about them. That is why, when teaching about Jesus, the religion of love must inculcate hatred of the perfidious Jews, who out of sheer malice crucified the one destined to bring harmony and eternal peace to humankind. And Salvation, too.

---

[3] Joseph Campbell, *The Masks of God: Occidental Mythology* (Penguin Compass, 1991), p. 28.

Appendix 2

Section II, n. 155

Bowl, Alexandria, Roman times (1st Century BCE and 1st Century CE), Ceramic, Alexandria Maritime Museum (C1_3557)

Bellow is the information on this item, kindly provided by David Fabre, Doctor in Egyptology, member of the European Institute of Submarine Archaeology

This bowl was discovered on the IEASM archaeological mission in the *Portus Magnus* of Alexandria in May 2008, close to the modern Corniche, at the foot of the peninsula that stretches towards the island of Antirhodos on the former coastline now submerged.

Bowl C1-3557 was found in an even context of the first half of the 1st century CE, associated with oriental sigillated, thin-walled goblets and imported culinary ceramic. This thin-walled ceramic, however, dates back to the 1st century BCE. It is a careened cup with handles, well preserved. Close forms are present in Pergamon, for production between the late 2nd century BCE and the early 1st century CE. Bearing in mind the technical characteristics and type of this specimen, this jug very likely comes from a workshop in the west of Asia Minor.

This bowl is engraved with *DIA CHRSTOU O GOISTAIS* made after baking as the incisions have taken away the slip. This inscription is at least enigmatic; it dates back either to the 1st century BCE (dating of the ceramic) or the first half of the 1st century CE (dating of the occupation) and offers different hypotheses of reading.

Different hypotheses of reading

For Pr. Bert Smith of Oxford University, it might be a dedication or a present made by a certain Chrestos belonging to an association (maybe religious) called *Ogoistais*. In this sense, Pr. Klaus Hallof, director of the Institute of Greek inscriptions in the Berlin-Brandenburg Academy of inscriptions believes that it is necessary to connect *"ogostaï"* to known Greek denominations of religious associations such as *Hermaistai, Athenaistai, Isiastai* which gathered worshippers of the god Hermes or the goddess Athena and Isis. "*Ogo*", according to this hypothesis, would be a divine form of expressing the god Osogo or Ogoa of whom Strabon and Pausanias talk with regard to a divinity worshipped in Milas, in Caria.

The goet?

According to the interpretation of Pr. André Bernand, Professor emeritus of French Universities, *Goistais* might be a mistaken graphic of *goes*, the *"goet"*, that is, the *"magician, the sorcerer, the charmer, the magus"*. This hypothesis becomes even more seducing as the expression introduced by *"dia"* is typical of these casters of chance and soothsayers well-known by the classical texts. According to this supposition, the writing could then be translated either as "*by Chres-*

tos/Christos the magician", or *"the magician by Chrestos/Christos"*.

Having said this, is it possible to specify the nature of the practised magic ritual with the help of this bowl?

A lecanomancia?

A certain number of elements lead us to imagine that this bowl was used by a magus to tell the future by evoking gods or the dead, questioning about the content of the vessel. This hypothesis could therefore be based on lecanomancia which is one of the oldest forms of artificial divination. It has been known in Mesopotamia probably since the 3rd millennium BCE; the soothsayer interprets the forms taken by the oil poured into a cup of water in an interpretation guided by manuals. There is one "hallucinating" variant: the medium, or the soothsayer themselves, goes into a kind of trance when studying the oil in the cup. They therefore see the divinities or supernatural beings appear that they call to answer their questions with regard to the future. Two Egyptian earthenware statuettes, dating from the Middle Empire, might be the first signs of lecanomancia in Egypt[4]. They show a kneeling child leaning his chin on a jug he is holding with his two hands. The shape of the vessel is very similar to that of the bowl discovered in the Portus Magnus in Alexandria (a bowl with two handles and careened belly). The position of the seer performing his art illustrates the practices described in the demotic and Greek scrolls.

Chrestos/Christos and Christ?

If Chrestos is a widely accepted name in Greek onomastics, *chrestos* or *christos* is the Greek word that translates the Hebrew *māšiah*, *"messia"*, *"Christ"* of the Christians. According to this interpretation of Pr. André Bernand, the goet would refer to Jesus-Christ to legitimise his magic abilities. Transformation of water into wine, multiplication

---

[4] One is conserved in the Royal Museum of Art and History in Brussels (former Mac Gregor Collection, E. 7421), and the other to the Metropolitan Museum of Arts in New York. This comes from the Licht's searches (no. 22.I.124).

of loafs, miraculous curing, resurrection… The story of Christ must have been veritable manna for the magician who could find (mythical) precedents to his questions and concerns.

To resort to "Christ" to support a magical practice does not mean belonging to the Christian religion. A pagan might appeal to the Christian God, new to them, simply because of his strangeness and the power attributed to him.

It should be remembered that in Alexandria paganism, Judaism and Christianity never evolved in isolation. All of these forms of religiousness came into magical practices that seduced both the humble layers of the population and the most well-off classes. It was in Alexandria where new religious constructions were made to propose solutions to the problem of man, of God's world. Cults of Isis, mysteries of Mithra, early Christianity bear witness to this.

> David Fabre,
> Doctor in Egyptology, member of the European Institute of Submarine Archaeology

Appendix 3

Section III, notes 56 and 90.

The rabbis pointed at a fundamental difference between the Judeo-*minim* and pagan-Christians. In spite of their defiant attitude towards Jewish authority and the Law, the Judeo-*minim* did not wish physical harm to befall Israel. In an imaginary dialogue, the rabbis posed a question to Jesus:

—Who is praiseworthy in that world?

—He answered: Israel!

—What about combating them?

—He answered: 'Sponsor their welfare, and don't sponsor their ruin. Whoever harms one of them is as if he had harmed the pupil of his eye.'

—How are you [Jesus] being punished?

—He answered: 'In scorching excrement'! As the rabbis taught: 'Whoever pokes fun on the sages will be punished in scorching excrements.

Obviously, "scorching excrement" is an allusion to the Eucharist, which according to Christian faith, is the *actual* flesh and blood of Jesus. Once ingested and digested by the digestive system of the faithful, is then excreted as waste material—certainly the most shocking manner to treat their Savior! See R. Simon b. Ṣemaḥ Duran, *Qeshet wu-Magen* (Leghorn, 5523/1763), 26a-b; cf. ibid, 54a and 54b *in fine*. See also *Studies in the Mishne Tora*, p. 231.

"Come and see," exclaimed a Talmudic sage, "How dissimilar are Jewish sinners (Jesus and the *minim*), from the prophets of the idolatrous nations (Paul and his followers)"![5]

---

[5] *Gittin* 57a.

There is archaeological evidence confirming the preceding and that some of the *minim* were patriotic and did not wish for the national destruction of Israel. In Talpiot, the area where Jesus' family was buried, it was found one ossuary where a Star of David, Israel's *national* symbol, was engraved. Let me quote a pertinent passage written by Jacobovici and Pellegrino:

> Jesus did not raise an army, nor did he strike any coins. But he and his followers clearly believed in his Davidic and messianic claims. Finely etched on the lid of the Talpiot ossuary of Jesus, son of Joseph, is a symbol. The mark was most probably made by whoever went through the heart-wrenching process of inserting Jesus' bones into the ossuary into its burial niche, where it was destined to remain for two thousand years. There on the lid, that unknown kin of Jesus, son of Joseph, carved a simple but unmistakable…star.[6]

---

[6] *The Jesus Family Tomb*, p. 212. Cf. above Section II, n. 48.

Appendix 4
Section IV, n. 25

The Hebrew people do not identify the signifier with the signified. Throughout the Ten Plagues in Egypt, Moses and Aaron would indicate with their staves the commencement of a plague (see *Ex* 7:10, 12, 19; 8:12; 9:23; 10:13; 14:17). If one were to identify the signifier (Moses' and Aaron's staves) with the signified (the wonder taking place), one would have to conclude that Moses was the author of these wonders. Because in the pagan mind, the signifier equals the signified, the Egyptians attributed the miracles to Moses and not to God. "And also the man Moses was very great in the sight of Pharaoh's servants and in the sight of the people" (*Ex* 11:3). Jews do not process reality in the same manner. Moses pointed with his staff at the splitting of the sea (*Ex* 14:16) and the return of the water over the Egyptians (*Ex* 14:26-27). Yet, the people did not attribute these miracles to Moses but to God. "And Israel saw the great work which the Lord did upon Egypt, and the people felt awe for the Lord, and they believed in the Lord, and in his servant Moses" (*Ex* 14:31).

INDICES

Index of References

HEBREW SCRIPTURES

GENESIS 1:1-31, p. 96; 1:3, p. 95; 1:27, pp. 1, 25, 82; 2:1-25, p. 96; 2:1, p. 310; 2:3, p. 96; 2:7, p. 82; 9:4, p. 200; 12:1, p. 22; 18:17-33, p. 259; 20:3-7, p. 17; 31:24, p. 17; 35:2, 4, p. 1. 48:16, p. 94.
EXODUS 1-40, p. 93; 1:9-11, p. 147*; 2:11-14, p. 22; 2:23-25, p. 22; 3:1-3, p. 22; 4:10, p. 76; 7:10, 12, 19, p. 321; 8:12, p. 321; 8:15, p. 166; 9:23, p. 321; 10:13, p. 321; 11:3, pp. 23, 321; 12:1-2, pp. 96, 108; 14:16, p. 321; 14:17, p. 321; 14:26-27, p. 321; 14:31, pp. 22, 23, 321; 15:1, p. 23; 15:24, p. 31*; 16:2, 8, 9, p. 31*; 16:11-27, p. 97; 19:1, p. 96; 19: 1-2, p. 108; 19:3, p. 42; 19:3-6, p. 260; 19:9, p. 266; 19:15-16, p. 109; 19:19, p. 73; 20:1, p. 45; 20:15, p. 73; 22:27 (28), p. 3; 24:7, p. 260; 31:18, p. 103; 33:9, 10, 20, p. 266.
LEVITICUS 18:5, p. 5*; 19:17, p. 4*; 19:18, pp. 83-84; 19:28, p. 172; 19:32, p. 8; 19:34, p. 84; 24:15-16, p. 3.
NUMBERS 1:1, p. 109; 9:1, p. 109; 5:26, pp. 26*, 74*; 10:11, p. 109; 12:3, p. 265; 14: 2, 27, 29, 34, 36, p. 31*; 14:4, p. 258*; 14:20, p. 85; 14:2, 27, 29, 34, 36, p. 31*; 16:15, p. 185; 17:6, 20, 25, p. 31*; 22:2-25:9, p. 17; 22:6, 12, p. 17; 24:14, p. 17; 25:1-3, 6, p. 17; 25:7, p. 162*; 32:22, p. 170.
DEUTERONOMY 1:12, p. 137*; 4:20, p. 93; 6:4, p. 21*; 6:5, p. 84; 9:10, p. 103; 11:1, p. 84; 14:1, p. 214; 17:6, p. 222; 19:15, p. 222; 27: 15-25, pp. 26*, 74*; 33:4, pp. 21*, 79, 298; 34:11-12, p. 266.
JOSHUA 9:18, p. 31*; 13:22, p. 162*; 24:1-28, p. 26*, 74*; 24:1-33, p. 269.
SAMUEL I, 2:24, p. 170; 12:3, p. 185; 16:17, p. 169; SAMUEL II 24:18-25, p. 292.
KINGS I, 8:41, 45, p. 6; 8:51, p. 93; 18:28, p. 196*; II, 17:9, p. 146*.
ISAIAH 2:2-4, p. 271; 2:5, p. 95*; 11:4, p. 169; 32:6, 141*; 49:17, p. 30*; 56:7, p. 6; 57:8, pp. 138, 148; 63:11, p. 44.
JEREMIAH 10:7-8, p. 301; 11:4, p. 93.
EZEKIEL 5:8, p. 7; 11:12, p. 7; 29:3, p. 257; 33:25-26, p. 194*; 37:19, p. 11.
HOSHEA 4:7-19, 12, p. 162*.
JONAH p. 301.
ZEPHANIA 3:9, p. 310.
ZECHARIA 5:4, p. 215*; 11:12-13, p. 206; 13:7, p. 205.
MALACHI 1:11, pp. 6, 301.

PSALMS 20:1-4, p. 44; 22: 1[2], p. 204; 29: 3-9, p. 259; 31:6, p. 205; 42, p. 246; 77:27, p. 259; 91:15, p. 73; 106:48, pp. 26*, 74*; 115, pp. 91, 98; 135, pp. 91, 98; 145:9, pp. 19, 301.
JOB 8:13, p. 141*; 13:16, p. 141*; 15:34, p. 141; 20:5, 141*; 27:8, 141*; 31:15, p. 19; 34:37, p. 259; 38:32, p. 186*.
DANIEL 7:13, p. 204*; 8:24, 11:16, p. 267.
SONG OF SONGS 1:11, p. 77*.
ECCLESIASTES 7:1, p. 170.
ESTHER 9:24, p. 211.
PROVERBS 3:4, p. 170; 6:23, 95*; 8:23, p. 95*; 14:15, p. 137; 17:13, p. 117.
NEHEMIAH 5:13, pp. 26*, 74*; 8:6, pp. 26*, 74*.
CHRONICLES I, 16:36, pp. 26*, 74*.

JEWISH HELLENISTIC LITERATURE

THE BOOK OF JUBILEES
19:14, p. 78.

PHILO
Allegorical Interpretations, 80, p. 271*. *The Embassy to Gaius*, 38, p. 235; 162, p. 235; 166, p. 235; 198, pp. 229, 235, 238, 244; 199-200, pp. 209-210; 201, pp. 237, 245; 256, pp. 237, 245, 270; 301, p. 235; 302, p. 235; 349, p. 243; 353, pp. 237, 245; 355, p. 236; 359, p. 243; 361, p. 230*; 362, pp. 237, 245; 368, pp. 231, 235, 237, 241, 246. *Flaccus*, 29, 33, 35, p. 229; 36-39, p. 233; 82, p. 230; 83-85, pp. 231*, 240; 84, p. 239; 96, p. 230. *The Migration of Abraham*, 25, p. 94*; 136-138, p. 99; 185, p. 99*. *Moses*, II, 198-206, p. 3*. *On Abraham*, I, 6, p. 93; VI, 38, p. 93. *On the Giants*, 66, p. 20*. *On Joseph*, VI, 29, p. 95*. *The Preliminary Studies*, 105, p. 94*. *The Special Laws*, I, 53, p. 3*; II, 145, p. 94*; 160, p. 97*; IV, 164, p. 298*.

JOSEPHUS
Against Apion, I, 25, p. 229*; 42, p. 224; 44-46, 73, p. 248*; II, 184-186, p. 298; 218, p. 224; 219, p. 224; 237, p. 4; p. 338, p. 236*. *Jewish Antiquities*, I, 113, p. 20; IV, 207, p. 4; XIV, 168, p. 181*; XVIII, 11-13, p. 132; 271, p. 224; 19.94, p. 242*; 271, p. 224. *Jewish Wars* II, 166, p. 130; 224-227, p. 228; 229, p. 227; III, 540, p. 240; VII, 43-44, p. 153.

TARGUM
Gn 2:7, p. 84; *Nu* 16:15, p. 185; 21:5, 7, p. 31*; *Dt* 4:28; 28:36, 64; 32:5, p. 2*.

PSEUDO-JONATHAN
Nu 16:15, p. 185*. *Mal* 1:11, p. 6*.

RABBINIC LITERATURE

TANNAITIC and TALMUDIC

MISHNA Berakhot 9:5, p. 140*; 9:7, p. 30*. Shebi'it 4:3; 5:9, p. 8*. Shabbat 8:7, p. 97*; 9:4, p. 97*. Pesaḥim 10:5, p. 94. Sheqalim 3:2, p. 170. Sukka 3:12, p. 97*; Rosh ha-Shana 4:3, p. 97*. Ta'aniyot 3:8, p. 130*. Nedarim 3:4, pp. 113*, 186*; Soṭa 3:4, p. 131*. Giṭṭin 5:8, p. 8*. Baba Meṣi'a 5:6, 6:1, p. 31*. Baba Batra, 9:3, p. 80*. 'Aboda Zara 2:3, p. 202*; 5:1-12, p. 227. Sanhedrin 4:5, pp. 6, 9, 11; 8:2, p. 97*; 10:2, p. 18*. Makkot 3:6, p. 172. 'Eduyot 5:7, p. 171. Abot 1:11, p. 140; 1:16, p. 118; 2:5, p. 207; 2:7, p. 170; 2:9, p. 130*; 2:12, p. 261*; 4:20, p. 139*; 5:19, pp. 18*, 162*. Ḥorayot 1:1-3:8, p. 102*; 3:8, p. 171. Ḥolin 7:6, p. 75*. Kelim 13:1, p. 186*. Ohalot 17:2, 3, p. 207*. Para 3:2, p. 30*.

TOSEFTA Berakhot 3:25, pp. 31*, 32*; 6:2, p. 118. Shabbat 13:5, p. 31*. Yom ha-Kippurim 2:10, p. 30*; 4:12, p. 131*. Ḥagiga 2:1, p. 118*. Nedarim 2:2, p. 113*. Giṭṭin 3:14, p. 8*. Baba Meṣi'a 4:22, 7:1, p. 31*. Shebu'ot 2:14, 186*. Sanhedrin 9:7, p. 188*. 13:2, p. 7*. Ḥolin 2:24, p. 152*.

TALMUD BABLI Berakhot 12a, p. 31*; 17a, p. 261*; 18b, p. 91*; 19a, p. 122*; 20a, p. 94*; 28a, p. 30*; 28b-29a, p. 31*; 31b, pp. 27*, 75*; 40a, p. 204; 54a, p. 140*; 55a, p. 95*; 58a, p. 8*; 61b, p. 94*; 63a, p. 30*. Shabbat 14b, p. 122*; 62b, p. 122; 63a; p. 85*; 72a, p. 1*; 75a, p. 137*; 104b, pp. 110, 161, 168*, 180*; 114a, p. 170; 116a, pp. 9*, 30*, 31*, 138; 116a-b, pp. 102, 127*; 119b, p. 310*; 133b, p. 84; 151b, p. 84. 'Erubin 21b, p. 122*; 53a, p. 20*. Pesaḥim 6a, p. 75*; 6b, p. 48; 56a, p. 31*; 86b, p. 131*; 94b, p. 8; 118a, p. 20*. Yoma 66b, p. 152; 69b, p. 141*; 70a, p. 171; 71a-b, p. 5*; 86b, p. 131*. Beṣa 18a, p. 140*; 32b, p. 90; 35b, p. 186*. Sukka 42a, p. 21*. Ta'aniyot 7a , p. 139*; 24a, p. 115*. Megilla 16a, p. 7; 17b, p. 31*; 21a, p. 81*; 25b, p. 2*; Mo'ed Qaṭan 16a, p. 85; 18b, p. 146. Ḥagiga 15b, p. 186*; 18b, p. 122*. Yebamot 24b, p. 309*; 64a, p. 85; 79a, p. 19*. Soṭa 4b, p. 122*; 40a, p. 170; 41b-42a, pp. 113, 141; 42a, p. 131*; 49b, p. 112*. Giṭṭin 14b, p. 113*; 27b, p. 138*; 45b, p. 138*; 56a, p. 187*; 56b, p. 294*; 57a, pp. 209, 319; 61b, p. 8*. Qiddushin 30b, p. 81; 31a, p. 57*; 33a, p. 8*. Baba Qamma 38a, pp. 4, 5*; 56a, p. 282*; 59b, p. 171*; 83a, p. 112*; 113a, p. 186*. Baba Meṣi'a 10b, p. 282*; 59b, pp. 27*, 75*; 114b, p. 18*. Baba Batra 10a, pp. 96*, 214; 12b, p. 130*; 15b, p. 36*; 47a, p. 185*; 145b, p. 31*. Sanhedrin 19a, p. 36*; 19a-b, p. 181*; 25b, p. 113*; 27b, p. 80*; 38b, p. 95*; 39b, p. 7*; 43a, pp. 112, 242*; 43b, p. 111; 49b, p. 48*; 59a, pp. 4*, 10; 61b, p. 1*; 63b, p. 2*; 66a, p. 3*; 102b, p. 139*; 103a, p. 131*; 103b, p. 146*; 105a, pp. 7*, 18*; 106b, p. 162*. Shebu'ot 39a, pp. 80*, 114. 'Aboda Zara 2a-3b, p. 242*; 3a, pp. 5, 225*; 3b, p. 94*; 4a, pp. 127*, 259*; 5a, p. 95; 14b, p. 152*; 16b-17a, p. 152*; 17b, p. 78*; 26b, p. 146*; 30a, p. 9*; 65a, p. 127*. Menaḥot 73b, p. 6; 110a, p. 6*. Ḥolin 94a, p. 8*; 100a-b, p. 75*; 106a, p. 122*. Bekhorot 8a, p. 233*. 'Arakhin 16b, p. 36*. Tamid 32a, p. 130*. Nidda 16a, p. 5*.

TALMUD YERUSHALMI Berakhot I, 4, 3c, p. 31*; IV, 3, 8a, p. 31*; VII, 3, 11c, p. 141*; IX,1,12d, p. 259*. Terumot VI, 2, 44b, p. 115*; VIII, 1, 45c, p. 115*. Sheqalim II, 7, 47a, p. 88*; VI, 1, 49d, pp. 75*, 77*. Megilla III, 7, 74c, p. 141*. Ta'aniyot II, 7, 65c, p. 31*. Mo'ed Qaṭan III, 8, 82c, p. 75*. Ketubbot V, 5, 30a, p. 19*. Baba Qamma VIII, 5, 6c, p. 19*. Baba Batra VIII, 8, 16c, pp. 9-10*. Sanhedrin VI, 10, 24d, p. 234*;

IX, 2, 27a, p. 140*. *Makkot* III, 12, 32b, p. 115*.

ABOT de-R. NATAN, A, XXXI, 46a, p. 95*.
MASSEKHET KALLA RABBATI III, 20, p. 4*.
YALQUT ha-TORA #771, p. 18*.

MIDRASHIM

MEKHILTA de-R. YISHMA'EL, p. 21, p. 261*; p. 153, p. 258*; p. 155, p. 31*; p. 220, p. 137*; p. 235, p. 77*; p. 317, p. 3*.

MEKHILTA de-R. SHIM'ON b. YOḤAI, p. 213, p. 3*.

SIFRA, 4a, p. 30*.
SIFRE BEMIDBAR, pp. 44-45, p. 171*; p. 191, p. 30*.
SIFRE DEBARIM, p. 83-84, p. 78*; p. 86, p. 80*; p. 218, p. 162*; p. 372, p. 78*; p. 381, pp. 30*, 31*.
BERESHIT RABBA, pp. 155-156, p. 83; p. 369, p. 91*; p. 460, p. 258*; p. 480, p. 141*; pp. 1246-1247, p. 94.
SHEMOT RABBA, (Vilna), vol. 1, 24d, p. 148*.
VAYYIQRA RABBA, pp. 155-156, p. 6*; pp. 176-179, p. 79*
DEBARIM RABBA, pp. 85-86, p. 19*.
SHIR HA- SHIRIM RABBA, (Vilna), vol. 2, 11d, p. 77*.
QOHELET RABBA, (Vilna), vol. 2, 23b, p. 91*.
ESTER RABBA, (Vilna), vol. 2, 12c, pp. 7-8*.
MIDRASH EKHA RABBATI, (Buber) I, 3, p. 97*.
MIDRASH TANḤUMA, *Vayyera*, I, p. 31-32*; *Ki-Tabo*, IV, p. 94*; *Naso*, XXX, p. 148*.
MIDRASH TEHILLIM, CVII, 4, p. 93; CXIV, 6, p. 93*.
AGGADAT ESTER, 16b-17a, pp. 7-8*.
MIDRASH SEKHEL ṬOB, *Bereshit* XXXVIII, p. 148*.
MIDRASH LEQAḤ ṬOB, XXXIII, 10, p. 113.
MISHNA OF R. ELIEZER, XII, p. 141*; XIX, p. 142*.
ZOHAR, vol. 3, 106a-b, p. 3*.

RABBINIC WORKS

'Arukh, s.v. GDF, p. 137*; s.v. ShḤR, pp. 185-186*.
Bayit Ḥadash, Ṭur Oraḥ Ḥayyim, 47:5, 2a, p. 5*.
Bene Ḥayye, 64a, p. 139*.
Bet E-lohim, 2a-c, p. 5*.
Birkat Mo'adekha le-Ḥayyim, vol. 2, 143d, p. 36.
Commentary to Psalms, R. Abraham ibn 'Ezra, XCLIX, 7, p. 310*.
Conciliator, vol. 1, p. 137, p. 259*.
Dibre Shalom, 89c-d, p. 6*.

Discourses on the Ecclesiastical and Civil Polity of the Jews, p. 126, p. 258*.
Doroth Harischonim, pp. 171-174, p. 31*.
Em la-Miqra, vol. 1, 1b-2a, 82b-83a, p. 258*; vol. 3, 46b, p. 194*; 59b-60b, 72b, p. 3*; vol. 4, 43a-b, p. 258*; 113b-114a, p. 164*; vol. 5, 4a-6a, 8b-10b, p. 9*; 153a, p. 9*; 171b, p. 162*; 175b, p. 9*.
Genizah Studies, vol. 1, pp. 225-226, p. 7*.
Gib 'at Sha'ul, p. 61, p. 259*; p. 257, p. 7*.
Guide I, 61, p. 259*; III, 29, pp. 11-12*; 32, p. 10.
Ḥiddushe ha-Rama, Giṭṭin, vol. 1, 326a, p. 137*.
Hitgallut ha-Sodot, p. 494, p. 9*.
Ḥobot ha-Lebabot, V, 3-4, pp. 141*.
Iggeret ha-Shmad (ha-Rambam), p. 37, p. 140.
Israel et l'Humanité, pp. 336-338, p. 310*.
Jewish and Christian Ethics, pp. 83-84, p. 13.
Keter Kehunna, Prologue, p. 15*; p. 1c, p. 9*.
Keter Shem Ṭob [vol. 1], pp. 57-58, p. 32*.
Kitab al Muḥadara wal-Mudhakara, p. 227, p. 9*.
Kuzari, IV, 23, pp. 10-11.
Mishnat R. Aharon, vol. 1, pp. 36-37, 243-245, p. 80*.
Mishne Tora (=MT), Yesode ha-Tora 6:8, pp. 138*, 139*, 142. De'ot 2:6, p. 8*; 3:3, p. 261*; 5:1-13, p. 170*. Talmud Tora 1:6, p. 21*; 3:2, p. 171; 4:2, p. 81; 6:9, p. 8*. 'Aboda Zara 1:2, p. 2*; 1:3, pp. 2*, 21*; 2:5, pp. 141, 146; 3:6, pp. 1-2; 10:5, p. 8*. Teshuba 3:7, pp. 137*, 141*; 3:14, p. 141*; 5:2, pp. 5*, 6*. Tefilla 9:3, pp. 26*, 74*. Sefer Tora 10:1, p. 46. Berakhot 10:11, p. 8*. Ma'akhalot Asurot 11:7, p. 11-12*. Shebu'ot 3:1, 2, p. 186*. Mattanot 'Aniyyim 1:9, p. 8*. Terumot 10:10, p. 115*. Me'ila 7:2, p. 282*. Gezela 5:9, p. 113*; 5:11, p. 186*; 11:2, p. 146*. Roṣeaḥ 4:10, p. 146*. Mekhira 18:1, p. 8*. 'Abadim 9:8, p. 19*. Naḥalot 9:1, p. 80*. 'Edut 1:14, p. 96*; 2:1, p. 96*; 10:4, pp. 113*, 186*; 11:10, p. 143. Mamrim 3:3, p. 142. Abel 1:1, p. 75*; 4:4, p. 88*; 14:12, p. 8*. Melakhim 3:9, p. 282*; 10:9, p. 10; 10:12, pp. 8*, 19*; 12:4, p. 310.
Oheb Ger, p. 123, p. 185*.
'Olat Shabbat, 112d, p. 169.
Oṣar ha-Ge'onim. Sanhedrin, p. 208, p. 114.
Peri Ḥadash, Ṭur Oraḥ Ḥayyim, 47:5, 2a, p. 5*.
Perush ha-Ge'onim, Seder Ṭaharot. Kelim 13:1, p. 186*.
Perush ha-Mishnayot (ha-Rambam): vol. 3, *Soṭa* 3:3, p. 140*; vol. 4, *Abot* 2:17, p. 142; 4:11, p. 140*; vol. 5, *Ḥolin* 1:2, p. 141*; 7:6, p. 75*; vol. 6, *Kelim* 13:1, p. 186*; vol. 7, *Para* 3:2, p. 30*.
Perush Rabbenu Ḥanan'el, on: Shabbat 75a, p. 137*; 116a, pp. 9*, 127*; Beṣa 73b, p. 185*; 'Aboda Zara 17b, p. 9*.
Preguntas, 125a-b, p. 205*.
Qeshet wu-Magen, 26a-b, 54a, 54b, p. 319.
Rama, Shulḥan 'Arukh: Oraḥ Ḥayyim, DLXXXI, 1, pp. 26*, 75*; DCXC, 1, p. 75*.
Sefer ha-Miṣvot (ha-Rambam), prohibition #65, pp. 237-238*.
Shalme Ṣibbur, 1a-4a, 4a-7c, p. 171*.
Shulḥan 'Arukh: Oraḥ Ḥayyim, LIII, 19, pp. 26*, 74*; CCXXIV, 7, p. 8*; CCXLIV,

7, p. 8*. *Yore De'a*, CCXLV, 5, p. 21*; CCXLVI, 9, p. 81; CCLI, 9, p. 171*. *Ḥoshen Mishpaṭ*, CCXXVIII, 6, p. 8*.
Teshubot ha-Rambam. 149, pp. 10, 11*; 263, p. 137*; 264, p. 142; 448, p. 12*.
Teshubot Radak, XVII, 9, p. 5.
Toledot Yiṣḥaq, 93b-94a, 18*.
Tosefet he- 'Arukh, s.v. tar'omet , p. 31*.
Words of Peace and Truth, pp. 13-14, p. 7*.
Yad Yosef, 175b-c, p. 5*.
Yefe To'ar. Bereshit, 271c, pp. 258-259*; *Vayyiqra*, 57a, 79*; 57b, p. 80.

CHRISTIAN SCRIPTURES

Matt 2:13-20, p. 233*; 4:1-11, p. 264; 5:8, p. 125; 5:17, p. 298; 5:19-20, p.151; 5:43-48, p. 126; 6:13, p. 263; 7:5, p. 36; 7:6-23, p. 127; 7:29, p. 103; 9:4, pp. 125, 147*; 9:9, p. 123; 9:10-11, p. 126; 9:12-13, p. 127; 9:13, p. 127*; 9:14, p. 116; 10:1, p. 264; 10:3, pp. 123, 124, 209; 10:5-6, p. 136; 10:34-36, p. 267; 11:9, p. 172; 11:11, p. 144; 11:19, p. 114,172; 11:12-20, p. 114; 12:1, p. 115; 12:14, p. 189; 12:8, pp. 116, 124; 12:28-29, p. 166; 12:46-52, p. 172; 14:14-33, p. 267; 15:11, pp. 114, 117, 118, 143; 15:12-20, p. 114; 15:24, p. 136; 18:17, p. 124; 18:21-35, p. 263; 19:3, p. 127; 20:2-13, p. 119; 20:26-28, p. 208; 21:1-3, pp. 184-185; 21:2-3, p. 293; 21:3, p. 186; 21:8-11, p. 210-211; 21:9, p. 187; 21:18-19, p. 115; 21:31, p. 125; 21:31-32, p. 125; 22:21, pp. 124, 189, 272*; 22:23, pp. 172, 205; 22: 29, pp. 172, 205, 265; 23:1-3, p. 143; 23:2-3, p. 151; 23:16-22, p. 182; 23:54, 56, p. 207; 24:29, 39, p. 268; 25:29, p. 190; 26: 2,4, 24, 64 p. 204; 26:3-4, p. 213; 26:5, p. 221; 26:14-15, p. 213; 26:17, p. 206; 26:24, p. 206; 26:25, p. 213; 26:26, p. 206; 26:26-29, p. 193; 26:29, p. 116; 26:31, p. 205; 26:37, 39, 40, 42, 43, 45, p. 208; 26:47, p. 221; 26:49-50, p. 210; 26:55, p. 210; 26:54, p. 206; 26:57, p. 218; 26:60, p. 222; 26:61, pp. 216, 237; 26:63-64, p. 217; 26:64, p. 204; 26:65, pp. 222, 237; 27:2, p. 221; 27:4, p. 222; 27:9-10, p. 205; 27:15, p. 218; 27:28, 29, 37, 41, p. 233; 27:38, p. 188; 27:25, pp. 191, 210; 27:1, p. 211; 27:20, p. 234; 27:22, pp. 234, 238; 27: 22-23, p. 234; 27:24, p. 234; 27:25, pp. 191, 210, 211, 225, 236, 237; 27:28, p. 233, 239; 27:32, p. 218; 27:33, pp. 207, 213; 27:38, p. 188; 27:42, p. 207; 27:46-47, p. 204; 27:57, pp. 128, 207; 27:57-60, pp. 128, 207; 28:1, p. 207; 28:2, pp. 29, 128, 132; 28: 6, p. 128; 28:13, p. 128; 28:15, p. 128.

Mk 2:5, 10, p. 265; 2:14, pp. 123, 209*; 2:18, p. 116; 2:24-28, pp. 116, 124; 3:11, pp. 166, 264; 3:11-12, p. 169; 3:15, pp. 166, 264; 3:21, pp. 151, 168, 169, 180, 192; 3:28, pp. 204*, 265; 3:28-30, p. 266; 3:31-33, p. 151; 3:31-32, p. 169; 3:31-35, p. 172; 3:33-34, pp. 29, 132; 4:21, p. 206; 6:7, p. 264; 6:7-11, p. 265; 7:1-5, p. 117; 7:6, pp. 120, 126, 172; 7:15, p. 114; 9:12, p. 204; 9: 31, p. 204; 11:1-10, pp. 184-185; 11:8-10, p. 211; 11:10, p. 187; 11:13-14, p. 115; 14:1, p. 189; 14:2, p. 221; 14:3-8, p. 119; 14:8-10, p. 210; 14:12, p. 206; 14:19, p. 208; 14:21, p. 204; 14:22, p. 206; 14:22-24, p. 193; 14:32-41, p. 208; 14:33-34, p. 208; 14:36, p. 208; 14:41, p. 204; 14:43, p. 222; 14:45, p. 213; 14:47, p. 211; 14:50, p. 209; 14:51-52, p. 163; 14:53, pp. 190, 218; 14:55-59, p. 222; 14:56, p. 217; 14:59, p. 217; 14:61, p. 204; 14:62, pp. 217, 263; 14:66, p. 213; 14:71-72, p. 215; 15:2, p. 223; 15:6, pp. 218, 239; 15:7, p. 217*; 15:8, pp. 233, 238; 15:9, p. 223; 15:13, pp. 234, 238; 15:14, pp. 223, 234, 238; 15:15, p. 222; 15:17, p.

233; 15:18, p. 234; 15:18-20, p. 233; 15:21, pp. 211, 218; 15:22, p. 207; 15:23, p. 128; 15:25, p. 217; 15:26, p. 234; 15:31, p. 207; 15:32, p. 233; 15:34, p. 209; 15:40, p. 214; 15:43-47, p. 128; 16:1, p. 214; 16:15-18, p. 265; 23:26, p. 218; 24:27, p. 205.

Lk 2:7, p. 112; 3:12, p. 124; 3:13, p. 114*; 4:28-29, pp. 173, 200; 4:41, p. 166; 5:10, p. 142; 5:27, p. 209*; 5:27-29, pp. 124; 6:5, p. 124; 6:27, 35, 48, p. 198; 7:28, p. 196; 7:34, p. 114; 7:36-40, pp. 118, 119-120; 7:36-50, p. 137*; 7:44, p. 121; 9:1, p. 264; 9:7, p. 265; 9:16, p. 206; 9:43, p. 265; 9:44-45, 46, p. 208; 9:53, pp. 135-136; 10: 3-15, p. 265; 10:12, p. 269; 10:13, p. 265; 10:16, pp. 196, 264; 10:17, pp. 263, 264; 10: 18, p. 264; 10:19, pp. 196, 264; 10: 20, p. 264; 10:30-35, p. 135; 10:33, p. 135; 11:20, p. 167; 11:23, p. 269; 11:37-39, pp. 116, 123; 11:39, pp. 126, 147*, 172; 11:39-40, p. 127*; 11:40-43, p. 117; 13:31, pp. 180, 223; 14:1, p. 123; 16:16, p. 144; 17:21, p. 196; 18:10-14, p. 125; 19:2, p. 123; 19:5, p. 124; 19:7, p. 114; 19:12-27, p. 126; 19:47, p. 189; 21:36, p. 204; 22:2, p. 189; 22:22, p. 204; 22:30, p. 116; 22:48, p. 204; 22:66, pp. 190, 218; 22:69, p. 204; 23:1, p. 234; 23:1-2, p. 188; 23:4, p. 234; 23: 5, pp. 234, 238; 23:6-16, p. 181; 23:11, pp. 223, 233; 23:17, pp. 218, 239; 23:19, p. 217*; 23: 21, 23, 23, 25, pp. 234, 238; 23:34, pp. 237, 245; 23:36, 37, pp. 223, 234; 23:38, p. 233; 23:40, p. 188*; 23:46, p. 205; 23:50-51, p. 213; 23:50-53, p. 128; 24:1, p. 129.

Jn 1:14, p. 262; 2:4, p. 172; 3:2, 26, p. 213; 6:25, p. 213; 6:27-29, p. 255; 6:53, p.116; 6:53-58, p. 193; 6:56, p. 116; 6:56-57, p. 196; 6:60, p. 199; 6:61, pp. 199, 203; 6:64, p. 199; 6:65, pp. 173*, 199; 6:66, pp. 173, 200; 6:67, p. 204; 6:68, p. 199; 7:5, pp. 173, 201; 7:12, pp. 173, 200; 7:19-20, p. 147*; 7:20, p. 180; 8:6, p. 103; 8:32, p. 299; 8:48-49, pp. 168, 180; 8:52, pp. 169, 180; 10:20, pp. 151, 169, 180; 10:30-33, p. 266; 11:53, p. 189; 12:1-3, p. 121; 12:1-6, p. 119; 12:2-4, p. 121; 12:5, p. 123; 12:8, p. 119; 13:2-4, p. 121; 13:3-16, p. 121; 13:12, p. 121; 13:23, p. 164*; 14:6, 7, 9, 11, 13, 17, p. 267; 18:10-11, p. 211; 18:13, p. 207; 18:24, p. 218; 18:29, p. 234; 18:31, p. 234; 18:36, p. 223*; 18:39, pp. 218, 239; 18:40, pp. 217*, 234; 19:2, 3, 5, 15, 19, 21, pp. 233-234; 19:4, p. 234; 19:6, 8, p. 234; 19:12, pp. 189, 234; 19:14, pp. 217, 233; 19:15, p. 233; 19:17, pp. 207, 218; 19:20, p. 213; 19:26, p. 172; 19:34, p. 242; 19:38, p. 128; 20:31, p. 214.

Acts 2:23, p. 232; 4:5, 6, p. 272; 4:13, pp. 211, 215; 4:19, p. 272; 5: 5, 6, 17, 21, 29, p. 272; 8:18-24, p. 264; 8:27, p. 264; 9:23-25, p. 158; 10:10-16, p. 114; 11:26, p. 153; 18:6, p. 237; 21:20-25, p. 159; 26:13, pp. 156, 160; 26:15, p. 160.

Rom 1:1, p. 160; 1:4, pp. 28, 160, 270; 1:16, pp. 255, 270; 3:19-20, p. 146*; 3:22-28, p. 255; 5: 1-2, 3, 9-10, p. 255; 5:14, 19, p. 274; 7:25, p. 255; 8:1, 2, p. 255; 9:5, p. 262; 9:21, pp. 263-264; 9:30-32, p. 255; 10:4, 8, 9, p. 255; 13:1-5, p. 271.

1*Cor* 1:24, p. 270; 2:4, pp. 110, 133*, 270, 2:14, p. 291; 3:33, p. 291; 5:1, p. 146; 5:1-2, p. 164; 6:9, 11-19, p. 164; 7:20, 21, 22, 23, pp. 153, 154, 156; 8:8, pp. 114-115; 11:24-34, p. 193; 15:21, p. 274; 15:57, p. 268; 16:21, pp. 233-234.
2*Cor* 3:7, p. 262*; 5:17, p. 291; 11:21-12:10, pp. 157, 158; 11: 1, 16, 17, 19, 21, 24-27, 28-29, pp. 157-158; 11:24-34, p. 193; 11:32-33, pp.158-159; 12:1-4, p. 158; 12:2-4, pp. 133*, 158; 12:7-9, pp. 157-158; 16:26, p. 295.

Gal 4:4, p. 28; 4:21-26, 30-31, p. 290; 5:1, p. 299; 5:5, p. 255; 5:12, p. 159; 5:24, p. 291; 6:15, p. 291.

Col 2:12, p. 291; 2:19, p. 258.

Book of Revelation 19:11-21, pp. 268-271
Heb 1:3, pp. 263 ; 1:4-6, p. 265; 2:15, p. 198; 6:6, p. 237.
Eph 5:22-24, p. 273.
1*Pet* 2:13-14, p. 272; 2:18-19, p. 293; 3:1, p. 273; 3:22, 265; 5:9-10, p. 255
1*Jn* 2:9, p. 154; 3:8, p. 166; 3:9, p. 201; 4:14, p. 299.

WESTERN WRITERS

A Dictionary… (M. Jastrow), 186*.
A Dictionary of Greek & Latin Legal Terms, 188*, 258*.
A History of Greek Literature, 58*.
A History of Greek Religion, 195*.
A History of Reading, 46*.
A History of Religious Ideas, 195*, 197*, 203*.
A Short History of Anti-Semitism, 225*, 228*.
Abraham and the Contemporary Mind, 20*, 80*, 85*, 90*, 96*.
"American Judaism," 306*.
An Empire of their Own, 92*.
The Anatomy of Human Destructiveness, 194*, 196*, 269*.
"…And so we came to Rome," 112*, 122*, 123*, 125*, 136*, 192*.
The Archetypes of the Collective Unconscious, 89*.
Are we all Nazis?, 295*, 296*.
"Authority," 160*.

The Bar Kokhba Syndrome, 3*.
Becoming American Women, 93*.
"Beliefs," 280*.
Beyond Psychology, 57*.
The Book of Job, 2*.
"Borges on Life and Death," 43*.

The Case of the Nazarene Reopened, 29*, 115*, 119*, 120*, 181*, 188*, 204*, 205*, 206*, 207*, 208*, 209*, 210*, 211*, 213*, 214*, 215*, 216*, 217*, 218*, 221*, 222*, 223*, 235*.
Catechism of the Catholic Church, 196, 197*, 198*, 214*, 273*.
"Charles V," 287.
Christian Antisemitism, 105*, 155*, 178*, 181*, 183*, 192*, 244*, 284*.
Christianity in Talmud and Midrash, 148*, 152*, 162*, 233*, 242*.
Civilization and its Discontents, 260*.
Claude Levi-Strauss, 52*.
The Classical Foundations of Modern Historiography, 60*.

The Common Background of Greek and Hebrew Civilization, 200*.
Communication and the Human Condition, 49*, 55*.
Communication as Culture, 59*.
Convergence Culture, 70*.
Conversations with Kafka, 46*.
Creativity, 42*, 52*.
"The Crucifixion of Jesus," 183*, 222*.

The Death of American Antisemitism, 308.
De la España que aún no Conocia, 287.
The Decline and Fall of the Roman Empire, 12.
"Demonology of the New Testament," 167.
Demons of the Inner World, 33, 147, 167, 168.
The Development of Greek Biography, 61.
Diogenes Laertius, 140.
The Divinity of the Roman Emperor, 214, 235, 258.
Documentos de Historia Americana, 286.
Doroth Harischonim, 31.
"The Dramatic Instinct of Early Christianity," 241.
Dynamics of Faith, 14.

The Emergence of the Christian Basilica, 241, 242.
"The Economy of Ideas," 43.
El Honor de Dios, 285, 286, 287, 288.
"El tiempo en la historiografia Antigua," 55.
Eros in Antiquity, 163.
Essays in Ancient and Modern Historiography, 272.
Essays on a Science of Mythology, 61.
Etudes Evangeliques, 202.
European Paganism, 194, 195.
"Eutychianism," 236.
Ezra Stiles and the Jews, 15.

Fathers and Sons in Athens, 56.
Fiction as History, 219, 247, 248.
"The First Settlement of the Jews in the United States," 304.
"Francisco Sanchez's Theory of Cognition" 99, 302.
From the Lower East Side to Hollywood, 92.
From Spanish Court to Italian Ghetto, 13.

The Garden of Adonis, 194, 201.
The Gnostic Religion, 203.
Gnosticism, 33, 164.
The Golden Bough, 146, 193, 194, 195, 196, 198, 202, 233.
Golden Doves with Silver Dots, 10, 27, 41, 45, 46, 47, 48, 50, 51, 54, 59, 65, 73, 75, 77, 78, 81, 83, 97, 214, 310.
The Great Escape, 92.

"Greek Animals," 194.
Greek in Jewish Palestine, 10.
The Greeks and the Irrational, 57.
Group Psychology, 253.
The Gutenberg Galaxy, 104.

Hakotel Hama'arabi, 73.
Ha-Vatican ve-Yisrael, 308.
The Heart of Man, 255, 256, 258.
Hellenistic Mystery-Religions, 196.
Hermetica, 165.
The Hero with a Thousand Faces, 49.
Histories, 193.
The History of the Church, 102, 133, 134, 150, 151, 152, 155, 166, 173.
History of Religions, 236.
Holy Images, 287.
Homo Mysticus, 10, 11, 41, 42, 43, 47, 51, 96, 97, 99, 227, 279.
Homo Necans, 197.
Horizontal Society, 1, 6, 7, 9, 12, 13, 19, 27, 30, 31, 42, 43, 44, 45, 46, 47, 48, 53, 58, 60, 66, 68, 75, 76, 78, 83, 85, 86, 91, 104, 109, 110, 112, 116, 124, 131, 137, 146, 148, 155, 169, 186, 219, 246, 252, 255, 257, 258, 259, 265, 268, 275, 276, 282, 289, 293, 294, 296, 297, 298, 301, 313.

"Imagination and Religious Pluralism," 302.
"The Importance of New Being," 86.
In His Image, 80.
The Individual and Society in the Middle Ages. 278, 279, 281, 291, 294, 295.
Indo-European Languages and Society, 198, 267.
"The Influence of the Old Testament on Puritanism," 304.
The Intrapsychic Self, 54.
In the Shadow of History, 5, 12, 171, 227, 255, 285, 287, 289.
"'Israel, My Firstborn,'" 151.

Jesus (Wilson), 103, 104, 105, 135, 179, 212.
"Jesus' Attitude towards the Law," 144.
The Jesus Family Tomb, 29, 127, 128, 129, 207, 320.
Jesus the Magician, 104, 111, 135, 167, 168, 174, 180, 182, 200.
The Jesus Mysteries, 114, 116, 134, 162, 313.
Jesus as others saw him, ii, 136.
The Jesus Papers, 151.
"The Jewish Christians," 31, 116, 128, 150, 151, 152, 205, 238.
Jewish Self-Hatred, 30.
Jews and Christians, iii.
"Josephus on Ancient Jewish Groups," 129.
"Josephus's Pharisees," 130.
Judaism, 261.
Judas Iscariot and the Myth of Jewish Evil, 203.

"Judeocristianismo," 150.

Kapital, 63, 311.
The King's Two Bodies, 186, 236, 262, 263, 272, 274, 275, 276.
Kosher Nation, 309.

La Conquête de l'Amérique, 284.
La Realidad Histórica de España, 289.
"Les Marranes," 289.
Leviathan, 187.
Libros de las Décadas del Nuevo Mundo, 286.
The Life of Jesus, 183, 209, 234.
Local Religion in Sixteenth Century Spain, 195.
Los Judios en America, 287.

"The Maccabean Uprising," 9.
Magic and Rhetoric, 165.
"Maimonides' Water-Clock," 99.
Masks Mimes and Miracles, 157, 159, 241.
The Masks of God, 34, 314.
The Mishna on Idolatry, 202, 227, 240.
Mission of Inquiry to the Jews, 15.
Moses and Monotheism, 194.
"Mystery and Spiritual Regeneration," 194, 202.
Myth of the Eternal Return, 53, 97.
Myth and Reality, 40, 41, 55, 60, 61, 63, 65, 69, 91, 100, 102, 106.
Myth and Society in Ancient Greece, 50, 62.
Myth and Tragedy, 87, 193.

The Naked Crowd, 43, 89.
"The Name of the Christians," 153, 154.
"New Light on Tannaitic Jewry," 110.
"Newton, Maimonidean," 259, 274.
Notebooks, 1914-1916, 47.
The Notebooks on Primitive Mentality, 34, 41, 53, 54.
"Notes et Melanges," 135, 136.

The Obedience Experiment, 281, 283.
"Of Cultural Intimidation," 66, 127.
Obeying Orders, 296.
Odyssey, 194.
Oheb Ger, 185.
'Olam ha-Tanakh, Bemidbar, 18.
On God and Society, 302, 303.
"On the Mystery and Worship of the Eucharist," 197.
"On the Origins of the Mysteries," 87.
Origen: Contra Celsum, 33, 124, 150, 151, 156, 180, 211, 265.

The Origin and History of Consciousness, 91.
The Origin of the Republican Form of Government, 278, 303, 305, 306, 307, 309.
"The Origin of the Term 'Gospel,'" i.
Orpheus, 195.

Pagan Monotheism in Late Antiquity, 265.
Papal Sins, 247, 273, 282, 300.
Parchment, Printing and Hypermedia, 43, 65, 103.
Paul and Hellenism, 159, 274.
Pax Romana and the Peace of Jesus Christ, 268.
The Persian Religion, 59.
Phaedrus, 57, 58, 59.
Philo (Wolfson), 95, 184, 236, 246, 272.
Philo and the Oral Law, 110, 212.
The Philosophy of the Church Fathers, 225, 246.
Plough, Sword, and Book, 65.
The Politics of Philo Judaeus, 272, 275.
"Politics and Religion," 261.
The Power of Myth, 96.
"Primitive Intellectual Mechanism," 51, 63.
Primitive Religion, 40.
Problems in General Linguistics, 45, 67, 82, 86.
The Prophets, 275.
Psychoanalysis and Religion, 279.
"The Psychology of the Child Archetype," 51, 52, 55, 254.

Quod Nihil Scitur, 99.

R. Eliezer ben Hyrcanus, 152.
"The Reason for the Persecution of Paul," 144, 147.
Religions in Four Dimensions, 294.
The Revolt of the Masses, 70, 71, 226.
Rites and Symbols of Initiation, 86, 100.
Roger Williams, 7.
"Runaway Paul," 157, 158, 159, 242.

The Sacred and the Profane, 40, 41, 53.
"Saints and Fanatics," 296.
The Secret Gospel, 114, 120, 127, 133, 137, 145, 146, 147, 148, 159, 162, 163, 164, 166, 196, 201, 215.
"Self-cooking Beef and the Drinks of Ares," 193.
Seven Sermons, 2.
Shamanism, 86, 88, 195, 202.
"The Significance of the Tantric Yoga," 51.
The Silver Age of Latin Literature, 231, 241.
Social Cognition, 64.
"Some Basic Problems Common to Anthropology and Modern Psychiatry," 52.

The Source, 13.
Spinoza's Critique of Religion, 140.
Spiritual and Demonic Magic, 165, 167, 168.
"The Splitting of the *Logos*," 302.
The Structure of Spanish History, 272, 289, 291.
Studies in the Cult of Y., 196, 201.
Studies in Historiography, 60.
Studies in the History of Philosophy and Religion, 236.
Studies in the Mishne Tora, 2, 75, 276, 319.
Summa Theologica, 104, 291.
Symbolism, the Sacred, and the Arts, 86, 89, 91.
Systematic Theology, 102, 155, 161.

Tancred, 15.
"The Third Person," 45.
The Torch in my Ear, 45, 69*.
Totem and Taboo, 198.
Treaties…of the United States of America, 307.
Tres Cronistas de Indias, 287.
The Trial and Death of Jesus, 116, 122, 188, 189, 190, 191, 192, 213, 221.
Tosefta Ki-Fshuṭah, 30, 31, 32, 118, 131.

Understanding Media, 49, 54, 63, 64, 65, 70, 72, 77, 92.
The Undiscovered Self, 66, 67, 68, 71, 91.
The Unknown Sanctuary, 10, 11, 13, 280.

Vatican Council II, 197, 299.

When Atheism Becomes Religion, 258.
When Religion Becomes Evil, 18.
Witchcraft, 202.
The Works of Joseph de Maistre, 303.

Names, Places and Subjects

ABBA B. KAHANA, R. 77.
ABENDANA, R. ISAAC 258.
ABGAR, KING 101.
ABRAHAM, PATRIARCH 19, 20, 21; disobeyed *Übermensch*-Nimrod, 161.
AGRIPPA, KING 113, 229, 232, 234.
AḤA, R. 77.
AHASUERUS 7.
ALCIBIADES 158.
ANTIOCHUS, KING 228, 298.

ALEXANDRIA Church of, 247; Cradle of: anti-Semitism, 225-231, and the Christian Scripture, 247-249; place of first recorded Pogrom, 225.
ALEXANDRIAN JEWRY 225, 226, 246; no Jewish heretics in, 225.
'AM HA-AREṢ definition of, 104.
'AQIBA, R. 3, 77, 122, 214
AQUINAS, ST. THOMAS Jews slaves of Church, 103, 104, 291
ARIMATHAEA Geographical name invented by *Christian Scripture*, 212.
ARIETI, SILVANO 20, 41, 42, 51, 52, 54, 63, 80.
ARIUS and rabbinic sages, 9; declared a heretic by Christian authorities, 245.
ASTYAGES, KING 193.
ATHEISM, ATHEIST 272, 275; intolerant of non-atheists, 251; Jewish, 45; political, 254, 258; societies, 171; *minim* worse than, 141.
AUTHORITY (*ezousía*) Christian concept of, 263-265, 270-271; exercise tyrannical dominion, 263; pagan deities endowed with, 263; political, is also divine, 271-272, 281, 290-297; resistance to, equals insubordination to God, 281; submission to, 273.

BALAAM, PROPHET 17-18, 38; code name for 'Jesus,' 162
BALAK, KING 17, 38.
BASS, LEON 283, 284.

BENAMOZEGH, R. ELIE 3, 12, 13, 162*, 164*, 194*.
BENEDICT OF NURSIA 103.
BENVENISTE, EMILE 44, 45, 59, 66, 81, 85, 198.
BERNARDIN, JOSEPH L., CARDINAL 308
BIBAS, R. JUDAH 14-15.
BONAR, ANDREW 14-15.
BRUNO, GIORDANO 59, 164.

CALIGULA 147, 231, 235, 236, 237, 240, 242, 243, 244, 245, 259, 263, 266, 267, 269, 301.
CAMPBELL, JOSEPH 34, 49, 51, 86, 96, 194, 314.
CANETTI, ELIAS 45, 69.
CARABAS 232-234, 239, 244.
CARVALHO, JOAQIM DE 99.
CARMEL, ABRAHAM I. 10.
CELSUS 124, 211, 248.
CHARLES V, KING 287.

CHRISTIAN(S), CHRISTIANITY anthropocentric concept of the universe, 257; anti-Semitism, central to Christianity, 38, promoted by Christianity missionaries, 16-17, 284-285; arrogance of, 109-110, 265; art and, 247-248; authority, 160, faith derives from 161; bad-mouth its victims Jews, iii, 18, and Native Americans, 284-285; and Jewish biographies of Jesus, 27-28, 135-136; champions of freedom, 7; changed the Hebrew concept of 'One God,' to one exclusive religion, 38; demands that Jews repudiate their own National Memory, 110-111, defrocking Israel, 252; disrespectful with 'Jews' and 'Judaism,' 34, turned site of Jewish Temple into a

garbage dump, 292; first persecuting religion, 14, pretext for, 15; freedom, more restrictive than submission to tyrants, 299; fundamental differences with Judaism, 10, 166; God, belief in, ancillary to belief in Jesus, 262-265, Christian God not God of Jews, 156, and the 'Mystery of the Kingdom,' 143-148; earthly king: godly concept of, 274-275, 'two bodies' of, 274, double nature of, 274-275; hatred of Jews, fundamental to, 178, 183, 203, 253; identified in rabbinic tradition with Balaam, 18; infallibility of, 28; "holy" and "religious" wars first introduced by, 16, and the 'religious enemy,' 16-17, 38, inspired Islam's idea of *ijtihad*, 16, 272; Jesus, depicted in terms of pagan lore, 34, as Cosmic-*Übermensch*, 169, 262, 276-277, model of, originated in Alexandria, 262; Jewish persecution of, a Christian invention, 147, 148; Jews, status of, as slaves of the Church, 291; Judaism and, alien to one other, iii-iv, 18-20, 23-24; Law, dead and deadly, ii-iii, 34; liturgy, greatest magical act ever, 168, 284, identifies earthly monarch with Jesus, 276, incorporates imperial symbols, 279-280, designed to promote Jewish hatred, 101-102; libertine practices among early, 145-148, 165; 'love,' 127, conditioned by hatred of Jews, 177, 252, 313, pretext for domination, 14-15, 286-288; liturgy, performed as a theatrical drama, 238-242; magic, belief in, fundamental to, 112-113, and demonology, 166-167, and sexual rituals, 165; mythical thinking, central to, 99-108, 161; narcissism, 250-253 254-256; 'Old' Testament, used by, as a mask to cover 'New' Testament, 92, 170-175, 293, 313; orgiastic communions, 146-147; pagan doctrines basic to, 13; philosophers, promoted hatred of Jews and Judaism, 301-302; peace, concept of, same as *Pax Romana*, 265-268; reason, must be submitted to faith, 102; reasoning, different than Jewish, 105; repudiates the Jesus of history, 32, 33-34, 37, 104-105, 110-113, 156, 261-262, and brand it as demonic prevarications, 249; rituals, exclusively from the pagan world, 34, 99-100; salvation, not depending on works, 255-256, gained gastronomically, 113; "Theology of Power", 261-271, designed to persecute undesirables, 147; time, linear, unknown to, 97, 100-102, mythical, begins with the birth of Jesus, 100-101, reversible, 100-101; saints, not always psychologically sound, 296; supported by Israel's enemies, 261; values of, alien to the *Hebrew Scripture*, 102-104, 134, transmitted from the first to the third person, 102, 150, 161, 250, 252; vilification of Jews, purpose of, iii-iv, 13-14, 17, 38; writing, regarded as debasing, 103-104.
CHRISTIAN SCRIPTURE complete text finalized *circa* 5th century, 102; main purpose of, promotion of anti-Jewish feelings, 269; intended as passion play and not as an historical document, 134.
CHRISTIANOUS Meaning of name, 153-155.
CHURCH alliance, Church-Monarch, 277-281, Church-Rome, 38; Church-Sword, 37-38; and magic, 168.
CICERO 60, 248.
COENA 121, 123, 124.
COHN, JUSTICE HAIM 116, 122, 187-188, 189, 190, 192.
CONQUISTADORES, improper to fault them with genocide, 92, 294.
CONSTANTINE, KING 37, 38, 276, 277, 294, 300, 303; mother of, built Church on the site of the Jewish Temple, 292; statue of him as god, 276.
CONSTANTINE'S ARCH 294.
CONSTANTINE'S SWORD 109, 300.
CUTHEANS, 135. See SAMARITAN(S)

CYAXARES, KING 193.

DAVID, KING 115, 211.
DAVID HA-KOHEN, R. 5.
DAWIDOWICZ, LUCY 283, 284.
"DAY OF FAITH" celebrates pact signed by Mussolini with Vatican, 277.
DICTATORSHIP socialist, religion of the State, 91, 273.
DIOGENES 140.
DIONYSUS 114, 134, 163*, 192.
DISRAELI, BENJAMIN 15.

EBIONITES 33, 151.
ECPHANTUS 274.
EICHMANN, ADOLF 283.
EL 'AZAR BEN 'ARAKH, R. 122.
ELIADE, MIRCEA 40, 53, 55, 60, 65, 86, 88, 96-97, 101, 194, 195, 197.
ELI'EZER BEN HORQANOS, R. 152-153.
ENLIGHTENMENT hostile against anything remotely 'Jewish,' 279, 302-303.
ESKIMO masks, 87; theology, 69, 103.
ESSENES 132.
EUCHARIST 102, 193-203; consumption of Jesus flesh and drinking his blood, 193-21; it constitutes "the perfection of spiritual life," 197, bringing about the "real" and "substantial" presence of Jesus, 197-200, thus the faithful experiences Jesus' agony, 100-102, 241, while at the same time defeating 'Devil/Angel of Death,' 198-199; magical character of, 167, and the miracle of "Transubstantiation," 167, 197, 198; pagan roots of, 12-13, diabolical imitations of, 203-204; it effects salvation gastronomically, 116, transforming *illo tempo* into *illud tempo*, 101, and spatial *here* into *there*, 101, helping thereby to promote further hatred of Jews, 101-102.
EUSEBIUS 102*, 133, 134, 150, 151, 173, 200*.

FLACCUS crucified Alexandrian Jews, 238; made torture of Jews a public spectacle, 239-240; model for future anti-Semitic politicians, 229-231; scourged Jewish victims before Crucifixion, 239.
FORNA, R. JACOB IBN 138.
FREEDOM of conscience, Christian champions of, 7; incompatible with the concept of *Übermensch*, 22; tyrannical, enjoyed by pagan deities, 257; unattainable in pagan and Christian societies, 296-301.
FRENCH REVOLUTION 62, 278.

GASPARRI, CARDINAL signs accord with Benito Mussolini, 277.
GEORGE III, KING 305.
GIBBON, SIR EDWARD malicious erudition of, 12-13.
GNOSTIC, GNOSTICISM 33*, 197*, Christian, 134; nudity and indiscriminate sexuality, 164, 175; Jesus came to destroy the God of the Jews, 203.
GOLGOTHA geographical name invented by *Christian Scripture*, 207, 213, 218.

GOSPEL(S) authors of, never witnessed the actual Trial of Jesus, 37; concocted Jesus' Trial, 37, 179, modeled on mocks-trial, 37, 178, 232-240; contradictions and inconsistencies, 33; copies of, destroyed by early Church authorities, 183; falsify history, 183, and Jesus' actual behavior to prevent cordial relations between Jews and Christians, 298; offer heathens an alternative to Judaism, 223; pander to Roman interest, 223; promote religious anti-Semitism, 1-2, 178, 212-220, 223; "Secret Gospel of Mark," 164-166; supersedes God's voice at Sinai, 252; suppresses historical Jesus, 33-34, 178-183; 221-223.

GREECE and ROME aversion to writing, 59; dictators, power of political, in, 68-69; orators, 68-69; organized along hierarchic lines, 56; society, essential inequality, 62.

HADRIAN, KING 294.
HALEVY, JOSPEH 135, 136, 204.
HEROD, KING 180-181, portrayed in the *Christian Scripture* as the 'fool' in mimic plays, 222-223.
HERODOTUS 59, 60, 193, 248, 262, 263.
HESCHEL, ABRAHAM JOSHUA 275.
HESS, RUDOLF 283.
HIMMLER, HEINRICH 283.
HITLER, ADOLF ii, 69, 253, 282, 283.
HOBBES, THOMAS 186.
ḤOFNI HA-ME'AGGEL 130*.
HOLY WAR introduced by Christianity, 16, 272.
HUMANITAS members of, inferior to Christians, 290-304.
HUXLEY, ALDOUS, 261.
HYPPOLYTUS 56.

ISIDORUS 236.
ISRAEL suffering of, proof of Christian superiority, 272.

JACOBS, JOSEPH ii, 136*.
JAMES, BROTHER OF JESUS 208; conformed to the rabbinic teachings, 299; canonicity of, contested, 299.
JAMES I, KING 275.
JASTROW, MARCUS 186.
JERICHO 136.
JESUS abusive of Jewish host, 121, 123-124, 133, 172, and rabbis, 133; addressed an analphabetic crowd, 104, 134, 135; agony of, modeled after Flaccus torturing of Jews, 238; alleged charges against, meaningless in Jewish law, 216; authority to forgive sins, 265; biography of, Jewish and Christian,189-200; 'Balaam,' code for 'Jesus,' 18; broke food taboos, 115-116; confiscated she-ass, 184-187, 289; demeanor of, not of a well-bred person, 171-173, respectful with Pilate, but abusive with rabbis and Jewish hosts, 123-124, 127-128, 133, 172, 174, and his own mother, 29, 133, 172-173, and loving and caring with prostitutes, 29, 120-121, 133; aversion to the washing of the hands, 117, 122, 123; demonology, 166-168; eating and drinking, importance of, 117, basis for the Eucharist, 117; earthly life and death, 178-183, as

others saw him, iii, 111, 112-113, 162-175, 264, as a magician, 111-113, 162; disciples of, 134, 204-213, 263-264, acted cowardly, 208-209, ate during Jewish public fasts, 117, and desecrated the Sabbath, 116, described as "the most wicked tax-collectors," 124, did not think much of him, 173, not men of letters, 134-135, knew not Hebrew, 204-206, Jewishly clueless, 206-207, misquote the *Scripture*, 205-206, were themselves publicans or connected to publicans, 128, stole Jesus' body, 129; described as, a "glutton and winebibber," 115, 146; disconnected from the general public, 172; 'exoteric' and 'esoteric' teachings, 148; family, background of, 124, close to "the ruling circles" (=*qarob la-malkhut*) 28, 114, 128, 184, 189; humble origins of, invented by *Luke*, 129-130; sumptuous burial grounds of family, 29; fasted on *Yom Kippur*, 117; feet-washing, fixation with, 119-120, 121, 123, with expensive oil, 119-120, 122; freedom from the Law, 145, 146, 147, 164, 200, 202; friend and defender of publicans and prostitutes, 124-130; insult, prone to, 118-119; 'legal' teachings, 144-147; libertine message, 200-202; life-style, opulent 113-124, passion for foot-massage; ministry, confirmed by his magic, 167; love of, people who did not know him loved him 173, but people who knew him, including his own family, did not love him, 174; power of, 261-267, mightier than Satan's and the Angel's, 264-265, obtained by invoking his name, 263-264; mother of, did not come to visit his tomb, 29, 133; paranoia, feelings of, 148, 168-169; Pharisees courteous with 130-132, alerted him of danger, 179, but he did not preach to love them, 126-127, 125-126, and never met a Pharisee that he did not insult, 133; practiced magic, 112-113, 166-168, had his entire body tattooed with magical spells, 111, 161, magic-wand of, 162, 163, 164; prostitutes, sponsored by men of means and, 133, came to visit his tomb, 29, 133; publicans, close association with, 29, 124-125, 128-129, regarded him as their spiritual guide, 125, he was courteous with them, 133, 172, and favored them and the prostitutes they patronized over the rabbis and Jews that invited him to eat, 125, 127; secret initiation rites, 144, consumption of his Blood and his Flesh, 146, 193-203, transferred to the Eucharist, 197, effects salvation, 255-256, but repealed his Jewish disciples, 199-201; seized private property for his own use, 182-187; spoke only Aramaic, not Hebrew, 103; state of mind, regarded as "madman" by the general public, his family, and rabbis, and therefore legally incompetent to stand trial, 152, 169-170, 180, 192; arrest of, 179; supreme Cosmocrator, 267-271; uncanny ability to read the mind of people whom he disliked, 120, 126-127, 172; wrote no books, 104, 105-106.
JOHANAN B. ZAKKAI, R. 97, 187.
JOHN THE BAPTIST 116, 124, 196.
JOSEPH OF ARIMATHEA had direct access to Pilate, 128-129; Jesus buried in the tomb of, 129-130; Jesus' disciple, 128-129, 207; powerful publican, 128-129.
JOSEPHUS 3, 4, 20, 129, 130, 131, 132, 135, 153, 181, 224, 227, 228, 236, 240, 242, 248, 298.
JOSHUA BEN ḤANANYA, R. 75, 139, 233.
JUDAH HA-LEVI, R. 10-11, 152.
JUDAH HA-NASI, R. 78.
JUDAISM against pagan idols in the Land of Israel, 2; bad-mouthed by Christianity, ii-iii, 13-14, 38, 177, 246, thereby excusing Christianity from common civility, 34, 313; centered on "the Book," 105; inspired the creation of the USA but not Christianity, 306-307; freedom, unattainable under pagan form of governance, 296-

297, it includes political and judicial institutions, 2; ineffective in Oedipal environments, 260; medium of communication, 23-24, 72-78, 109; Law, freely contracted by the people and ratified at Sinai-Moab, 25-26, 72-74, the supreme rule of Israel, 18, 25-27, Christian sages recognized the exceptionality of the Jewish Law, 302-303; Messiah, a human and not a Cosmic *Übermensch*, 181-182; pagan humanity, created in the image of God, 72-72, not wicked and worthless, 5, pious are saved, 7, their sages are to be respected, 7-8, and human fellowship, 18, may offer sacrifice at the Jewish Temple, 6; pluralistic, 28; publicans regarded as brigands, 213-214; rejects Paul's notion of human hierarchy, 259-260, 'liberty,' 298-299, submission to tyrants, 271; refuses to bow down to the religious and or political *Übermensch*, 19-20; religious enemy, impossible according to, 12-13, 16-17, 253, 301; salvation depends on "works," 255-256; theocentric concept of the universe, 259-260; time, linear not cyclical, 97-98, intercrossing with space, 96-97.
JUDAISTIC ERRORS 33, 34, 155; imputing of, an absolute condition to Christian love, 313.
JUNG, KARL GUSTAV 51, 52, 54, 55, 66, 67, 89, 91, 254.

KOTLER, R. AHARON 80.
KYRIOS title of Jesus, 116, 117, 139*, 184-190; meaning, in Judaism, 139, 220, 273-274, in Greek, 184, 186; Paul urges Christian wives to submit to husbands in quality of, 273-274.

LAZARUS member of publican family, 123, 162, 163.
LEOPOLD, KING 284, 290.
LEVI tax-collector and Jesus' friend, 124.
LEVI-STRAUSS, CLAUDE 52.
LIDA, ROSA 291.
LINDO, E.H. 259.
LUKE member of publican family, 123.

MACCOBY, HYAM 159.
MAIMONIDES, R. MOSES 10, 11, 46, 140, 141, 142, 152, 309.
MAISTRE, JOSEPH DE 302.
MANETHO 228.
MARX, KARL, 62, and Marxism, incorporated Christian doctrines and structures, 254.
MASKS Christian, 85-92; kabuki, 89, 91, 313; *minut*, 137-148; psychological, 88-89; role of, in rituals, 86*; garment and dress as, 86-87; and *persona*, 88-89; and time, 87-88; manipulation of, 89; 'Old', used as, of 'New' Testament, 92, 313; saints and, 296.
MATTHEW 36, 103, 128, 181, 237; a publican, 123-124, 132, 209, 215; Jew-hater, 216, 238; malicious fabrications by, 218; moral standard of, 201*-202*.
MAYHEW, REV. JONATHAN 2.
MCLUHAN, MARSHAL 49*, 63, 64, 69, 76, 77*, 95, 108.
ME'IR, R. 4.
MEMORY national of Israel, linear, 108, it begins at Sinai, 108-109.
MILITES CHRISTI 16.

MIN, MINIM, MINUT abandoned Jerusalem after Arab conquest, 32; R. Eli'ezer b. Horqanos and the, 152; expelled from Christendom, 148-152; Jews regarded Jesus as a *min*, 29-30; and the Judeo-Christians, 29-32; meaning of term, 148; and "The Mystery of the Kingdom," 142-147; the sin of, 137-143; some were patriotic, 319-320.
MOB members of, behave as tyrants with Jews, 236.
MOMIGLIANO, ARNALDO 55*, 61.
MOSES 2, 17, 22, 42, 43, 73, 75, 76, 84, 85, 96, 149, 200, 265, 266, 271, 297; everyone can be like, 6; not a Jewish *Übermensch*, 22-23; unlike Jesus, did not seized anyone's donkey, 185.
MUJTAHIDIN 16.
MUSSOLINI, BENITO 69, 253, 276, 277. See "DAY OF FAITH."
MYTH(S), MYTHICAL, MYTHOLOGICAL abhors history, 49-55, 100; and Book, 40-48; and Christianity, 99-105, 155-157, 161, 176; conveyance of, 53, 74; definition of, 49-56; escape from, 92-99; excludes dialogue and dissention, 27, 41, 75; graffiti and, 41; the medium of, 24, 49-55, and the modern media, 62-72, 76, 77; mental model of, 40, 63-65; myth-centered-cultures, 85; mythical knowledge, 52-53, 55; and "oral transmission," 42, 53, 58; "palelogic thinking," 41-42; space, 41, 53-54, 100; structures of, 56-73; time, begins with the birth of Jesus, 100-101, reversible, 100-101 ; "third-party," 24; unprovable, 25, 28, 40.
MYTHRAS story of, model of Jesus' Passion, 201.

NATIVE AMERICANS 92, 296; Christian debate as to whether they were human or beast, 286; extermination of Native population in the Americas and Africa, 284-290, 294; offered as Sacrifices to the Christian deity, 287; described as "Ugly, lazy, stupid, and dumb," 288; treated as sub-humans, 288; US Supreme Court ruling on *Tee-Hit-Ton Indians*, 288-289.
NAZI atrocities, 295; war criminals, found to be 'normal,' 282, and innocent, 296.
NEBRODES, see "NIMROD"
NEUSNER, PROFESSOR JACOB ii, iii*.
NICHOLLS, WILLIAM 244, 284*, 296.
NIMROD, KING 19-23, 161, 270; first *Übermensch* in history, 20.
NOVA CREATURA, 290-291, 294 cannot be charged for crimes against *humanitas*, 294.

OBEDIENCE, see SUBMISSION/OBEDIENCE
ORATORY AND MAGIC 165.
ORIGEN 33*, 124*, 150*, 151*, 156, 180*, 211*, 248, 265*, 266*.
ORIGINAL SIN 271.
ORTEGA Y GASSET, JOSE 70-71, 91, 226.
ORWELL, GEORGE 68.

PALAGGI, R. ḤAYYIM 35, 36*.
PALLIERE, AIME 10, 11, 13, 279.
PAUL 18*, 127*, 133, 144*, 145, 146*, 153; associated with the more libertine branch of Christianity, 159; clashed with Judeo-Christians, 150*, 155; consumption of Jesus' blood and flesh, 196; Damascus, epiphany, on the road to, 156-160; divine

rights of tyrants, 271-273; God of Israel, depicted as a sadomasochist deity, 147*; "ministration of death," 262*; hardships of, modeled after Alcibiades, 158; *hybris*, 161, "Jesus' slave," 153, perceived Jesus in terms of pagan spirituality, 154-155; Jews, wretched and unworthy, 291, legal status of "slaves," 290-291; justification by faith and not works, 255, 299*; liberty, without law, 298-299; mimic actor, 157-161; met post-*mortem* Jesus, 156; opposition to libertine practices, 201*-202*; "Original Sin," doctrine of, introduced by, 274; "Renegade of the Law," 155, 298-299; repudiates circumcision, 156, 159; "runaway fool," 157-159; 'salvation,' 262*, 270, 279; son of converts, 156; theological imperative to obey "authority" (*exousia*) of monarchs, 281, 295, 306; *Übermensch*, 156; uncircumcised, 156; wives, inferior to husbands, 273.

PAX ROMANA 268.
PEDRO MARTIR, 286.
PETER 208-211, 213; described as "uneducated and untrained," 211, 215; entrusted with the "keys of heaven," 215; guilty of perjury, 215; title "Christ, the son of the living God," proposed by, 215.
PHARISEES accurate interpreters of the Law, 129-130; addressed Jesus respectfully, 120, alerted him from impeding danger, 180; bad mouthed by Jesus and his disciples, 133, 310; exposed religious frauds, 131-133; loved by the people, 131-132; Jesus, affronted the, 125, and was the foe of, 130-133, had no reason to seek his death, 188, he never met a, whom he did not insult, 29, 117-118, 121, 123-125; ; meaning of term, 131; men of grit, 132-133; sit in the seat of Moses, 144, 151; they submitted a question to him, 103; washed hands before eating, 117.
PHILIP II, KING 262.
PHILO 2*, 3, 20*, 21*, 37, 93, 94*, 95*, 97*, 98, 99*, 184*, 229-241, 243, 244*, 245*, 246, 272, 318*.
PILATE, PONTIUS 202, 210; bloodthirsty ruler, 192, did not release prisoners for Jewish holydays, 218, 239, in charge of collecting imperial taxes in Judea, 188-189, sent Jesus to be judged by Herod, 180; code-name in Rabbinic literature, 162*; complied with the demands of Joseph of Arimathea, 128; Jesus, he flogged him before Crucifixion, 223, 239; 'Jews' counseling Pilate, 189; meaning of name, 162, 233; portrayed in the *Christian Scripture* as the 'fool' in mimic plays, 222-223, afraid of the Jewish authorities and Jewish public, 234-235.
POPE JOHN PAUL II 197.
POPE PIUS XI 277, 300.
POPE PIUS XII anti-Semitic policies of, 277, 294-295.
POPE PAUL III 286.
POPE PAUL VI 197*.
POPE JOHN PAUL XXIII 308.
POWER (*dinamis*) Jesus', 264-265, authority by virtue of, 161, equals God's, 25, 267; Jesus' disciples awarded with, 261; salvation effected through, 270.
PROCLUS 267*.
PROPHET BALAAM 17, 18, 38, 162*.
PROPHET ELIJAH 204 associated with Pineḥas 18; Christians confused 'Eli/God' with 'Eli/Elijah,' 205.
PROPHET ISAIAH 6, 138, 219*, 271.
PROPHET JEREMIAH 93, 205, 206, 219*.

PROPHET MALACHI 6, 301.
PROPHET SAMUEL 169.
PROSTITUTES 133, 171, 172 treated with deference by Jesus, 29.
PUBLICANS, behaved worse than heathens, 124; enemies of the Pharisees, 131-132; hated by Jews, 126; Jesus was regarded as their spiritual guide, 124; most powerful Roman Citizens, 112; pander to the mighty, 113; part of Jesus' entourage, 142; regarded by Jews as brigands, 215; resented Jews were 'idle' on the Sabbath, 116, 124; self-hating Jews and informers, 132; sumptuous tombs, 127; supported Jesus, 123-128; treated with deference by Jesus, 29.
PYTHAGORAS 58*, 104.

QAROB la-MALKHUT associated with bandits, 114, and publicans, 127-128; connection with the *minim*, 30; differences between them and pagan-Christians, 319-320; expelled from the Synagogue, 31; "flatterers" and "hypocrites," 30, 113, 140-141; ideology and theology, 30, 137-143, invoked the Holy Trinity, 31; love and social connections between Jesus and them, 127-129, 184; reputation for malice and vindictiveness, 113-114; men of great wealth and influence, 112; no evidence that they were persecuted by Jews, 146-147; self-hating Jews, 30, collaborated with Roman forces, 31, making Roman occupation possible, 114; political foes of Israel, 32; sumptuous life style, burial grounds, 127, 129, meals, 121-123, patronized expensive prostitutes, 132-133; sneered at the masses below, 121-122; tactic of slandering those whom they wronged, 209-210.

RANK, OTTO 57.
RELIGIOUS ENEMY concept alien to Israel and the entire ancient world, 1, 12, invented by Christians to target Jews, 11-14, 16, 38, 105, 253, 301; Jews did not perceived Christian and Moslems, as, 11, 301.
RITUAL CONSUMPTION of human blood, 194-196, and human flesh, 192-193. See EUCHARIST.
ROMAN(S) apotheosis of kings and emperors, 180, 214, 262-263, 275; authorities, 28, 29*, 31, 192; aversion to writing, 59; catacombs, 163; Catholic mass, performed as a religious drama, 241; criminal jurisdiction over Judea, 191, did not crucify common bandits, 188; Empire, Christian defense of, 192, 220, Christian Roman Empire, 292; "Empire of Evil," 32; genocide of Jews, 3*; Jesus' family close to, governing circles, 57; Jews regarded as "slaves" by, 214; law, 179, 188, 191, 210, 212*, 216, 218, 219, 221, 231, 234,; mime acting and mimic theater, 241*; mock trials, 15; orators, 69; organized along hierarchical lines, 61; slave mentality, 66; strict with official titles, 187; thought themselves superior to others, 30.
ROME 56, 59, 61, 69, 137, 214, 247, 270, 301; alliance Church-Rome, 38; arch enemy of Israel, 38; charged Jesus with sedition, 111, did not crucify common bandits, 188; executed Jesus for seizing property illegally, 184, 186, 187; crushed Israel militarily, but not politically, 110, 223;promoted political anti-Semitism, 178.
RUSSELL, BERTRAND 282, 299.

SACHS, CHIEF RABBI LORD JONATHAN 311.
SADDUCEES 132, 172, 189, 205.
SAMARITAN(S), called by Jews "Cutheans," 135; 'Good,' identity of, 133-136.

SAMUEL (Emora), contact with Christians, 9.
SANCHEZ (S), FRANCISCO 99*.
SHALOM concept of, 301-309.
SIMON BEN KOSEBA 110*.
SIMONIDES 59.
SMITH, PROFESSOR MORTON 111, 143, 146, 162, 201*.
SOCRATES 57, 58, 59, 61, 68, 69, 91, 104, 158.
SOLOMON, KING 6, 93, 95*, 122*.
STALIN 69, 253, 282.
STRAUS, OSCAR 7, 277-278*, 299-300, 303, 304*, 305*.
STRAUSS, LEO 140.
SUBMISSION/OBEDIENCE to the Christian authorities, 271-274, the higher powers, 268-270, 272, and tyrants 268-269, 276-278, 296-299, in quality of "faithful Christian," 270; in military law, 296*.

TACITUS 60*.
TALPIOT sumptuous tombs of Jesus' family, found at, 29, 127.
ṬARFON, R. 137, 138, 139, 146, 148.
TAX-COLLECTORS, 29, 114, 184-190.
THEATER importance of in the formation of Christianity, 237-241; Kabuki, 92; mimic, 157-159, 222-224.
THUCYDIDES 59.
TILLICH, PAUL 102*.
TINNEIUS RUFUS, ROMAN GOVERNOR OF JUDEA 214.
TITUS, ROMAN EMPEROR 187, 293.
TITUS' ARCH 294.
TORA constitution of the Jewish Nation, 296-301; "cool medium," 72-78; evolutionary gift to humanity, 296-308; internalized by the Jewish people, 27; permitted the Jewish people to govern themselves *without* military force, 296-297; rejects the notion of sovereign immunity, 282*; vowel-less text of, 78-85.
TRAJAN 294.
TRIAL AND CRUCIFIXION account of, in Christian Scripture, 178-180, 184, 190-192; demand suppression of historical rationality, 136; designed to promote hatred of Jews, 178; documentation pertaining to, destroyed by Christian authorities, 219; incredible inventions, 179; guilt imputed on all Jews, including children, 236; minutes of said 'trial' disappeared, 183; name of place of Crucifixion invented by *Christian Scripture*, 213; modeled on a famous mock-trial described in Philo, 37, popular among the mobs in Alexandria, 229-241
TYRANT(S) divine right of, 267-273; identification with gods, 253-254, 266; Israel's natural enemy, 257.

ÜBERMENSCH Christian Monarch, conceived as earthly *Übermensch*, 272, and the "Alliance Church-Monarch," 273-285; issues command from 1st person platform, 24, 148-149, 156; God of Israel, not *Übermensch*, 25-26; 'Holy See,' robust relation with, 272-273; Jesus conceived as Cosmic *Übermensch*, 33, 149; Nimrod first, 20-21, 22, 290; people in mental bondage to the, 21-24; personal status, needs not to provide evidence, 27-28; 'Salvation' equals incorporation into the body of *Übermensch*,

262.

VATICAN celebrates pact signed with Mussolini, 277.
VETUS ADAM /NOVUS ADAM 262.
VICTOR EMMANUEL III, KING 276.

WAND, MAGIC in sex-magic, 162-165.
WILLIAM, ROGER 7*.

XENOPHON 61*.

YAHUDA, A. S. 73*.
YANNAI, R. 78-80.
YOḤANAN, R. 19
YOḤANAN, B. ZAKKAI, R. 185

ZACCAHEUS chief publican, disciple of Jesus, 123.

BIBLIOGRAPHY

BIBLICAL LITERATURE

Biblia Rabinica = *Miqra'ot Gedolot*. 4 vols. Venice, 5308/1548.

Targum Anqelos = *Targum Onqelos*. In *Miqra'ot Gedolot*.

The Bible in Aramaic. Ed. Alexander Sperber. Leiden: E. J. Brill, 1962.

Targum Neophyti 1. Ed. Alejandro Díez Macho. 6 vols. Madrid and Barcelona: Consejo de Investigaciones Científicas, 1968-1979.

Targum Pseudo-Jonathan. Ed. M. Ginsburger, *Pseudo-Jonathan*. Berlin: S. Calvary, 1903.

Sharaḥ. Arabic version. R. Seʻadya Gaon. Ed. J. Derenbourg, *Version Arabe du Pentateuque*. Paris : Ernest Leroux, 1893.

JEWISH HELLENISTIC LITERATURE

The Book of Jubilees. In *Apocrypha*. Ed. R. H. Charles. Oxford: Clarendon Press, 1978.

Josephus. *Complete Works*. 10 vols. Loeb Classical Library.

Philo. *Complete Works*. 10 vols. and 2 Supplements. Loeb Classical Library.

RABBINIC LITERATURE

TANNAITIC and TALMUDIC

Mishna. In Maimonides' *Perush ha-Mishnayot*. Ed. and tr. R. Joseph Qafiḥ. 7 vols. Jerusalem: Mossad Harav Kook, 1967.

Tosefta. Ed. M. S. Zuckermandel. Jerusalem: Wahrman Books, 5035/1975.

Tosefta. Ed. Saul Lieberman. *Zeraʻim-Neziqin*. New York: Jewish Theological

Seminary, 1955-2001.

Talmud Yerushalmi. Venice, 5283/1523.

Talmud Babli. Standard Edition. 18 vols. Vilna: Re'em, 5668/1908.

Mss. *Sanhedrin.* Yad ha-Rab Herzog; Firenzi, III.

Tractate 'Abodah Zarah. Ed. Shraga Abramson. New York: The Jewish Theological Seminary of America, 1957.

Abot de-R. Natan. Ed. Salomon Schechter. Vienna, 5647/1887.

Yalquṭ ha-Tora. Venice, 5326/1566.

Massekhet Kalla Rabbati. Ed. Michael Higger. Brooklyn: Moinester Publishing, 1936.

MIDRASHIM

Mekhilta de-R Yishma'el. Eds. H. S. Horovitz and I. A. Rabin. Jerusalem: Wahrmann Books, 1970.

Mekhilta de-R. Shim'on b. Yoḥai. Eds. J. N. Epstein and E. Z. Melamed Jerusalem: Mekize Nirdamim, 1955.

Sifra. Ed. Isaac Hirsch Weiss. Vienna, 5622/1862.

Sifre Bemidbar. Ed. H. Horovitz. Jerusalem: Wahrman Books, 1966.

Sifre Debarim. Ed. Louis Finkelstein. New York: The Jewish Theological Seminary of America, 1969.

Sifre Zuṭa. Ed. Menahem Kahana. Jerusalem: Magnes Press, 2002.

Bereshit Rabba. Eds. J. Theodor and Ch Albeck. 3 vols. Jerusalem: Wahrman Books, 1965.

Midrash Rabba ['al ha-Tora ve-Ḥamesh Megilloṯ]. 2 vols. Vilna. Reprinted: Jerusalem, 5735/1975.

Vayyiqra Rabba. Ed. Mordecai Margulies. 5 vols. Jerusalem: American Academy for Jewish Research, 1960.

Debarim Rabba. Ed. Saul Lieberman. Jerusalem: Wahrman Books, 1974.

Qohelet Rabba. In *Midrash Rabba* ['al ha-Tora ve-Ḥamesh Megilloṯ]. Vilna, Reprinted: Jerusalem, 5735/1975.

Shir ha-Shirim Rabba. In *Midrash Rabba* ['al ha-Tora ve-Ḥamesh Megilloṯ]. Vilna. Reprinted: Jerusalem, 5735/1975.

Ester Rabba. In *Midrash Rabba* ['al ha-Tora ve-Ḥamesh Megilloṯ]. Vilna. Reprinted: Jerusalem, 5735/1975.

Midrash Ekha Rabbati. Ed. S. Buber. Vilna, 1899.

Midrash Tanḥuma. 2 vols. Warsaw, 5611/1851.

Midrash Tanḥuma. Ed. S. Buber. 2 vols. Vilna, 5645/1885.

Midrash Tehillim. Ed. Salomon Buber. New York: Om Publishing, 1947.

Aggadat Ester. Ed. Salomon Buber. Cracow, 5657/1897.

Leqaḥ Ṭob (Pesiqta Zoṭrata). Ed. S. Baber. Jerusalem, 5720/1960.

Midrash Ekha. Ed. Salomon Buber. Vilna, 1899.

Midrash Sekhel Ṭob. Ed. S. Buber. Berlin, 5660/1900.

Debarim Rabba. Ed. Saul Lieberman. Jerusalem: Wahrman Books, 1974.

The Mishna of R. Eli'ezer. Ed. H. G. Enelow. New York, Jewish Theological Seminary, 1933.

Zohar. 3 vls. Leghorn, 5618/1858.

RABBINIC WRITERS

R. Aharon Kotler. *Mishnat R. Aharon.* Vol. 1. Jerusalem: Beth Midrash Gavoha-Lakewood, 5744/1984.

R. Baḥye ibn Faquda. *Ḥobot ha-Lebabot.* Ed. and tr. R. Joseph Qafiḥ. Jerusalem, 5733/1973.

Benamozegh, R. Elie. *Em la-Miqra.* 5 vols. Leghorn, 1862-1863.

——— *Israel et l'Humanité.* Paris: Ernest Leroux, 1914.

——— *Jewish and Christian Ethics.* San Francisco: Emanuel Blochman, 5633-1873.

R. David Cohen de Lara. *Keter Kehunna (Lexicon Thalmudico),* N.p. 1667.

Genizah Studies. Ed. Louis Ginzberg. Vol. 1. New York: Jewish Theological Seminary, 1928.

R. Ḥanan'el. *Perush.* In Talmud, Standard Edition.

> *Perush R. Ḥanan'el. Shabbat.* Ed. R. David Matzger. Jerusalem: Makhon Leb Sameaḥ, 5755/1995.

R. Ḥayyim Algazi. *Bene Ḥayye.* Orta-Kivvae, 5479/1719.

R. Ḥayyim Palaggi. *Birkat Mo'adekha le- Ḥayyim.* Vol. 2. Izmir, 5611/1851.

R. Henry Pereira Mendes. *The Jewish Religion Ethically Presented* (New York: Published by the Author, 1904)

R. Isaac Abendana. *Discourses on the Ecclesiastical and Civil Polity of the Jews.* London, 1706.

R. Isaac Adrebe. *Dibre Shalom.* Venice, 5346/1586.

R. Isaac Caro. *Toledot Yiṣḥaq.* Riva di Trento, 5318/1558.

R. Israel Moses Ḥazzan. *Words of Peace and Truth* (London, Samuel Meldola: 5605/1845.

R. Jacob Israel Algazi. *Shalme Ṣibbur.* Salonika, 5550/1790.

R. Joel ibn Shu'eb. *'Olat Shabbat.* Venice, 5337/1577.

Maran Joseph Caro. *Shulḥan 'Arukh, Oraḥ Ḥayyim.* Standard Edition.

R. Joseph ibn 'Aqnin. *Hitgallut ha-Sodot.* Ed. and tr. A.S. Halkin. Jerusalem: Mekize Nirdamim, 1964.

R. Joseph Ṣarfati. *Yad Yosef.* Amsterdam, 5460/1700.

R. Judah ha-Levi. Arabic Original, *Kitab al-Radd wa-al Dalil fi-al Din Dhalil.* Ed. H. Baneth. Jerusalem: Magness Press, 1977. Hebrew version: *Kuzari.* Ed. and trans. Yehuda Even Shmuel. Tel-Aviv: Dvir Publishing, 1994.

R. Manasseh Ben Israel. *The Conciliator.* 2 vols. London: 5602-1842.

R. Meir Abul'afya. *Ḥiddushe ha-Rama. Giṭṭin.* Ed. R. A. Shoshana, vol. 1. Jerusalem: 5745/1985.

R. Moses de Ṭrani. *Bet Elohim.* Venice, 5336/1576.

R. Moses ibn 'Ezra. *Kitab al-Muḥadara wal-Mudhakara.* Ed. and tr. A. S. Halkin. Jerusalem: Mekize Nirdamim, 1975.

R. Moses Iserlin (Rama). *Shulḥan 'Arukh. Oraḥ Ḥayyim.* Standard Edition.

R. Moses Maimonides. *Guide.* Arabic Original, *Dalalat al- Ḥa'irin.* Eds. Issachar Joel and Solomon Munk. Jerusalem, 1931.

—— *Iggeret ha-Shemad,* in *Iggerot ha-Rambam,* vol. 1. Ed. and tr. Isaac Shailat. 2 vols. Maaleh Adumim: Maaliyot Press, 5748/1988.

—— *Mishne Tora.* Standard Edition.

—— *Perush ha-Mishnayot.* Ed. and tr. R. Joseph Qafiḥ. 7 vols. Jerusalem: Mossad Harav Kook, 1967.

—— *Sefer ha-Miṣvot,* ed. and tr. R. Joseph Qafiḥ (Jerusalem: Mossad Harav Kook, 1971.

—— *Teshubot ha-Rambam.* Ed. and tr. J. Blau. 4 vols. Jerusalem: Mekize Nirdamim, 1975-1986.

R. Nathan b. Yeḥi'el. *'Arukh, Aruch Completum.* Ed. Alexander Kohut. 8 vols. Vienna and Berlin: Menora, 1926.

R. Nissim Gerondi. *Perush.* In R. Isaac Alfasi. Standard Edition.

Oṣar ha-Geonim. Sanhedrin. Ed. R. Ch. Z. Tobias. Jerusalem, Mossad Harav

Kook, 1966.

Perush ha-Geonim 'al Ṭahorot. Ed. J. N. Epstein. Berlin: Mekize Nirdamim, 1924.

R. Samuel Yafe Ashkenazi. *Yefe To'ar. Bereshit*. Venice, 5357/1595.

—— *Yefe To'ar, Vayyiqra*. Constantinople, 5408/1648.

R. Saul Levi Mortera. *Gib'at Sha'ul*. Brooklyn, NY, 5751-1991.

—— *Preguntas*. In *Obstaculos y Oposiciones*. Ms. EH 48 D 38, Hebrew University, Jerusalem.

R. Shem Ṭob Gaguine. *Keter Shem Ṭob*. [Vol. 1]. England, 5694/1934.

R. Simon b. Ṣemaḥ Duran. *Qeshet wu-Magen*. Leghorn, 5523/1763.

WESTERN WRITERS and LITERATURE

Arieti, Silvano. *Abraham and the Contemporary Mind*. New York: Basic Books, 1981.

—— *Creativity*. New York: Basic Books, 1976.

—— *The Intrapsychic Self*. New York: Basic Books, 1967.

—— "Primitive Intellectual mechanism in Psycho-Pathological Conditions." *American Journal of Psychotherapy* 4 (1959).

—— "Some Basic Problems Common to Anthropology and Modern Psychiatry." *American Anthropologist* 58 (1956).

Askenasy, Hans. *Are We All Nazis?* Secaucus, N.J.: Lyle Stuart Inc.,1978.

Baigent, Michael. *The Jesus Papers*. San Francisco: Harper, 2006.

Barlow, John Perry. "The Economy of Ideas: A Framework for Rethinking Patents and Copyrights in the Digital Age." *Wired*. March, 1994.

Barnes, Albert. *The Book of Job,* vol. 1. New York: Leavitt, Trow, & Company, 1845.

Baumgarten, Albert I. "Josephus on Ancient Jewish Groups from a Social Scientific Perspective." In eds. S.J.D. Cohen and J. Schwartz. *Studies on Josephus and the Varieties of Ancient Judaism*. Leiden: E.J. Brill: 2007.

Belkin, Samuel. *In His Image*. New York: Abelard-Schuman, n.d.

—— *Philo and the Oral Law*. Cambridge, Mass.: Harvard University Press, 1940.

Benveniste, Émile. *Indo-European Languages and Society*. Coral Gables, Florida: University of Miami Press, 1973.

—— *The Persian Religion*. Paris: Libraire Orientaliste Paul Guenther, 1929.

—— *Problems in General Linguistics*. Coral Gables, Florida: University of Miami, 1971.

Bevan, Edwyn. *Holy Images*. London: George Allen, 1940.

Bickerman, Elias. "The Maccabean Uprising: An Interpretation." *The Jewish Expression*. Ed. Judah Goldin. New Haven: Yale University Press, 1976.

—— "The Name of Christians." In idem, *Studies in Jewish and Christian History*. Part Three. Leiden : E.J. Brill, 1986.

Blakeslee, Spencer. *The Death of American Antisemitism*. Westport, Connecticut: Praeger, 2000.

Bonar, Andrew A. *Mission of Inquiry to the Jews*. Philadelphia: Presbyterian Board of Publication, 1839.

Borges, Jorge Luis. "Borges on Life and Death." Amelia Barili, *New York Times Book Review*, July 13, 1986.

Bowersock, G. W. *Fiction as History*. Berkeley: University of California Press, 1997.

Branscomb, B. H. "The Dramatic Instinct of Early Christianity." *Journal of Bible and Religion* 9 (1941).

Buhle, Paul. *From the Lower East Side to Hollywood: Jews in American Popular Culture*. London: Verso, 2004.

Burkert, Walter. *Homo Necans*. Berkeley: University of California Press, 1983.

Burrows, Millar. "The Origin of the Term 'Gospel.'" *Journal of Biblical Literature* 44 (1925).

Campbell, Joseph. *The Hero with a Thousand Faces*. London: Fontana Press, 1993.

—— *The Masks of God: Occidental Mythology*. Penguin Compass, 1991.

—— *The Power of Myth*. New York: Anchor Books, 1988.

Canetti, Elias. *The Torch in my Ear*. New York: Farrar, Strauss and Giroux, 1982.

Carey, James W. *Communication as Culture*. New York: Rutledge, 1992.

Castro, Américo. *De la Espana que aun no conocía*. Vol. 1. Mexico: Finisterre, 1972.

—— *La Realidad Histórica de Espana*. Mexico City: Editorial Porrua, 1975.

—— *The Structure of Spanish History*. Princeton, N.J.: Princeton University Press, 1954.

Catechism of the Catholic Church. Promulgated by Pope John Paul II. Città del

Vaticano. Libreria Editrice Vaticana, 1994.

Christian, William A. Jr. *Local Religion in Sixteenth Century Spain.* Princeton, N.J.: 1989.

Cohn, Haim. *The Trial and Death of Jesus.* London: Weidenfeld and Nicolson, 1972.

Conybeare, F. C. "Demonology of the New Testament." *Jewish Quarterly Review* 8 (1896) and 9 (1897)

Deibert, Ronald J. *Parchment, Printing and Hypermedia.* NY: Columbia University Press, 1997.

Detienne, Marcel. *The Garden of Adonis.* Princeton, N.J.: Princeton University Press, 1994.

—— and Vernant, Jean-Pierre. *Myth and Tragedy in Ancient Greece.* New York: Zone Books, 1990.

Diogenes Laertius. Loeb Classical Library.

Disraeli, Benjamin. *Tancred.* Westport, Connecticut: Greenwood Press, 1970.

Dodds, E.R. *The Greeks and the Irrational.* Berkeley: University of California Press, 1968.

Dowden, Ken. *European Paganism.* London: Rutledge, 2000.

Durand, Jean-Louis. "Greek Animals." In Marcel Detienne and Jean-Pierre Vernant, *The Cuisine of Sacrifice among the Greeks.* Chicago: Chicago University Press, 1989.

Eliade, Mircea. *A History of Religious Ideas.* Vol. 2. Chicago: Chicago University Press, 1984.

—— "Mystery and Spiritual Regeneration." In ed. Joseph Campbell. *Man and Transformation.* Princeton, N. J.: Princeton University Press, 1972

—— *Myth and Reality.* New York: Harper & Row, 1963.

—— *The Myth of the Eternal Return.* Princeton: Princeton University Press, 1991.

—— *Rites and Symbols of Initiation.* New York: Harper Torch Books, 1975.

—— *The Sacred and the Profane.* San Diego: Harcourt Brace and Company, 1987.

—— *Shamanism: Archaic Techniques of Ecstasy.* Princeton, N. J.: Princeton University Press, 1974.

—— *Symbolism, the Sacred, and the Arts.* New York: Continuum, 1992.

Elmslie, W.A.L. *The Mishna on Idolatry 'Aboda Zara.* Cambridge: Cambridge University Press, 1911.

Eros in Antiquity. Photographs by A. Mulas. New York: The Erotic Art Book Society, 1978.

Etchart, Martha B. *Documentos de Historia Americana*. Buenos Aires: Cesarini Hnos., 1971.

Eusebius. *The History of the Church*. Tr. G.A. Williamson. Middlesex, England: Penguin, 1983.

Faur, José. "Francisco Sanchez's Theory of Cognition and Vico's *verum/factum*." *New Vico Studies* 5 (1987).

—— *Golden Doves with Silver Dots: Semiotics and Textuality in Rabbinic Tradition*. Bloomington, Indiana: Indiana University Press, 1986.

—— *Homo Mysticus*. Syracuse, N.Y.: Syracuse University Press, 1999.

—— *Horizontal Society*. 2 vols. Boston: Academic Studies Press, 2008.

—— "Imagination and Religious Pluralism: Maimonides, ibn Verga, and Vico." *New Vico Studies* 10 (1992)

—— *In the Shadow of History*. Albany, N.Y.: SUNY, 1992.

—— "Maimonides' Water-Clock and its Epistemological Implications: Sánchez's *modus sciendi* and Vico's *verum-factum*," Jewish Responses to Early Modern Science. The Van Leer Institute, Jerusalem, May 15-18, 1995.

—— *The Naked Crowd: The Jewish Alternative to Cunning Humanity*. Fort Lee, N.J.: Derusha Publishing, 2009.

—— "Newton, Maimonidean." *Review of Rabbinic Judaism* 6 (2003).

—— "Of Cultural Intimidation and Other *Miscellanea*: Bar-Sheshakh *vs.* Raba." *Review of Rabbinic Judaism* 5 (2002).

—— "The Splitting of the *Logos*: Some Remarks on Vico and Rabbinic Tradition." *New Vico Studies* 3 (1985)

—— *Studies in the Mishne Tora* (Heb.) Jerusalem: Mossad Harav Kook, 1978.

—— "The Third Person in Semitic Grammatical Theory and General Linguistics." *Linguistica Biblica*, Bonn, 46 (1979)

Ferdinandy, Michael de. "Charles V." *Encyclopaedia Britannica*, 14th Edition.

Fishkoff, Sue. *Kosher Nation*. New York: Schocken Books, 2010.

Fiske, Susan T. and Taylor, Shelley E. *Social Cognition*. New York: McGraw, 1991.

Frazer, Sir James George. *The Golden Bough*. Parts II-V. London: Macmillan and Co., 1919.

Freke, Timothy, and Gandy Peter. *The Jesus Mysteries*. New York: Three Rivers Press, 1999.

Freud, Sigmund. *Civilization and its Discontent.* Garden City, N.Y.: Doubleday & Company, 1958.

——— *Group Psychology and the Analysis of the Ego.* New York: Bantam Books, 1960.

——— *Moses and Monotheism.* New York: Vintage Book, 1955.

——— *Totem and Taboo.* New York: Vintage Books, 1946.

Fromm, Eric. *The Anatomy of Human Destructiveness.* New York: Holt, Rinehart and Winston, 1973.

——— *The Heart of Man.* NY: Harper & Row, 1964.

——— *Psychoanalysis and Religion.* New Haven: Yale University Press, 1950.

Gabler, Neal. *An Empire of their Own: How the Jews Invented Hollywood.* New York: Doubleday, 1988.

García Proodian, Lucía. *Los Judíos en América.* Madrid: Instituto Arias Montano, 1966.

Gellner, Ernst. *Plough, Sword, and Book.* Chicago: Chicago University Press, 1988.

Gibbon, Edward. *The Decline and Fall of the Roman Empire.* New York: The Modern Library, n.d.

Gilat, Y.D. *R. Eliezer ben Hyrcanus.* Ramat-Gan: Bar-Ilan University Press, 1984.

Gilman, Sander L. *Jewish Self-Hatred.* Baltimore: Johns Hopkins Baltimore University Press, 1986.

Ginsberg, H. L. "New Light on Tannaitic Jewry and on the State of Israel of the Years 132-135 C.E." In *The Jewish Expression.* Ed. Judah Goldin. New Haven: Yale University Press, 1976.

Goldin, Hyman E. *The Case of the Nazarene Reopened.* Clark, NJ: The Lawbook Exchange, 2003.

Goodenough, Erwin R. *The Politics of Philo Judaeus.* New Haven: Yale University Press, 1938.

Gordon, Cyrus H. *The Common Background of Greek and Hebrew Civilizations.* New York: W. W. Norton, 1965.

Hadas, Moses. *A History of Greek Literature.* New York: Columbia University Press, 1950.

Halevy, Isaak. *Doroth Harischonim*, vol. 5. Frankfurt: Louis Golde, 1918.

Halévy, Joseph. *Études Evangeliques.* Premier Fascicule. Paris: Ernest Leroux, 1903.

——— "Nótes et Mélanges," *Revue des Études Juives,* 4 (1882).

Harkabi, Yehoshafat. *The Bar Kokhba Syndrome*. Chappaqua, N.Y.: Russel Books, 1983.

Hartog, François. "Self-cooking Beef and the Drinks of Ares. In Marcel Detienne and Jean-Pierre Vernant, *The Cuisine of Sacrifice among the Greeks*. Chicago: Chicago University Press, 1989.

Hedges, Chris. *When Atheism Becomes Religion*. New York: Free Press, 2008.

Herford, R. Travers. *Christianity in Talmud and Midrash*. London: Williams & Norgate, 1903.

Herodotus. *Histories*. Penguin Classics.

Heschel, Abraham J. *The Prophets*. New York: The Burning Bush Press, 1962.

Hobbes, Thomas. *Leviathan*. Penguin Classics.

Homer, *Odyssey*. Penguin Classics.

Hughes, Pennethorne. *Witchcraft*. Pelican Book.

Huxley, Aldous. "Beliefs." In *Collected Essays*. New York: Harper & Row, 1971.

—— "Politics and Religion." In *Collected Essays*. New York: Harper & Row, 1971.

Jacobovici, Simcha and Pellegrino, Charles. *The Jesus Family Tomb*. San Francisco: Harper, 2007.

Jacobs, Joseph. *Jesus as others saw him*. New York: Bernard G. Richards Co., 1925.

Jastrow, Marcus. *A Dictionary*. New York: The Judaica Press, 1992.

Jenkins, Henry. *Convergence Culture*. New York: New York University Press, 2006.

Jonas, Hans. *The Gnostic Religion*. Boston: Beacon Press, 1963.

Jung, C. G. *The Archetypes of the Collective Unconscious* Princeton, N.J.: Princeton University Press, 1981.

—— "The Psychology of the Child Archetype." In *Essays on a Science of Mythology*. Princeton, N.J.: Princeton University Press, 1993.

—— *The Undiscovered Self*. New York: A Mentor Book, 1957.

Kantorowicz, Ernst H. *The King's Two Bodies*. Princeton, N.J. Princeton University Press, 1957.

Kaufmann, Walter. *Religions in Four Dimensions*. New York: Reader's Digest Press, 1976.

Kerényi, C. *Essays on a Science of Mythology*. Princeton, N.J.: Princeton University Press, 1993.

Kimball, Charles. *When Religion Becomes Evil.* San Francisco: Harper San Francisco, 2002.

Kirsch, J. P. "Eutychianism." *The Catholic Encyclopedia.* Vol. 5. New York: Robert Appelton Company, 1909.

Kohut, George A. *Ezra Stiles and the Jews.* New York: Philip Cowen, 1902.

Koppers, Wilhelm. "On the Origins of the Mysteries in the Light of Ethnology and Indology." In ed. Joseph Campbell. *The Mystic Vision.* Princeton, N.J.: Princeton University Press, 1982.

Lerner, Daniel. "The Coercive Ideologist in Perspective." In *World Revolutionary Elites.* Eds. Harold D. Lasswell and Daniel Lerner. Cambridge, Mass. M.I.T. Press, 1965.

Lévy-Bruhl, Lucien. *The Notebooks on Primitive Mentality.* New York: Harper and Row, 1978.

Lieberman, Saul. *Greek in Jewish Palestine.* New York: Philipp Feldheim, 1965.

—— *Tosefta Ki-Fshutah.* 10 vols. New York: Jewish Theological Seminary, 1955-2001.

Luzzato, Samuel David. *Oheb Ger.* Cracow, 1895.

Maccoby, Hyam. *Judas Iscariot and the Myth of Jewish Evil.* New York: The Free Press, 1992.

—— *Paul and Hellenism.* Philadelphia: Trinity Press, 1991.

Maistre, Joseph de. *On God and Society.* Chicago: Henry Regnery, 1967.

—— *The Works of Joseph de Maistre.* New York: Schocken Books, 1971.

Manguel, Alberto. *A History of Reading.* Viking, Penguin, 1996.

Mártir de Anglería, Pedro. *Libros de las Décadas del Nuevo Mundo.* Buenos Aires: Editorial Bajel, 1944.

Marton, Kati. *The Great Escape: Nine Jews that Fled Hitler and Changed the World.* New York: Simon & Schuster, 2007.

Marx, Karl. *Kapital.* Chicago: Encyclopedia Britanica, 1952.

Mason, Steve ."Josephus's Pharisees: the Narratives." In eds. Jacob Neusner and Bruce D. Chilton. *In Quest of the Historical Pharisees.* Waco, Texas: Baylor University Press, 2007.

Mayhew, Reverend Jonathan. *Seven Sermons.* Reprinted in *Religion in America.* New York: Arno Press, 1969.

McLuhan, Marshall. *The Gutenberg Galaxy.* Toronto: University of Toronto

Press, 1997.

——— *Understanding Media.* Cambridge, Mass.: MIT Press, 1998.

Méchoulan, Henry. *El Honor de Dios.* Barcelona: Editorial Argos Vergara, 1981.

Ménard, J. E. "Judeocristianismo." In *Enciclopedia de la Biblia*, vol. 4. Barcelona: Ediciones Garriga, 1969.

Mendes, Meir. *Ha-Vatican ve-Israel.* Jerusalem: The Hebrew University, The Leonard Davis Institute for International Relations, 1983.

Michelson, Carl. "Authority." In *A Handbook of Christian Theology.* New York: Meridian Books, 1958.

Michener, James. *The Source.* New York: Random House, 1965.

Miller, Arthur G. *The Obedience Experiments.* New York: Praeger Special Studies, 1974.

Momigliano, Arnaldo. *The Classical Foundations of Modern Historiography.* Berkeley: The University of California Press, 1990.

——— *Essays in Ancient and Modern Historiography.* Middletown, Conn.: Wesleyan University Press, 1982.

——— *The Development of Greek Biography.* Cambridge, Mass.: Harvard University Press, 1993.

——— *Studies in Historiography.* New York: Harper & Row, 1966.

——— "El tiempo en la historiografía Antigua." In *La Historiografía Griega.* Barcelona: Editorial Crítica.

Moore, George Foot. *History of Religions.* Vol. 2. Edinburgh: T&T Clark, 1965.

——— *Judaism.* Vol. 2, 3. Cambridge, Mass.: Harvard University Press, 1966.

Morais, Vamberto. *A Short History of Anti-Semitism.* New York: W.W. Norton, 1976.

Neumann, Eric. *The Origins and History of Consciousness.* Princeton, N. J.: Princeton University Press, 1993.

Neusner, Jacob. *Jews and Christians: The Myth of a Common Tradition.* Binghamton, N.Y.: Global Publications, 2001.

Nicholls, William. *Christian Antisemitism.* Northvale, New Jersey: Jason Aronson Inc., 1993.

——— "Saints and Fanatics: The problematic connection between religion and spirituality." *Judaism* 46 (1996).

Nicoli, Allardyce. *Masks Mimes and Miracles.* New York: Cooper Square Publishing, 1963.

Nilsson. Martin P. *A History of Greek Religion.* New York: W.W. Norton & Company, 1964.

'Olam ha-Tanakh. Bemidbar. Jerusalem: Rebibim, 1985.

Origen: *Contra Celsum.* Tr. Henry Chadwick. Cambridge: Cambridge University Press, 1953.

Ortega y Gasset, José. *The Revolt of the Masses.* New York: W.W. Norton, 1957.

Osiel, Mark J. *Obeying Orders: Atrocity, Military, Discipline, and the Law of War.* New Brunswick and London: Transaction Publishers, 1999.

Pagan Monotheism in Late Antiquity. Eds. Polymnia Athanassiadi and Michael Frede. Oxford: Oxford University Press, 1999.

Pallière, Aimé. *The Unknown Sanctuary.* Preface by Abraham I. Carmel. New York: Bloch Publishing Company, 1971.

Paz, Octavio. *Claude Lévi-Strauss: An Introduction.* New York: Dell Publishing, 1978.

Pearce, W. Barnet. *Communication and the Human Condition.* Carbondale and Edwardsville: Southern Illinois University, 1989.

Pellegrino, Charles. See Jacobovici, Simcha and Pellegrino, Charles.

Pines, Shlomo. "'Israel, My Firstborn' and the Sonship of Jesus." In *Studies in Mysticism and Religion presented to Gershom G. Scholem.* Ed. E. E. Urbach *et al.* Jerusalem: Magness Press, 1967.

—— "The Jewish Christians...," (Heb.). *Proceedings of the Israel Academy of Science and Humanities.* II (1966).

Phaedrus. In *Collected Works of Plato.* Tr. by B. Jowett. New York: Greystone Press, n.d.

Pope John Paul. "On the Mystery and Worship of the Eucharist." In *Vatican Council* II. Ed. Austin Flannery, O.P. Collegeville, MN: The Liturgical Press, 1982.

Radin, Paul. *Primitive Religion.* New York: Dover Publications, 1957.

Rank, Otto. *Beyond Psychology.* New York: Dover, 1958.

Reinach, Solomon. *Orpheus.* New York: Horace Liveright, 1930.

Renan, Ernest. *The Life of Jesus.* Boston: Little, Brown and Company, 1915.

Reizenstein, Richard. *Hellenistic Mystery-Religions.* Pittsburgh, Pa.: The Pickwick Press, 1978.

Revah, Israel Salvador. "Les Marranes." *Revue des Études Juives* 118 (1959-1960).

Ribi, Alfred. *Demons of the Inner World.* Boston: Shambhala, 1990.

Romilly, Jacqueline de. *Magic and Rhetoric in Ancient Greece.* Cambridge, Mass.: Harvard University Press, 1975.

Rosenblatt, Samuel. "The Crucifixion of Jesus from the Standpoint of Pharisaic Law." *Journal of Biblical Literature,* 75 (1956).

Salas, Alberto M. *Tres Cronistas de Indias: Pedro Mártir de Anglería, Gonzalo Fernández de Oviedo, Fray Bartolomé de las Casas.* México: Fondo de Cultura Económica, 1959. á, í *T̩, t̩,* É, ó, é

Sánchez(s), Francisco. *Quod nihil scitur.* In ed. Joaquim de Carvalho. *Opera.* Coimbra, 1955.

Schreier, Barbara A. *Becoming American Women: Clothing and the Jewish Immigrant Experience, 1880-1920.* Chicago: Chicago Historic Society, 1994.

Scott, Walter. *Hermetica.* Vol. 1. Oxford: Oxford University Press, 1925.

Selbie, W. B. "The Influence of the Old Testament on Puritanism." In ed. I. Abrahams *et al, The Legacy of Israel.* Oxford: Clarendon Press, 1928.

Sinai, Yuval. "*Net̩el.*" www.Netanya.ac.il

Smith, Morton. "Jesus' Attitude towards the Law." *Fourth World Congress of Jewish Studies.* Vol. 1. Jerusalem: World Union of Jewish Studies, 1967.

——— *Jesus the Magician.* New York: Harper & Row, 1978.

——— "The Reason for the Persecution of Paul and the Obscurity of Acts." In *Studies in Mysticism and Religion presented to Gershom G. Scholem.* Jerusalem: Magness Press, 1967.

——— *The Secret Gospel.* New York. Harper & Row, 1973.

——— *Studies in the Cult of Y....* 2 vols. Ed. Shaye J. D. Cohen. Leiden: E. J. Brill, 1996.

Socrates. *Phaedrus.* In *Collected Works of Plato.* Tr. by B. Jowett. New York: Greystone Press, n.d.

Souter, Alexander. *A Pocket Lexicon to the Greek of the New Testament.* Oxford: Clarendon Press, 1917.

Sperber, Daniel. *A Dictionary of Greek & Latin Legal Terms.* Ramat-Gan: Bar Ilan University Press, 1984.

Strange, James Riley. *The Emergence of the Christian Basilica in the Fourth Century.* Binghamton, New York: Global Publication, Binghamton University, 2000.

Straus, Oscar. "American Judaism." In *The American Spirit.* New York: The Century Co., 1918.

——— "The First Settlement of the Jews in the United States." In idem, *The American Spirit.* New York: The Century Co., 1918.

—— *The Origin of the Republican Form of Government in the United States.* New York: G. P. Putnam's Son, 1885.

—— *Roger Williams: The Pioneer of Religious Liberty.* New York: D. Appleton-Century Company, 1936.

Strauss, Barry S. *Fathers and Sons in Athens.* Princeton, N.J.: Princeton University Press, 1993.

Strauss, Leo. *Spinoza's Critique of Religion.* New York: Schocken Books, 1965.

Summer, Walter C. *The Silver Age of Latin Literature.* London: Methuen, 1920.

Taylor, Lily Ross. *The Divinity of the Roman Emperor.* Middletown, Connecticut, 1931.

Taylor, Shelley E. See Fiske, Susan T. *Social Cognition,* 2nd ed. New York: McGraw, 1991.

Tillich, Paul. *Dynamics of Faith* (New York: Harper & Row, 1957.

—— "The Importance of New Being for Christian Theology." In ed. Joseph Campbell. *Man and Transformation.* Princeton, N.J.: 1972.

—— *Systematic Theology.* Vol. 1. Chicago: Chicago University Press, 1953.

Thomas Aquinas. *Summa Theologica.* English version by Timothy Mc Dermot, *Summa Theologiæ.* London: Eyre and Spottiswoode, 1989.

Todorov, Tzevetan. *La conquête de l'Amérique.* Paris: Editions du Soleil, 1982.

Treaties and other International Acts of the United States of America. Volume 2, Documents 1-40; 1776-1818. Ed. Hunter Miller. United States Government Printing Office, Washington: 1931.

Ullmann, Walter. *The Individual and Society in the Middle Ages.* Baltimore, Maryland: Hopkins University Press, 1966.

Vatican Council II. Ed. Austin Flannery, O.P. Collegeville, MN: 1983.

Vernant, Jean-Pierre. *Myth and Society in Ancient Greece.* New York: Zone Books, 1990.

—— and Vidal-Naquet, Pierre. *Myth and Tragedy in Ancient Greece.* New York: Zone Books, 1990.

Vidal-Naquet, Pierre and Vernant, Jean-Pierre. *Myth and Tragedy in Ancient Greece.* New York: Zone Books, 1990.

Walaskay, Paul W. *'... And so we came to Rome.'* Cambridge: Cambridge University Press, 2005.

Walker, Benjamin. *Gnosticism.* Wellingborough, Northamptonshire: The Aquarian Press, 1983.

Walker, D. F. *Spiritual and Demonic Magic.* Notre Dame: University of Notre Dame, 1975.

Wellborn, Laurence L. "Runaway Paul," *Harvard Theological Review* 92 (1999).

Wengs, Klaus. *Pax Romana and the Peace of Jesus Christ.* Philadelphia: Fortress Press, 1987.

Will, Garry. *Papal Sins.* New York: Image Books, 2001.

Wilson, A. N. *Jesus.* New York: W. W. Norton, 1992.

Wittgenstein, Ludwig. *Notebooks,* 1914-1916. New York: Harper & Row, 1961.

Wolfson, Harry. *Philo.* 2 vols. Cambridge, Mass.: Harvard University Press, 1948.

—— *The Philosophy of the Church Fathers.* Vol. 1. Cambridge, Mass.: Harvard University Press, 1956.

—— *Studies in the History of Philosophy and Religion.* Vol. 2. Cambridge, Mass.: Harvard University Press, 1977.

Yahuda, Abraham Shalom. *Hakotel Hama'arabi.* Jerusalem: 5728/1968.

Yerushalmi, Yosef. *From Spanish Court to Italian Ghetto* (New York: Columbia University, 1971.

Zimmer, Heinrich. "The Significance of the Tantric Yoga." In ed. Joseph Campbell, *Spiritual Disciplines.* Princeton: Princeton University Press, 1985.

ABOUT THE AUTHOR

JOSÉ FAUR is Professor Emeritus at the Law School, Netanya College, Netanya, Israel where he taught since 1996. He obtained his Ph.D. in Semitic Philology at the University of Barcelona in 1964. He taught at the JTS and Bar-Ilan University and published numerous articles in Hebrew, Spanish, French, Italian and English. Previous publications include: *Studies in the Mishne Tora* (Heb.) (Mossad Harav Kook, 1978); *Golden Doves with Silver Dots: Semiotics and Textuality in Rabbinic Tradition* (Indiana UP, 1986); *In the Shadow of History: Jews and Conversos at the Dawn of Modernity* (SUNY, 1992); *Homo Mysticus: A Guide to Maimonides' Guide for the Perplexed* (Syracuse UP, 1998); *The Horizontal Society: Understanding the Covenant and Alphabetic Judaism* (Academic Studies Press, 2002).

www.ingramcontent.com/pod-product-compliance
Lightning Source LLC
Chambersburg PA
CBHW022047160426
43198CB00008B/153